How To Read Classical Tibetan • Volume One

Summary of the General Path

ལམ་སྤྱིའི་དོན་བསྡུ་བ་

HOW TO READ CLASSICAL TIBETAN • VOLUME ONE

SUMMARY OF THE GENERAL PATH

ལམ་སྤྱིའི་དོན་བསྡུ་བ་

by

Craig Preston

Excerpted from

The Great Treatise on the Stages of the Path to Enlightenment

SNOW LION
BOSTON & LONDON

Snow Lion
An imprint of Shambhala Publications, Inc.
Horticultural Hall
300 Massachusetts Avenue
Boston, Massachusetts 02115
www.shambhala.com

For more information from the author, visit www.giganticom.com.

9 8 7 6 5 4

Printed in the United States of America

♾ This edition is printed on acid-free paper that meets the American National Standards Institute Z39.48 Standard.
♻ Shambhala Publications makes every effort to print on recycled paper. For more information please visit www.shambhala.com.
Distributed in the United States by Random House, Inc., and in Canada by Random House of Canada Ltd

Designed and typeset by Gigantic Computing

Library of Congress Cataloging-in-Publication Data

Preston, Craig, 1950–
How to read classical Tibetan / Craig Preston.
v. cm.
"Excerpted from 'The great treatise on the stages of the path to enlightenment'"—v. 1, t.p.
Contents: v. 1. Summary of the general path.
ISBN 978-1-55939-178-8 (alk. paper)
1. Tibetan language—Textbooks for foreign speakers—English. 2. Tibetan language—Readers—Buddhism. I. Tsoṅ-kha-pa Blo-bzaṅ-grags-pa, 1357–1419. Lam rim chen mo. Selections. Tibetan & English. II. Title.
PL3613.P74 2003

Contents

Introduction

Summary of the General Path

Appendix

Ven. Segyu Choepel Rinpoche and Craig Preston

Introduction

Acknowledgments

The writing of this book has occupied me on and off from the fall of 1999 until the spring of 2002. I would like to thank by name many—my teachers, students, friends, and family—who have contributed both directly and indirectly to this dependent-arising.

Buddha and teachers who have come before

Thanks to Buddha, who taught the path to Buddhahood, the harmony of dependent-arising and emptiness animated by compassion, in accordance with the needs and capacities of his trainees!

Thanks to all in the transmission of his teaching of dependent-arising from the Country of Superiors and the Land of the Snows to the Land of the Free and the Home of the Brave!

My teachers

Thanks to my teachers! When I began studying Classical Tibetan at the University of Virginia from 1978 to 1982, I had the great good fortune to have Joe Wilson, Elizabeth Napper, and Jeffrey Hopkins as my teachers. The kindness, skill, patience, and wisdom of all three gave me the foundation from which to develop my approach to teaching Classical Tibetan. In gratitude I offer this book, so that others might benefit from your kindness.

My students

Thanks to my students! Special thanks to my long-time Ithaca students Susan Krafft and Steven Rhodes. During the writing of this book, they heard quite a bit about topics not directly related to their own reading, often in conflicting formulations. Their patience has given me the space to work things out to produce the final form this book has taken. My only regret with regard to teaching is that life's demands inevitably take my students away from me eventually. I feel a special debt to those students who stick around for years so we can read the good stuff together.

Everybody who benefits from this book owes Susan Krafft a special debt of gratitude. She has been enormously generous with her time, applying her excellent editing and proofreading skills throughout all phases of this book. She has made this a better book with her kindness.

I give thanks also to the students to whom I have taught this material while I wrote early versions. In the fall of 1999, I taught Daniel Hirshberg, Beth Dart, and Dr. Maura Santangelo. I must thank Rhonda Fleming, although she is not a Tibetan language student, for her timely encouragement.

Much of this was written in the summer of 2000 while I was teaching at the Dharma Farm in Charlottesville, Virginia. I want to thank my morning class: Liza Pascal, Annabella Pitkin, Christopher Kelley, and David Stainton. You were a high wattage class and I certainly had a lot of fun! Thanks also to my afternoon grammar class; you all contributed to this dependent-arising as we went through verb classes and case declensions together. In particular, I want to thank Ven. Segyu Choepel Rinpoche for his encouragement and exhortation to finish this book quickly.

Back in Ithaca for fall 2000, I want to thank my "anthropology" class: Heather Harrick, Sienna Craig, Abraham Zablocki, and Lauren Cottrell. Abraham and Sienna are finishing their doctoral studies in anthropology at Cornell University here in Ithaca; Heather and Lauren each is the mother of two daughters. That these four busy adults make time for additional study is itself an inspiration to make the most of our opportunities.

During the summer of 2001, I taught a second Dharma Farm Summer Intensive, this time in Taos, New Mexico. In particular I want to thank Rachael Ryer, Jennifer Garlick, and Boston Russell for being excellent students; Susan Krafft who shared much of the teaching; and again Ven. Segyu Choepel Rinpoche for his encouragement and exhortation to practice.

My friends

Thanks to my friends! I am deeply appreciative of all the help I've received over the years from my Dharma Farm colleagues: Bill Magee, Dan Perdue, and Paul Hackett. Thanks, guys.

Thanks to Sidney Piburn and Jeff Cox of Snow Lion Publications who have done so much for Tibetan Buddhism in translation. And special thanks to Steven Rhodes, my editor at Snow Lion, who helped me correct an appalling number of inconsistencies at the end.

I can't write without music

Special thanks to my dear friend Charles d'Orban, Musical Director and Deacon of the First Church of the Big Beat; together we immersed ourselves in Avant-Garde Jazz, Hard Bop, and Free Jazz during the writing of this book. Thanks to Miles Davis for his first and second quintets; thanks to John Coltrane for everything leading up to *Ascension;* special thanks to Rudy Van Gelder for the Village Vanguard sessions in the first week of November, 1961.

I also want to thank the staff of Café Charles—Suzi, Lauren, and Laurie—for keeping it real, as well as Fela's road band, and the whole crew from Motown. Special thanks to Holland-Dozer-Holland.

I was going to Dead shows before you were born

Thanks to everyone responsible: band, crew, tapers, deadheads. Special thanks to the rhythm devils for the jam out of *William Tell*; to Phil Lesh for *The Eleven* (one of my all-time favorite tunes); to Bobby Weir for all those great cowboy songs; to Tom Constanten for too often overlooked counterpoint; to soul man Ron McKernan for his sage counsel on *Alligator, Caution,* and *Lovelight;* and finally to Garcia and Hunter for all those great songs. Finally, I want to thank a deadhead I never got to hang out with, but from whom I have received so much: thanks Dick.

Special mention: 8/24/68 (such a fine *Other One*), 1/26/69, 2/11/69, the run from 2/27/69 to 3/2/69, the outstanding run at Boston's Ark from 4/21/69 to 2/23/69, 11/8/69, and, I guess, the whole spring of 1969; thanks for those dreamy *Dark Stars* from the fall of 1973. Thanks to Donna-Jean for singing like an angel.

Thanks to Buddy Holly. And thanks to the actual man behind it all, Otha Ellas Bates, Ellas McDaniel, the great Bo Diddley.

My Ithaca crew

Thanks to the whole crew in Ithaca, especially Josh and Crow.

My family

Thanks to my mother-in-law Dorothea Mitchell Queen, my favorite pianist; thanks to my father-in-law Merritt Queen, an all around great guy and deep thinker. Thanks to my kids: Sam, Betsy, and Emily. You're the best. Thanks to Jack and Willie who spend the most time with me. Most of all, in ways both vast and profound, thanks to my wife, Bethany Queen — you know our love won't fade away.

Ithaca, New York, April 2002

Using This Book to Learn to Read Classical Tibetan

I teach Classical Tibetan in two phases. In the first phase, I teach students the range of recurrent patterns of Tibetan syntax systematically. In the second phase, as we begin to read Tibetan books, I teach students to recognize in the sentences we are reading the recurrent patterns illustrated by the paradigms memorized in the first phase. My intention with this book is to make the transition from the first phase to the second phase easier for my own students by always explaining everything in terms of what's going on in any given sentence. To get the most out of this book, I recommend that you prepare yourself by doing the same preliminary study that my own students do.

Preliminary Study

I begin with Joe B. Wilson's excellent *Translating Buddhism from Tibetan* (hereinafter *TBFT*). I introduce students to the written language following *TBFT* Sections One and Two, (Chapters 1–13). This covers

- the alphabet,
- pronunciation rules,
- words and particles,
- "the science of the dots," and
- the basic verb-last structure of Tibetan.

I also require students to use the excellent cassette tape of pronunciation drills and exercises prepared by Tenzin Namgyal and Sidney Piburn of Snow Lion Publications.

At this point in a beginner's class, I stop going through the chapters in *TBFT* and concentrate instead on the appendices. For those of you unfamiliar with the later chapters of *TBFT,* Section Three of *TBFT,* (Chapters 14-19), presents very clearly and with many examples the various constructions of Classical Tibetan. In addition, *TBFT* also provides comprehensive basic vocabulary and a wealth of doctrinal material about Tibetan Buddhism. If you haven't already familiarized yourself with the later material in *TBFT,* I really do suggest you study that thoroughly before attempting this book. I am assuming familiarity with that material and will not duplicate that basic language instruction here because it is done so well there. As you work your way through this book, I hope you will have your copy of *TBFT* near at hand. I have found that the students who go back to *TBFT* and frequently re-read Wilson's explanations are the ones who learn the material.

In my own classes for beginners, once we complete Chapters 1–13, we focus on the memorization of paradigm sentences found in Appendices Four and Five. Rather than organizing class time around the remaining Chapters 14–19 in *TBFT,* I organize classes around exposition and memorization of the paradigm sentences found in the appendices on the eight verb classes (Appendix Four) and the eight cases of declension (Appendix Five). These appendices provide students with paradigm sentences which introduce the elements of Tibetan syntax systematically.

I require that students **memorize the paradigm phrases and sentences**. Committing these paradigm sentences to memory allows us to have a shared analytical vocabulary for articulating precisely the relationships that occur in Tibetan sentences. This is what I teach my students in the first phase; my hope is other students will learn these basics from *Translating Buddhism from Tibetan* before using this material.

What you should be able to do from memory at the end of phase one

When you have memorized the paradigms in Appendices Four and Five, you should be able to do the following:

- Name the eight classes of verbs and all their subclasses;
- Name the eight cases of declension of nouns, and the subclasses;
- Say and write the Tibetan paradigm sentence for each verb and noun type; and
- Understand the grammar of every paradigm

Everyone who has studied with me knows that this is the core of how I teach.

On using this book to start phase two of your study

The first phase introduces students systematically to the range of recurrent elements of Tibetan syntax. In the second phase, as we begin to read Tibetan books, I teach students to recognize in the sentences we are reading the recurrent patterns illustrated by the paradigms memorized in the first phase. In the beginning stages of language study, you should learn the structure of Tibetan syntax through memorizing paradigm phrases and sentences. In the second phase you should learn to recognize the syntax illustrated by the memorized paradigms when reading new material. While you read the "Summary of the General Path," you should develop facility in

- **recognizing** the syntactic relationships you encounter,
- **understanding** the meaning signified, and in
- **translating** that meaning correctly into English.
- To this end, memorizing the paradigm sentences is the indispensable key to **connecting** your understanding of the relationships illustrated by the paradigms with patterns in new Tibetan sentences. Recognizing the recurrence of a pattern you have memorized as a paradigm allows you to understand the new passage.

I find that students who make the effort to memorize the paradigms learn to read Tibetan correctly.

This book is primarily about the Tibetan sentences

The early stages of learning to read a new language tend to be unlike later stages of topical study when one can read the new language. Once you know how to read Tibetan, your focus of study is the meaning of the text being studied, not the structure of the sentences themselves. At the beginning of language study, understanding the structure of the sentences themselves is the proper focus of a student's attention. With this in mind, I have tried to present here the sentences of the "Summary of the General Path" in the way appropriate to the special needs of students learning to read Tibetan.

What to read first?

I have experimented with a number of different approaches to the puzzle of what to read first with students after we have finished the presentation of the eight classes of verbs and eight cases of declension.

- I began learning Tibetan with a **Collected Topics** text. This is a good place to start to develop systematic familiarity with Buddhist philosophy, but owing to the idiosyncratic structure of debate texts, it is less well-suited to exposing students to a wide range of syntactic constructions.
- I have also used the fourteen-stanza poem on the **Three Principal Aspects of the Path** by Tsong-kha-pa. The chief problem with verse is that key elements of syntax may be omitted due to the requirements of meter. I have found it more helpful for students to begin with narrative Tibetan.
- The passage I have annotated here for Tibetan language students is the **Summary of the General Path** excerpted from Tsong-kha-pa's *The Great Treatise on the Stages of the Path to Enlightenment.*

While the focus of the "Summary of the General Path" is the narrative summary of the topics of meditation for an individual practitioner through three developmental stages (termed "the beings of the three capacities"), the focus of my book is the **Tibetan sentences themselves.**

Beginners need complete redundancy

Beginners have special needs simply because they are beginners. Beginning students don't know the vocabulary (the words and particles), and they couldn't put the words and particles together correctly into sentences anyway because no one has shown them the syntax: the rules for how the language "works." The form this book takes is my solution to the challenge of meeting a beginner's two needs: **learning vocabulary** and **understanding structure.** I have said quite a bit about the structure of these sentences and the vocabulary found therein, and a lot of it is repetitive. Indeed, I have adopted a procedure I call complete redundancy: I have tried to **identify and explain everything, every time.** I have tried to reproduce graphically the same language instruction I present in class on the board as I teach this material to beginning Tibetan students.

Learning to read Tibetan is largely a matter of memorizing vocabulary and learning to recognize the recurrent patterns forming phrases, clauses, and sentences from words and particles. Accordingly, as I teach students to read Tibetan, I begin with identifying the words and particles that make up larger syntactic elements. Then I identify the various elements of Tibetan syntax, explain the rules for their occurrence and, most importantly, I identify the relationship signified by the syntax. Once a student understands the relationship signified by the syntax, she can translate the Tibetan correctly.

The general structure of each chapter

I have broken the exposition of the "Summary of the General Path" into ten chapters. Chapters are divided into six parts: text, overview of the syntactic structure of the passage, detailed exposition, complete glossary, review, and additional text for the advanced student.

- **Text** Each chapter starts with successive portions of the "Summary," a few lines in length. Later chapters have longer passages.
- **Overview** I have divided the passage into units to facilitate the analysis of the syntax.
- **Detailed exposition of each unit** I diagram each unit completely. When diagramming, I have identified three levels of meaning: the type of particle or word, its lexical meaning, and the level of syntactic function: agents, subjects, objects, complements, qualifiers, and verbs.
- **Glossary for every particle and word as it occurs** For each and every particle and word, in the order in which they occur, I have identified both the general range of uses and indicated the specific contextual use within the passage for every occurrence. (In addition, at the end of the book there is a glossary of every particle and word in alphabetical order.)
- **Review** Another look at the original passage and key vocabulary encountered in the passage; hopefully you will have already learned the vocabulary and can read the passage easily.
- **Additional text for the advanced student** For the advanced student, I have ended each chapter with an annotated commentary on Tsong-kha-pa's text from a commentary called *The Four Interwoven Annotations.*

As you read through the charts of the sentences in Tsong-kha-pa's text, take the time to understand every part of every sentence. It will take you a while to get familiar with the syntax of Tibetan sentences. I find that students need about 60 class-hours for the exposition of this material, plus study on their own.

Use the glossaries to learn vocabulary

In addition to learning to recognize and understand the recurring patterns of syntax, a major task for the beginner is learning new vocabulary. Indeed, I was moved to write this beginner's reader in large part after watching new students struggle with the complexities of Tibetan dictionary order. I thought their time would be better spent if I identified the particles and words so that students could spend their time learning vocabulary rather than looking for it. Accordingly, I have given full translation equivalents for **every** particle and word with **every** occurrence.

A suggestion for how to learn the vocabulary

Now, one more word of advice. I'm giving you complete and total vocabulary redundancy. You save a lot of time by not needing to look up words. Put this time saved to good use: **learn the vocabulary. Write each word out at least 10 times**; learn to spell the words by writing them over and over again. Learn the verb forms so that you can identify the tenses. May each and every one of you find a learning strategy that works for you! Here's what I did: because learning to spell the words was tedious and stressful, I never set about to "learn" the words. Instead I'd start writing them out, as if I were practicing handwriting. I'd tell myself I'd learn them later; now I was just writing them out. I'd find that if I wrote a word ten times, I had learned it, and it was *mine.*

Where to find more detail on meaning of the text

I have written this book with the needs of beginning students of Tibetan in mind. When I learned Tibetan, everyone in my class was primarily interested in the details of Buddhist philosophy, but that is not always the case. These days, I rarely get students with any systematic philosophical training, but often they have considerable experience with spoken Tibetan. For example, of the four students reading this material with me in fall 2000, three of the four have considerable proficiency in modern spoken Tibetan. Two are graduate students in anthropology who have already done field work in the Himalayan region and the third is an American married to a Tibetan. All three have far more fluency in modern spoken Tibetan than I, yet they are just beginning to learn to read technical Buddhist Tibetan precisely.

I have tried to be comprehensive regarding the words, particles, and elements of syntax within the sentences themselves, but, for the most part, I have not commented upon the text in terms of its meaning. Rather than listening to anything I would have to say about the text itself, my hope is that you will become interested in the topics mentioned in the "Summary" and read the whole of *The Great Treatise on the Stages of the Path* itself—in Tibetan, of course. And just to check your understanding, there is a translation entitled *The Great Treatise on the Stages of the Path to Englightenment,* translated by the

Lamrim Chenmo Translation Committee, Joshua Cutler, editor-in-chief, Guy Newland, editor, published by Snow Lion Publications.

Ways in which I depart from Wilson's system:
Descriptive idiosyncrasies of this book

For the most part, I have followed the system of describing Tibetan syntax created by Jeffrey Hopkins, and developed by Elizabeth Napper and Joe Wilson. I have departed from them in a few key ways which I will identify in a moment. The careful reader ought be aware of these differences so as not to be confused with differences in usage between this book and Wilson's *Translating Buddhism from Tibetan.*

My use of the terms "subject" and "agent" contrasted

I use the word **subject** exclusively within **intransitive** constructions, and I use the word **agent** exclusively within **transitive** constructions. This is **not** how these words are usually used in English grammar, and this is **not** how Wilson uses them. In brief, I have adopted this convention because I have seen it significantly reduces the time it takes for students to recognize and understand the differences between transitive and intransitive constructions.

Here is an example of how I use these terms and why I assign the meanings I do. In the transitive English sentence "Buddha taught the doctrine," English grammar holds "Buddha" to be the **subject** of the sentence. Likewise, in the intransitive sentence "the wheel turns," English grammar holds "wheel" to be the **subject** of the sentence. I have not followed this convention when I describe Tibetan syntax. I have found that students have difficulty distinguishing transitive Tibetan constructions from intransitive Tibetan constructions. Tibetan frequently leaves important syntactic elements out, far more so than in English. The problem is often this: you have the noun "wheel" and a verb "turn." Is this a transitive construction or an intransitive construction? Is some unstated agent turning the wheel, and if so, who might that be? Or is the sentence just "the wheel turns" and no person is acting as an agent? Learning to read Tibetan accurately requires mastering this sort of distinction.

When I introduce verbs I identify them as either ཐ་དད། **transitive** (trans.) or ཐ་མི་དད། **intransitive** (intr.) following the comprehensive verb form chart at the end of *The Great Tibetan-Chinese Dictionary.* Transitive verbs have agents (expressed or implied) separate from objects; intransitive verbs do not have agents or objects. Every time you come across a verb you should ask yourself which is it—intransitive or transitive. I have identified verb forms repeatedly in this book in hopes that you will learn them.

There is a great benefit to my admittedly idiosyncratic use of "agent" and "subject." Whereas in traditional English grammar the term "subject" is ambiguous in that the construction in which it occurs can be either transitive or intransitive, with my usage you will know unambiguously whether we're dealing with a transitive construction (**agent** of **transitive** verb) or intransitive construction (**subject** of **intransitive** verb). Remember, Tibetan uses unstated elements far more than English does. A Tibetan sentence is not conclusively intransitive just because a sentence doesn't have an explicit agent.

My use of the terms "qualifier" and "complement" contrasted

I have been fascinated by Wilson's descriptions of how Tibetan grammar employs complements and qualifiers. Indeed, I have thought long and hard about what appear to me to be the occasional contradictions or inconsistencies in his presentation. Compare, for example, Wilson's different descriptions of the following sentence found on pages 412, 479–80, and 601:

གངས་རི་མིག་ཤེས་ལ་སྔོན་པོར་སྣང་།	Snow mountains appear to be blue to the eye consciousness.

After much thought, I have concluded that qualifiers differ from complements in the following manner. **Qualifiers** are words, phrases and clauses that **qualify the action expressed by the verb** by showing how, when, where, why, for whose benefit and the like. In this I am confident I am following Wilson's descriptive scheme.

Complements are another matter. As far as I'm concerned, complements are syntactic units that **complete the subject** of an intransitive verb or that **complete the object** of a transitive verb. The subject or object will either be the complement, appear as the complement, or be perceived as the complement. I do not say, as Wilson often does, that a verb has a complement. In my descriptive system, only subjects and objects have complements.

Overview of how I describe the eight basic syntactic elements

I present Tibetan grammar in terms of eight basic building blocks of Tibetan syntax. On the most basic level of syntactic function, Classical Tibetan has eight elements: agents of transitive verbs, objects of transitive verbs, complements of objects, subjects of intransitive verbs, complements of subjects, qualifiers of verbs, transitive verbs, and intransitive verbs. Any of these syntactic functions may be filled by a single word, or by phrases and clauses made up of words and particles. The following chart illustrates the order in which these elements may be found in a typical Classical Tibetan sentence, together with cases in which the declined elements may be found.

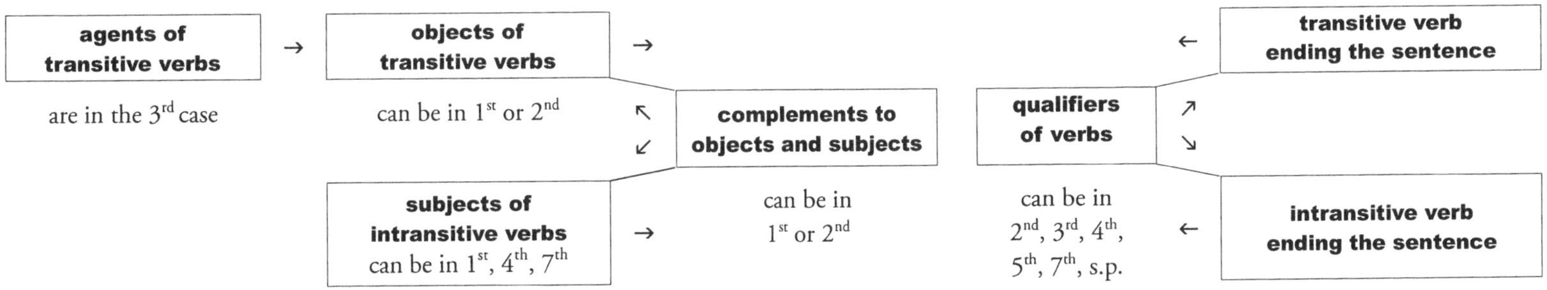

Agents of transitive verbs	The **agent** of a transitive verb is the one who, or that which, performs the action indicated by the transitive verb. Transitive verbs have agents separate from objects. Put another way, agents of transitive verbs act on objects different from themselves. Agents may be expressed or understood; Tibetan frequently uses implied agents in transitive constructions. Agents are nouns or noun equivalents (nouns, noun phrases, verbal noun clauses).
Objects of transitive verbs	**Objects** of transitive verbs are acted upon by agents different from themselves. Objects are nouns or noun equivalents. Objects themselves may have complements.
Complements to objects	**Complements to objects** are syntactic units that **complete** the **object** in the sense that complements **tell more about the object** in three ways. The object may **be the complement,** or may **appear as the complement,** or may **be conceived of as the complement.**
Subjects of intransitive verbs	The **subject** of an intransitive verb is the person, place, thing, or idea that is *doing* or *being* something. Intransitive verbs have subjects, either expressed or implied, but do not have objects. Subjects are nouns or noun equivalents. Subjects may have complements.
Complements to subjects	**Complements to subjects** are syntactic units that **complete** the **subject** of an intransitive verb in the sense that **complements tell more about the subject** in three ways. The subject may **be the complement,** or the subject may **appear as the complement,** or the subject may **be conceived of as the complement.**
Qualifiers of verbs	**Qualifiers** are syntactic units that **qualify the action expressed by the verb.** They qualify verbs by answering these questions: **how? when? where? for whom? why? because of what?** and **for what purpose?**
Transitive verbs	**Transitive verbs** are verbs that take direct objects, expressed or implied, separate from the agent.
Intransitive verbs	**Intransitive verbs** are those verbs that do not take objects.

Example of a sentence containing an agent of a transitive verb, object of the verb, complement to the object, and transitive verb

This transitive sentence has an agent, object, complement to the object, and transitive verb. Notice how the complement tells you more avbout the object.

	agents will usually come first, but may also follow objects		only transitive verbs can have objects	in a transitive construction, complements tell you more about the object		verbs end sentences	
syntax with transitive verbs	**agent of transitive verb** →		**object of transitive verb** →←	**complement to the object**		← **transitive verb**	
syntactic function	agent of transitive verb འདོད་ →		object of transitive verb འདོད་ →←	complement to the object		← transitive verb (ag-nom) present tense	
	ཁ་ཅིག་	གིས་ →	སེམས་ →←	གང་ཟག་གི་མཚན་གཞི་	ར་	← འདོད་	དོ།།
type of word or particle	pronoun	3rd case particle	noun	noun phrase (n. + 6th + n.)	fused 2nd case particle	verb	terminating syntactic particle
lexical meaning	someone		mind	illustration of the person		assert	
translation	*Some assert mind to be an illustration of the person.*						

Four of the eight basic syntactic functions are present in this transitive sentence

ཁ་ཅིག་	**Agent of transitive verb**	The **agent** ཁ་ཅིག་ *someone* of the transitive verb འདོད་ *assert* is marked with 3rd case particle གིས་
སེམས་	**Object of the transitive verb**	The **object** སེམས་ *mind* of transitive verb འདོད་ *assert* is in the first case, thus has no case particle marking it.
གང་ཟག་གི་མཚན་གཞི་	**Complement to the object**	The **complement** གང་ཟག་གི་མཚན་གཞི་ *illustration of the person* completes the object in the sense that the object (mind) is being perceived as the complement (an illustration of the person). It is marked with a 2nd case particle ར་ fused to the suffixless final syllable.
	No qualifier in this sentence qualifying the action expressed by the verb	
འདོད་	**Transitive verb**	**Transitive verbs** are those verbs that take direct objects, expressed or understood, separate from the agent.

No subject in this sentence because the verb is transitive and thus takes an agent

No complement to the subject in this sentence because the verb is transitive and thus takes an agent, not a subject

Example of a sentence containing an agent, object, qualifier of the verb, and transitive verb

This transitive sentence contains four of the eight possible different syntactic functions: Agent, object, qualifier (showing place of activity), and transitive verb.

	agents will usually come first, but may also follow objects			only transitive verbs can have objects		qualifiers qualify the action expressed by the verb by showing how, when, where, for whom, and because of what.			verbs end sentences
syntax with transitive verbs	**agent of transitive verb**		→	**object of transitive verb**	→	**qualifier of verb**		→←	**transitive verb**
syntactic function	agent of transitive verb བསྟན་		→	object of transitive verb བསྟན་	→	qualifier of verb: place of activity		→←	transitive verb (ag-nom) past tense
	སངས་རྒྱས་	གྱིས་	→	ཆོས་	→	རྒྱ་གར་	ལ་	→←	བསྟན།
type of word or particle	noun	3rd case particle		noun		noun	2nd case particle		verb
lexical meaning	Buddha			doctrine		India			taught
tranlsation	*Buddha taught the doctrine in India.*								

Four of the basic eight syntactic functions are present in this transitive sentence.

སངས་རྒྱས་	**Agent of transitive verb**	The agent སངས་རྒྱས་ *Buddha* of the transitive verb བསྟན་ *taught* is marked with 3rd case particle གྱིས་
ཆོས་	**Object of transitive verb**	The **object** ཆོས་ *the doctrine* of transitive verb བསྟན་ *taught* is in the first case, thus has no case particle marking it.
རྒྱ་གར་	**Qualifier of verb**	The **qualifier** རྒྱ་གར་ *India* qualifies the action expressed by the verb by showing the place of activity. It is marked with a 2nd case particle ལ་
བསྟན།	**Transitive verb**	**Transitive verbs** are those verbs that take direct objects, expressed or understood, separate from the agent.

No subject because the verb is transitive and thus takes an agent

No complement to the object in this sentence

No complement to the subject in this sentence because there is no subject in a transitive sentence.

Example of a sentence containing a subject of an intransitive verb, qualifier of the verb, complement to the subject, and intransitive verb

Here is an example of an intransitive sentence with four of the eight possible different syntactic functions: Subject, qualifier, complement to the subject, and intransitive verb.

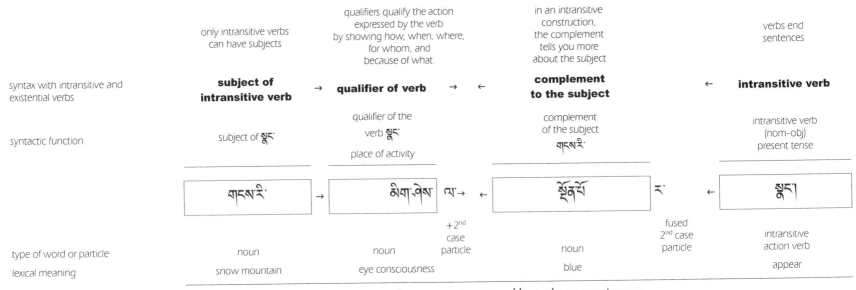

	only intransitive verbs can have subjects	qualifiers qualify the action expressed by the verb by showing how, when, where, for whom, and because of what.		in an intransitive construction, the complement tells you more about the subject		verbs end sentences
syntax with intransitive and existential verbs	**subject of intransitive verb** →	**qualifier of verb** →		← **complement to the subject**		← **intransitive verb**
syntactic function	subject of སྣང་	qualifier of the verb སྣང་ place of activity		complement of the subject གངས་རི་		intransitive verb (nom-obj) present tense
	གངས་རི་ →	མིག་ཤེས་	ལ་ →	← སྔོན་པོ་	ར་	← སྣང་།
type of word or particle	noun	noun	+2nd case particle	noun	fused 2nd case particle	intransitive action verb
lexical meaning	snow mountain	eye consciousness		blue		appear
translation	*Snow mountains appear blue to the eye consciousness.*					

Four of the basic eight syntactic functions are present in this intransitive sentence

No agent in this sentence because the verb is intransitive and takes a subject, not an agent

No object in this sentence because the verb is intransitive and only transitive verbs take objects

གངས་རི་	**Subject of the intransitive verb**	The **subject** གངས་རི་ *snow mountains* of the intransitive verb སྣང་ *appear* is unmarked because it is in the first case.
སྔོན་པོ་	**Complement to the subject**	The **complement** སྔོན་པོ་ *blue* completes the subject in the sense that the subject (snow mountains) are perceived as being the complement (blue). It is marked with a 2nd case particle ར་ fused to the suffixless final syllable.
མིག་ཤེས་	**Qualifier of the intransitive verb**	The verb སྣང་ *appear* is qualified by མིག་ཤེས་ *the eye consciousness* marked with 2nd case particle ལ་ indicating it as the place of activity.
སྣང་	**Intransitive verb**	**Intransitive verbs take subjects,** but do not take either agents or objects.

Introducing the "Summary of the General Path"

The Tibetan text presented here, "Summary of the General Path" occurs at the conclusion of *The Great Treatise on the Stages of the Path / Stages of the Path to Enlightenment Thoroughly Teaching All the Stages of Practice of the Three Types of Beings* (often abbreviated as *The Great Treatise on the Stages of the Path,* or simply as *The Great Stages of the Path)* by Tsong-kha-pa Lo-sang-drak-a, who lived from 1357 to 1419. This is an enormously detailed work—over 1,000 pages long. In it, Tsong-kha-pa presents how to properly practice the Great Vehicle Buddhism of the Perfection Vehicle. Tsong-kha-pa later wrote a companion book on the Mantra Vehicle known as the *Great Stages of Secret Mantra.* Together these two books present how a meditator integrates the two branches of the Great Vehicle: the Perfection and Mantra vehicles.

Tsong-kha-pa wrote *The Great Treatise on the Stages of the Path* outside Lhasa, Tibet's capital city, in 1402. To place this within a historical perspective, consider the following:

- Tsong-kha-pa wrote 350 years after Atisha composed the *Lamp for the Path*—the short text on which Tsong-kha-pa states he bases *The Great Stages of the Path.*
- Tsong-kha-pa wrote 750 years after Chandrakirti in India wrote his influential commentaries on Nagarjuna. Tsong-kha-pa takes Chandrakirti's commentaries on Nagarjuna as his basis for presenting the Middle Way Consequence School view of emptiness.
- Tsong-kha-pa wrote 1,200 years after Nâgârjuna wrote his *Treatise on the Middle Way.*

The general outline for The Great Stages of the Path

The Great Stages of the Path presents the sequence of mind training practiced by a single individual, from the beginning of one's religious life up through Buddhahood, according to the Perfection Vehicle form of Great Vehicle Buddhism. The text is organized around an individual's progression through three developmental stages termed the practices of the beings of the three capacities: small, middle and great. Before saying a bit about the practices of the beings of the three capacities, I will mention the general outline of topics Tsong-kha-pa discusses in *The Great Stages of the Path.*

- The greatness of the teaching's author, Atisha.
- The greatness of the teaching.
- How to listen to and how to explain the teachings.
- How to rely on your spiritual guide.
- What to do during your actual meditation sessions.
- What to do between your sessions.
- Eliminating misconceptions about the interrelation between a meditator's analytical meditations and stabilizing meditations.
- How to make the most out of leisure and opportunity: the eight freedoms from conditions making practice difficult, and the ten conditions of opportunity making fruitful practice possible.
- How to develop certainty regarding the general structure of the path.
- How to train the mind in the stages of the paths **shared with beings of small capacity:** mindfulness of death, reflecting on the already accumulated causes of bad migrations in future lifetimes, how to go for refuge to the Buddha, Doctrine and Spiritual Community, how to train in the precepts of refuge, how to develop the faith of conviction in actions and effects, reflecting on the varieties of karma, and how to engage in virtuous actions and disengage from non-virtuous actions after having reflected on cause and effect.
- How to train the mind in the stages of the paths **shared with beings of middle capacity:** how to develop the attitude of seeking liberation from cyclic existence through reflecting on suffering and its origins, and reflecting on the twelve links of dependent-origination.
- Understanding that the nature of the path leading to liberation is the three trainings: ethics, meditative stabilization, and wisdom.
- How to train the mind in the stages of the paths **shared with beings of great capacity:** the altruistic aspiration to Buddhahood is the door of entry for the Great Vehicle, how to train in the altruistic aspiration, and how to train in the Bodhisattva deeds—the six perfections—after having generated the altruistic aspiration to enlightenment.

- Extensive presentation of concentration: how to generate calm abiding.
- Extensive presentation of wisdom: how to generate special insight realizing emptiness according to Chandrakirti's Middle Way Consequence School.
- How, after you have trained in the paths common to the beings of the three capacities, you should enter the paths of the Mantra Vehicle.

How to train the mind in the stages of the paths shared with beings of the three capacities

The Great Stages of the Path presents the mind training of a single individual from the beginning of one's religious life up through how to achieve Buddhahood. The text is organized around an individual's progression through three developmental stages termed the practices of the beings of the three capacities: small, middle and great. An individual's training starts with the practices of a being of small capacity, then graduates to practices for beings of middle capacity, and finally to practices for beings of great capacity. These are the three developmental stages a single individual progresses through as the factors of wisdom and compassion are developed.

Practices in common with beings of small capacity

In brief, an individual at the stage of a being of small capacity has understood the predicament of being caught in cyclic existence and has turned to religious practice so that future rebirths will be good. The topics herein are the certainty of death and indefiniteness of when death will come, and the suffering in bad migrations of hell beings, hungry ghosts, and animals. This leads to a consideration of the benefits of the refuge provided by the three jewels: Buddha, the teacher of refuge; the Doctrine, which is the actual refuge; and the Spiritual Community of Superiors. The relation of actions to their effects is considered at length, leading to the adopting of the ten virtuous actions and abandoning of the ten non-virtuous actions, together with the ways to purify the effects of negative actions already accumulated.

Practices in common with beings of middle capacity

A being of middle capacity has seen not just the suffering of bad migrations, but the whole sphere of cyclic existence as pervaded by suffering. Renunciation—the thought definitely to leave cyclic existence—is developed. In this section Tsong-kha-pa discusses the organizational principle of the four truths for Superiors, with special attention to true sufferings and true sources, and the mechanism of the twelve links of dependent origination. Finally, Tsong-kha-pa identifies the afflictions and the path to liberation.

Practices in common with beings of great capacity

The final section discusses the practices of beings of great capacity: bodhisattvas, beings under the influence of great compassion. Beings of great capacity, seeing the faults of cyclic existence and feeling a special closeness to all sentient beings, seek the enlightenment of Buddhahood so that they might optimally lead all sentient beings to their own Buddhahood. In this section Tsong-kha-pa presents the generation of the altruistic aspiration to enlightenment and the six perfections in which a bodhisattva trains: generosity, ethics, patience, effort, concentration, and wisdom.

Tsong-kha-pa's extensive presentation of calm abiding and special insight

Tsong-kha-pa's discussion of emptiness occurs in his presentation of how to train in the final two perfections, concentration and wisdom. Concentration is discussed in the technical context of how to develop the one-pointedness of mind termed "calm abiding." One-pointedness of mind alone is not enough to accomplish the bodhisattva's object of attainment, her own Buddhahood, so that she may accomplish her object of intent, leading all sentient beings to their own state of Buddhahood. Buddhism teaches that concentration alone will never overturn cyclic existence, much less transform the mind into a Buddha's omniscient consciousness. The most innately held misconceptions that actively bind individuals in cyclic existence are overcome only through repeated, prolonged meditation on emptiness. Accordingly, about one third of the 1,000+ pages of *The Great Stages of the Path* is devoted to Tsong-kha-pa's presentation of how to develop the wisdom consciousness understanding emptiness, termed "special insight."

A final overview at the end: Summary of the General Path

While Tsong-kha-pa's brilliant and controversial treatment of emptiness occupies over 300 pages of *The Great Stages of the Path*, meditation on emptiness is not the focus of the "Summary of the General Path" presented in this book. Rather, in this passage Tsong-kha-pa is summarizing the basic structure of the complete path, an individual's entire journey from the beginning of one's religious life up to Buddhahood.

I chose this extract for a beginner's reader for a number of reasons. The vocabulary found herein is quintessentially basic Great Vehicle Buddhism. Further, in recognition of how slowly beginning Tibetan students proceed, I wanted to choose a text that presented major ideas in a straightforward manner. In this summary, Tsong-kha-pa outlines the major topics of meditation for a practitioner at each of the three stages. Each sentence offers profound insight into how individuals might transform their minds from self cherishing into minds of altruism, the very core of Buddhist meditative practice. My hope is that it will hold your attention as strongly as it has held mine.

Complete Tibetan Text for the "Summary of the General Path"

ད་ནི་ལམ་སྤྱིའི་དོན་བསྡུ་བ་ཅུང་ཟད་བརྗོད་པར་བྱ་སྟེ། ཐོག་མར་ལམ་གྱི་རྩ་བ་བཤེས་གཉེན་བསྟེན་ཚུལ་ལ་ཐུག་པས་དེའི་བདར་ཤ་བཅད། དེ་ནས་དལ་བ་ལ་སྙིང་པོ་ལེན་འདོད་བཙོས་མ་མིན་པ་བསྐྱེད་ན་དེས་རྒྱུན་དུ་བསླབ་པ་ལ་ནང་ནས་བསྐུལ་བས་དེ་བསྐྱེད་པའི་ཕྱིར་དུ་དལ་འབྱོར་གྱི་སྐོར་རྣམས་བསྒོམ། དེ་ནས་ཚེ་འདི་དོན་དུ་གཉེར་བའི་བློ་སྔ་མ་ལོག་ན་འཇིག་རྟེན་ཕྱི་མ་ལ་དོན་གཉེར་དྲག་པོ་མི་འབྱུང་བས་ལུས་ཐོབ་པ་རིང་དུ་མི་སྡོད་པའི་མི་རྟག་པ་དང་ཤི་ནས་ངན་འགྲོར་འཁྱམ་ཚུལ་བསྒོམ་པ་ལ་འབད། དེའི་ཚེ་འཇིགས་པ་དྲན་པའི་བློ་རྣལ་མ་སྐྱེ་བས་སྐྱབས་གསུམ་གྱི་ཡོན་ཏན་ལ་སྙིང་ཐག་པ་ནས་ངེས་པ་བསྐྱེད་ལ་སྐྱབས་འགྲོ་ཐུན་མོང་བའི་སྡོམ་པ་ལ་གནས་ཤིང་དེའི་བསླབ་བྱ་ལ་བསླབ། དེ་ནས་དཀར་ནག་ཆོས་ཐམས་ཅད་ཀྱི་གཞི་ཆེན་པོ་ལས་འབྲས་ལ་ཡིད་ཆེས་པའི་དད་པ་སྒོ་དུ་མ་ནས་བསྐྱེད་ལ་བརྟན་པར་བྱས་ཏེ། དགེ་མི་དགེ་བཅུའི་འཇུག་ལྡོག་ལ་འབད་ཅིང་སྟོབས་བཞིའི་ལམ་དུ་རྒྱུན་དུ་ཞུགས་པ་ཞིག་བྱ། དེ་ལྟར་སྐྱེས་བུ་ཆུང་ངུའི་ཆོས་སྐོར་རྣམས་ཚགས་སུ་ཚུད་པ་ན་འཁོར་བ་སྤྱི་དང་བྱེ་བྲག་གི་ཉེས་དམིགས་མང་དུ་བསམས་ལ། འཁོར་བ་སྤྱི་ལས་བློ་ཅི་ལྡོག་བྱ། དེ་ནས་འཁོར་བ་གང་ལས་འབྱུང་བའི་རྒྱུ་ལས་དང་ཉོན་མོངས་པའི་ངོ་བོ་ངོས་བཟུང་ནས་དེ་སྤོང་འདོད་བཙོས་མ་མིན་པ་བསྐྱེད། འཁོར་བ་ལས་གྲོལ་བའི་ལམ་བསླབ་པ་གསུམ་སྤྱི་ལ་ངེས་པ་དྲང་ཞིང་ཁྱད་པར་དུ་རང་གིས་གང་ཁས་བླངས་པའི་སོ་སོར་ཐར་པ་ལ་འབད་པར་བྱའོ། །དེ་ལྟར་སྐྱེས་བུ་འབྲིང་གི་ཆོས་སྐོར་རྣམས་ཚགས་སུ་ཚུད་པ་ན། རང་ཉིད་སྲིད་མཚོར་ལྟུང་བ་ཇི་འདྲ་བ་དེ་བཞིན་དུ། མ་རྣམས་ཀྱང་དེ་འདྲ་བར་སོང་བ་ཡིད་ལ་བྱས་ཏེ། བྱམས་པ་དང་སྙིང་རྗེའི་རྩ་བ་ཅན་བྱང་ཆུབ་ཀྱི་སེམས་སྦྱངས་ལ་འདི་ཅི་སྐྱེ་ལ་འབད་དགོས་ཏེ། དེ་མེད་ན་སྤྱོད་པ་ཕྱིན་དྲུག་དང་རིམ་གཉིས་སོགས་རྨང་མེད་པའི་ཐོག་བྱེད་པ་དང་འདྲ་བར་འགྱུར་བ་ཡིན་ནོ། །དེ་ལ་སྦྱོང་བའི་རྣམ་པ་ཐབ་ཐུབ་རྒྱུད་ལ་སྐྱེས་ན་ཆོ་གས་བཟུང་ལ། དེའི་བསླབ་བྱ་ལ་འབད་ནས་སྨོན་པ་ཅི་བརྟན་བྱ། དེ་ནས་བྱང་སེམས་ཀྱི་སྤྱོད་པ་རླབས་ཆེ་བ་རྣམས་མཉན་ལ། ལྡོག་འཇུག་གི་མཚམས་རྣམས་ཤེས་པ་དང་དེ་ལ་སློབ་འདོད་དྲག་པོ་བསྐྱེད། བློ་དེ་དག་སྐྱེས་པ་ན་འཇུག་པའི་སྡོམ་པ་ཆོ་གས་བཟུང་ལ། རང་རྒྱུད་སྨིན་པར་བྱེད་པའི་ཕྱིན་དྲུག་དང་གཞན་རྒྱུད་སྨིན་བྱེད་ཀྱི་བསྡུ་བཞི་སོགས་ལ་བསླབ། ཁྱད་པར་དུ་རྩ་ལྟུང་ལ་འབད་པ་དྲག་པོས་སྲོག་བསྟོས་བྱ། ཟག་པ་ཆུང་འབྲིང་དང་ཉེས་བྱས་རྣམས་ཀྱིས་མ་གོས་པ་ལ་འབད་ཅིང་གོས་ནའང་ཕྱིར་འཆོས་པ་ལ་འབད་དོ། །དེ་ནས་ཕར་ཕྱིན་ཐ་མ་གཉིས་ལ་ཁྱད་པར་དུ་བསླབ་དགོས་པས་བསམ་གཏན་སྐྱོང་ལུགས་ལ་མཁས་པར་བྱས་ལ་ཏིང་ངེ་འཛིན་བསྒྲུབ། བདག་མེད་

པ་གཉིས་ཀྱི་ལྟ་བ་རྟག་ཆད་དང་བྲལ་བའི་རྣམ་དག་ཅིག་རྒྱུད་ལ་ཅི་སྐྱེ་བྱས་ཏེ། རྙེད་པ་དང་ལྟ་ཐོག་དེར་བཞག་ནས་སྐྱོང་བའི་སྐྱོང་ཚུལ་རྣམ་དག་ཤེས་པར་བྱས་ལ་བསྐྱང་ངོ་། །དེ་འདྲ་བའི་བསམ་གཏན་དང་ཤེས་རབ་གཉིས་ལ་ཞི་ལྷག་གི་མིང་བཏགས་པ་ཡིན་གྱི། ཕར་ཕྱིན་ཐ་མ་གཉིས་ལས་ཟུར་པ་ཞིག་མེད་པས་བྱང་སེམས་ཀྱི་སྡོམ་པ་བཟུང་ནས་དེའི་བསླབ་བྱ་ལ་སློབ་པའི་གསེབ་ནས་འོང་བ་ཡིན་ནོ། །འདི་ཡང་འོག་མ་འོག་མ་བསྒོམས་ཀྱིན་གོང་མ་གོང་མ་ལ་ཐོབ་འདོད་ཆེར་འགྲོ་བ་དང་གོང་མ་གོང་མ་མཉན་པ་ན་འོག་མ་འོག་མ་ལ་བསླབ་འདོད་ཇེ་ཆེ་ཇེ་ཆེར་འགྲོ་བ་ཞིག་བྱུང་ན་གནད་དུ་སོང་བ་ཡིན་གྱི། ལྷ་མ་རྣམས་ཅི་ཡང་མེད་པར་སེམས་ཀྱི་གནས་ཆ་རེ་ཙམ་དང་ལྟ་བའི་གོ་བ་ཙམ་རེ་ལ་ནུས་པ་སྤྲུག་ལོ་བྱས་ཀྱང་གནད་དུ་འགྲོ་ཤིན་ཏུ་དཀའ་བས་ལམ་གྱི་ལུས་ཡོངས་སུ་རྫོགས་པ་ཞིག་ལ་ངེས་པ་འདྲོངས་དགོས་པ་ཡིན་ནོ། །དེ་རྣམས་བསྒོམ་པའི་ཚེ་ཡང་རྟོག་པ་སྦྱོང་བར་བྱས་ནས་བློ་རྣམས་ཆ་མཉམ་དགོས་ཏེ། འདི་ལྟར་ལམ་ལ་འཁྲིད་པའི་བཤེས་གཉེན་ལ་གུས་པ་ཆུང་བར་སྣང་ན་ལེགས་ཚོགས་ཐམས་ཅད་ཀྱི་རྩ་བ་འཆད་པས་བསྟེན་ཚུལ་ལ་འབད། དེ་བཞིན་དུ་བསླབ་པ་ལ་སྤྲོ་ཤུགས་ཆུང་ན་དལ་འབྱོར་གྱི་སྙིང་དང་ཚེ་འདི་ལ་མངོན་ཞེན་ཆེ་བར་སོང་ན་མི་རྟག་པ་དང་ངན་འགྲོའི་ཉེས་དམིགས་བསྒོམ་པ་ལ་གཙོ་བོར་བྱ་དགོས། ཁས་བླངས་པའི་བཅས་པ་རྣམས་ལ་གཡེལ་བར་སྣང་ན་ལས་འབྲས་ལ་ངེས་པ་ཆུང་བ་ཡིན་སྙམ་དུ་བསམས་ལ། ལས་འབྲས་བསྒོམ་པ་ལ་གཙོ་བོར་བྱ། འཁོར་བ་མཐའ་དག་ལ་སྐྱོ་ཤས་ཆུང་ན་ཐར་པ་དོན་གཉེར་གྱི་བློ་ཚིག་ཙམ་དུ་འགྲོ་བས་འཁོར་བའི་ཉེས་དམིགས་རྣམས་བསམ། ཅི་བྱེད་སེམས་ཅན་གྱི་དོན་དུ་བྱེད་པའི་བློ་ཤུགས་དྲག་མི་སྣང་ན་ཐེག་ཆེན་གྱི་རྩ་བ་འཆད་པས་སྨོན་སེམས་རྒྱུ་དང་བཅས་པ་ལ་མང་དུ་སྦྱང་། རྒྱལ་སྲས་ཀྱི་སྡོམ་པ་བླངས་ནས་སྤྱོད་པ་ལ་སློབ་པ་ནའང་མཚན་མར་འཛིན་པའི་འཆིང་བ་ཤུགས་དྲག་པར་སྣང་ན་རིགས་ཤེས་ཀྱིས་མཚན་མར་འཛིན་པའི་བློས་བཟུང་བའི་དམིགས་གཏད་ཐམས་ཅད་བཤིག་ལ། ནམ་མཁའ་ལྟ་བུ་དང་སྒྱུ་མ་ལྟ་བུའི་སྟོང་ཉིད་ལ་བློ་སྦྱང་། སེམས་དགེ་བའི་དམིགས་པ་ལ་མི་སྡོད་པའི་རྣམ་གཡེང་གི་བྲན་དུ་གྱུར་པར་སྣང་ན་རྩེ་གཅིག་པའི་གནས་ཆ་ལ་གཙོ་བོར་སྐྱོང་བར་གོང་མ་རྣམས་གསུང་སྟེ། དེས་མཚོན་ནས་མ་བཤད་པ་རྣམས་ཀྱང་ཤེས་པར་བྱ་ལ། མདོར་ན་ཕྱོགས་རེ་བར་མ་སོང་བར་རྒྱུད་དགེ་བའི་ཕྱོགས་ཐམས་ཅད་ལ་བཀོལ་དུ་རུང་བ་ཞིག་དགོས་སོ། །

The Title Sentence of *The Great Treatise on the Stages of the Path*

༄༅། །སྐྱེས་བུ་གསུམ་གྱིས་ཉམས་སུ་བླང་བའི་རིམ་པ་ཐམས་ཅད་ཚང་བར་སྟོན་པའི་བྱང་ཆུབ་ལམ་གྱི་རིམ་པ་བཞུགས་སོ། །

Before we get to the "Summary of the General Path," let's take a moment to look at the title of the book. Titles of Tibetan books are sentences ending with an honorific verb of living. In this chart I have parsed the entire sentence. I will discuss how the internal parts of the syntax operate starting on page xxvii. The title is a rather complex sentence because it contains two nested verbal adjective clauses. Because space is often limited within sentence diagrams, I have used abbreviations. A table of abbreviations used in sentence diagrams may be found on page 219.

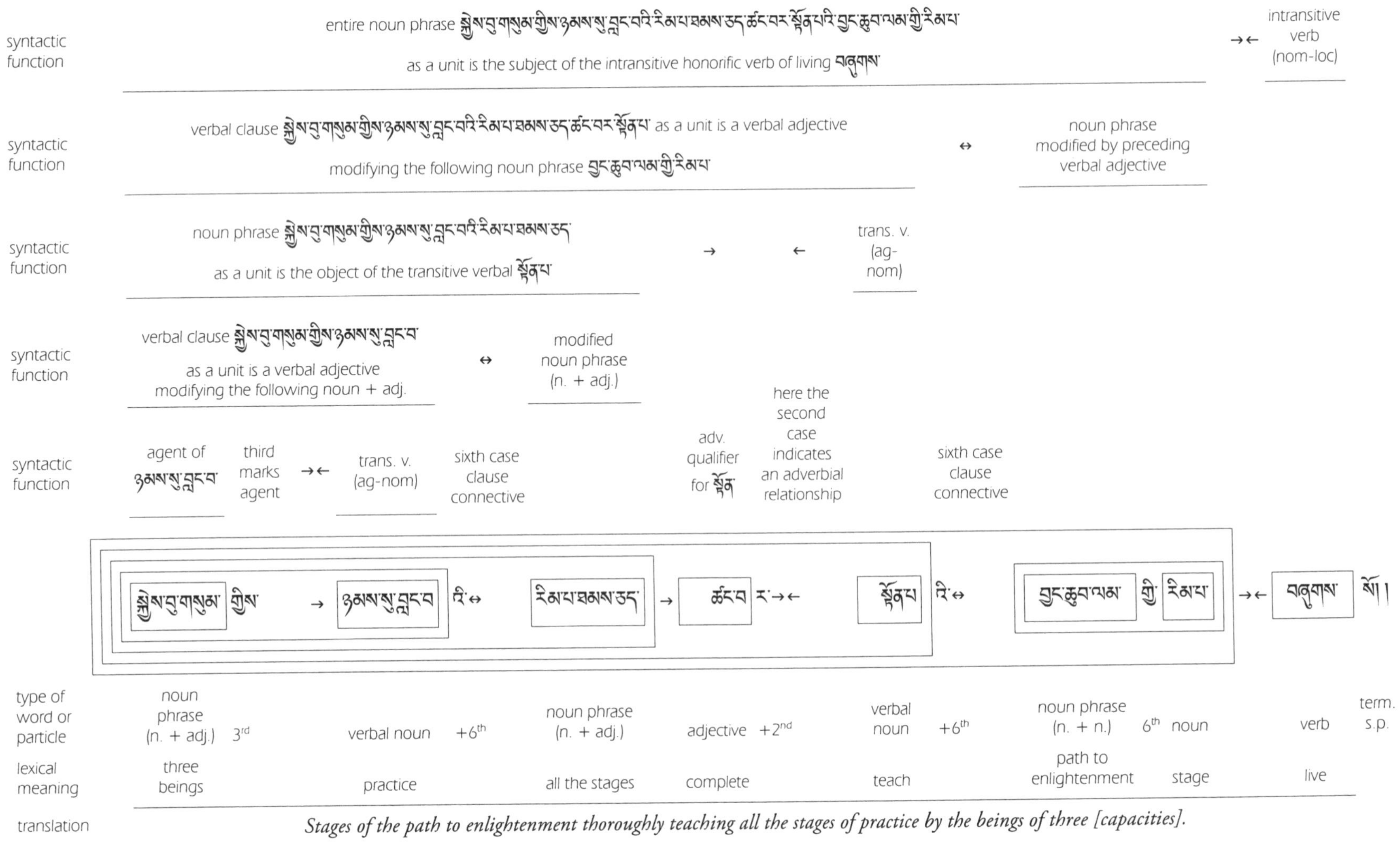

Glossary of particles and words in title sentence

In this glossary you will find all the particles and words in the title, **listed in the order in which they appear.** I have also included a glossary for the entire book in alphabetical order as an appendix. You may find a chart of key terms and abbreviations used in the glossaries on page 219. Order of verb tenses: present, past, future, plus imperative if the verb has one; intransitive verbs often do not have an imperative form.

༄༅	ཡིག་མགོ་ a beginning ornament
སྐྱེས་	intr. v. (nom-obj), *be born, arise, be created*
	སྐྱེ་སྐྱེས་སྐྱེ། ཐ་མི་དད།
བསྐྱེད་	trans. v. (ag-nom), *produce, generate, create, give birth to*
	སྐྱེད་བསྐྱེད་བསྐྱེད་སྐྱེད། ཐ་དད།
སྐྱེས་བུ་	n., *(sentient) being*
གསུམ་	n. or adj., *three;* here: adjective
སྐྱེས་བུ་གསུམ་	noun phrase (n. + adj.), *beings of the three [capacities]*
སྐྱེས་བུ་གསུམ་གྱིས་	noun phrase (n. + adj.) + 3rd case particle marking the agent of the transitive verb ཉམས་སུ་བླང་ *practice, train*
གྱིས་	particle; depending on how it is used, it will be either 1) a syntactic particle creating an adverbial construction, 2) a syntactic particle marking the qualifier of an intransitive nom-s.p. verb of absence, or 3) case particle marking the 3rd case
གིས་ཀྱིས་གྱིས་འིས་ཡིས་	are five equivalent particles
ཉམས་སུ་བླང་	trans. v. (ag-nom) (future tense), *practice, train*
	ཉམས་སུ་ལེན། ཉམས་སུ་བླངས། ཉམས་སུ་བླང་། ཉམས་སུ་ལོངས། ཐ་དད།
ཉམས་སུ་བླང་བ་	verbal noun, *practicing*
ཉམས་སུ་བླང་བའི་	verbal n. + fused 6th case particle
འི་	particle fused to suffixless final syllable; depending on how it is used, it will be either 1) a syntactic particle following a verb or verb phrase signifying conjunction or disjunction, or 2) a 6th case particle following nouns, pronouns, postpositions, and adjectives
རིམ་པ་	n., *stage*
ཐམས་ཅད་	adj., *all*
རིམ་པ་ཐམས་ཅད་	noun phrase (n. + adj.), *all the stages*
ཚང་	intr. v. (nom-obj), *be complete, be full*
	ཚང་ཚང་ཚང་། ཐ་མི་དད།
ཚང་བ་	adj., *complete*
ཚང་བར་	adj. + 2nd case particle fused to suffixless final syllable
ར་	particle fused to suffixless final syllable; depending on how it is used, it will be either 1) a verb-modifying syntactic particle within a verb phrase, or 2) a case particle following nouns, pronouns, postpositions, and adjectives marking the 2nd, 4th and 7th cases
སྟོན་	trans. v. (ag-nom), *teach*
	སྟོན་བསྟན་བསྟན་སྟོན། ཐ་དད།
སྟོན་པ་	verbal n., *teacher, teaching*
སྟོན་པའི་	verbal n. + 6th case particle fused to suffixless final syllable
འི་	particle fused to suffixless final syllable; depending on how it is used, it will be either 1) a syntactic particle following a verb or verb phrase signifying conjunction or disjunction, or 2) a 6th case particle following nouns, pronouns, postpositions, and adjectives
གི་ཀྱི་གྱི་འི་ཡི་	are five equivalent particles
བྱང་ཆུབ་	n., *enlightenment*
ལམ་	n., *path*
བྱང་ཆུབ་ལམ་	noun phrase (noun + understood 6th + noun), *path to enlightenment;* abbreviation for བྱང་ཆུབ་ཀྱི་ལམ་

བྱང་ཆུབ་ཀྱི་ལམ་	noun phrase (n. + 6th case particle + n.), *path to enlightenment;* here, the 6th case particle is connecting two nouns wherein the first noun is the destination of the second
བྱང་ཆུབ་ལམ་གྱི་	noun phrase + 6th case particle
གྱི་	particle; depending on how it is being used, it will be either 1) a syntactic particle following a verb or verb phrase signifying conjunction or disjunction, or 2) a 6th case particle following nouns, pronouns, postpositions, and adjectives
གི་ཀྱི་གྱི་འི་ཡི་	are five equivalent particles
གི་	used following words ending with the suffix letters ག་ and ང་
ཀྱི་	used following words ending with the suffix letters ད་ བ་ and ས་
གྱི་	used following words ending with the suffix letters ན་མ་ར་ and ལ་
འི་	used following words ending with the suffix letter འ་ and following suffixless final syllables. when འིས་ is fused to a suffixless final syllable, the འི goes away and all that's left is a fused ས་
ཡི་	used following any letter when an extra syllable is required to complete a line of verse
རིམ་པ་	n., *stage*
བཞུགས་	intr. v. (nom-loc), *live* (h). This verb is the honorific used in place of གནས་ or སྡོད་ བཞུགས་བཞུགས་བཞུགས་བཞུགས། ཐ་མི་དད།
གནས་	intr. v. (nom-loc), *abide, dwell* གནས་གནས་གནས་གནས། ཐ་མི་དད།
སྡོད་	intr. v. (nom-loc), *dwell, remain, sit* སྡོད་བསྡད་བསྡད་སྡོད། ཐ་མི་དད།
བཞུགས་སོ། །	final verb + sentence-ending terminating syntactic particle
སོ་	terminating s.p., following a syllable ending with the suffix letter ས་

The title sentence is a subject and an intransitive verb; the subject is composed of a complex noun phrase

The titles of Tibetan books are sentences ending with the honorific verb of living བཞུགས་ *live, reside.* The entire noun phrase preceding the verb is the subject of the honorific verb of living བཞུགས་

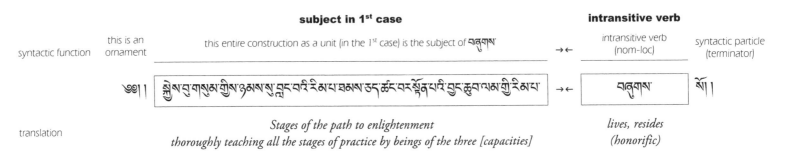

		subject in 1st case		intransitive verb	
syntactic function	this is an ornament	this entire construction as a unit (in the 1st case) is the subject of བཞུགས་	→←	intransitive verb (nom-loc)	syntactic particle (terminator)
	༄༅། །	སྐྱེས་བུ་གསུམ་གྱིས་ཉམས་སུ་བླང་བའི་རིམ་པ་ཐམས་ཅད་ཚང་བར་སྟོན་པའི་བྱང་ཆུབ་ལམ་གྱི་རིམ་པ་	→←	བཞུགས་	སོ། །
translation		*Stages of the path to enlightenment thoroughly teaching all the stages of practice by beings of the three [capacities]*		*lives, resides (honorific)*	

The subject is a noun phrase modified by a verbal adjective

While the syntax of the sentence is simple, just a subject and a verb, the syntax within the subject is complex. The essential noun phrase—stages of the path to enlightenment—is modified by a preceding verbal adjective which contains within it yet another verbal adjective construction! We will look at each part separately.

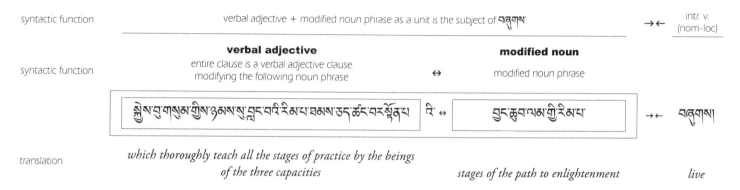

syntactic function	verbal adjective + modified noun phrase as a unit is the subject of བཞུགས་			→←	intr. v. (nom-loc)
syntactic function	**verbal adjective** entire clause is a verbal adjective clause modifying the following noun phrase	↔	**modified noun** modified noun phrase		
	སྐྱེས་བུ་གསུམ་གྱིས་ཉམས་སུ་བླང་བའི་རིམ་པ་ཐམས་ཅད་ཚང་བར་སྟོན་པ	འི་ ↔	བྱང་ཆུབ་ལམ་གྱི་རིམ་པ་	→←	བཞུགས།
translation	*which thoroughly teach all the stages of practice by the beings of the three capacities*		*stages of the path to enlightenment*		*live*

The verbal adjective diagrammed above contains within it a second nested verbal adjective

The tricky part here is recognizing that the verbal adjective modifying the noun phrase "stages of the path to enlightenment" contains within it a second verbal adjective. Notice how the following diagram explains how the innermost verbal adjective clause functions.

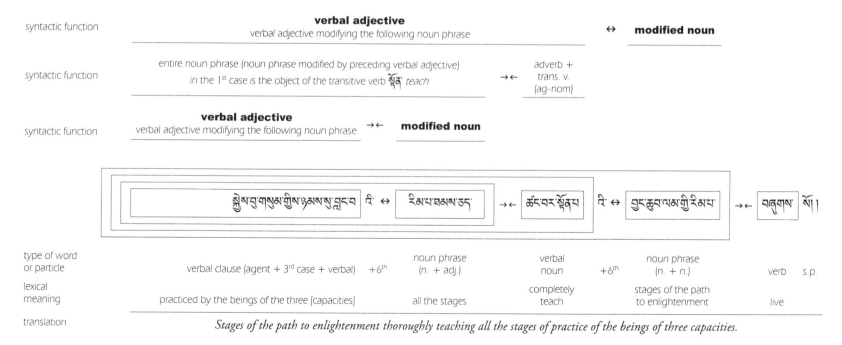

syntactic function	**verbal adjective** verbal adjective modifying the following noun phrase					↔	**modified noun**				
syntactic function	entire noun phrase (noun phrase modified by preceding verbal adjective) in the 1st case is the object of the transitive verb སྟོན་ *teach*			→←	adverb + trans. v. (ag-nom)						
syntactic function	**verbal adjective** verbal adjective modifying the following noun phrase	→←	**modified noun**								
	སྐྱེས་བུ་གསུམ་གྱིས་ཉམས་སུ་བླང་བ	འི་ ↔	རིམ་པ་ཐམས་ཅད་	→←	ཚང་བར་སྟོན་པ	འི་ ↔	བྱང་ཆུབ་ལམ་གྱི་རིམ་པ་	→←	བཞུགས་	སོ།	
type of word or particle	verbal clause (agent + 3rd case + verbal)	+6th	noun phrase (n. + adj.)		verbal noun	+6th	noun phrase (n. + n.)		verb	s.p.	
lexical meaning	practiced by the beings of the three [capacities]		all the stages		completely teach		stages of the path to enlightenment		live		
translation	*Stages of the path to enlightenment thoroughly teaching all the stages of practice of the beings of three capacities.*										

The syntax of the innermost verbal adjective in the subject of the title sentence

Here is a diagram of the syntax of a noun phrase, "all the stages practiced by beings of the three [capacities]" composed of a noun phrase "all the stages," modified adjectivally by a preceding verbal adjective, "practiced by beings of the three [capacities]."

	verbal adjective verbal adjective modifying the following noun phrase				modified noun
syntactic function	agent of ཉམས་སུ་བླང་བ་	the 3rd case here marks the agent of the transitive verb →←	trans. v. (ag-nom)		
	སྐྱེས་བུ་གསུམ་	གྱིས་→	← ཉམས་སུ་བླང་བ	འི་↔	རིམ་པ་ཐམས་ཅད་
type of word or particle	noun phrase (n. + adj.)	3rd	verbal noun	+6th	noun phrase (n. + adj.)
lexical meaning	three beings		practice		all the stages

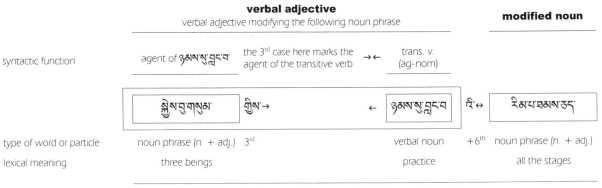

all the stages of practice of the beings of three capacities.

Notice how the agent is a compound (noun + adjective) declined as a unit in the 3rd case

སྐྱེས་བུ་གསུམ་ noun phrase (noun + adjective) *beings of the three [capacities].* That this compound means *beings of the three [capacities]* is not obvious merely from the words. As is often the case with technical Tibetan, significant content may be implicit, becoming apparent only when one is familiar with the content of a work as a whole.

སྐྱེས་བུ་གསུམ་གྱིས་ noun phrase (noun + adjective)+ 3rd case particle, *beings of the three [capacities].*
The 3rd case is here marking the noun phrase as the **agent** of the transitive verb ཉམས་སུ་བླང་ *practice*

གྱིས་ case and syntactic particle; here: case particle marking the 3rd case

Grammar review • The three distinct uses of the 5 equivalent particles གིས་ཀྱིས་གྱིས་འིས་ཡིས་

གིས་ཀྱིས་གྱིས་འིས་ཡིས་ are five equivalent particles. Each is used in three ways; depending on how it is used, any given instance of this particle will be either:

1) a syntactic particle creating an adverbial construction,
2) a syntactic particle marking the qualifier of an intransitive nom-s.p. verb of absence, or
3) a case particle marking the 3rd case; the three main uses of the 3rd case are **agents** of transitive verbs, qualifiers marking **means** by which something is accomplished, and **reasons** why something exists or some action is undertaken

Grammar review • Understanding verbal adjective clauses

As we have seen in the book's title, nouns are often modified adjectivally by a verbal clause which precedes them and to which they are joined with a 6th case particle. The noun thus modified is often the **understood** subject, agent, object, qualifier, or complement of that verbal clause. You can understand the relationship signified by the verbal adjective by recasting the relationship between the verbal adjective and modified noun within a sentence in standard verb-last syntax.

1. The basic syntax of the verbal adjective

Here is the verbal clause composed of just agent (marked with the 3rd case particle) and verbal (in the past tense).

syntactic function	agent of the transitive (ag-nom) verb ཉམས་སུ་བླང་བ་	3rd case marking agent of the transitive verb	→←	transitive verb (ag-nom)
	སྐྱེས་བུ་གསུམ་	གྱིས་→	←	ཉམས་སུ་བླང་བ་
type of word or particle	noun + adjective compound	3rd case		verbal noun
translation	*practiced by beings of the three [capacities]*			

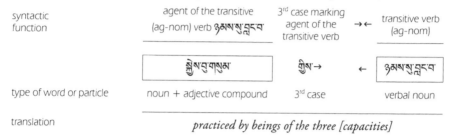

2. Here the verbal clause is an adjective modifying the noun + adj. compound following it

syntactic function	verbal adjective modifies following noun + adj. compound རིམ་པ་ཐམས་ཅད་				+6th case clause connective	modified noun + adj. compound
	སྐྱེས་བུ་གསུམ་	གྱིས་	→←	ཉམས་སུ་བླང་བ་	འི་ ↔	རིམ་པ་ཐམས་ཅད་
type of word or particle	noun + adj. comp	3rd		verbal noun	+6th case	noun + adj. compound
translation	*all the stages which are practiced by beings of the three [capacities]*					

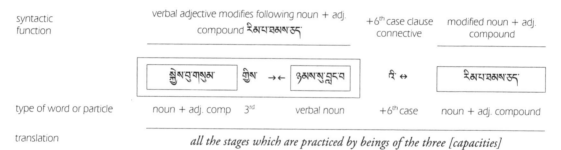

3. Recasting the clause as a sentence (i.e., verb-last syntax), we see the relationship signified by the verbal adjective is between a transitive verb and its object

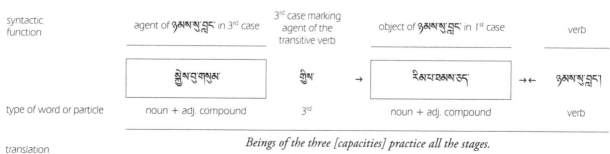

syntactic function	agent of ཉམས་སུ་བླང་ in 3rd case	3rd case marking agent of the transitive verb		object of ཉམས་སུ་བླང་ in 1st case		verb
	སྐྱེས་བུ་གསུམ་	གྱིས་	→	རིམ་པ་ཐམས་ཅད་	→←	ཉམས་སུ་བླང་།
type of word or particle	noun + adj. compound	3rd		noun + adj. compound		verb
translation	*Beings of the three [capacities] practice all the stages.* Or, in the passive voice: *All the stages are practiced by beings of the three [capacities].*					

Grammar review • The 6th case can connect two nouns otherwise having the relationship of destination and subject

བྱང་ཆུབ་ལམ་ noun phrase (noun + understood 6th + noun), *paths **to** enlightenment* (the path leads to the destination); abbreviation for བྱང་ཆུབ་ཀྱི་ལམ་

	བྱང་ཆུབ་	ཀྱི་	ལམ་
type of word or particle	noun	6th	noun
lexical meaning	enlightenment		path

noun phrase (n. + 6th + n.), *paths to enlightenment;* here, the 6th case particle is connecting two nouns wherein the 1st noun is the destination of the 2nd noun. Wilson call this the sixth case imitating the second case. The path **leads** to enlightenment. This is **not** *the path OF enlightenment,* as if the path were composed of enlightenment. In general, **paths are consciousnesses.** To speak of paths to enlightenment is to use the word path metaphorically. Just as one progresses to a destination by way of a path, one progresses to the city of enlightenment by means of newly generating consciousnesses that appreciate the faults of cyclic existence and the benefits of compassion and altruism, as well as eliminate superimposing consciousnesses that prevent us from understanding phenomena as they actually exist.

Grammar review • The 6th case can signify that the 2nd noun is composed of the 1st noun in a literal sense

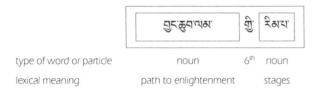

	བྱང་ཆུབ་ལམ་	གྱི་	རིམ་པ་
type of word or particle	noun	6th	noun
lexical meaning	path to enlightenment		stages

བྱང་ཆུབ་ལམ་གྱི་རིམ་པ་ noun phrase (noun phrase + 6th case particle + noun), *stages of the paths to enlightenment;* the path is composed of stages

བྱང་ཆུབ་ལམ་གྱི་ noun phrase + 6th case particle

གྱི་ particle; either 1) a syntactic particle following a verb or verb phrase signifying conjunction or disjunction, or 2) a 6th case particle following nouns, pronouns, postpositions, and adjectives

Grammar review • Dual use of the 5 equivalent particles གི་ཀྱི་གྱི་འི་ཡི་

གི་ཀྱི་གྱི་འི་ཡི་ are five equivalent particles; either 1) a syntactic particle following a verb or verb phrase signifying conjunction or disjunction, or 2) a 6th case particle following nouns, pronouns, postpositions, and adjectives

གི་ used following words ending with the suffix letters ག་ and ང་

ཀྱི་ used following words ending with the suffix letters ད་ བ་ and ས་

གྱི་ used following words ending with the suffix letters ན་མ་ར་ and ལ་

འི་ used following words ending with the suffix letter འ་ and following suffixless final syllables

ཡི་ used following any letter when an extra syllable is required to complete a line of verse

Alternate formulations of the book's title

Tibetan books are often cited by abbreviated titles. These frequently seen abbreviated formulations of the title are noun phrases (compound noun + adjective)

ལམ་རིམ་ཆེན་མོ་

	ལམ་		རིམ་	ཆེན་མོ་
type of word or particle	compound noun	[understood 6th case particle]	noun	adjective + feminine lexical particle
lexical meaning	path		stage	great
translation	*Great Stages of the Path*			

ལམ་རིམ་ཆེན་པོ་

	ལམ་		རིམ་	ཆེན་པོ་
type of word or particle	compound noun	[understood 6th case particle]	noun	adjective
lexical meaning	path		stage	great
translation	*Great Stages of the Path*			

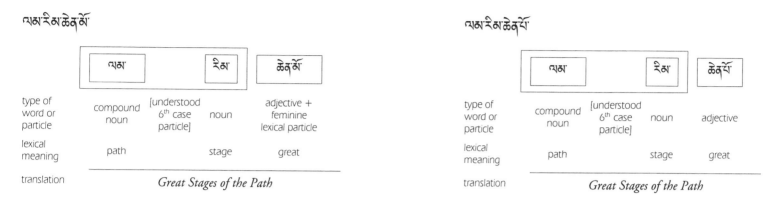

Related vocabulary • Related honorific and non-honorific verbs

བཞུགས་ this is an intransitive verb belonging to the class of verbs of living (nom-loc), *live* (honorific). This verb is the honorific used in place of གནས་ or སྡོད་

བཞུགས་བཞུགས་བཞུགས་བཞུགས། ཐ་མི་དད།

The common syntax for the class of nominative-locative (nom-loc) verbs is a **subject in the 1st** (nominative) **case** and a **principal qualifier in the 7th** (locative) **case**; the qualifier will qualify the verb by showing **place** of existing, living, and dependence, or that in reference to which an attitude is held or a cognitive state is referring.

These are related non-honorific verbs

གནས་ intr. v. (nom-loc), *abide, dwell*

གནས་གནས་གནས་གནས། ཐ་མི་དད།

སྡོད་ intr. v. (nom-loc), *dwell, remain, sit*

སྡོད་བསྡད་བསྡད་སྡོད། ཐ་མི་དད།

བཞུགས་སོ། final verb + sentence-ending terminating syntactic particle

སོ་ terminating s.p., following a syllable ending with the suffix letter ས་

Title sentence review

སྐྱེས་བུ་གསུམ་གྱིས་ཉམས་སུ་བླང་བའི་རིམ་པ་ཐམས་ཅད་ཚང་བར་སྟོན་པའི་བྱང་ཆུབ་ལམ་གྱི་རིམ་པ་བཞུགས་སོ།།

1. Write out the title sentence, boxing and identifying every element of syntax.

2. Vocabulary self test. For each word, can you identify what part of speech it is (noun, pronoun, adjective, verb, adverb, postposition) and what it means? For each syntactic particle, can you identify what class of syntactic particle it belongs to and how it is used?

ཡིག་མགོ་	ཉམས་སུ་བླང་	ཚང་བ་	ཀྱི་	སྟོན་
༄༅	ཉམས་སུ་བླང་བ་	འི་	གྱི་	སྟོན་པ་
གནས་	ཐམས་ཅད་	ཡི་	གྱིས་	སྟོད་
གསུམ་	བཞུགས་	རིམ་པ་	བྱང་ཆུབ་	སྐྱེས་
གི་	བསྐྱེད་	ལམ་	བྱང་ཆུབ་ལམ་	སྐྱེས་བུ་
	ཚང་	སོ་	བྱང་ཆུབ་ཀྱི་ལམ་	

Summary of the General Path

Chapter One

ད་ནི་ལམ་སྤྱིའི་དོན་བསྡུ་བ་ཅུང་ཟད་བརྗོད་པར་བྱ་སྟེ། ཐོག་མར་ལམ་གྱི་རྩ་བ་བཤེས་གཉེན་བསྟེན་ཚུལ་ལ་ཐུག་པས་དེའི་བདར་ཤ་བཅད། དེ་ནས་དལ་བ་ལ་སྙིང་པོ་ལེན་འདོད་བཅོས་མ་མིན་པ་བསྐྱེད་ན་དེས་རྒྱུན་དུ་བསྒྲུབ་པ་ལ་ནང་ནས་བསྐུལ་བས་དེ་བསྐྱེད་པའི་ཕྱིར་དུ་དལ་འབྱོར་གྱི་སྐོར་རྣམས་བསྒོམ།

Division of the passage into units to facilitate the analysis of the syntax

In order to facilitate the process of diagramming the syntactic structure of each chapter's text selection, I have divided the text into units based on grammatical structure and function that can be diagrammed within the space available on the page. This process of subdivision is somewhat arbitrary, with the limits imposed by the page size being the final determinate. Chapter One is composed of three sentences. Parts 1 and 2 each form a sentence. Parts 3, 4, and 5 together form a sentence.

1

ད་ནི་ལམ་སྤྱིའི་དོན་བསྡུ་བ་ཅུང་ཟད་བརྗོད་པར་བྱ་སྟེ།

2

ཐོག་མར་ལམ་གྱི་རྩ་བ་བཤེས་གཉེན་བསྟེན་ཚུལ་ལ་ཐུག་པས་དེའི་བདར་ཤ་བཅད།

3

དེ་ནས་དལ་བ་ལ་སྙིང་པོ་ལེན་འདོད་བཅོས་མ་མིན་པ་བསྐྱེད་ན་

4

དེས་རྒྱུན་དུ་བསྒྲུབ་པ་ལ་ནང་ནས་བསྐུལ་བས་

5

དེ་བསྐྱེད་པའི་ཕྱིར་དུ་དལ་འབྱོར་གྱི་སྐོར་རྣམས་བསྒོམ།

Identification of subdivisions

The topic covered in Chapters One through Seven is the mode of procedure of the general path. Tsong-kha-pa does not provide any topical subdivisions within the "Summary of the General Path." The well-known commentary on *The Great Treatise on the Stages of the Path,* called *The Four Interwoven Annotations,* explicitly identifies the topical progression within Tsong-kha-pa's exposition by introducing four subheadings placed at the beginning of the text appearing in Chapters 1, 8, 9, and 10 of this book. The first section, composed of our Chapters 1–7, is entitled "the mode of procedure of the general path." Here Tsong-kha-pa summarizes the stages of practice of the beings of the three capacities.

Part 1 • ད་ནི་ལམ་སྤྱིའི་དོན་བསྡུ་བ་ཉུང་ཟད་བརྗོད་པར་བྱ་སྟེ།

Part 1 is a transitive sentence with an implied agent. The "Summary of the General Path" begins with the author, Tsong-kha-pa, announcing a new topic. The section begins with a simple transitive sentence beginning with an introductory adverb. As is frequently seen in Tibetan, the **agent** of the transitive verb བརྗོད་པར་བྱ་ *[I] will discuss* is **implied from context.** I recommend you approach each new sentence first by reading the sentence aloud repeatedly. The flow of ideas in Tibetan sentences is from left to right. A large part of learning to read Tibetan is learning to become comfortable with the order of the flow of ideas in Tibetan syntax. I found that reading each new sentence out loud **over and over** was indispensable to the process of learning to read Tibetan.

syntactic function	implied agent of transitive verb	adverbial qualifier of བརྗོད་པར་བྱ་	punctuational syntactic particle sets off a word or noun phrase for rhetorical emphasis without changing the declension.	noun phrase ལམ་སྤྱིའི་དོན་བསྡུ་བ་ is the object of བརྗོད་པར་བྱ་		adverbial qualifier of བརྗོད་པར་བྱ་	trans. v. (ag-nom)	continuative syntactic particle following verb indicating that more relevant information follows
		ད་	ནི་	ལམ་སྤྱི	འི་ དོན་བསྡུ་བ	ཉུང་ཟད་	བརྗོད་པར་བྱ་	སྟེ།
type of word or particle	implied agent "I"	adverb	syntactic particle	noun + adj. compound	+6th compound noun	adverb qualifying the following verb	verb phrase (verbal infinitive + st. f. aux.)	continuative syntactic particle when following a verb
lexical meaning	[I]	now		general path	summary	briefly	[I] will discuss	

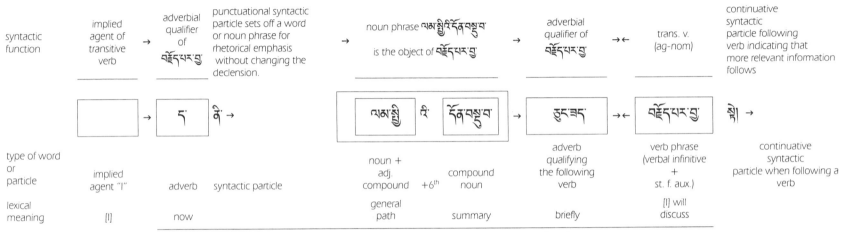

Now I will discuss briefly the summary of the general path.

Glossary for Part 1

ད་ adv., *now*

ནི་ punctuational syntactic particle, sets off a word or noun phrase for rhetorical emphasis without changing the declension. Here ནི་ follows an adverb; true adverbs (i.e., words that are adverbs as opposed to adverbial constructions utilizing syntactic particles or the 2nd case) are not declined.

ལམ་ n., *path.* A path is a mind one cultivates through meditation. Here, from the context, path refers to the entire path leading to the state of Buddhahood.

སྤྱི་ n., *generality*

ལམ་སྤྱི་ *general path.* This is a noun + adjective compound acting as a unit. Adjectives can follow the nouns they modify to create a noun + adjective compound.

སྤྱིའི་ n. + 6th case particle fused to suffixless, single-syllable word

འི་ particle fused to suffixless final syllable; depending on how it is being used, it will be either 1) a syntactic particle following a verb or verb phrase signifying conjunction or disjunction, or 2) a 6th case particle following nouns, pronouns, postpositions, and adjectives

གི་ཀྱི་གྱི་འི་ཡི་ These five particles are equivalent

གི་ used following words ending with the suffix letters ག་ and ང་

ཀྱི་ used following words ending with the suffix letters ད་ བ་ and ས་

གྱི་ used following words ending with the suffix letters ནམར་ and ལ་

འི་ used following words ending with the suffix letter འ་ and following suffixless final syllables. when འིས་ is fused to a suffixless final syllable, the འི goes away and all that's left is a fused ས་

ཡི་ used following any letter when an extra syllable is required to complete a line of verse

དོན་ n., *object, meaning, purpose*

བསྡུ་ trans. v. (ag-nom), *gather, collect*

སྡུད་བསྡུས་བསྡུ་སྡུས། ཐ་དད།

འདུས་ intr. v. (nom-obj), *be gathered, be included*

འདུད་འདུས་འདུ་འདུས། ཐ་མི་དད་

བསྡུ་བ་ n., *collection*

དོན་བསྡུ་བ་ compound noun, *summary, summation;* literally, it is a verbal clause *condensed meaning,* more elegantly translated as *summary.*

མཇུག་བསྡུ་བ་ compound noun, *conclusion*

ལམ་གྱི་འི་དོན་བསྡུ་བ་ noun phrase (n. + 6th case particle + n.), *summary of the general path,* **considered as a unit** it is the object of the transitive verb བརྗོད་ པར་བྱ་

ཅུང་ཟད་ adv., *slightly, a little, briefly*

ཅུང་ཟད་ The absence of a case particle following the adverb does not indicate the 1st case because adverbs are not declined.

བརྗོད་པར་བྱ་ verb phrase (verbal infinitive + strong future auxiliary), *[I] will express* or *[you] should express*

བརྗོད་ trans. v. (ag-nom), *set forth, express*

རྗོད་བརྗོད་བརྗོད་རྗོད། ཐ་དད།

བརྗོད་པར་ verbal infinitive; here, the fused ར་ is a syntactic particle modifying a verb to create a verbal infinitive within the verb phrase བརྗོད་པར་བྱ་ *[I] will express;* it is **not** a case particle marking the 2nd, 4th or 7th cases because it does not follow a noun—it is within a verb phrase

སུ་རུ་ཏུ་དུ་ར་ are the five syntactic particles used to modify verbs to create infinitives within verb phrases

བྱ་ trans. v. (future tense) (ag-nom), *do, make, perform, take;* here: strong future auxiliary

བྱེད་བྱས་བྱ་བྱོས། ཐ་དད།

བརྗོད་པར་བྱ་སྟེ། verb phrase + continuative syntactic particle showing sequence by indicating that more relevant information will follow.

ཏེ་ སྟེ་ and དེ་ are equivalent syntactic particles; either 1) continuative syntactic particles following verbs and verb phrases showing sequence, or 2) punctuational syntactic particles following words or phrases marking appositives

ཏེ་ follows words ending with suffix letters ནརལས་

སྟེ་ follows suffixless words and words ending with suffix letters གངབམའ་

དེ་ follows words ending with suffix letter ད་

Grammar review • Understanding how verbs function is the key to understanding a Tibetan sentence

བརྗོད་ transitive verb that takes an agent in the 3rd case and an object in the 1st case (ag-nom), *set forth, express*

བརྗོད་པར་བྱ་ verb phrase (verbal infinitive + strong future auxiliary), *[I] will express* or *[you] should express* . Because this verb phrase may sometimes imply **"I"** and other times imply **"you"** as its agent, as translator you need to determine **who** the agent is from context. Here, at the beginning of a new topic, the author Tsong-kha-pa is indicating that he will now discuss briefly the summary of the general path.

བརྗོད་པར་ verbal infinitive; here, the fused ར་ is a syntactic particle modifying a verb to create a verbal infinitive within the verb phrase བརྗོད་པར་བྱ་ *[I] will express* or *[you] should express;* it is **not** a case particle marking the 2nd, 4th or 7th cases because it does not follow a noun—it is within a verb phrase.

བྱ་ trans. v. (future tense) (ag-nom), *do, make, perform, take;* here: strong future auxiliary བྱེད་བྱས་བྱ་བྱོས། ཐ་དད།

Grammar review • Important parts of Tibetan sentences often are implied by context

As is often the case in Tibetan, when the author is speaking in the first person, as in "I will discuss," the pronoun "I" is implied. Tibetan sentences often have implied syntactic elements such as implied **agents** or **subjects**. The seeming omission of such important elements can contribute to the challenge of learning to read Tibetan for those accustomed to the convention of English to have all the elements explicitly present. In Tibetan, the unstated elements can be absent **because the sentence isn't about the implied elements**. Here the sentence isn't about **who** is doing the stating (the absent, implied element), but rather about **what** is being stated (the explicit element).

implied agent	→	ད་ནི་ལམ་སྤྱིའི་དོན་བསྡུ་བ་ཅུང་ཟད་བརྗོད་པར་བྱ་སྟེ།
The agent of བརྗོད་པར་བྱ་ is implied		*Now, I will set forth briefly the summary of the general path.*

Grammar review • Tibetan modifies verbs adverbially in three different ways

Classical Tibetan qualifies verbs adverbially in three different ways: with adverbs, and with words or phrases marked with either a *la* group particle (considered in Wilson's system to be the second case), or with a syntactic particle. The first sentence of the "Summary of the General Path" is somewhat unusual in that it has has two adverbs in it. More frequently seen are two other ways (illustrated below) of qualifying verbs adverbially. Words and phrases are often used to qualify verbs adverbially by a use of the 2nd case, which Wilson calls the adverbial identity construction. Finally, five particles, in addition to marking the 3rd case, also signify adverbial constructions, most frequently with verbs of existence.

1. Tibetan modifies verbs adverbially with words that are adverbs

ད་ adverb, *now* ཅུང་ཟད་ adverb, *slightly, a little, briefly*

2. Tibetan modifies verbs adverbially with words or phrases marked as 2nd case adverbial identity constructions

བདེན་པར་ཡོད་པ་ verb phrase (adverb + verbal noun) *truly existent*

བདེན་པར noun + 2nd case particle (here marking an adverbial identity) fused to suffixless syllable, *truly*

ར་ particle fused to suffixless final syllable. Depending on how it is used, this particle will be either
1) a verb-modifying syntactic particle within a verb phrase, or
2) a case particle following nouns, pronouns, postpositions, and adjectives marking the 2nd, 4th and 7th cases

3. Tibetan modifies verbs of existence adverbially with words or phrases marked with the syntactic particles གིས་ཀྱིས་གྱིས་འིས་ཡིས་

རང་བཞིན་གྱིས་ཡོད་པ་ verb phrase (noun + syntactic particle + verbal noun), *inherently existent*

རང་བཞིན་གྱིས་ noun + syntactic particle creating an adverbial construction, *inherently*

གིས་ཀྱིས་གྱིས་འིས་ཡིས་	are five equivalent particles used in three ways; any given instance of this particle will be either 1) a syntactic particle creating an adverbial construction, 2) a syntactic particle marking the qualifier of an intransitive nom-s.p. verb of absence, or 3) case particle marking the 3rd case. The three main uses of the 3rd case are **agents** of transitive verbs, and qualifiers marking **means** by which something is accomplished, and **reasons** why something exists or some action is undertaken.
གིས	used following words ending with the suffix letters ག and ང
ཀྱིས་	used following words ending with the suffix letters ད་བ་ and ས་
གྱིས་	used following words ending with the suffix letters ནམར་ and ལ་
འིས་	used following words ending with the suffix letter འ་ and following suffixless final syllables. When འིས་ is fused to a suffixless final syllable, the འི is eliminated and all that's left is a fused ས་
ཡིས་	used following any letter when an extra syllable is required to complete a line of verse

Grammar review • The three equivalent syntactic particles ཏེ་ སྟེ་ and དེ་ are syntactic particles indicating apposition or continuation

1. Following nouns or noun phrases, ཏེ་ སྟེ་ and དེ་ act as punctuation by marking apposition with following nouns or noun phrases

Used as **punctuational** syntactic particles, they mark appositional relationships. They follow a **noun** or **noun phrase** and themselves are followed by a **noun** or **noun phrase** in apposition with the first.

འཁོར་བ་སྤྱི་དང་བྱེ་བྲག་གི་ཉེས་དམིགས་ཏེ་སྐྱོན་སྡུག་བསྔལ་རྣམས་ཞིབ་པར་མང་དུ་བསམས་ལ།

You should reflect frequently and in detail on the faults of cyclic existence in general and in particular: its defects and sufferings.

འཁོར་བ་སྤྱི་དང་བྱེ་བྲག་གི་ཉེས་དམིགས་ཏེ་ (*faults of cyclic existence in general and in particular*) and སྐྱོན་སྡུག་བསྔལ་རྣམས་ (*defects and sufferings*) are noun phrases in apposition

2. Following verbs, ཏེ་ སྟེ་ and དེ་ indicate continuation

དེ་ནི་ལམ་སྤྱིའི་དོན་བསྡུ་བ་ཙུང་ཟད་བརྗོད་པར་བྱ་སྟེ། *Now I will set forth a brief summation of the general path.*

The sentence ends with a continuative syntactic particle སྟེ་ following a final verb. This is a frequently seen construction indicating that more relevant information will immediately follow. Used as a **continuational s.p.**, they follow **core verbs** and **verbs with auxiliaries** whose action has been completed, indicating that what follows is a continuation of the previous thought.

Part 2 • ཐོག་མར་ལམ་གྱི་རྩ་བ་བཤེས་གཉེན་བསྟེན་ཚུལ་ལ་ཐུག་པས་དེ་ཉིད་བདར་ཤ་བཅད།

Part 2 is a complete sentence. It begins with a clause stating a reason acting as a unit as a qualifier qualifying the action expressed by the transitive verb བཅད།

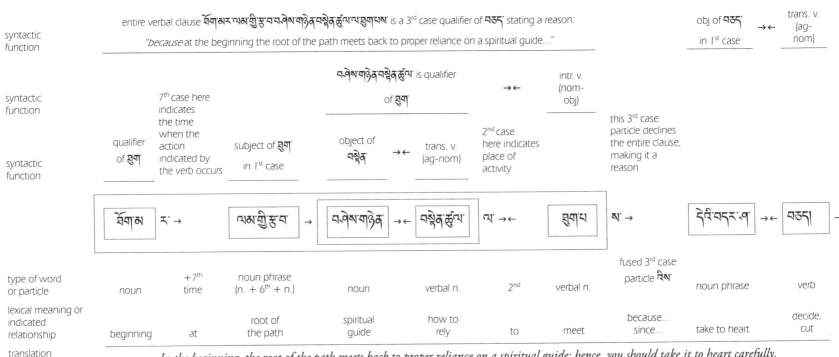

syntactic function	entire verbal clause ཐོག་མར་ལམ་གྱི་རྩ་བ་བཤེས་གཉེན་བསྟེན་ཚུལ་ལ་ཐུག་པས་ is a 3rd case qualifier of བཅད་ stating a reason: "*because* at the beginning the root of the path meets back to proper reliance on a spiritual guide..."								obj of བཅད་ in 1st case →←	trans. v. (ag-nom)
syntactic function				བཤེས་གཉེན་བསྟེན་ཚུལ་ is qualifier of ཐུག་		→←	intr. v. (nom-obj)			
syntactic function	qualifier of ཐུག་	7th case here indicates the time when the action indicated by the verb occurs	subject of ཐུག་ in 1st case	object of བསྟེན་ →←	trans. v. (ag-nom)	2nd case here indicates place of activity		this 3rd case particle declines the entire clause, making it a reason		
	ཐོག་མ	ར་ →	ལམ་གྱི་རྩ་བ →	བཤེས་གཉེན →←	བསྟེན་ཚུལ	ལ་ →←	ཐུག་པ	ས་ →	དེ་ཉིད་བདར་ཤ་ →←	བཅད། →
type of word or particle	noun	+7th time	noun phrase (n. + 6th + n.)	noun	verbal n.	2nd	verbal n.	fused 3rd case particle ཡིས་	noun phrase	verb
lexical meaning or indicated relationship	beginning	at	root of the path	spiritual guide	how to rely	to	meet	because... since...	take to heart	decide, cut
translation	*In the beginning, the root of the path meets back to proper reliance on a spiritual guide; hence, you should take it to heart carefully.*									

Glossary for Part 2

ཐོག་མ་ n., *beginning*

ཐོག་མར་ n. + 7th case particle fused to suffixless final syllable, *at the beginning*

ར་ particle fused to suffixless final syllable; either 1) a verb-modifying syntactic particle within a verb phrase, or 2) a case particle following nouns, pronouns, postpositions, and adjectives marking the 2nd, 4th and 7th cases. Here, the ར་ is here marking the 7th case, and from among the eight uses of the 7th case, the meaning signified is the time when an action is done.

ལམ་ n., *path*

ལམ་གྱི་ n. + 6th case particle, *of the path*

གྱི་ གི་ཀྱི་གྱི་འི་ཡི་ are five equivalent particles; depending on how they are used, they are either 1) syntactic particles following a verb or verb phrase signifying conjunction or disjunction, or 2) 6th case particles following nouns, pronouns, postpositions, and adjectives. གྱི་ in the context of ལམ་གྱི་རྩ་བ་ is a type connective whereby the first noun narrows the scope of the second noun. Which root? The root of the path

རྩ་བ་	n. and adj., *root, main, principal*
ལམ་གྱི་རྩ་བ་	noun phrase, *root of the path.* This noun phrase is a unit. It does not have a case marking particle following it because it is in the 1st case (also called the nominative case). It is the subject of the nominative-objective action verb ཐུག་ *meet.*
བཤེས་གཉེན་	n., (Sanskrit, *kalyānamitra) spiritual friend, spiritual guide*
བསྟེན་	trans. v. (ag-obj), *adhere to, rely on, stay close to* སྟེན་བསྟེན་བསྟེན་བསྟེན། ཐ་དད།
རྟེན་	intr. v. (nom-loc), *depend on, rely on* རྟེན་བརྟེན་བརྟེན་རྟེན། ཐ་མི་དད།
ཚུལ་	n., *mode;* the addition of ཚུལ་ to the verbal noun or verbal clause means *how to* or *proper;* in this case, *proper reliance on a spiritual guide*
བསྟེན་ཚུལ་	comp. n., *proper reliance, mode of reliance;* i.e., the correct way to go about relying
བཤེས་གཉེན་བསྟེན་	verbal clause (object + verb), *reliance on a spiritual guide.* བཤེས་གཉེན་ is the object of the transitive verb བསྟེན་
བསྟེན་ཚུལ་ལ་	comp. n. + 2nd case particle
ལ་	particle; either 1) a syntactic particle following a verb or verb phrase signifying conjunction or disjunction, or 2) a case particle following nouns, pronouns, postpositions, and adjectives marking the 2nd, 4th and 7th cases
བཤེས་གཉེན་བསྟེན་ཚུལ་ལ་	verbal clause + 2nd case particle ལ་. This is a verbal clause qualifying the action expressed by the verb ཐུག་ *meets [back to something]* by indicating the **place of activity,** i.e., the locus of the action expressed by the verb. Where does the root of the path meet back to? Proper reliance on a spiritual guide.
ཐུག་	intr. v. (nom-obj), *meet, meet back, derive from;* also used to mean *rely on* ཐུག།ཐུག།ཐུག། ཐ་མི་དད་
ཐུག་པས་	verbal n. + 3rd case particle fused to suffixless final syllable; here, 3rd case signifies a reason
ས་	abbreviation of the particle ཡིས་ (when ཡིས་ is fused to a suffixless final syllable, the ཡི goes away and all that's left is a fused ས་); either 1) syntactic particle creating an adverbial construction, 2) syntactic particle marking the qualifier of an intransitive nom-s.p. verb of absence, or 3) case particle marking the 3rd case
དེ་	limiting adj. and pronoun, *that those*
དེའི་	limiting adj. + fused 6th case particle fused to suffixless, single-syllable word
འི་	particle fused to suffixless final syllable; either 1) a syntactic particle following a verb or verb phrase signifying conjunction or disjunction, or 2) a 6th case particle following nouns, pronouns, postpositions, and adjectives
བདར་ཤ་བཅད་	verbal phrase, *take to heart,* this is used idiomatically to mean *decide after having investigated and analyzed*
བཅད་	trans. v. (ag-nom) (past tense), *cut, eliminate, decide, judge* གཅོད་བཅད་གཅད་ཆོད། ཐ་དད།
འཆད་	intr. v. (nom-obj), *be severed, be cut* འཆད་ཆད་འཆད། ཐ་མི་དད།

Notes on Part 2: The entire introductory clause is declined in the 3rd case, making the clause a reason qualifying a later verb

ལམ་གྱི་རྩ་བ་བཤེས་གཉེན་བསྟེན་ཚུལ་ལ་ཐུག་པས་ — the entire verbal clause ལམ་གྱི་རྩ་བ་བཤེས་གཉེན་བསྟེན་ཚུལ་ལ་ཐུག་པ་ is declined in the 3rd case, signified by the fused ས་, indicating that the clause as a whole states a reason. This entire construction is now a qualifier of the final verb བཅད་

ས་ — abbreviation of the particle ཡིས་ (when ཡིས་ is fused to a suffixless final syllable, the ཡི goes away and all that's left is a fused ས་); depending on how it is being used, it will be either 1) a syntactic particle creating an adverbial construction, 2) a syntactic particle marking the qualifier of an intransitive nom-s.p. verb of absence, or 3) a case particle marking the 3rd case

Exploring the meaning of དེའི་བདར་ཤ་བཅད།

དེའི་བདར་ཤ་བཅད་ — means *take to heart,* in the sense of making a decision after investigation and analysis (བརྟག་དཔྱད་བྱས་ནས་ཐག་ཆོད།)

བཅད་ — trans. v. (ag-nom) (past tense), *cut, eliminate, decide, judge;* གཅོད་བཅད་གཅད་ཆོད། ཐ་དད།

བརྟག་དཔྱད་བྱས་ནས་ཐག་ཆོད་ — this verbal clause means *decide, having investigated and analyzed*

བརྟག་དཔྱད་བྱས་ — *have investigated and have analyzed;* this is an abbreviation for two verbs in the past tense with strong past auxiliaries: བརྟག་པར་བྱས་དང་དཔྱད་པར་བྱས་

བརྟག་དཔྱད་བྱས་ནས་ — the particle ནས་ following verbs and verb phrases is a syntactic particle marking adverbs, participles or disjunction

The syntax of བརྟག་དཔྱད་བྱས་ནས་ཐག་ཆོད་

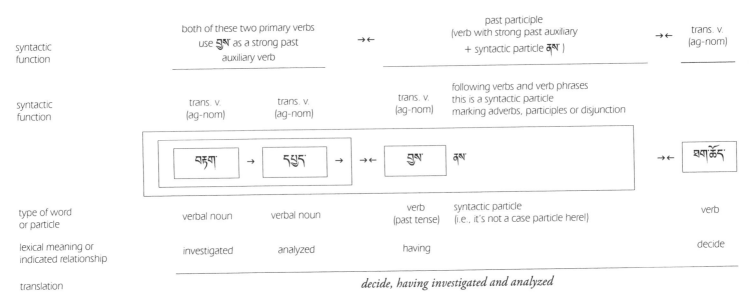

syntactic function	both of these two primary verbs use བྱས་ as a strong past auxiliary verb		→← past participle (verb with strong past auxiliary + syntactic particle ནས་)		→←	trans. v. (ag-nom)
syntactic function	trans. v. (ag-nom)	trans. v. (ag-nom)	trans. v. (ag-nom)	following verbs and verb phrases this is a syntactic particle marking adverbs, participles or disjunction		
	བརྟག →	དཔྱད →	→← བྱས་	ནས་	→←	ཐག་ཆོད་
type of word or particle	verbal noun	verbal noun	verb (past tense)	syntactic particle (i.e., it's not a case particle here!)		verb
lexical meaning or indicated relationship	investigated	analyzed	having			decide
translation	*decide, having investigated and analyzed*					

Parts 3, 4, and 5 make up a complete sentence

I have separated this single Tibetan sentence into three meaning units. Part 3 is a conditional clause. Part 4 concludes the thought begun with the previous conditional clause. Parts 3 and 4 considered as a unit qualify the final verb བསྒོམ། *meditate on* by stating a reason why one should so meditate. Part 5 concludes the sentence with a transitive construction qualified by a 4th case qualifier indicating the purpose for which the action indicated by the verb (meditation on the topics of leisure and opportunity) is undertaken.

3	4	5
དེ་ནས་དལ་བ་ལ་སྙིང་པོ་ལེན་འདོད་བཅོས་མ་མིན་པ་བསྐྱེད་ན་	དེས་རྒྱུན་དུ་བསྒྲུབ་པ་ལ་ནང་ནས་བསྐུལ་བས་	དེ་བསྐྱེད་པའི་ཕྱིར་དུ་དལ་འབྱོར་གྱི་སྐོར་རྣམས་བསྒོམ།
Then, when you generate the non-simulated wish to extract the essence with respect to leisure,	*it will urge you on to practice from within.*	*Hence, in order to generate it you should meditate on the topics concerning leisure and fortune.*

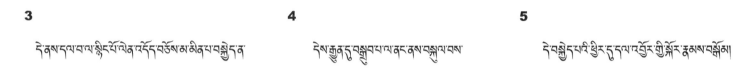

Part 3 • དེ་ནས་དལ་བ་ལ་སྙིང་པོ་ལེན་འདོད་བཅོས་མ་མིན་པ་བསྐྱེད་ན་

Part 3 is a conditional, transitive clause

This is not a sentence expressing a complete thought. This clause ends with the frequently seen conditional syntactic particle ན་ following a verb.

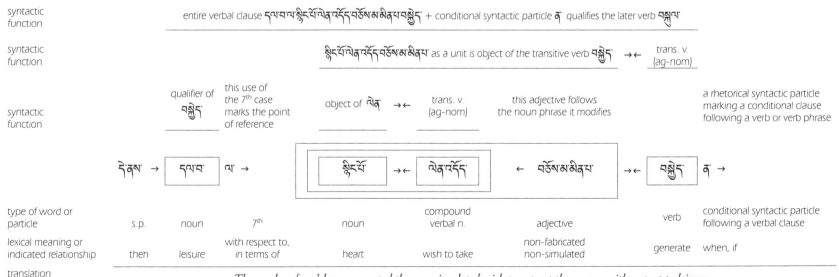

syntactic function: entire verbal clause དལ་བ་ལ་སྙིང་པོ་ལེན་འདོད་བཅོས་མ་མིན་པ་བསྐྱེད་ + conditional syntactic particle ན་ qualifies the later verb བསྐུལ་

syntactic function: སྙིང་པོ་ལེན་འདོད་བཅོས་མ་མིན་པ་ as a unit is object of the transitive verb བསྐྱེད་ →← trans. v. (ag-nom)

	དེ་ནས་ →	དལ་བ་	ལ་ →	སྙིང་པོ་ →←	ལེན་འདོད་	← བཅོས་མ་མིན་པ་	→← བསྐྱེད་	ན་ →
syntactic function		qualifier of བསྐྱེད་	this use of the 7th case marks the point of reference	object of ལེན་ →←	trans. v. (ag-nom)	this adjective follows the noun phrase it modifies		a rhetorical syntactic particle marking a conditional clause following a verb or verb phrase
type of word or particle	s.p.	noun	7th	noun	compound verbal n.	adjective	verb	conditional syntactic particle following a verbal clause
lexical meaning or indicated relationship	then	leisure	with respect to, in terms of	heart	wish to take	non-fabricated non-simulated	generate	when, if

translation: *Then, when [you] have generated the non-simulated wish to extract the essence with respect to leisure...*

Glossary for Part 3

དེ་ནས་ s.p., *then;* literally, *after that.* དེ་ནས་ is often glossed as དེའི་རྗེས་སུ་ meaning *after that.*

རྗེས་ postposition, *after.* རྗེས་ is a word—a postposition—meaning *after.*

དེའི་རྗེས་ The postposition རྗེས་ *after* is connected to དེ་ (the pronoun it modifies), *that,* with a fused 6th case particle འི་

Most of the relationships expressed in English with prepositions are indicated in Tibetan through declining nouns by adding case endings. Additionally, Tibetan does have actual words which are postpositions. They are connected to the noun they modify with a sixth case particle and are themselves declined.

དེའི་རྗེས་སུ་ དེའི་རྗེས་ is then declined as a compound in the 7th case as indicated by the case particle སུ་ This use of the 7th case signifies the time when an event happens.

དལ་བ་ n., *leisure*

དལ་བ་ལ་ n. + 7th case particle here signifying the general referential context

ལ་ particle; either 1) a syntactic particle following a verb or verb phrase signifying conjunction or disjunction, or 2) a case particle following nouns, pronouns, postpositions, and adjectives marking the 2nd, 4th and 7th cases

སྙིང་པོ་ n., *heart*

ལེན་འདོད་ verb phrase (verb + auxiliary verb), *want to take, wish to take.* In compound verb phrases, the syntax preceding the verb is governed by the first verb (here ལེན་), not the second, auxiliary, verb འདོད་; abbreviation for ལེན་པར་འདོད་

ལེན་ trans. v. (ag-nom), *take, obtain, grasp, seize, take up, obtain, appropriate*

ལེན་བླངས་བླང་ལོངས། ཐ་དད།

ལེན་པར་འདོད་ verb phrase (verbal infinitive + auxiliary verb) *want to take, wish to take*

ལེན་པར་ verbal infinitive; here, the fused ར་ is a syntactic particle modifying a verb to create a verbal infinitive within the verb phrase ལེན་པར་འདོད་ *[I, you] want to take;* it is **not** a case particle marking the 2nd, 4th or 7th cases because it does not follow a noun—it is within a verb phrase

འདོད་ trans. v. (ag-nom), *want, wish, assert.* This verb is listed in the *Great Word Treasury* as ཐ་མི་དད།, but I think it is a transitive ag-nom verb.

འདོད་འདོད་འདོད། ཐ་མི་དད།

བཅོས་ trans. v. (ag-nom), *fabricate, make up;* by extension, *simulate*

འཆོས་བཅོས་བཅོས་ཆོས། ཐ་དད།

བཅོས་མ་ n. or adjective, *simulated, fabricated, made up*

བཅོས་མ་མིན་པ་ This adjective (actually a verbal clause), means *not fabricated, non-simulated.* This term is used in a way that the English translation does not sufficiently convey. བཅོས་མ་མིན་པ་ signifies the stage of development which arises when one has cultivated a topic in meditation through the application of prolonged effort such that the qualities of the topic arise naturally and spontaneously.

བཅོས་མ་ A two-syllable word meaning something *fabricated* or *made up.*

མིན་ negative lexical suffix particle which is added to the end to create a word meaning *non-fabricated.*

བསྐྱེད་ trans. v. (ag-nom), *produce, generate, create, give birth to*

སྐྱེད་བསྐྱེད་བསྐྱེད་སྐྱེད། ཐ་དད།

སྐྱེས་ intr. v. (nom-obj), *be born, arise, be created*

སྐྱེ་སྐྱེས་སྐྱེ། ཐ་མི་དད།

བསྐྱེད་ན་ verb + conditional syntactic particle

ན་ particle; either 1) a rhetorical syntactic particle marking a conditional clause following a verb or verb phrase, or 2) a case particle following nouns, pronouns, postpositions, and adjectives marking the 2nd, 4th and 7th cases

Part 4 • དེས་རྒྱུན་དུ་བསྒྲུབ་པ་ལ་ནང་ནས་བསྐུལ་བས་

Part 4 concludes the thought begun with the conditional clause in Part 3, and it is itself a qualifying reason

As we have seen, Part 3 is a conditional clause. Part 4 concludes the thought begun with the previous conditional clause. Parts 3 and 4 considered as a unit qualify the final verb བསྒོམ་ *meditate on* in Part 5 by stating **the reason why one should so meditate.** Part 5 concludes the sentence with a transitive construction qualified by a 4th case qualifier indicating the purpose for which the action indicated by the verb (meditation on the topics of leisure and opportunity) is undertaken.

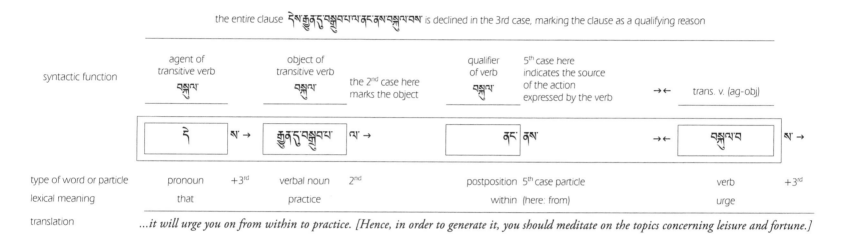

the entire clause དེས་རྒྱུན་དུ་བསྒྲུབ་པ་ལ་ནང་ནས་བསྐུལ་བས་ is declined in the 3rd case, marking the clause as a qualifying reason

syntactic function	agent of transitive verb བསྐུལ་		object of transitive verb བསྐུལ་	the 2nd case here marks the object	qualifier of verb བསྐུལ་	5th case here indicates the source of the action expressed by the verb	→←	trans. v. (ag-obj)	
	དེ	ས་ →	རྒྱུན་དུ་བསྒྲུབ་པ	ལ་ →	ནང་	ནས་	→←	བསྐུལ་བ	ས་ →
type of word or particle	pronoun	+3rd	verbal noun	2nd	postposition	5th case particle		verb	+3rd
lexical meaning	that		practice		within	(here: from)		urge	
translation	*...it will urge you on from within to practice. [Hence, in order to generate it, you should meditate on the topics concerning leisure and fortune.]*								

Glossary for Part 4

དེ་ limiting adj., used also as a pronoun, *that, that one, those*

དེས་ limiting adjective དེ used as a pronoun declined in the 3rd case. Because དེ་ is a suffixless syllable, the 3rd case particle གིས་ is abbreviated as a ས་ and fused to the suffixless syllable. Because དེ་ *that* is being used as a pronoun, it stands for, i.e., takes the place of, some unstated noun. You should always determine whether དེ་ is acting as an adjective or as a pronoun, and when it is a pronoun, you should identify what དེ་ refers to. Here, the referent of དེས་ is དལ་བ་ལ་སྙིང་པོ་ལེན་འདོད་བཅོས་མ་མིན་པ་, *the non-simulated wish to extract the essence of leisure and opportunity,* or, more colloquially in English, *to make the most of one's resources and opportunities.*

ས་ abbreviation of the particle གིས་ (when གིས་ is fused to a suffixless final syllable, the གི goes away and all that's left is a fused ས་); either 1) syntactic particle creating an adverbial construction, 2) syntactic particle marking the qualifier of an intransitive nom-s.p. verb of absence, or 3) case particle marking the 3rd case. The three main uses of the 3rd case are: agents of transitive verbs, qualifiers stating reasons, and qualifiers stating the means by which something is done.

རྒྱུན་ n., *stream*

རྒྱུན་དུ་ n. + 2nd here: adverbial sense of *continuously*

དུ་ particle; either 1) a verb-modifying syntactic particle within a verb phrase, or 2) a case particle following nouns, pronouns, postpositions, and adjectives marking the 2nd, 4th and 7th cases

རྒྱུན་དུ་བསྒྲུབ་པ་ n., *practice;* literally, *continuously achieve*

སྒྲུབ་ trans. v. (ag-nom), *achieve, attain, accomplish, complete; prove*

སྒྲུབ་བསྒྲུབས་བསྒྲུབ་སྒྲུབས། ཐ་དད།

གྲུབ་ intr. v. (nom-obj), *be established, be proven, exist*

འགྲུབ་གྲུབ་འགྲུབ། ཐ་མི་དད།

སྒྲུབ་པ་ n., *accomplishment, achievement, proof*

སྒྲུབ་པ་ལ་ n. + 2nd case marking object of trans. v. བསྐུལ་

ལ་ particle; either 1) a syntactic particle following a verb or verb phrase signifying conjunction or disjunction, or 2) a case particle following nouns, pronouns, postpositions, and adjectives marking the 2nd, 4th and 7th cases

ནང་ postposition, *in, inside, within*

ནང་ནས་ This is the postposition ནང་ *in, inside, within,* declined with the 5th case particle ནས་ Here, ནང་ནས་ is a 5th case qualifier showing **source**. The **action** expressed by the verb བསྐུལ་ *urge* (you to practice) is **qualified** by the postpositional phrase ནང་ནས་ indicating that the source of the urging is *from within.* In shorthand, ནང་ནས་ is postpositional qualifier in the 5th case showing source. The six main uses of the 5th case are: source, instrument, separation, comparison, inclusion, and logical sequence.

ནས་ particle; either 1) a syntactic particle following verbs and verb phrases marking adverbs, participles or disjunction, or 2) a case particle marking the 5th case

བསྐུལ་ trans. v. (ag-obj), *urge on*

སྐུལ་བསྐུལ་བསྐུལ་སྐུལ། ཐ་དད།

བསྐུལ་བ་ verbal noun, *urging*

བསྐུལ་བས་ verbal noun + 3rd case particle fused to suffixless final syllable

ས་ abbreviation of the particle ཡིས་ (when ཡིས་ is fused to a suffixless final syllable, the ཡི goes away and all that's left is a fused ས་); either 1) syntactic particle creating an adverbial construction, 2) syntactic particle marking the qualifier of an intransitive nom-s.p. verb of absence, or 3) case particle marking the 3rd case

The verbal noun phrase རྒྱུན་དུ་བསྒྲུབ་པ་

རྒྱུན་དུ་བསྒྲུབ་པ་ verbal clause, taken as a whole, this means *practice*. Literally, *continuously achieve.*

རྒྱུན་དུ་བསྒྲུབ་པ་ལ་ verbal clause, declined in the 7th case, the clause becomes a referential qualifier of བསྐུལ་, i.e., that which one is being urged to do. The non-simulated wish will urge you on *to practice.*

Vocabulary enrichment regarding the verb བསྐུལ་

བསྐུལ་ trans. v. (past and future forms), translated here as *urged on* means བྱེད་དུ་འཇུག་པ་ *made to do,* and གསལ་འདེབས་ *visualize*
I take an understood "you" as the object of བསྐུལ་ *the non-simulated wish to extract the essence with respect to leisure will urge you on.*

བྱེད་དུ་འཇུག་པ་ adding འཇུག་ to a simple infinitive creates a **causative sense,** *[the subject] is made to do [something]*

བྱེད་དུ་ infinitive; here, དུ་ is a verb modifying syntactic particle creating the simple infinitive *to do.*

འཇུག་ Unlike auxiliary verbs, འཇུག་ as a causative **does** control the syntax of the preceding sentence when it is used as a causative.

གསལ་འདེབས་ trans. v. (ag-nom), *visualize* འདེབས་བཏབ་གདབ་ཐོབ། ཐ་དད།

Part 5 • དེ་བསྐྱེད་པའི་ཕྱིར་དུ་དལ་འབྱོར་གྱི་སྐོར་རྣམས་བསྒོམ།

Part 5 illustrates the use of the 4th case to indicate the purpose for which an action is done

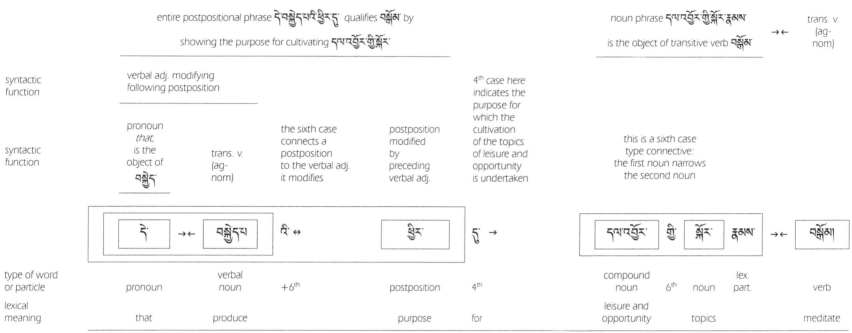

entire postpositional phrase དེ་བསྐྱེད་པའི་ཕྱིར་དུ་ qualifies བསྒོམ་ by showing the purpose for cultivating དལ་འབྱོར་གྱི་སྐོར་

noun phrase དལ་འབྱོར་གྱི་སྐོར་རྣམས་ is the object of transitive verb བསྒོམ་ →← trans. v. (ag-nom)

	དེ་	→←	བསྐྱེད་པ	འི་ ↔	ཕྱིར་	དུ་ →	དལ་འབྱོར་	གྱི་	སྐོར་	རྣམས་	→←	བསྒོམ།
syntactic function	verbal adj. modifying following postposition					4th case here indicates the purpose for which the cultivation of the topics of leisure and opportunity is undertaken						
syntactic function	pronoun *that,* is the object of བསྐྱེད་		trans. v. (ag-nom)	the sixth case connects a postposition to the verbal adj. it modifies	postposition modified by preceding verbal adj.		this is a sixth case type connective: the first noun narrows the second noun					
type of word or particle	pronoun		verbal noun	+6th	postposition	4th	compound noun	6th	noun	lex. part.		verb
lexical meaning	that		produce		purpose	for	leisure and opportunity		topics			meditate

[...it will urge you on from within to practice.] Hence, in order to generate it you should meditate on the topics concerning leisure and fortune.

Glossary for Part 5

དེ་ limiting adj. used as pronoun, *that, those;* here it refers to the wish to take up the essence in terms of leisure and opportunity

བསྐྱེད་ trans. v. (ag-nom), *produce, generate, create, give birth to*

སྐྱེད་བསྐྱེད་བསྐྱེད་སྐྱེད། ཐདད།

དེ་བསྐྱེད་ verbal clause (object + verb) *producing that;* the limiting adjective དེ་ is here being used as a pronoun *that,* serving as the object of the transitive verbal བསྐྱེད་ *produce*

བསྐྱེད་པ་ verbal n., *production, producing*

བསྐྱེད་པའི་ verbal n. + 6th case particle fused to suffixless final syllable

འི་ particle fused to suffixless final syllable; either 1) a syntactic particle following a verb or verb phrase signifying conjunction or disjunction, or 2) a 6th case particle following nouns, pronouns, postpositions, and adjectives

ཕྱིར་ adverb, *again, back*

ཕྱིར་ postposition indicating intention, *for the sake [of something], for the purpose [of something]*

ཕྱིར་དུ་ post. + 4th case particle, *for the purpose [of something]*

ཏུ་ — particle; either 1) a verb-modifying syntactic particle within a verb phrase, or 2) a case particle following nouns, pronouns, postpositions, and adjectives marking the 2nd, 4th and 7th cases

དེ་བསྐྱེད་པའི་ཕྱིར་ཏུ་ — here, ཕྱིར་ is a postposition. It is connected to the verbal adjective preceding it with a 6th case particle. The entire compound is then declined in the 4th case to create a qualifier expressing the purpose for which an action is done.

དལ་འབྱོར་ — compound noun, *the (eight) leisures and (ten) endowments.* Abbreviation for དལ་བ་དང་འབྱོར་བ

དལ་བ་ — n., *leisure*

འབྱོར་བ་ — n., *opportunity*

དལ་འབྱོར་གྱི་ — compound noun + 6th case particle

གྱི་ — particle; either 1) a syntactic particle following a verb or verb phrase signifying conjunction or disjunction, or 2) a 6th case particle following nouns, pronouns, postpositions, and adjectives

སྐོར་ — trans. v. (ag-nom), *turn* སྐོར་སྐོར་སྐོར་སྐོར། ཐ་དད།

འཁོར་ — intr. v. (nom-obj), *be turned* འཁོར་འཁོར་འཁོར། ཐ་མི་དད།

སྐོར་ — n., *topic*

དལ་འབྱོར་གྱི་སྐོར་ — noun phrase (compound n. + 6th case particle + n.), *the topics of leisure and opportunity*

དལ་འབྱོར་གྱི་སྐོར་རྣམས་ — noun phrase + lexical pluralizing particle, *the topics of leisure and opportunity*

རྣམས་ — optional lexical pluralizing particle (remember, without a pluralizing particle, Tibetan nouns are ambiguous as to number)

བསྒོམ། — trans. v. (ag-nom), *meditate on, cultivate*

སྒོམ་བསྒོམས་བསྒོམ་སྒོམས། ཐ་དད།

གོམས་ — intr. v. (nom-loc), *be accustomed to* གོམས་གོམས་གོམས། ཐ་མི་དད།

Where to find "how to rely on a spiritual guide" in The Great Treatise on the Stages of the Path

To give you a sense of the enormous detail found within *The Great Treatise on the Stages of the Path,* what follows are the subdivisions of the topic "how to rely on a spiritual guide." Each of the six major topic headings is cross-referenced to the Tibetan text and to the corresponding sections of the Lamrim Chenmo Translation Committee's translation of *The Great Treatise on the Stages of the Path*. As you can see, this one sentence summarizes over 20 pages of original Tibetan and translation.

		translation	*Great Treatise*
དེ་ལྟར་ན་བཤེས་གཉེན་བསྟེན་ཚུལ་ལ་དྲུག	*How to rely on a spiritual guide has six sections:*	69	34.8
བསྟེན་བྱ་དགེ་བའི་བཤེས་གཉེན་གྱི་མཚན་ཉིད།	*The defining characteristic of the object of reliance, the spiritual guide;*	70	34.8
སྟེན་བྱེད་སློབ་མའི་མཚན་ཉིད།	*The defining characteristic of the student who relies;*	75	38.15
དེས་དེ་ཇི་ལྟར་བསྟེན་པའི་ཚུལ།	*How the student relies on the teacher;*	77	40.4
བསྟེན་པའི་ཕན་ཡོན།	*The advantages of reliance [on a spiritual guide];*	87	49.15
མ་བསྟེན་པའི་ཉེས་དམིགས།	*The disadvantages of not relying [on a spiritual guide]; and*	89	52.1
དེ་དག་གི་དོན་བསྡུ་བའོ། །	*The summary of those [sections].*	91	54.7

Chapter One Self Test

ད་ནི་ལམ་སྤྱིའི་དོན་བསྡུ་བ་ཙུང་ཟད་བརྗོད་པར་བྱ་སྟེ། ཐོག་མར་ལམ་གྱི་རྩ་བ་བཤེས་གཉེན་བསྟེན་ཚུལ་ལ་ཐུག་པས། དེའི་བདར་ཤ་བཅད། དེ་ནས་དལ་བ་ལ་སྙིང་པོ་ལེན་འདོད་བཅོས་མ་མིན་པ་
བསྐྱེས་ན་དེས་རྒྱུན་དུ་བསྒྲུབ་པ་ལ་ནང་ནས་བསྐུལ་བས་དེ་བསྐྱེད་པའི་ཕྱིར་དུ་དལ་འབྱོར་གྱི་སྐོར་རྣམས་བསྒོམ།

Write out the passage, boxing and identifying every syntactic element

Look, it's really up to you to learn to read Tibetan. If you get to this point and can't read the passage at all, it is because you can't remember the explanations. If you can't remember the explanations of the syntax, it is because you haven't said the explanations aloud enough. If you were in my class, I'd ask: what is the verb? Is it transitive or intransitive? What class of verbs does it belong to? If it's transitive, is the agent expressly stated or is the agent implied? The answer to everything I ask is right here on the page. Here's an example for the first sentence.

syntactic function	implied agent of transitive verb →	adverbial qualifier of བརྗོད་པར་བྱ →		object of བརྗོད་པར་བྱ in 1st case →			adverbial qualifier of བརྗོད་པར་བྱ →←	trans. v. (ag-nom)	continuative syntactic particle following verb
	implied agent "I" →	ད	ནི →	ལམ་སྤྱི	འི	དོན་བསྡུ་བ →	ཙུང་ཟད →←	བརྗོད་པར་བྱ	སྟེ། →
type of word or particle		adverb	s.p.	noun + adjective compound	+6th	compound noun	adverb qualifying the following verb	verb phrase (verbal infinitive + strong future auxiliary)	continuative syntactic particle
lexical meaning	[I]	now		general path		summary	briefly	[I] will set forth, discuss	following verbs, this indicates that more relevant information follows

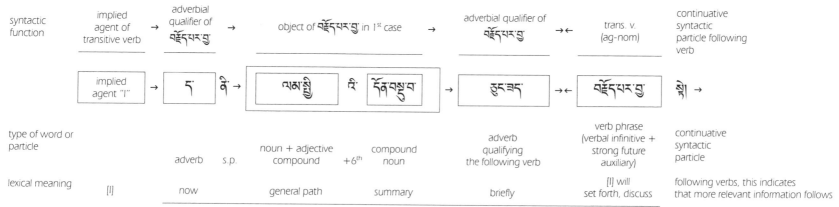

Now I will discuss briefly the summary of the general path.

Ask yourself questions as you review

1. What is the verb? — བརྗོད་པར་བྱ *I will discuss*
2. Is it transitive or intransitive? — It is transitive
3. Is the agent expressed or implied? — It is an implied "I"
4. In what case does this verb take its object? — 1st case—nominative
5. What is the object? — ལམ་སྤྱིའི་དོན་བསྡུ་བ *summary of the general path*
6. What is the particle ནི doing? — It is a punctuational syntactic particle, setting off a word or noun phrase for rhetorical emphasis without changing the declension.
7. What is the word ཙུང་ཟད doing? — It is an adverb qualifying the action expressed by the verb.
8. What is the particle སྟེ doing? — It is a continuative syntactic particle following a verb indicating that more relevant information follows.

Vocabulary

For each word, can you identify what part of speech it is (noun, pronoun, adjective, verb, adverb, postposition) and what it means?
For each syntactic particle, can you identify what class of syntactic particle it belongs to and how it is used?

ཐོག་མ་	བཅོས་མ་མིན་པ་	ལམ་
ཅུང་ཟད་	བདར་ཤ་བཅད་	ལེན་
ཏེ་	བཤེས་གཉེན་	རྟེན་
ཐུག་	བརྗོད་	རྒྱུན་
ད་	བརྗོད་པར་བྱ་	སྙིང་པོ་
དལ་བ་	བསྟེན་	སྟེ་
དེ་ནས་	བསྟེན་ཚུལ་	སྐྱེས་
དོན་	བསྡུ་	སྐྱེ་
དོན་བསྡུ་བ་	བསྡུ་བ་	རྩ་བ་
ནི་	བསྐྱེད་	སུ་རུ་ཏུ་དུར་
བཅད་	ཚུལ་	
བཅོས་	འདོད་	
བཅོས་མ་	འདུས་	

Recognition of verb forms

For each verb, you should know the translation, whether the verb is transitive or intransitive, and to what Wilson verb class it belongs.

བྱེད་བྱས་བྱ་བྱོས།

སྟེན་བསྟེན་བསྟེན་བསྟེན།

རྟེན་བརྟེན་བརྟེན་རྟེན།

ཐུག་ཐུག་ཐུག

གཅོད་བཅད་གཅད་ཆོད།

ཆད་ཆད་འཆད

ལེན་བླངས་བླང་ལོངས།

འདོད་འདོད་འདོད།

འཆོས་བཅོས་བཅོས་ཆོས།

སྐྱེད་བསྐྱེད་བསྐྱེད་སྐྱེད།

Translation of Tsong-kha-pa's text

ད་ནི་ལམ་སྤྱིའི་དོན་བསྡུ་བ་ཅུང་ཟད་བརྗོད་པར་བྱ་སྟེ། ཐོག་མར་ལམ་གྱི་རྩ་བ་བཤེས་གཉེན་བསྟེན་ཚུལ་ལ་ཐུག་པས་དེའི་བདར་ཤ་བཅད། དེ་ནས་དལ་བ་ལ་སྙིང་པོ་ལེན་འདོད་བཅོས་མ་མིན་པ་བསྐྱེད་ན་དེས་རྒྱུན་དུ་བསྒྲུབ་པ་ལ་ནང་ནས་བསྐུལ་བས་དེ་བསྐྱེད་པའི་ཕྱིར་དུ་དལ་འབྱོར་གྱི་སྐོར་རྣམས་བསྒོམ།

Now I will set forth a brief summation of the general path. Initially, the root of the path meets back to the mode of relying on a spiritual guide. Therefore, [after careful deliberation] you should take it to heart. Then, when you have generated the non-simulated wish to extract the essence in terms of leisure, it will urge you on to practice from within. Therefore, in order to generate it, you should meditate on the topics concerning leisure and opportunity.

Annotations for Tsong-kha-pa's text in Chapter One

We have been looking at Tsong-kha-pa's text without annotations. For advanced students who will benefit from more detail, here is Tsong-kha-pa's text as supplemented by the annotations from *The Four Interwoven Annotations,* 827.4-828.2. Tsong-kha-pa's text is in the large font and the annotations are in the small font.

གཉིས་པ་ལ་ལམ་སྤྱིའི་དོན་བསྡུས་པ་ ད་ནི། དེ་དག་གི་གནད་ཉེ་བར་བསྡུས་པའི་ ལམ་སྤྱིའི་དོན་བསྡུ་བ་ ལ་ལམ་སྤྱིའི་རྗེས་འགྲོ་དང་། སྒོམ་པ་གནད་དུ་སོང་མ་སོང་གི་ཁྱད་པར་དང་། རྟོག་ཞིབ་མོས་གནད་དུ་སོ་སོར་བསྒྲུན་ཚུལ་གོང་མའི་གསུང་དག་དང་། ཕྱོགས་རེ་བ་མ་ཡིན་པའི་ཉམས་སུ་ལེན་པར་གདམས་པ་བཞི་ལས། དང་པོ་དོན་སྤྱིར་རྗེས་འགྲོ་ཅུང་ཟད་བརྗོད་པར་བྱ་སྟེ། ཐོག་མར་ གང་ལས་ཀྱང་གལ་ཆེ་བ་ ལམ་གྱི་རྩ་བ་བཤེས་གཉེན་བསྟེན་ཚུལ་ལ་ཐུག་ པ་ཡིན་ པས་ བཤེས་གཉེན་བསྟེན་ཚུལ་ དེའི་དོན་ལ་ངེས་པ་རྣམ་དག་བསྐྱེད་པའི་ བདར་ཤ་བཅད་ ནས་བསྒོམ་པ་གཞིར་བཟུང་། དེ་ནས་ དེའི་རྗེས་སུ་བཤེས་གཉེན་བསྟེན་པའི་དགོས་པ་ དལ་བ་ དང་འབྱོར་པ་ཚང་བའི་རྟེན་ ལ་སྙིང་པོ་ལེན་ པ་དེ་ཡིན་པས་སྙིང་པོ་ལེན་ འདོད་བཅོས་མ་མིན་པ་བསྐྱེད་ པར་བྱས་ ན་ ལེན་འདོད་ཀྱི་བློ་ དེས་ དུས་ རྒྱུན་དུ་ ཆོག་ཙམ་ལ་མི་འཛེམ་པར་སྙིང་ཐག་པ་ནས་ལག་ལེན་དུ་ སྒྲུབ་པ་ལ་ རང་གི་ ནང་ནས་བསྐུལ་བ་ ར་བྱེད་པ་ཡིན་པ ས་ ན་དེ་འདྲའི་བློ་ དེ་བསྐྱེད་པའི་ཕྱིར་དུ་ དལ་འབྱོར་གྱི་ངོ་བོ་དང་རྙེད་དཀའ་དོན་ཆེ་ལུགས་སོགས་དལ་འབྱོར་གྱི་སྐོར་རྣམས་ དམིགས་ལེགས་པར་ཕྱེད་པར་བྱས་ནས་ བསྒོམ་ པར་བྱ་དགོས། །

Part 2, the summary of the general path

The summary of the general path condensing the essential points has four parts:
- the mode of procedure of the general path,
- the difference between successful and unsuccessful cultivation of the path,
- advice of earlier [lamas] to enhance your practice with fine discrimination, and
- advice to practice without becoming partial.

Now I will discuss briefly the summary of the general path. At the beginning, what is most important is that the root of the path meets back to proper reliance on your spiritual guide. Because this is so, you should take proper reliance on your spiritual guide as the foundation of your meditation through taking it to heart by generating pure certainty about the meaning of proper reliance on your spiritual guide.

Then, after that, since the purpose of reliance on your spiritual guide is to extract the essence of your complete basis of leisure and opportunity, you should generate the non-simulated wish to extract the essence. When you have done so, that mind wanting to take up the essence will urge you on from within, continuously, to practice, from the depths of your heart, not just verbally. Therefore, for the purpose of generating such a mind, you must meditate on the topics of leisure and opportunity: the entity of [the conditions of] leisure and opportunity, that they are difficult to find and are of great importance, etc., through differentiating the features well.

Chapter Two

དེ་ནས་ཚེ་འདི་དོན་དུ་གཉེར་བའི་བློ་སྣ་མ་ལོག་ན་འཇིག་རྟེན་ཕྱི་མ་ལ་དོན་གཉེར་དྲག་པོ་མི་འབྱུང་བས་ལུས་ཐོབ་པ་རིང་དུ་མི་སྡོད་པའི་མི་རྟག་པ་དང་ཤི་ནས་ངན་འགྲོར་འཁྱམ་ཚུལ་བསྒོམ་པ་ལ་འབད། དེའི་ཚེ་འཇིགས་པ་དྲན་པའི་བློ་རྣལ་མ་སྐྱེ་བས། སྐྱབས་གསུམ་གྱི་ཡོན་ཏན་ལ་སྙིང་ཐག་པ་ནས་ངེས་པ་བསྐྱེད་ལ། སྐྱབས་འགྲོ་ཐུན་མོང་བའི་སྡོམ་པ་ལ་གནས་ཤིང་དེའི་བསླབ་བྱ་ལ་བསླབ།

Division of the passage into units to facilitate the analysis of the syntax

Chapter Two is two sentences which I have subdivided into five parts. We will look at each part separately.

Parts 1 and 2 together are a complete sentence. Part 1 is a conditional clause acting as a reason qualifier for the principal verb in Part 2: འབད། The basic form of Part 2 is: "Strive at cultivating A and B!"

1

དེ་ནས་ཚེ་འདི་དོན་དུ་གཉེར་བའི་བློ་སྣ་མ་ལོག་ན་འཇིག་རྟེན་ཕྱི་མ་ལ་དོན་གཉེར་དྲག་པོ་མི་འབྱུང་བས

2

ལུས་ཐོབ་པ་རིང་དུ་མི་སྡོད་པའི་མི་རྟག་པ་དང་། ཤི་ནས་ངན་འགྲོར་འཁྱམ་ཚུལ་བསྒོམ་པ་ལ་འབད།

Part 3 is a verbal clause declined in the 3rd case indicating a reason. Parts 4 and 5 are relatively simple transitive constructions. Together the three parts form a single sentence.

3

དེའི་ཚེ་འཇིགས་པ་དྲན་པའི་བློ་རྣལ་མ་སྐྱེ་བས།

4

སྐྱབས་གསུམ་གྱི་ཡོན་ཏན་ལ་སྙིང་ཐག་པ་ནས་ངེས་པ་བསྐྱེད་ལ།

5

སྐྱབས་འགྲོ་ཐུན་མོང་བའི་སྡོམ་པ་ལ་གནས་ཤིང་དེའི་བསླབ་བྱ་ལ་བསླབ།

Part 1 • དེ་ནས་ཚེ་འདི་དོན་དུ་གཉེར་བའི་བློ་སྣ་མ་ལོག་ན་འཇིག་རྟེན་ཕྱི་མ་ལ་དོན་གཉེར་དྲག་པོ་མི་འབྱུང་བས་

entire construction ཚེ་འདི་དོན་དུ་གཉེར་བའི་བློ་སྣ་མ་ལོག་ན་འཇིག་རྟེན་ཕྱི་མ་ལ་དོན་གཉེར་དྲག་པོ་མི་འབྱུང་བས་ is qualifying the later verb བཤད་ by stating a reason

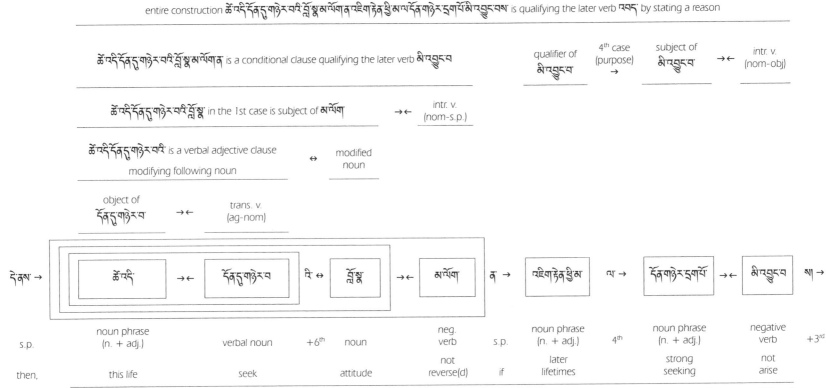

ཚེ་འདི་དོན་དུ་གཉེར་བའི་བློ་སྣ་མ་ལོག་ན་ is a conditional clause qualifying the later verb མི་འབྱུང་བ | qualifier of མི་འབྱུང་བ | 4th case (purpose) → | subject of མི་འབྱུང་བ | →← | intr. v. (nom-obj)

ཚེ་འདི་དོན་དུ་གཉེར་བའི་བློ་སྣ་ in the 1st case is subject of མ་ལོག་ | →← | intr. v. (nom-s.p.)

ཚེ་འདི་དོན་དུ་གཉེར་བའི་ is a verbal adjective clause modifying following noun | ↔ | modified noun

object of དོན་དུ་གཉེར་བ | →← | trans. v. (ag-nom)

དེ་ནས་ →	ཚེ་འདི་	→←	དོན་དུ་གཉེར་བ	འི་ ↔	བློ་སྣ་	→←	མ་ལོག་	ན་ →	འཇིག་རྟེན་ཕྱི་མ་	ལ་ →	དོན་གཉེར་དྲག་པོ་	→←	མི་འབྱུང་བ	ས་ →
s.p.	noun phrase (n. + adj.)		verbal noun	+6th	noun		neg. verb	s.p.	noun phrase (n. + adj.)	4th	noun phrase (n. + adj.)		negative verb	+3rd
then,	this life		seek		attitude		not reverse(d)	if	later lifetimes		strong seeking		not arise	

Then, if the attitude of seeking [your own welfare just for] this lifetime is not overcome, a strong seeking of [your own welfare] in future lives will not arise. Therefore...

Part 1 begins with an intransitive conditional clause and ends with another intransitive clause stating the result of this contingency

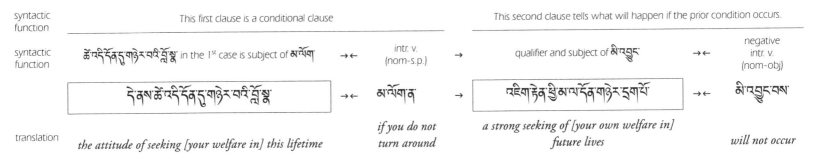

syntactic function	This first clause is a conditional clause				This second clause tells what will happen if the prior condition occurs.		
syntactic function	ཚེ་འདི་དོན་དུ་གཉེར་བའི་བློ་སྣ་ in the 1st case is subject of མ་ལོག་	→←	intr. v. (nom-s.p.)	→	qualifier and subject of མི་འབྱུང་	→←	negative intr. v. (nom-obj)
	དེ་ནས་ཚེ་འདི་དོན་དུ་གཉེར་བའི་བློ་སྣ་	→←	མ་ལོག་ན་	→	འཇིག་རྟེན་ཕྱི་མ་ལ་དོན་གཉེར་དྲག་པོ་	→←	མི་འབྱུང་བས་
translation	*the attitude of seeking [your welfare in] this lifetime*		*if you do not turn around*		*a strong seeking of [your own welfare in] future lives*		*will not occur*

Glossary for Part 1

དེ་ནས་	an introductory syntactic particle translated *then;* (literally, pronoun དེ་ + 5th case ནས་: *after that*).
དེ་ནས་	often glossed as དེའི་རྗེས་སུ་ *after that*
དེའི་རྗེས་སུ་	pronoun + 6th case particle fused to suffixless syllable + postposition + 7th case particle: *after that*
རྗེས་	postposition, *after*
ཚེ་	n., *life*
འདི་	limiting adj. sometimes used as a pronoun, *this, these*
ཚེ་འདི་	noun phrase (n. + adj.), *this lifetime*
དོན་དུ་གཉེར་	trans. phrasal v. (ag-nom), *seek* གཉེར་གཉེར་གཉེར་གཉེར། ཐ་དད།
དོན་དུ་གཉེར་བ་	verbal noun, *seeking*
དོན་དུ་གཉེར་བའི་	verbal noun + 6th case particle fused to suffixless final syllable
འི་	particle fused to suffixless final syllable; depending on how it is being used, any instance of this particle will be either 1) a syntactic particle following a verb or verb phrase signifying conjunction or disjunction, or 2) a 6th case particle following nouns, pronouns, postpositions, and adjectives
བློ་སྣ་	n., *orientation, attitude, perspective*
ཚེ་འདི་དོན་དུ་གཉེར་བའི་བློ་སྣ་	the noun བློ་སྣ་ *perspective, orientation* is modified by the preceding verbal adjective ཚེ་འདི་དོན་དུ་གཉེར་བའི་ as a unit
མ་ལོག་	negative intr. v. (nom-s.p.), *not be reversed, not be turned.* This intransitive verb is usually qualified by a noun in the 5th case from which the 1st case subject is separated ལོག་ལོག་ལོག ཐ་མི་དད།
མ་	negative lexical prefix particle
མ་མི་	equivalent negative lexical prefix particles that precede the word they negate
མིན་མེད་	equivalent negative lexical suffix particles that follow the word they negate
མ་ལོག་ན་	negative verb + conditional syntactic particle creating a conditional clause, *if [something] is not reversed, ...*
ན་	particle; depending on how it is being used, any instance of this particle will be either 1) a rhetorical syntactic particle marking a conditional clause following a verb or verb phrase, or 2) a case particle following nouns, pronouns, postpositions, and adjectives marking the 2nd, 4th and 7th cases
སྡོག་	trans. v. (ag-s.p.), *isolate from, reverse from.* This transitive verb is usually qualified by a noun in the 5th case from which the 3rd case agent is separated སྡོག་བསྡོགས་བསྡོག་སྡོགས། ཐ་དད།
ཚེ་འདི་དོན་དུ་གཉེར་བའི་བློ་སྣ་མ་ལོག་	ཚེ་འདི་དོན་དུ་གཉེར་བའི་བློ་སྣ་ as a unit is now the subject of the verb མ་ལོག་ *not reversed*
ཚེ་འདི་དོན་དུ་གཉེར་བའི་བློ་སྣ་མ་ལོག་ན་	the addition of the syntactic particle ན་ after the verb མ་ལོག་ creates a conditional clause which qualifies the later verb མི་འབྱུང་
འཇིག་	trans. v. (ag-nom), *destroy, break,* and intr. v. (nom-obj), *disintegrate* འཇིག་བཤིག་གཞིག་ཤིགས། ཐ་དད། འཇིག་ཞིག་འཇིག ཐ་མི་དད།
རྟེན་	intr. v. (nom-loc), *depend on, rely on* རྟེན་བརྟེན་བརྟེན་རྟེན། ཐ་མི་དད།
རྟེན་	n., *basis, support*
འཇིག་རྟེན་	compound n., *the world;* literally: *disintegrating basis*
ཕྱི་མ་	adj., *later*
འཇིག་རྟེན་ཕྱི་མ་	noun phrase (n. + adj.), *later lives*

འཇིག་རྟེན་ཕྱི་མ་ལ་ — the noun phrase (n. + adj.) འཇིག་རྟེན་ཕྱི་མ་ is declined in the 4th case. The meaning signified is not the place of activity (that would be in the 2nd case), or the general referential context with respect to which དོན་གཉེར་དྲག་པོ་ *strong striving* མི་འབྱུང་ *will not arise* (that would be in the 7th case). The 4th case here indicates a verb-qualifying construction stating the purpose for which the action was undertaken.

ལ་ — particle; depending on how it is being used, any instance of this particle will be either 1) a syntactic particle following a verb or verb phrase signifying conjunction or disjunction, or 2) a case particle following nouns, pronouns, postpositions, and adjectives marking the 2nd, 4th and 7th cases

དོན་གཉེར་ — abbreviation for དོན་དུ་གཉེར་ *seek*

དོན་དུ་གཉེར་ — trans. phrasal v. (ag-nom), *seek* གཉེར་གཉེར་གཉེར་གཉེར། ཐ་དད།

དྲག་པོ་ — adj., *strong*

མི་འབྱུང་ — negative intr. v. (nom-obj), *arise, come forth, emerge, occur, appear*

འབྱུང་ — intr. v. (nom-obj), *arise, come forth, emerge, occur, appear*

འབྱུང་བྱུང་འབྱུང་། ཐ་མི་དད།

མ་མི་ — negative lexical prefix particles that precede the word they negate

མིན་མེད་ — negative lexical suffix particles that follow the word they negate

མི་འབྱུང་བས་ — verbal noun + 3rd case particle fused to suffixless final syllable. From among the three uses of the 3rd case (agent of transitive verbs, qualifiers stating the means by which something is done, and qualifiers stating the reasons for something) the 3rd case here is marking a reason: the entire conditional clause (if A is not reversed, B will not happen) is qualifying the later verb འབད་ by stating the reason why one should strive at meditating on the causes of reversing A.

ས་ — abbreviation of the particle རིས་ (when རིས་ is fused to a suffixless final syllable, the རི goes away and all that's left is a fused ས་); depending on how it is being used, any instance of this particle will be either 1) syntactic particle creating an adverbial construction, 2) syntactic particle marking the qualifier of an intransitive nom-s.p. verb of absence, or 3) case particle marking the 3rd case

འབྱུང་བ་ — n., *element, arising*

Qualifiers stating a reason often come first

The entire construction as a unit is declined in the 3rd case, here signifying that it is a reason qualifying the later verb འབད་ *strive*. To put the reason and conclusion in one enormous sentence, we can see how the concluding verb clause ending with strive, "you should strive at meditating on impermanence—the fact that the body gained will not last for long—and on the mode of wandering in bad migrations upon dying," is qualified by the clause stating the reason why this is so: "if you do not turn around the attitude of striving [for your welfare in only] this lifetime, a strong striving for [your welfare in] future lives will not arise."

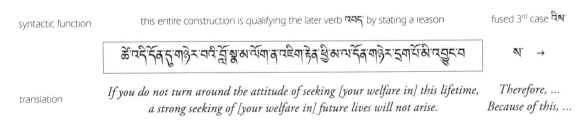

syntactic function	this entire construction is qualifying the later verb འབད་ by stating a reason	fused 3rd case རིས་
	ཚེ་འདི་དོན་དུ་གཉེར་བའི་བློ་སྣ་མ་ལོག་ན་འཇིག་རྟེན་ཕྱི་མ་ལ་དོན་གཉེར་དྲག་པོ་མི་འབྱུང་བ	ས་ →
translation	*If you do not turn around the attitude of seeking [your welfare in] this lifetime, a strong seeking of [your welfare in] future lives will not arise.*	*Therefore, ...* *Because of this, ...*

Part 2 • ལུས་ཐོབ་པ་རིང་དུ་མི་སྡོད་པའི་མི་རྟག་པ་དང་། ཤི་ནས་ངན་འགྲོར་འཁྱམ་ཚུལ་བསྒོམ་པ་ལ་འབད།

Part 2 in abbreviated form is "Strive at cultivating A and B."

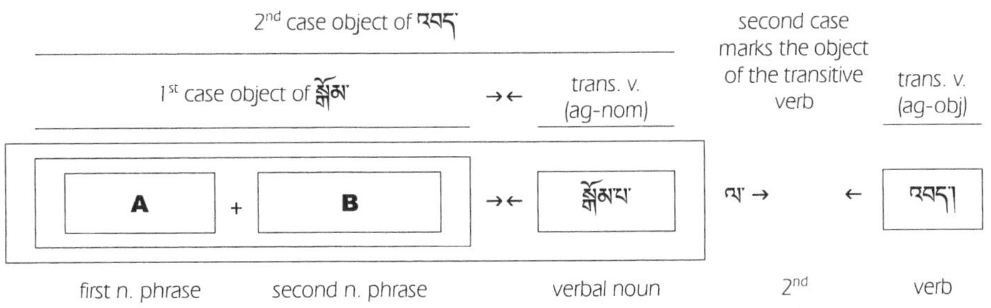

Part 2 diagrammed in full

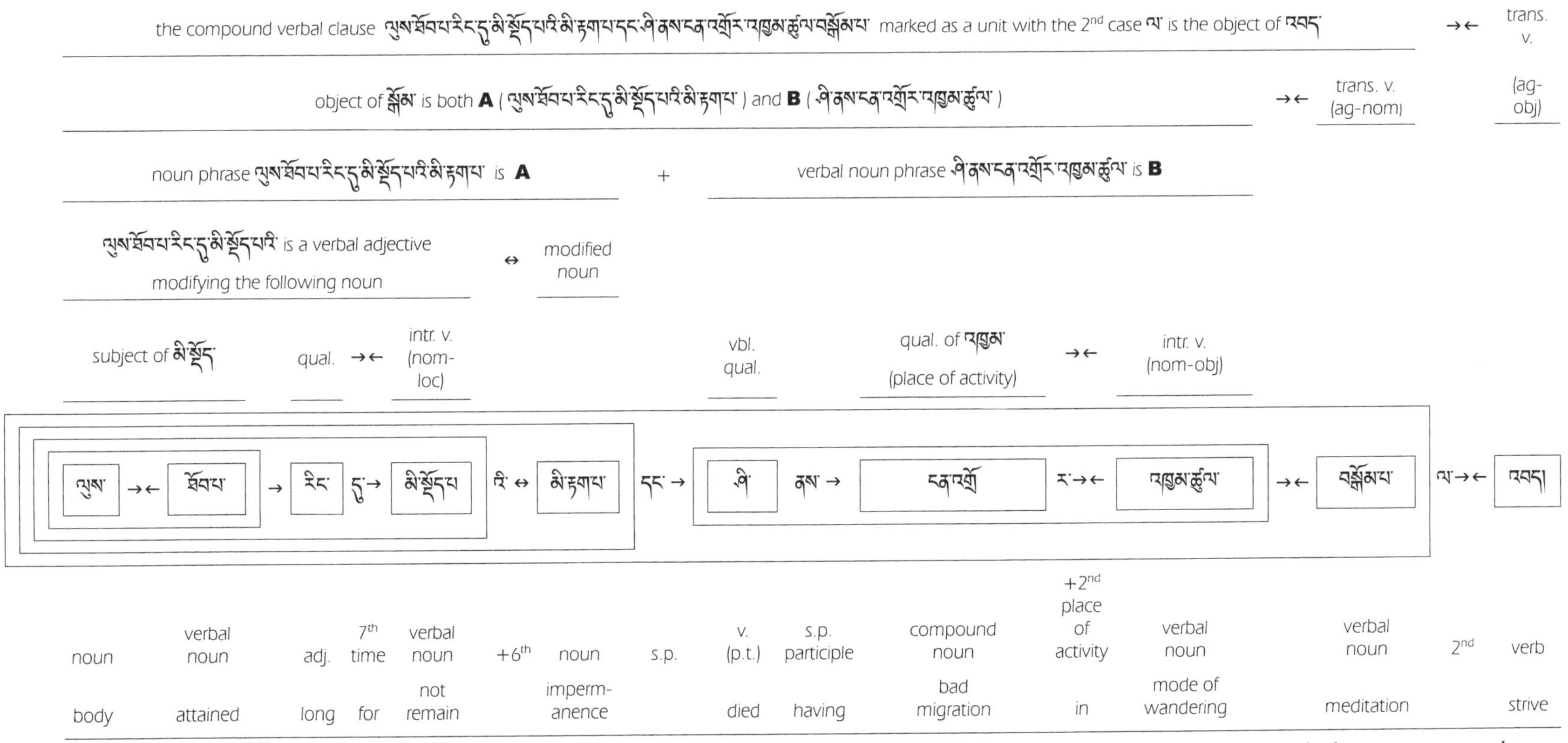

You should strive at meditating on impermanence—the fact that the body gained will not last for long—and on the mode of wandering in bad migrations upon dying.

Glossary for Part 2

ལུས་ n., *body, corpus*

ཐོབ་ intr. v. (nom-obj) (past tense), *attain, obtain, get*

འཐོབ་ཐོབ་འཐོབ། ཐ་མི་དད།

ཐོབ་པ་ n., *acquisition, attainment*

ལུས་ཐོབ་པ་ this is a verbal clause composed of a subject ལུས་ *body,* and verb ཐོབ་པ་ *the body gained.* It serves as the subject of མི་སྡོད་པ་ *not remain*

རིང་ adj., *long*

རིང་དུ་ adj. + 7th case particle qualifies verb of living མི་སྡོད་ *not remain*

དུ་ particle; depending on how it is being used, any instance of this particle will be either 1) a verb-modifying syntactic particle within a verb phrase, or 2) a case particle following nouns, pronouns, postpositions, and adjectives marking the 2nd, 4th and 7th cases

མི་སྡོད་ negative intr. v. (nom-loc), *not remain*

སྡོད་ intr. v. (nom-loc), *remain*

སྡོད་བསྡད་བསྡད་སྡོད། ཐ་མི་དད།

མི་སྡོད་པ་ negative verbal n., *the non-remaining*

མི་སྡོད་པའི་ negative verbal n., *the non-remaining,* + 6th case particle

འི་ particle fused to suffixless final syllable; either 1) a syntactic particle following a verb or verb phrase signifying conjunction or disjunction, or 2) a 6th case particle following nouns, pronouns, postpositions, and adjectives

ལུས་ཐོབ་པ་རིང་དུ་མི་སྡོད་པའི་ this a verbal clause is a verbal adjective modifying the following noun མི་རྟག་པ་ If མི་རྟག་པ་ occurred before the verbal མི་སྡོད་པ, it would be a qualifier stating a reason: *Because* of being impermanent, the body gained will not last long.

མི་རྟག་པ་ n., *impermanent, impermanent phenomena*

རྟག་པ་ n., *permanence, permanent phenomena*

མ་མི་ equivalent negative lexical prefix particles that precede the word they negate

མིན་མེད་ equivalent negative lexical suffix particles that follow the word they negate

དང་ particle, used three ways: 1) continuative syntactic particle used following nouns and noun phrases (*and* or with negative verb *or*); 2) syntactic particle marking the qualifier of an intr. nom-s.p. v. of conjunction, as in ང་རང་མི་སྡུག་པ་དང་ཕྲད་ན་ *if we meet with unpleasantness;* and 3) syntactic particle marking the qualifier of an intr. nom-s.p. v. of disjunction, as in རྟོག་པ་དང་བྲལ་ *free from conceptuality*

ཤི་ intr. v. (nom-obj), *die*

འཆི་ཤི་འཆི་ཤི ཐ་མི་དད།

ཤི་ནས་ this is a verb ཤི་ *die* + continuative syntactic particle indicating a sequence of actions: *having died.* This qualifies འཁྱམ་ *wander,* by showing **when** the wandering happens.

ནས་ particle; depending on how it is being used, any instance of this particle will be either 1) a syntactic particle following verbs and verb phrases marking adverbs, participles or disjunction, or 2) a case particle after nouns and noun phrases marking the 5th case.

ངན་འགྲོ་ n., *bad migrations*

ངན་འགྲོར་ noun + fused 2nd case particle (place of activity). This construction acts to qualify འཁྱམ་ *wander* by showing **where** one wanders: in bad migrations.

ར་ particle fused to suffixless final syllable; depending on how it is being used, any instance of this particle will be either 1) a verb-modifying syntactic particle within a verb phrase, or 2) a case particle following nouns, pronouns, postpositions, and adjectives marking the 2nd, 4th and 7th cases

འཁྱམ་ intr. v. (nom-obj), *wander*

འཁྱམ་འཁྱམས་འཁྱམ་འཁྱོམས། ཐ་མི་དད།

འཁྱམ་ཚུལ་ compound n., *mode of wandering*

ཤི་ནས་ངན་འགྲོར་འཁྱམ་ཚུལ་ noun phrase, *how, having died, you will wander in bad migrations,* this complex verbal noun as a unit is the object of the transitive verb བསྒོམ་ *meditate*

བསྒོམ་ trans. v. (ag-nom) (future tense), *meditate on*

སྒོམ་བསྒོམས་བསྒོམ་སྒོམས། ཐ་དད།

གོམས་ intr. v. (nom-loc), *be accustomed to, be familiar with*

གོམས་གོམས་གོམས། ཐ་མི་དད།

བསྒོམ་པ་ verbal n., *meditation*

བསྒོམ་པ་ལ་ verbal n. + 2nd case particle marking the object of transitive verb འབད་ *strive to, strive at, make effort in*

ལ་ particle; depending on how it is being used, any instance of this particle will be either 1) a syntactic particle following a verb or verb phrase signifying conjunction or disjunction, or 2) a case particle following nouns, pronouns, postpositions, and adjectives marking the 2nd, 4th and 7th cases

འབད་ trans. v. (ag-obj), *strive to, strive at, make effort in*

འབད་འབད་འབད་འབོད། ཐ་དད།

Notes on Part 2

The syntax of Part 2 employs an implied agent ("you") twice with transitive verbs. The first unstated agent goes with the transitive verb བསྒོམ་ *meditate on.*

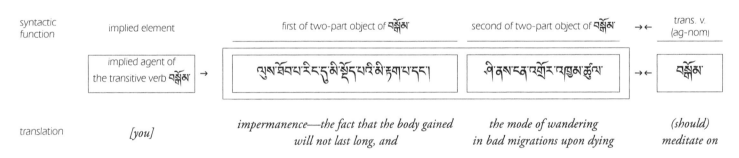

syntactic function	implied element	first of two-part object of བསྒོམ་	second of two-part object of བསྒོམ་	→←	trans. v. (ag-nom)
	implied agent of the transitive verb བསྒོམ་ →	ལུས་ཐོབ་པ་རིང་དུ་མི་སྡོད་པའི་མི་རྟག་པ་དང་།	ཤི་ནས་ངན་འགྲོར་འཁྱམ་ཚུལ་	→←	བསྒོམ་
translation	*[you]*	*impermanence—the fact that the body gained will not last long, and*	*the mode of wandering in bad migrations upon dying*		*(should) meditate on*

The second unstated agent goes with the transitive verb འབད་ *strive at.*

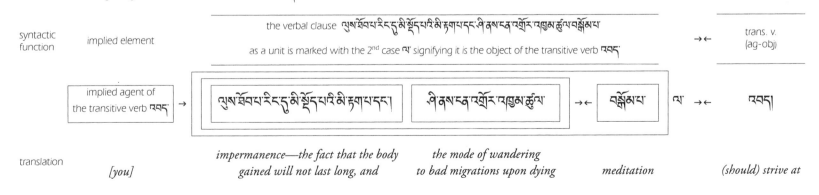

syntactic function	implied element	the verbal clause ལུས་ཐོབ་པ་རིང་དུ་མི་སྡོད་པའི་མི་རྟག་པ་དང་ཤི་ནས་ངན་འགྲོར་འཁྱམ་ཚུལ་བསྒོམ་པ་ as a unit is marked with the 2nd case ལ་ signifying it is the object of the transitive verb འབད་					→←	trans. v. (ag-obj)
	implied agent of the transitive verb འབད་ →	ལུས་ཐོབ་པ་རིང་དུ་མི་སྡོད་པའི་མི་རྟག་པ་དང་།	ཤི་ནས་ངན་འགྲོར་འཁྱམ་ཚུལ་	→←	བསྒོམ་པ་	ལ་	→←	འབད།
translation	*[you]*	*impermanence—the fact that the body gained will not last long, and*	*the mode of wandering to bad migrations upon dying*		*meditation*			*(should) strive at*

Parts 3 and 4

3

དེའི་ཚེ་འཇིགས་པ་དྲན་པའི་བློ་རྣལ་མ་སྐྱེ་བས།

Since at that time a natural attitude mindful of fright will be generated,

4

སྐྱབས་གསུམ་གྱི་ཡོན་ཏན་ལ་སྙིང་ཐག་པ་ནས་ངེས་པ་བསྐྱེད་ལ།

you should, from the depths of your heart, generate ascertainment with respect to the qualities of the three refuges.

5

སྐྱབས་འགྲོ་ཐུན་མོང་བའི་སྡོམ་པ་ལ་གནས་ཤིང་དེའི་བསླབ་བྱ་ལ་བསླབ།

as well as dwell in the vow of common refuge and train in its points of training.

Part 3 is a qualifier stating a reason

It is acting as a reason (signified by declining the clause as a unit in the 3rd case) qualifying the later verb བསྐྱེད་.

Parts 3 and 4 contrast related intransitive and transitive verbs

Parts 3 and 4 offer an interesting contrast between related intransitive and transitive verbs. Part 3 uses the future intransitive form སྐྱེ་ *will be produced* in a clause qualifying the transitive verb བསྐྱེད་ *[you should] generate* ending Part 4.

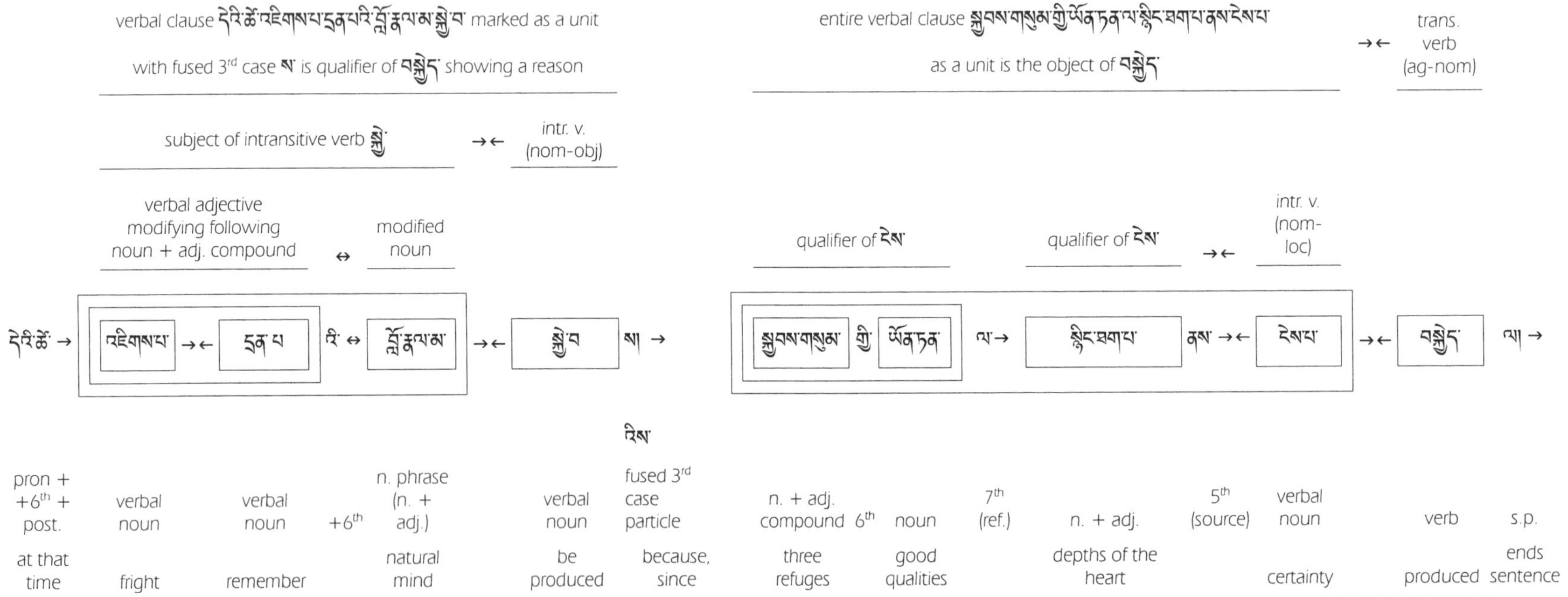

Since at that time a natural attitude mindful of fright will be produced, you should, from the depths of your heart, generate certainty about the qualities of the three refuges.

Glossary for Parts 3 and 4

དེ་ relative pronoun and adjective, *that, those*

དེའི་ relative pronoun + 6th case particle fused to suffixless single-syllable word

འི་ particle fused to suffixless final syllable; depending on how it is being used, any instance of this particle will be either 1) a syntactic particle following a verb or verb phrase signifying conjunction or disjunction, or 2) a 6th case particle following nouns, pronouns, postpositions, and adjectives

ཚེ་ n. or postposition, *time, lifetime*

འཇིགས་ intr. v. (nom-loc), *fear*

འཇིགས་འཇིགས་འཇིགས། ཐ་མི་དད།

འཇིགས་པ་ verbal n., *fright*

དྲན་ trans. v. (ag-nom), *remember, be mindful of*

དྲན་དྲན་དྲན་དྲན། ཐ་དད།

དྲན་པ་ verbal noun, *remember*

དྲན་པའི་ verbal noun, *remember,* + fused 6th case particle

འི་ particle fused to suffixless final syllable; depending on how it is being used, any instance of this particle will be either 1) a syntactic particle following a verb or verb phrase signifying conjunction or disjunction, or 2) a 6th case particle following nouns, pronouns, postpositions, and adjectives

བློ་ n., *mind*

རྣལ་མ་ adj., *natural*

འཇིགས་པ་དྲན་པའི་བློ་རྣལ་མ་ The subject of the nom-obj verb *is produced* is the noun phrase (noun+ adj.) *natural mind* modified by a verbal adjective which precedes it *mindful of fright.*

སྐྱེ་ intr. v. (nom-obj), *be produced, be generated, be born, arise*

སྐྱེ་སྐྱེས་སྐྱེ། ཐ་མི་དད།

བསྐྱེད་ trans. v. (ag-nom), *create, produce, generate, give birth to*

སྐྱེད་བསྐྱེད་བསྐྱེད་སྐྱེད། ཐ་དད།

སྐྱེ་བས་ verbal noun + 3rd case particle fused to suffixless final syllable

ས་ abbreviation of the particle ཡིས་ (when ཡིས་ is fused to a suffixless final syllable, the ཡི goes away and all that's left is a fused ས་); it is either 1) syntactic particle creating an adverbial construction, 2) syntactic particle marking the qualifier of an intransitive nom-s.p. verb of absence, or 3) case particle marking the 3rd case

སྐྱབས་ n., *refuge*

གསུམ་ adj., *three*

སྐྱབས་གསུམ་ noun phrase (noun + adjective), *the three refuges*

སྐྱབས་གསུམ་གྱི་ noun phrase + 6th case particle

གྱི་ particle; depending on how it is being used, any instance of this particle will be either 1) a syntactic particle following a verb or verb phrase signifying conjunction or disjunction, or 2) a 6th case particle following nouns, pronouns, postpositions, and adjectives

ཡོན་ཏན་ n., *good qualities*

ཡོན་ཏན་ལ་ n. + 7th case particle marking qualifier of intransitive nom-loc verb ངེས་ *be certain*

ལ་ particle; depending on how it is being used, any instance of this particle will be either 1) a syntactic particle following a verb or verb phrase signifying conjunction or disjunction, or 2) a case particle following nouns, pronouns, postpositions, and adjectives marking the 2nd, 4th and 7th cases

སྙིང་ n., *heart, essence*

ཐག་པ་ n., *distance, depth*

སྙིང་ཐག་པ་ནས་ noun phrase + 5th case particle signifying source.

ནས་ particle; depending on how it is being used, any instance of this particle will be either 1) a continuative syntactic particle following verbs and verb phrases, or 2) a 5th case particle

ངེས་ intr. v. (nom-loc), *be certain, ascertain.* This verb takes a qualifier in the 7th case: that of which the subject is certain is marked with a ལ་ particle signifying the referential use of the 7th case
ངེས་ངེས་ངེས། ཐ་མི་དད།

ངེས་པ་ verbal n., *certainty, ascertainment*

བསྐྱེད་ trans. v. (ag-nom) (past tense), *create, produce, generate, give birth to*
སྐྱེད་བསྐྱེད་བསྐྱེད་སྐྱེད། ཐ་དད།

སྐྱེས་ intr. v. (nom-obj), *be produced, be generated, be born, arise*
སྐྱེ་སྐྱེས་སྐྱེ། ཐ་མི་དད།

བསྐྱེད་ལ། verb + syntactic particle following verb signifying conjunction *and* + । (a *shay*)

ལ་ particle; depending on how it is being used, any instance of this particle will be either 1) a syntactic particle following a verb or verb phrase signifying conjunction or disjunction, or 2) a case particle following nouns, pronouns, postpositions, and adjectives marking the 2nd, 4th and 7th cases

---

Notes on Parts 3 and 4

Grammar review • Parts 3 and 4 offer an interesting contrast between related intransitive and transitive verbs

སྐྱེ་	intransitive verb (nom-obj), *be produced, be generated, be born, arise*	སྐྱེ་སྐྱེས་སྐྱེ། ཐ་མི་དད།	This verb never takes an object because it is intransitive.
བསྐྱེད་	transitive verb (ag-nom), *create, produce, generate, give birth to*	སྐྱེད་བསྐྱེད་བསྐྱེད་སྐྱེད། ཐ་དད།	This verb takes an agent and an object, although — as here — the agent may be implied by context.

The syntax of Part 3 is a subject (in the 1st case) and the intransitive verb

Part 3 uses the future form of the intransitive སྐྱེ་ *will be produced* in a clause qualifying the later transitive verb བསྐྱེད་ *[you should] generate* ending Part 4.

The syntax of Part 4 is an unstated agent, an object (verbal clause in the 1st case), and the transitive verb

Agents of transitive verbs are often unstated because they are general and obvious from context. Part 4 isn't about **who** should generate ascertainment (you should), it's about **what** should be generated, i.e., *ascertainment with respect to the qualities of the three refuges.*

	Part 3			**Part 4**				
syntactic function	subject of intransitive verb སྐྱེ་	→←	intr. v. (nom-obj)	unstated element	→	entire verbal clause as a unit is the object of བསྐྱེད་	→←	trans. verb (ag-nom)
དེའི་ཚེ་	འཇིགས་པ་དྲན་པའི་བློ་རྒྱལ་མ་	→←	སྐྱེ་བས། →	unstated agent of the transitive verb བསྐྱེད་	→	སྐྱབས་གསུམ་གྱི་ཡོན་ཏན་ལ་སྙིང་ཐག་པ་ནས་ངེས་པ་	→←	བསྐྱེད་ལ།
translation	*Since at that time a natural attitude mindful of fright will be generated,*			*[you should,] from the depths, generate ascertainment with respect to the qualities of the three refuges.*				

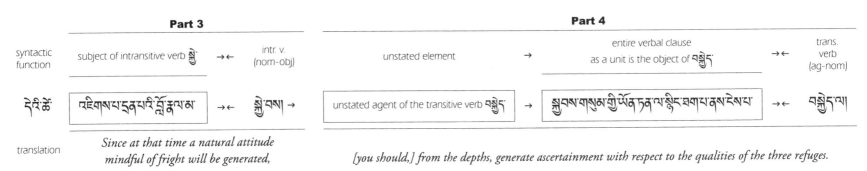

Grammar review • Understanding how verbal adjective clauses modify nouns

Nouns and noun phrase are frequently modified by verbal adjective clauses which precede them and to which they are connected with a 6th case particle. Sometimes the relationship is obvious, but sometimes it is not. The 6th case is used to signify a wide range of relationships between nouns and noun equivalents. It is often necessary to recast the verbal clause in standard verb-last syntax in order to understand precisely what relationship obtains between the modifying adjective and the modified noun.

1. Start with the basic pattern: verbal adjective + 6th case particle + noun

verbal clause	+	6th case particle གི་ཀྱི་གྱི་འི་ཡི་	+	noun or noun phrase modified adjectivally by the preceding verbal adjective clause

2. A verbal adjective modifying a following noun phrase

This example is a noun phrase itself composed of a verbal adjective and a noun phrase; it is not a complete sentence. It does not end with a terminal verb. The modified noun phrase བློ་རྣལ་མ་ *natural mind,* is narrowed by the preceding verbal adjective འཇིགས་པ་དྲན་པའི་ *which remembers fear.* It is merely a noun phrase composed of a verbal adjective and the noun phrase—*natural mind*—it modifies.

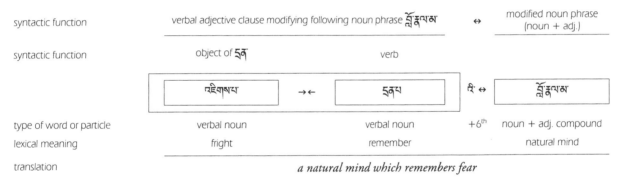

syntactic function	verbal adjective clause modifying following noun phrase བློ་རྣལ་མ་			↔	modified noun phrase (noun + adj.)
syntactic function	object of དྲན་		verb		
	འཇིགས་པ་	→←	དྲན་པ	འི་ ↔	བློ་རྣལ་མ་
type of word or particle	verbal noun		verbal noun	+6th	noun + adj. compound
lexical meaning	fright		remember		natural mind
translation	*a natural mind which remembers fear*				

3. Here, the verbal adjective and modified noun phrase are recast as a sentence with verb-last syntax

If we were to rearrange the noun phrase into verb-last sentence syntax, the noun being modified by the verbal adjective would occur before the verb. Its syntactic role would be as a **qualifier indicating the agent** by which the action indicated by the verb is accomplished.

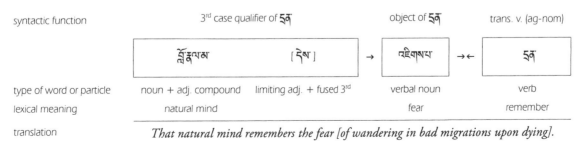

syntactic function	3rd case qualifier of དྲན་			object of དྲན་		trans. v. (ag-nom)
	བློ་རྣལ་མ་	[དེས་]	→	འཇིགས་པ་	→←	དྲན་
type of word or particle	noun + adj. compound	limiting adj. + fused 3rd		verbal noun		verb
lexical meaning	natural mind			fear		remember
translation	*That natural mind remembers the fear [of wandering in bad migrations upon dying].*					

Part 5 • སྐྱབས་འགྲོ་ཐུན་མོང་བའི་སྡོམ་པ་ལ་གནས་ཤིང་དེའི་བསླབ་བྱ་ལ་བསླབ།

Part 5 is a compound sentence composed of an intransitive clause followed by a transitive clause.

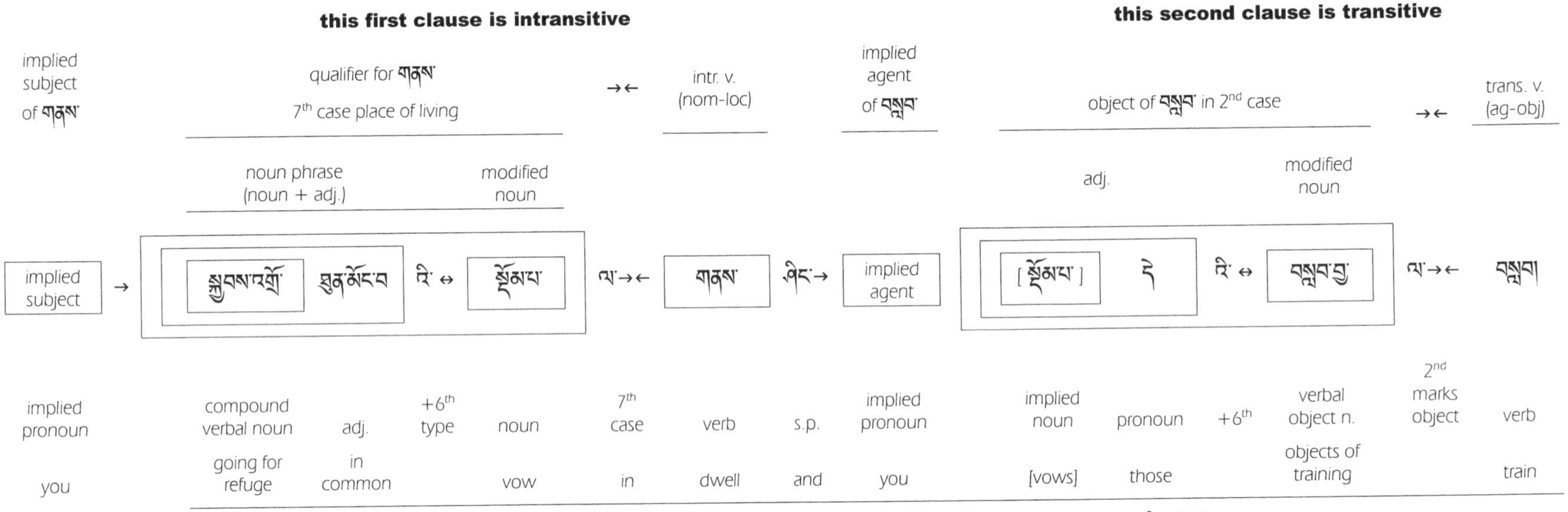

You should dwell in the vow of common refuge and train in its points of training.

Glossary for Part 5

སྐྱབས་འགྲོ་ n., *refuge;* literally, a verbal clause: *go [for] refuge*

ཐུན་མོང་བ་ adj., *common, shared*

ཐུན་མོང་བའི་ adj. + fused 6th case particle

འི་ particle fused to suffixless final syllable; depending on how it is being used, any instance of this particle will be either 1) a syntactic particle following a verb or verb phrase signifying conjunction or disjunction, or 2) a 6th case particle following nouns, pronouns, postpositions, and adjectives

སྡོམ་ trans. v. (ag-nom), *vow, promise*

སྡོམ་བསྡམས་བསྡམ་སྡོམས། ཐ་དད།

སྡོམ་བསྡོམས་བསྡོམ་སྡོམས། ཐ་དད། alternate past and future forms

སྡོམ་པ་ n., *vow, promise*

སྡོམ་པ་ལ་ n. + 7th case particle signifying place of living or remaining

ལ་ particle; either 1) a syntactic particle following a verb or verb phrase signifying conjunction or disjunction, or 2) a case particle following nouns, pronouns, postpositions, and adjectives marking the 2nd, 4th and 7th cases

གནས་ intr. v. (nom-loc), *abide, dwell* གནས་གནས་གནས་གནས། ཐ་མི་དད།

གནས་ n., *place, abode, location,* and also *status, state, situation, source, object, topic* and *basis* (whew!)

གནས་པ་ verbal n., *dwelling, remaining, one who dwells or remains*

ཤིང་	continuative syntactic particle used following verbs and verb phrases, *and*
ཅིང་ཞིང་ཤིང་	are three equivalent continuative syntactic particle used following verbs and verb phrases
ཅིང་	after words ending with the letters གདབ་ and with the secondary suffix ད་ (which is invisible)
ཞིང་	after words ending with the letters ང་ན་མ་འ་ར་ལ་ and with suffixless final syllables
ཤིང་	after words with ས་ and with the secondary suffix ས་
དེ་	adj. and pronoun, *that, those*
དེའི་	relative pronoun + 6th case particle fused to suffixless single-syllable word
འི་	particle fused to suffixless final syllable; depending on how it is being used, any instance of this particle will be either 1) a syntactic particle following a verb or verb phrase signifying conjunction or disjunction, or 2) a 6th case particle following nouns, pronouns, postpositions, and adjectives
བསླབ་	trans. v. (ag-obj) (future tense), *train* སློབ་བསླབས་བསླབ་སློབས། ཐ་དད།
བསླབ་བྱ་	verbal object noun, *object of training;* verbal object nouns are formed by adding བྱ་ (the strong future auxiliary) to the future form of the verb.
བྱ་	trans. v. (ag-nom) (future tense), *do, make, perform, take*, also the strong auxiliary བྱེད་བྱས་བྱ་བྱོས། ཐ་དད།
བསླབ་བྱ་ལ་	verbal object noun + 2nd case particle marking the object of the transitive verb བསླབ་ *train*
ལ་	particle; either 1) a syntactic particle following a verb or verb phrase signifying conjunction or disjunction, or 2) a case particle following nouns, pronouns, postpositions, and adjectives marking the 2nd, 4th and 7th cases
བསླབ་	trans. v. (ag-obj), *train* སློབ་བསླབས་བསླབ་སློབས། ཐ་དད།

Notes on Part 5

Grammar review • The agents of transitive verbs, and the subjects of intransitive verbs, are often implied by context

The basic syntax of this compound sentence is "Abide in A, and train in B." The subject of the intransitive verb གནས་ *abide* is implied, as is the agent of the transitive verb བསླབ་ *train in.* As is often the case in Tibetan, when the author is speaking to the reader, as in "You should dwell," the pronoun "you" is unstated. In contrast with English sentences, Tibetan sentences routinely have unstated syntactic elements such as unstated agents or subjects. English sentences use short pronouns such as "it" or "you", while Tibetan sentences often omit the subject or agent entirely. This can be confusing at first for those accustomed to the convention of English to have all the elements explicitly present. In Tibetan, the unstated elements can be absent because the sentence isn't about them. Here the sentence isn't about *who* (the absent element) should be dwelling within the confines of the moral discipline assumed with the vow, but rather about *where* (the explicit element) you should dwell—in the vow of common refuge.

Grammar review • Adjectives that precede nouns often narrow the scope of the modified noun

སྐྱབས་འགྲོ་ཐུན་མོང་བའི་སྡོམ་པ་ noun phrase སྐྱབས་འགྲོ་ཐུན་མོང་བ་ (n. + adj.) *common refuge* + fused 6th case particle འི་ connecting it to the following noun སྡོམ་པ་ *vow, promise.* The scope of the second noun སྡོམ་པ་ *vows* is narrowed by the first noun phrase སྐྱབས་འགྲོ་ཐུན་མོང་བ་ *common refuge*

འི་ particle fused to suffixless final syllable; either 1) a syntactic particle following a verb or verb phrase signifying conjunction or disjunction, or 2) a 6th case particle following nouns, pronouns, postpositions, and adjectives

སྐྱབས་འགྲོ་ཐུན་མོང་བའི་སྡོམ་པ་ལ་ n. phrase (adj. + n.) + 7th case particle signifying place of living or remaining

ལ་ particle; either 1) a syntactic particle following a verb or verb phrase signifying conjunction or disjunction, or 2) a case particle following nouns, pronouns, postpositions, and adjectives marking the 2nd, 4th and 7th cases

Grammar review • Three equivalent continuative syntactic particles follow verbs and verb phrases

སྐྱབས་འགྲོ་ཐུན་མོང་བའི་སྡོམ་པ་ལ་གནས་ཤིང་ The first sentence in Part 5 ends with a verb followed by a conjunctive syntactic particle ཤིང་

ཅིང་ཞིང་ཤིང་ are three equivalent continuative syntactic particles **most frequently used following verbs and verb phrases**

ཅིང་ is used after words ending with the letters ག་ད་བ་ and with the secondary suffix ད (which is invisible)

ཞིང་ is used after words ending with the letters ང་ན་མ་འ་ར་ལ་ and with suffixless final syllables

ཤིང་ is used after words with ས་ and with the secondary suffix ས་

Grammar review • Learn to recognize verbal object nouns

དེའི་བསླབ་བྱ་ noun phrase (pronoun + 6th case particle + verbal object noun), *their objects of training*

དེ་ adj. and pronoun, *that, those*

དེའི་ relative pronoun + 6th case particle fused to suffixless single-syllable word

འི་ particle fused to suffixless final syllable; either 1) a syntactic particle following a verb or verb phrase signifying conjunction or disjunction, or 2) a 6th case particle following nouns, pronouns, postpositions, and adjectives

བསླབ་བྱ་ verbal object noun, *object of training;* verbal object nouns are formed by adding the strong future auxiliary to the future form of the verb

བྱ་ trans. v. (ag-nom) (future tense), *do, make, perform, take;* also used as the strong auxiliary verb. བྱེད་བྱས་བྱ་བྱོས། ཐ་དད།

བསླབ་ trans. v. (ag-obj) (future tense), *train* སློབ་བསླབས་བསླབ་སློབས། ཐ་དད།

Chapter Two Self Test

Write out the passage, boxing and identifying every syntactic element.

དེ་ནས་ཚེ་འདི་དོན་དུ་གཉེར་བའི་བློ་སྣ་མ་ལོག་ན་འཇིག་རྟེན་ཕྱི་མ་ལ་དོན་གཉེར་དྲག་པོ་མི་འབྱུང་བས་ལུས་ཐོབ་པ་རིང་དུ་མི་སྡོད་པའི་མི་རྟག་པ་དང་། ཤི་ནས་ངན་འགྲོར་འཁྱམ་ཚུལ་བསྒོམ་པ་ལ་འབད།
དེའི་ཚེ་འཇིགས་པ་དྲན་པའི་བློ་སྣལ་མ་སྐྱེ་བས། སྐྱབས་གསུམ་གྱི་ཡོན་ཏན་ལ་སྙིང་ཐག་པ་ནས་ངེས་པ་བསྐྱེད་ལ། སྐྱབས་འགྲོ་ཐུན་མོང་བའི་སྡོམ་པ་ལ་གནས་ཤིང་དེའི་བསླབ་བྱ་ལ་བསླབ།

Vocabulary

For each word, can you identify what part of speech it is (noun, pronoun, adjective, verb, adverb, postposition) and what it means?
For each syntactic particle, can you identify what class of syntactic particle it belongs to and how it is used?

དེ་ནས་	བསྒོམ་	འཇིགས་	དྲག་པོ་
འཇིག་རྟེན་ཕྱི་མ་	བསྒོམ་པ་	འཇིགས་པ་	དྲན་
གསུམ་	བསྐྱེད་	འདི་	དྲན་པ་
གོམས་	མ་	འབད་	བློ་
ངན་འགྲོ་	མི་	འཁྱམ་	བློ་སྣ་
ཐོབ་	མ་ལོག་	འཁྱམ་ཚུལ་	རྗེས་
ཐོབ་པ་	མི་འབྱུང་	འབྱུང་	རྟག་པ་
དང་	མི་རྟག་པ་	འབྱུང་བ་	རྟེན་
དེ་	མི་སྡོད་	རིང་	རྟེན་
དེ་ནས་	མི་སྡོད་པ་	རིང་དུ་	སྣལ་མ་
དེའི་རྗེས་སུ་	མིན་	ལ་	སྡོག་
དོན་གཉེར་	མེད་	ལུས་	སྡོད་
དོན་དུ་གཉེར་	ཚེ་	ཤི་	སྐྱབས་
དུ་	ཚེ་འདི་	ཤི་ནས་	སྐྱེ་
ན་	འཇིག་	-ས་	
ནས་	འཇིག་རྟེན་	ཕྱི་མ་	

Translation of Tsong-kha-pa's text

དེ་ནས་ཚེ་འདིའི་དོན་དུ་གཉེར་བའི་བློ་སྣ་མ་ལོག་ན་འཇིག་རྟེན་ཕྱི་མ་ལ་དོན་གཉེར་དྲག་པོ་མི་འབྱུང་བས་ལུས་ཐོབ་པ་རིང་དུ་མི་སྡོད་པའི་མི་རྟག་པ་དང་ཤི་ནས་ངན་འགྲོར་འཁྱམ་ཚུལ་བསྒོམ་པ་ལ་འབད། དེའི་ཚེ་འཇིགས་པ་དྲན་པའི་བློ་རྣལ་མ་སྐྱེ་བས། སྐྱབས་གསུམ་གྱི་ཡོན་ཏན་ལ་སྙིང་ཐག་པ་ནས་ངེས་པ་བསྐྱེད་ལ། སྐྱབས་འགྲོ་ཐུན་མོང་བའི་སྡོམ་པ་ལ་གནས་ཤིང་དེའི་བསླབ་བྱ་ལ་བསླབ།

Then, if the attitude of seeking [one's own welfare just for] this lifetime is not overcome, a strong seeking of [your own welfare] in future lives will not arise. Therefore, you should strive at meditating on impermanence—the fact that the body gained will not last long—and on the manner whereby one wanders in bad migrations upon dying. Since at that time a natural attitude mindful of fright will be generated, you should, from the depths, generate certainty with respect to the qualities of the three refuges [—the Buddha, the Doctrine, and the Spiritual Community—to protect you from the fright of bad migrations], as well as dwell in the vow of common refuge and train in its points of training.

Annotations for Tsong-kha-pa's text in Chapter Two

Here is Tsong-kha-pa's text as supplemented by *The Four Interwoven Annotations,* 828.2–829.1

དེའི་རྗེས་ དེ་ནས་ སྙིང་པོ་ལེན་འདོད་ཀྱིས་བསྒྲུབ་པའི་དགོས་པ་ནི་ཚེ་འདིའི་བློ་སྣ་ལོག །ཕྱི་མ་ཕན་ཆད་ཀྱི་དོན་གཉེར་སྐྱེ་བ་དེ་ཡིན་པས་དེ་ལ་ ཚེ་འདིའི་དོན་དུ་གཉེར་བའི་ བློ་སྣ་ངེས་པར་ལྡོག་དགོས་ཏེ་ བློ་སྣ་ དེ་ མ་ལོག་ན་འཇིག་རྟེན་ཕྱི་མ འི་དོན་ ལ་དོན་ དུ་ གཉེར་ ནས་བསྒྲུབ་པའི་དོན་གཉེར་ དྲག་པོ་མི་འབྱུང་བ་ ཡིན་པ ས་ ན་ཚེ་འདིའི་བློ་སྣ་ལོག་པའི་ཐབས་སུ་ ལུས་ཐོབ་པ་འདི་ཚེ་འདིར་ རིང་དུ་མི་སྡོད་ ཅིང་མྱུར་དུ་འཆི་ལ། དེ་ཡང་ནམ་འཆི་ལ་ངེས་པ་མེད་པ་འཆི་བའི་ཚེ་ཆོས་མ་གཏོགས་པ་གང་གིས་ཀྱང་མི་ཕན་པའི་ཚུལ་བསམས་ པའི་མི་རྟག་པ་ འི་སྒོར་ལ་འབད་པ་དང་ཤི་ནས་ ཀྱང་མེད་དེ་མི་འགྲོ་བར་སྐྱེ་དགོས་ཤིང་། དེ་ཡང་ཚེ་རབས་ཐོག་མ་མེད་པའི་ལས་ཀྱི་བག་ཆགས་དང་ཚེ་འདིའི་བྱ་བ་ལ་དཔགས་ན་ ངན་འགྲོར་འཁྱམ་ དགོས་པའི་ ཚུལ་ ཞིབ་ཏུ་ བསྒོམ་པ་ལ་འབད་ དགོས། དེ་ལྟར་འབད་པ་ དེའི་ཚེ་ བློ་དེ་ལ་བསྒོམས་པའི་མཐུས་ངན་འགྲོའི་ འཇིགས་པ་དྲན་པའི་བློ་རྣལ་མ་ ཚུགས་ཐུབ་མེད་པ་ཞིག་ སྐྱེ་བ་ ཡིན་པ ས་ བློ་དེ་འདྲ་སྐྱེ་བ་ན་འཇིགས་པ་དེ་ལས་སྐྱོབ་ནུས་པའི་སྐྱབས་འཚོལ་བའི་བློ་ངེས་པར་སྐྱེ་བས་དེའི་ཚེ་སངས་རྒྱས་དང་ཆོས་དང་དགེ་འདུན་ཏེ་ སྐྱབས་ དེ་ གསུམ་གྱིས་ འཇིགས་པ་དེ་ལས་སྐྱོབ་ནུས་པའི་སྐུ་གསུང་ཐུགས་ཁྱད་པར་དུ་མཁྱེན་བརྩེ་ནུས་པའི་ ཡོན་ཏན་ རྣམས་ ལ་སྙིང་ཐག་པ་ནས་ངེས་བསྐྱེད་ པར་བྱས་ ལ་སྐྱབས་ སུ་འགྲོ་བ་དང་སྐྱབས་ འགྲོ་ཐུན་མོང་བའི་སྡོམ་པ་ ནས་དེ་ ལ་གནས་ཤིང་ དེ་ལས་མི་འདའ་བ་དང་སྐྱབས་འགྲོ་ དེའི་བསླབ་བྱ་ རྣམས་ལ་ངེས་པར་ བསླབ་ དགོས་སོ། །

Then, since the purpose for being urged to want to extract the essence is turning your mind from this life and generating seeking for later lives, you must definitely turn your mind from this life. If you don't reverse that attitude, strong seeking for your welfare in future lifetimes will not occur. Therefore, as a method for turning your mind from this lifetime, you should work at the topics of impermanence: this body you have obtained won't remain here long and you will die quickly. Furthermore, when you will die is uncertain. At the time of death, except for the Dharma, nothing helps. You must work at meditating in detail how, when you die, you don't become non-existent; you must be reborn. You must wander in bad migrations due to accumulating predispositions from actions over a limitless continuum of lives and the actions of this life. When you work at this, due to the power of cultivating that mind which cannot even help itself, a natural sense of fear of bad migrations will be produced. When you have generated that mind, you will definitely generate a mind seeking a refuge which is able to protect you from that fear. That is when you will generate certainty, from the depths of your heart, about the good qualities of the three refuges: the Buddha, the Doctrine, and the Spiritual Community—the body, speech and mind that are able to protect you from that fright, and in particular the capacities of wisdom and mercy. You should go for refuge and abide in that refuge through the vows of common refuge. You must not stray from that [refuge] and [you must] definitely train in the precepts of that refuge.

Chapter Three

དེ་ནས་དཀར་ཆོས་ཐམས་ཅད་ཀྱི་གཞི་ཆེན་པོ་ལས་འབྲས་ལ་ཡིད་ཆེས་པའི་དད་པ་སྒོ་དུ་མ་ནས་བསྐྱེད་ལ་བརྟན་པར་བྱས་ཏེ།
དགེ་མི་དགེ་བཅུའི་འཇུག་ལྡོག་ལ་འབད་ཅིང་སྟོབས་བཞིའི་ལམ་དུ་རྒྱུན་དུ་ཞུགས་པ་ཞིག་བྱ།

Division of the passage into units to facilitate the analysis of the syntax

Chapter Three is one Tibetan sentence that I have divided into four parts. Part 1 is a complete sentence when translated. Parts 2, 3, and 4 together form a complete sentence when translated. We will look at Parts 1 and 2 together, then Parts 3 and 4.

1

དེ་ནས་དཀར་ཆོས་ཐམས་ཅད་ཀྱི་གཞི་ཆེན་པོ་ལས་འབྲས་ལ་ཡིད་ཆེས་པའི་དད་པ་སྒོ་དུ་མ་ནས་བསྐྱེད་ལ་

2

བརྟན་པར་བྱས་ཏེ།

3

དགེ་མི་དགེ་བཅུའི་འཇུག་ལྡོག་ལ་འབད་ཅིང་

4

སྟོབས་བཞིའི་ལམ་དུ་རྒྱུན་དུ་ཞུགས་པ་ཞིག་བྱ།

Part 1

While Part 1 is a portion of a Tibetan sentence, it is a complete sentence in English.

1

དེ་ནས་དཀར་ཆོས་ཐམས་ཅད་ཀྱི་གཞི་ཆེན་པོ་ལས་འབྲས་ལ་ཡིད་ཆེས་པའི་དད་པ་སྒོ་དུ་མ་ནས་བསྐྱེད་ལ་

Then, you should generate from many viewpoints the faith of conviction in the great basis for all wholesome activities, actions and their effects.

2

བརྟན་པར་བྱས་ཏེ།

When you have made [that faith] firm, ...

Part 1 is about the object (the explicit element), not about the agent (the implicit element)

Part 1 is a sentence composed of an implied agent ("you"), a transitive verb ("should generate"), a qualifier in the 5th case showing the source of the action expressed by the verb ("from many viewpoints"), and an object in the 1st case composed of two noun phrases in apposition ("the great basis for all wholesome activities—faith of conviction in actions and their effects"). Part 2 begins a new sentence with a verb phrase for which the agent ("you") and object ("the faith of conviction") are implied.

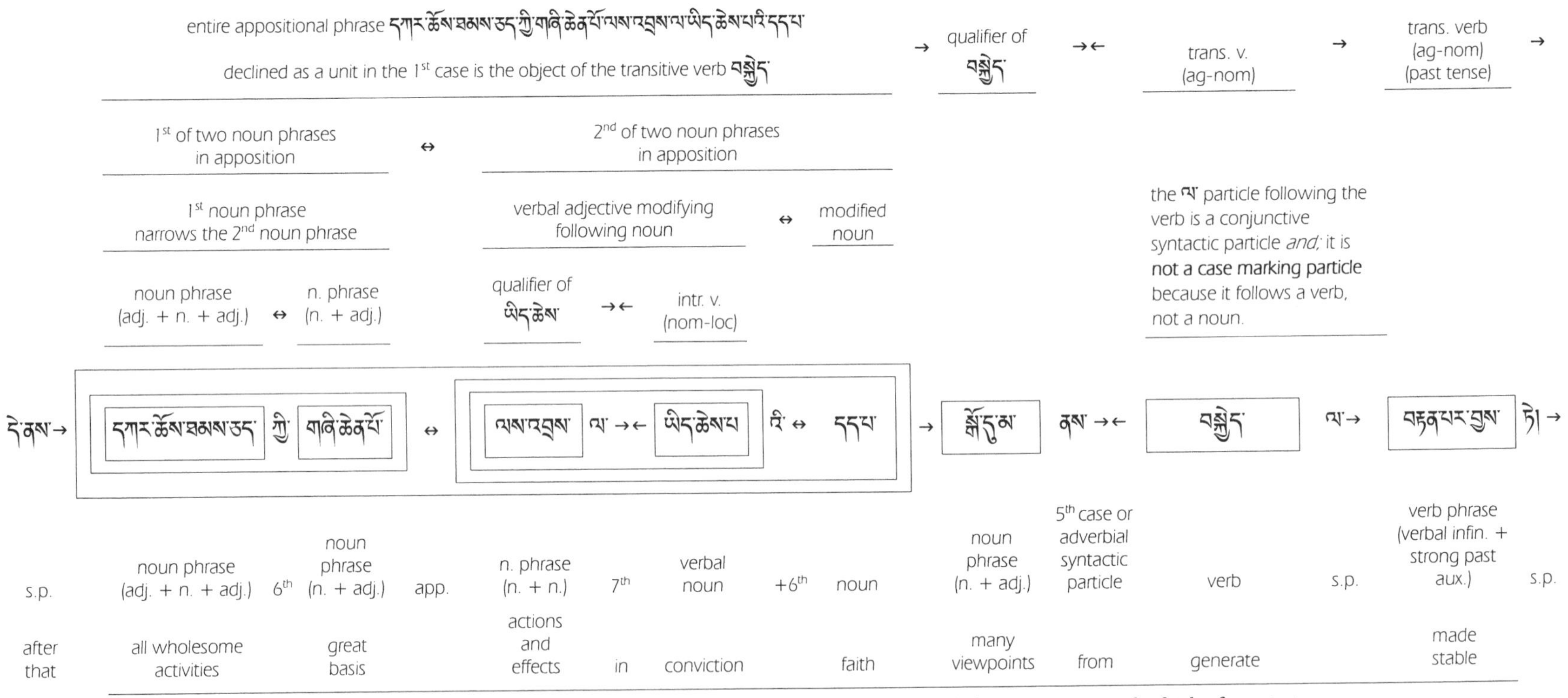

Then, you should generate from many viewpoints the great basis for all wholesome activities, the faith of conviction in actions and their effects. Having made that [faith] stable,...

Glossary for Part 1

དེ་ནས་	a syntactic particle translated *then* (literally, *after that*)
དེ་ནས་	དེའི་རྗེས་སུ་ *after that*
དེའི་རྗེས་སུ་	pronoun + 6th case particle fused to suffixless syllable + postposition + 7th case particle: *after that*
རྗེས་	postposition, *after*
དཀར་	adj., *white, wholesome,* abbreviation for དཀར་པོ་
དཀར་པོ་	adj., *white, wholesome*
ཆོས་	n., *phenomena, religion,* and many other meanings. This is the Tibetan translation of the Sanskrit *dharma*
དཀར་ཆོས་	noun phrase (adj. + n.), *wholesome activities;* abbreviation for དཀར་པོའི་ཆོས་

ཐམས་ཅད་ adj., *all*

དཀར་ཆོས་ཐམས་ཅད་ noun phrase (adj. + n. + adj.), *all wholesome practices*

དཀར་ཆོས་ཐམས་ཅད་ཀྱི་ noun phrase + 6th case particle

ཀྱི་ particle; either 1) a syntactic particle following a verb or verb phrase signifying conjunction or disjunction, or 2) a 6th case particle following nouns, pronouns, postpositions, and adjectives

གཞི་ n., *basis*

ཆེན་པོ་ adj., *big, large, great*

ལས་ n., *action;* Sanskrit: *karma*

འབྲས་ abbreviation of འབྲས་བུ་ n., *effect*

འབྲས་བུ་ n., *effect*

ལས་འབྲས་ noun phrase (n. + n.), *actions and [their] effects*

ལས་འབྲས་ལ་ noun phrase + 7th case particle

ལ་ particle; either 1) a syntactic particle following a verb or verb phrase signifying conjunction or disjunction, or 2) a case particle following nouns, pronouns, postpositions, and adjectives marking the 2nd, 4th and 7th cases

ཡིད་ཆེས་པའི་དད་པ་ n. phrase (verbal adjective + 6th + noun), *faith of conviction*

དད་ intr. v. (nom-loc), *have faith in, be interested in*

དད་དད་དད། ཐ་མི་དད།

དད་པ་ n., *faith*

སྒོ་ n., *door, approach*

དུ་མ་ adj., *many*

སྒོ་དུ་མ་ noun phrase (n. + adj.), *many doors,* and by extension *many points of view*

སྒོ་དུ་མ་ནས་ *from many points of view.* The function of the particle ནས་ can be understood either as 5th case particle marking a noun phrase as the **source** from which the faith of conviction is generated, or as a syntactic particle creating an adverb showing **how** the faith of conviction is generated.

ནས་ particle; depending on how it is being used, it will be either 1) a syntactic particle following verbs and verb phrases marking adverbs, participles or disjunction, or 2) a case particle marking the 5th case following nouns, pronouns, postpositions, and adjectives

ནས་ n., *barley*

བསྐྱེད་ trans. v. (ag-nom), *create, produce, generate, give birth to*

སྐྱེད་བསྐྱེད་བསྐྱེད་སྐྱེད། ཐ་དད།

སྐྱེས་ intr. v. (nom-obj), *be produced, be generated, be born, arise*

སྐྱེ་སྐྱེས་སྐྱེ། ཐ་མི་དད།

བསྐྱེད་ལ་ the ལ་ particle following the verb བསྐྱེད་ **is a conjunctive syntactic particle** *and;* it **is not a case marking particle** because it follows a verb, not a noun.

ལ་ particle; either 1) a syntactic particle following a verb or verb phrase signifying conjunction or disjunction, or 2) a case particle following nouns, pronouns, postpositions, and adjectives marking the 2nd, 4th and 7th cases

བརྟན་པར་བྱས་ verb phrase (verbal infinitive + strong past auxiliary), *[I, you] have made [something] stable*

བརྟན་ trans. v. (ag-nom), *stabilize, make firm* རྟེན་བརྟན་བརྟན་རྟེན། ཐ་དད།

བརྟན་པར་ verbal infinitive; here, the fused ར་ is a syntactic particle modifying a verb to create an infinitive within the verb phrase བརྟན་པར་བྱས་ *having made [something] stable;* it is **not** a case particle marking the 2nd, 4th or 7th cases because it does not follow a noun—it is within a verb phrase

བྱས་ trans. v. (past tense) (ag-nom), *do, make, perform, take;* here: strong past auxiliary

བྱེད་བྱས་བྱ་བྱོས། ཐ་དད།

སུ་རུ་ཏུ་དུ་ར་ are the five syntactic particles used to modify verbs to create infinitives within verb phrases

བརྟན་པར་བྱས་ཏེ། verb phrase + continuative syntactic particle showing sequence by indicating that more relevant information will follow.

ཏེ་ སྟེ་ and དེ་ are equivalent syntactic particles; either 1) continuative syntactic particles following verbs and verb phrases showing sequence, or 2) punctuational syntactic particles following words or phrases marking appositives

ཏེ་ follows words ending with suffix letters ན་ར་ལ་ས་

སྟེ་ follows suffixless words and words ending with suffix letters ག་ང་བ་མ་འ་

དེ་ follows words ending with suffix letter ད་

Grammar review • Noun phrases are often arranged in apposition to add more detail to an exposition

དཀར་ཆོས་ཐམས་ཅད་ཀྱི་གཞི་ཆེན་པོ་ and ལས་འབྲས་ལ་ཡིད་ཆེས་པའི་དད་པ་ are two noun phrases in apposition. Taken as a unit, it is the object of the transitive verb བསྐྱེད་ *produce*

དཀར་ཆོས་ཐམས་ཅད་ཀྱི་གཞི་ཆེན་པོ་ noun phrase (noun phrase + 6th + noun phrase), *the great basis for all wholesome activities.* The first noun phrase དཀར་ཆོས་ཐམས་ཅད་ narrows the meaning of the second noun phrase གཞི་ཆེན་པོ་ Which great basis? the great basis for all wholesome activities

དཀར་ adj. *wholesome;* abbreviation for དཀར་པོ་ adj., *white,* by extension *wholesome.* I translate the white/black oppositional pair as wholesome/unwholesome when they are used metaphorically.

ལས་འབྲས་ལ་ཡིད་ཆེས་པའི་དད་པ་ noun phrase (verbal adjective + modified noun), *the faith of conviction in actions and effects*

ལས་འབྲས་ compound noun phrase (n. + n.), *actions and effects;* an abbreviation for ལས་དང་འབྲས་བུ་

ལས་འབྲས་ལ་ compound noun ལས་འབྲས་ + 7th case ལ་ creates a qualifier signifying **the general context or reference of an action or state of mind**; here: what one has faith in.

Grammar review • Conjunctive syntactic particles following verbs

སྒོ་དུ་མ་ནས་བསྐྱེད་ལ་ the ལ་ particle following the verb བསྐྱེད་ is a conjunctive syntactic particle *and;* it is **not a case marking particle** because it follows a verb, not a noun.

ལ་ particle; either 1) a syntactic particle following a verb or verb phrase signifying conjunction or disjunction, or 2) a case particle following nouns, pronouns, postpositions, and adjectives marking the 2nd, 4th and 7th cases

Grammar review • The verb phrase བརྟན་པར་བྱས་ཏེ།

བརྟན་པར་བྱས་ verb phrase (verbal infinitive + strong past auxiliary), *[I, you] have made [something] stable*

བརྟན་པར་ verbal infinitive; here, the fused ར་ is a syntactic particle modifying a verb to create an infinitive within the verb phrase བརྟན་པར་བྱས་ *[I, you] have made [something] stable;* it is **not** a case particle marking the 2nd, 4th or 7th cases because it does not follow a noun—it is within a verb phrase

བྱས་ trans. v. (past tense) (ag-nom), *do, make, perform, take,* also, as here, the strong past auxiliary verb བྱེད་བྱས་བྱ་བྱོས། ཐ་དད།

བརྟན་པར་བྱས་ཏེ། verb phrase + continuative syntactic particle ཏེ། indicates that something relevant follows

Parts 2, 3, and 4 form a compound sentence • བརྟན་པར་བྱས་ཏེ། དགེ་མི་དགེ་བཅུའི་འཇུག་ལྡོག་ལ་འབད་ཅིང་སྟོབས་བཞིའི་ལམ་དུ་རྒྱུན་དུ་ཞུགས་པ་ཞིག་བྱ།

compound verbal clause དགེ་མི་དགེ་བཅུའི་འཇུག་ལྡོག is object in 2nd case of འབད →← trans. v. (ag-obj) | qualifier of ཞུགས in 2nd case | adverbial identity qualifier →← intr. v. (nom-obj)

n. + adj. compound modifying following n. ↔ modified noun

བརྟན་པར་བྱས་ཏེ། →		
དགེ་མི་དགེ ↔	n. phrase (n. + n.)	virtuous and nonvirtuous
བཅུ	adj.	ten
འི ↔	+6th	
འཇུག་ལྡོག	2 verbal nouns	engaging and disengaging
ལ	2nd	marks object
→← འབད	verb	strive
ཅིང	s.p.	and
སྟོབས་བཞིའི་ལམ	n. phrase + 6th + noun	path of the four powers
དུ	2nd	marks place
→ རྒྱུན	noun	stream
དུ →←	2nd	creates adverb
ཞུགས་པ་ཞིག་བྱ།	verb + imperative	be involved with

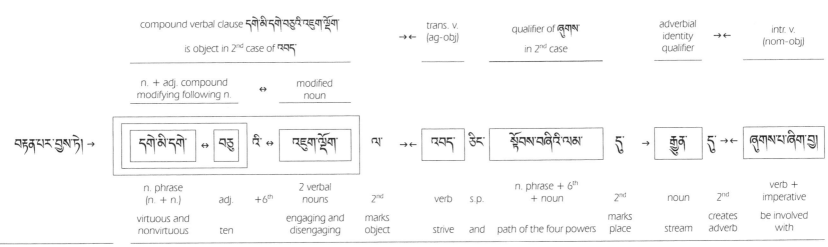

When you have made [that faith] firm, ... *...you should strive at engaging in the ten virtuous actions and disengaging from the ten non-virtuous actions, and you should be involved continuously with the paths of the four powers.*

Glossary for Parts 2, 3, and 4

བརྟན — trans. v. (ag-nom), *stabilize, make firm* རྟོན་བརྟན་བརྟན་རྟོན། ཐ་དད།

བརྟན་པར — verbal infinitive; here, the fused ར is a syntactic particle modifying a verb to create an infinitive within the verb phrase བརྟན་པར་བྱས *having made [something] stable;* it is **not** a case particle marking the 2nd, 4th or 7th cases because it does not follow a noun—it is within a verb phrase

སུ་རུ་ཏུ་དུ་ར — are the five syntactic particles used to modify verbs to create infinitives within verb phrases

བྱས — trans. v. (past tense) (ag-nom), *do, make, perform, take;* here: strong past auxiliary
བྱེད་བྱས་བྱ་བྱོས། ཐ་དད།

བརྟན་པར་བྱས་ཏེ། — verb phrase + continuative syntactic particle showing sequence by indicating that more relevant information will follow.

ཏེ་ སྟེ་ and དེ — are equivalent syntactic particles; either 1) continuative syntactic particles following verbs and verb phrases showing sequence, or 2) punctuational syntactic particles following words or phrases marking appositives

དགེ་བ — n., *virtuous (actions)*

མི་དགེ — n., *non-virtuous (actions)*

དགེ་མི་དགེ — noun phrase (n. + n.), *virtuous and non-virtuous (actions)*

བཅུ — n., adj., *ten*

དགེ་མི་དགེ་བཅུ — noun phrase (comp. n. + adj.), *the ten virtuous actions and the ten non-virtuous actions*

དགེ་མི་དགེ་བཅུའི — noun phrase + 6th case particle fused to suffixless single-syllable word

འི་ particle fused to suffixless final syllable; either 1) a syntactic particle following a verb or verb phrase signifying conjunction or disjunction, or 2) a 6th case particle following nouns, pronouns, postpositions, and adjectives

འཇུག་ trans. v. (ag-obj), *enter, engage, apply;* by extension: *be involved in*

འཇུག་འཙུག་གཞུག་ཆུག ཐ་དད།

འཇུག་ intr. v. (nom-obj), *enter, engage, apply;* by extension: *supplement*

འཇུག་ཞུགས་འཇུག་ཞུགས། ཐ་མི་དད།

ལྡོག་ intr. v. (nom-s.p.), *be isolated, be reversed*

ལྡོག་ལྡོག་ལྡོག ཐ་མི་དད།

ལོག་ intr. v. (nom-s.p.), *be reversed, be turned*

ལོག་ལོག་ལོག ཐ་མི་དད།

འཇུག་ལྡོག་ compound verbal noun, *engaging and disengaging*

འཇུག་ལྡོག་ལ་ compound verbal noun + 2nd case particle marking the object of the transitive verb འབད་ *strive at, work at*

ལ་ particle; either 1) a syntactic particle following a verb or verb phrase signifying conjunction or disjunction, or 2) a case particle following nouns, pronouns, postpositions, and adjectives marking the 2nd, 4th and 7th cases

འབད་ trans. v. (ag-obj), *strive*

འབད་འབད་འབད་འབོད། ཐ་དད།

ཅིང་ continuative syntactic particle used following verbs and verb phrases, *and*

ཅིང་ཞིང་ཤིང་ are three equivalent continuative syntactic particle used following verbs and verb phrases, *and*

ཅིང་ follows words ending with the letters གདབ་ and with the secondary suffix ད་ (which is invisible)

ཞིང་ follows words ending with the letters ངནམའརལ་ and with suffixless final syllables

ཤིང་ follows words ending with ས་ and with the secondary suffix ས་

སྟོབས་ n., *power*

བཞི་ n., adj., *four*

སྟོབས་བཞི noun phrase (n. + adj.), *the four powers*

སྟོབས་བཞི གཉེན་པོ་སྟོབས་བཞི *four powers of [overcoming non-virtues by] antidotes*

རྟེན་གྱི་སྟོབས་ *power of reliance*

གཉེན་པོའི་སྟོབས་ *power of [overcoming non-virtues by] antidotes*

རྣམ་པར་སུན་འབྱིན་པའི་སྟོབས་ *power of repentance*

ཉེས་པ་ལས་སླར་ལྡོག་པའི་སྟོབས་ *power of not engaging in non-virtues again*

སྟོབས་བཞིའི་ noun phrase (n. + adj.) + 6th case particle fused to suffixless syllable

འི་ particle fused to suffixless final syllable; either 1) a syntactic particle following a verb or verb phrase signifying conjunction or disjunction, or 2) a 6th case particle following nouns, pronouns, postpositions, and adjectives

ལམ་ n., *path*

ལམ་དུ་ n. + 2nd case particle marking the qualifier of the intransitive nom-obj verb ཞུགས་

དུ་ particle; either 1) a verb-modifying syntactic particle within a verb phrase, or 2) a case particle following nouns, pronouns, postpositions, and adjectives marking the 2nd, 4th and 7th cases

རྒྱུན་ n., *stream, continuum*

རྒྱུན་དུ་ n. + 2nd case particle; here: adv., *continuously*

དུ་ particle; either 1) a verb-modifying syntactic particle within a verb phrase, or 2) a case particle following nouns, pronouns, postpositions, and adjectives marking the 2nd, 4th and 7th cases

ཞུགས་ intr. v. (past tense) (nom-obj), *be engaged*

འཇུག་ཞུགས་འཇུག་ཞུགས། ཐ་མི་དད།

འཇུག་འཙུག་གཞུག་ཆུག ཐ་དད།

ཞུགས་པ་ཞིག་བྱ་ verb + imperative: *[You] should engage...*

Deciphering two qualifiers or objects when paired with two verbs • དགེ་མི་དགེ་བཅུའི་འཇུག་ལྡོག

	A	B				C	D
	དགེ	མི་དགེ	← བཅུ	འི	↔	འཇུག	ལྡོག
type of word or particle	noun	noun	adj.	+6th		verb	verb
lexical meaning	virtue	nonvirtue	ten			engage	disengage
translation	*engaging in the ten virtues and disengaging from the ten nonvirtues*						

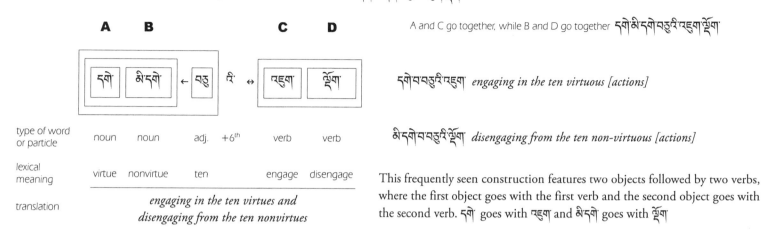

A and C go together, while B and D go together དགེ་མི་དགེ་བཅུའི་འཇུག་ལྡོག

དགེ་བ་བཅུའི་འཇུག *engaging in the ten virtuous [actions]*

མི་དགེ་བ་བཅུའི་ལྡོག *disengaging from the ten non-virtuous [actions]*

This frequently seen construction features two objects followed by two verbs, where the first object goes with the first verb and the second object goes with the second verb. དགེ goes with འཇུག and མི་དགེ goes with ལྡོག

Notes on Parts 3 and 4

འཇུག་ལྡོག — compound n., *engagement and disengagement.* These are not really verbs, but rather the abbreviation for འཇུག་པ་དང་ལྡོག་པ two verbal nouns in a list.

དགེ་མི་དགེ་བཅུའི་འཇུག་ལྡོག — *engagement in the ten virtues and disengagement from the ten non-virtues.* The 6th case here narrows the general scope of the two verbal nouns.

དགེ་མི་དགེ་བཅུའི་འཇུག་ལྡོག་ལ — དགེ་མི་དགེ་བཅུའི་འཇུག་ལྡོག is marked with the 2nd case particle ལ. This is the object of the transitive agentive-objective verb འབད *strive*

འབད་ཅིང — the continuative syntactic particles ཞིང་ཤིང and ཅིང occur conjunctively after verbs in compound sentences. Often the verbal auxiliaries with the sentence's final verb will also apply to the first verb.

སྟོབས་བཞིའི་ལམ་དུ་རྒྱུན་དུ་ཞུགས — ཞུགས is the past tense of the intr. v. (nom-obj), *be involved [with something]*. It follows the regular nom-obj syntax of intransitive action verbs, but rather than meaning *enter,* its meaning is extended to *be involved with.*

སྟོབས་བཞིའི་ལམ་དུ — the 2nd case particle དུ marks the noun phrase སྟོབས་བཞིའི་ལམ as a qualifier of ཞུགས signifying place of activity.

New Vocabulary • The four antidotal powers སྟོབས་བཞི།

སྟོབས་བཞི — གཉེན་པོ་སྟོབས་བཞི། *the four antidotal powers*

- རྟེན་གྱི་སྟོབས — *the power of [reliance on] a basis*
- གཉེན་པོའི་སྟོབས — *the power of [overcoming non-virtues by] antidotes*
- རྣམ་པར་སུན་འབྱིན་པོའི་སྟོབས — *the power of repentance*
- ཉེས་པ་ལས་སླར་ལྡོག་པའི་སྟོབས — *the power of not engaging in non-virtues again*

Grammar review • Shared verb forms

Tibetan has many pairs of related verbs, one transitive and one intransitive. Sometimes these pairs of related verbs share one or more verbs forms. འཇུག་ is such a verb form, since both the **present tense of the transitive verb** and the **present tense of the intransitive verb** are spelled the same.

འཇུག་ this is both the present tense of the transitive verb and the present tense of the intransitive verb.

འཇུག་ trans. v. (ag-obj), causative, in the sense of *make something happen* འཇུག་འཙུག་གཞུག་ཆུག ཐ་དད།

འཇུག་ intr. v. (nom-obj), *enter, engage, apply;* by extension: *supplement* འཇུག་ཞུགས་འཇུག་ཞུགས། ཐ་མི་དད།

New Vocabulary • The ten virtues and the ten non-virtues དགེ་མི་དགེ་བཅུ།

three physical non-virtues

སྲོག་གཅོད་	*killing*
མ་བྱིན་པར་ལེན་	*stealing*
ལོག་གཡེམ་	*sexual misconduct*

four verbal non-virtues

བརྫུན་པ་	*lying*
ཕྲ་མ་	*divisive speech, slander*
ཚིག་རྩུབ་	*hurtful speech*
ངག་འཁྱལ་	*idle gossip*

three mental non-virtues

བརྣབ་སེམས་མེད་པ་	*covetousness*
གནོད་སེམས་ཀྱི་ཞེ་སྡང་མེད་པ་	*malicious intent*
ལོག་ལྟ་དང་བྲལ་བའི་ཡང་དག་པའི་ལྟ་བ་	*wrong view*

three physical virtues

སྲོག་གཅོད་སྤོང་བ་	*abandoning killing*
མ་བྱིན་པར་ལེན་སྤོང་བ་	*abandoning stealing*
ལོག་གཡེམ་སྤོང་བ་	*abandoning sexual misconduct*

four verbal virtues

བརྫུན་པ་སྤོང་བ་	*abandoning lying*
ཕྲ་མ་སྤོང་བ་	*abandoning divisive speech, slander*
ཚིག་རྩུབ་སྤོང་བ་	*abandoning hurtful speech*
ངག་འཁྱལ་སྤོང་བ་	*abandoning idle gossip*

three mental virtues

བརྣབ་སེམས་མེད་པོ་སྤོང་བ་	*abandoning covetousness*
གནོད་སེམས་ཀྱི་ཞེ་སྡང་མེད་པ་སྤོང་བ་	*abandoning malicious intent*
ལོག་ལྟ་དང་བྲལ་བའི་ཡང་དག་པའི་ལྟ་བ་སྤོང་བ་	*abandoning wrong view*

Chapter Three Self Test

Write out the passage, boxing and identifying every syntactic element.

དེ་ནས་དཀར་ཆོས་ཐམས་ཅད་ཀྱི་གཞི་ཆེན་པོ་ལས་འབྲས་ལ་ཡིད་ཆེས་པའི་དད་པ་སྒོ་དུ་མ་ནས་བསྐྱེད་པ་བསྟན་པར་བྱས་ཏེ། དགེ་མི་དགེའི་འཇུག་ལྡོག་ལ་འབད་ཅིང་སྤོབས་བཞིའི་ལམ་དུ་རྒྱུན་དུ་ཞུགས་པ་ཞིག་བྱ།

Vocabulary

For each word, can you identify what part of speech it is (noun, pronoun, adjective, verb, adverb, postposition) and what it means?
For each syntactic particle, can you identify what class of syntactic particle it belongs to and how it is used?

ཀྱི་	དགེ་བ་	བསྐྱེད་པ་	ལས་འབྲས་
དེ་ནས་	དགེ་མི་དགེ་	མི་དགེ་	ལོག་
གཞི་	དད་	ཞིང་	ཤིང་
གཉེན་པོའི་སྟོབས་	དད་པ་	ཞུགས་	སུ་རུ་ཏུ་དུ་ར་
ཅིང་	དེ་	འཇུག་	བྲས་
ཅིང་ཞིང་ཤིང་	དེའི་རྗེས་སུ་	འཇུག་	རྗེས་
ཆེན་པོ་	དུ་	འཇུག་ལྡོག་	རྒྱུན་
ཆོས་	དུ་མ་	འབད་	རྒྱུན་དུ་
ཏེ་	ནས་	འབྲས་བུ་	ལྡོག་
ཏེ་ སྟེ་ and དེ་	བཅུ་	འི་	སྒོ་
ཐམས་ཅད་	བཞི་	ཡིད་ཆེས་པའི་དད་པ་	སྟེ་
དཀར་	བསྟན་	ལ་	སྤོབས་
དཀར་ཆོས་	བསྟན་པར་བྱས་	ལམ་	སྤོབས་བཞི་
དཀར་པོ་	བསྐྱེད་	ལས་	སྐྱེས་

Translation of Tsong-kha-pa's text

དེ་ནས་དཀར་ཆོས་ཐམས་ཅད་ཀྱི་གཞི་ཆེན་པོ་ལས་འབྲས་ལ་ཡིད་ཆེས་པའི་དད་པ་སྒོ་དུ་མ་ནས་བསྐྱེད་ལ་བརྟན་པར་བྱས་ཏེ། དགེ་མི་དགེ་བཅུའི་འཇུག་ལྡོག་ལ་འབད་ཅིང་སྟོབས་བཞིའི་ལམ་དུ་རྒྱུན་དུ་ཞུགས་པ་ཞིག་བྱ།

Then, you should generate from many viewpoints the faith of conviction in actions and their effects—this being the great basis for all wholesome practices. Having made that faith firm, you should strive at engaging in virtues and disengaging from non-virtues, abiding continuously in the path of the four powers.

Annotations for Tsong-kha-pa's text in Chapter Three

Here is Tsong-kha-pa's text as supplemented by *The Four Interwoven Annotations,* 829.1–829.5

དེ་ལྟར་སྐྱབས་སུ་སོང་བ་དེ་ནས་སྐྱབས་སུ་སོང་བའི་དགོས་པ་ནི་སྐྱབས་སུ་སོང་བ་ཞེས་བྱ་བ་དེ་སངས་རྒྱས་ལ་སྐྱབས་སྟོན་པ་པོ། ཆོས་ལ་སྐྱབས་དངོས། དགེ་འདུན་ལ་སྐྱབས་བསྒྲུབ་པའི་གྲོགས་སུ་བཟུང་ནས་ཡིད་ཆེད་པར་བྱས་པ་དེ་ཡིན་པས་ན་ནད་ཀྱི་གཉེན་པོར་སྨན་ཟ་དགོས་པ་བཞིན་དུ་འཇིགས་པ་དེའི་གཉེན་པོ་ཆོས་བྱེད་དགོས། དེ་ཡང་ངན་འགྲོ་འགོག་པ་ལ་མི་དགེ་བ་སྤང་དགོས། བདེ་འགྲོ་ཐོབ་པ་ལ་དགེ་བ་བསྒྲུབ་དགོས་དེ་ཡིན་པས་ན་སྐབས་འདིར་སྐྱབས་སུ་སོང་ནས་དེའི་བསླབ་བྱ་ལ་སློབ་པའི་སྐབས་སུ་དཀར་ནག་གི་ལས་འབྲས་བསམས་དེ་བླང་དོར་ཚུལ་བཞིན་དུ་བྱེད་པ་དེ་ཉིད་ཡིན་པའི་ཕྱིར། དེ་ནས་དཀར་ཆོས་ཐམས་ཅད་ཀྱི་གཞི་ཆེན་པོ་ལས་འབྲས་ལ་ཡིད་ཆེས་པའི་དད་པ་ ཐབས་ཀྱི་ སྒོ་དུ་མ་ནས་བསྐྱེད་ པར་བྱས་ ལ་ ཉིད་ བརྟན་པར་བྱས་ཏེ། དད་པ་དེས་ཀུན་ནས་བླང་བའི་ དགེ་བ་ བཅུ་དང་ མི་དགེ་བ་བཅུའི་འཇུག་ལྡོག་ལ་ ཅི་ནས་ཀྱང་ འབད་ཅིང་ མི་དགེ་བ་སྔར་བྱས་རྣམས་འདག་པའི་ཆེད་དུ་ སྟོབས་བཞི་ ཚང་བ འི་ བཤགས་པའི་ ལམ་ སྒོལ་ དུ་རྒྱུན་དུ་ བར་མ་ཆད་པར་ ཞུགས་པ་ཞིག་ གལ་ཆེ་བས་དེ་ནི་ཅི་ནས་ བྱ་ དགོས་སོ། །

Translation of Tsong-kha-pa's text with annotations, 829.1-829.5

The purpose for having gone for refuge in that way is to develop faith in the refuges through holding Buddha as the teacher of refuge, the Doctrine as the actual refuge, and the Spiritual Community as your assisters in achieving refuge.

Just as [someone who is ill] must ingest medicine as an antidote for the illness, we must take the doctrine as an antidote for that fear [of falling into a bad migration upon dying through the force of already accumulated causes]. Furthermore, in order to stop bad migrations, you must abandon non-virtue; in order to attain happy migrations, you must accomplish virtue. Accordingly, in this context of training in the precepts of refuge, you should contemplate wholesome and harmful actions and their effects and then you should properly take up [wholesome activities] and discard [harmful activities].

Then, you should generate from many viewpoints the method that is the great basis of all wholesome activities, the faith of conviction in actions and their effects. When you have made that faith stable, due to that faith you should strive at engaging in the ten virtues that are extensively taken up and disengaging from the ten non-virtues however much you can.

In order to purify the non-virtuous actions done earlier, you should become involved continuously, without interruption, in the path system by means of complete confession within the four powers. Because this is so important, you must do it as much as you can.

Chapter Four

དེ་ལྟར་སྐྱེས་བུ་ཆུང་ངུའི་ཆོས་སྐོར་རྣམས་ཚིགས་སུ་ཚུད་པ་ན་འཁོར་བ་སྤྱི་དང་བྱེ་བྲག་གི་ཉེས་དམིགས་མང་དུ་བསམས་ལ། འཁོར་བ་སྤྱི་ལས་བློ་ཅི་ལྡོག་བྱ། དེ་ནས་འཁོར་བ་གང་ལས་འབྱུང་བའི་རྒྱུ་ལས་དང་ཉོན་མོངས་པའི་ངོ་བོ་ངོས་བཟུང་ནས་དེ་སྤོང་འདོད་བཅོས་མ་མིན་པ་བསྐྱེད། འཁོར་བ་ལས་གྲོལ་བའི་ལམ་བསླབ་པ་གསུམ་གྱི་ལ་ངེས་པ་དྲང་ཞིང་ཁྱད་པར་དུ་རང་གིས་གང་ཁས་བླངས་པའི་སོ་སོར་ཐར་པ་ལ་འབད་པར་བྱའོ། །

Division of the passage into units to facilitate the analysis of the syntax

I have subdivided Chapter Four into seven parts to facilitate the discussion of its grammar and syntax. I have also used points that come up as points of departure for more generalized observations useful for those learning to read Classical Tibetan.

1

དེ་ལྟར་སྐྱེས་བུ་ཆུང་ངུའི་ཆོས་སྐོར་རྣམས་ཚིགས་སུ་ཚུད་པ་ན

2

འཁོར་བ་སྤྱི་དང་བྱེ་བྲག་གི་ཉེས་དམིགས་མང་དུ་བསམས་ལ།

3

འཁོར་བ་སྤྱི་ལས་བློ་ཅི་ལྡོག་བྱ།

4

དེ་ནས་འཁོར་བ་གང་ལས་འབྱུང་བའི་རྒྱུ་ལས་དང་ཉོན་མོངས་པའི་ངོ་བོ་ངོས་བཟུང་ནས

5

དེ་སྤོང་འདོད་བཅོས་མ་མིན་པ་བསྐྱེད།

6

འཁོར་བ་ལས་གྲོལ་བའི་ལམ་བསླབ་པ་གསུམ་གྱི་ལ་ངེས་པ་དྲང་ཞིང

7

ཁྱད་པར་དུ་རང་གིས་གང་ཁས་བླངས་པའི་སོ་སོར་ཐར་པ་ལ་འབད་པར་བྱའོ། །

Part 1 • དེ་ལྟར་སྐྱེས་བུ་ཆུང་ངུའི་ཆོས་སྐོར་རྣམས་ཚགས་སུ་ཆུད་པ་ན

Part 1 is a conditional clause ending with the syntactic particle ན་ meaning "when"

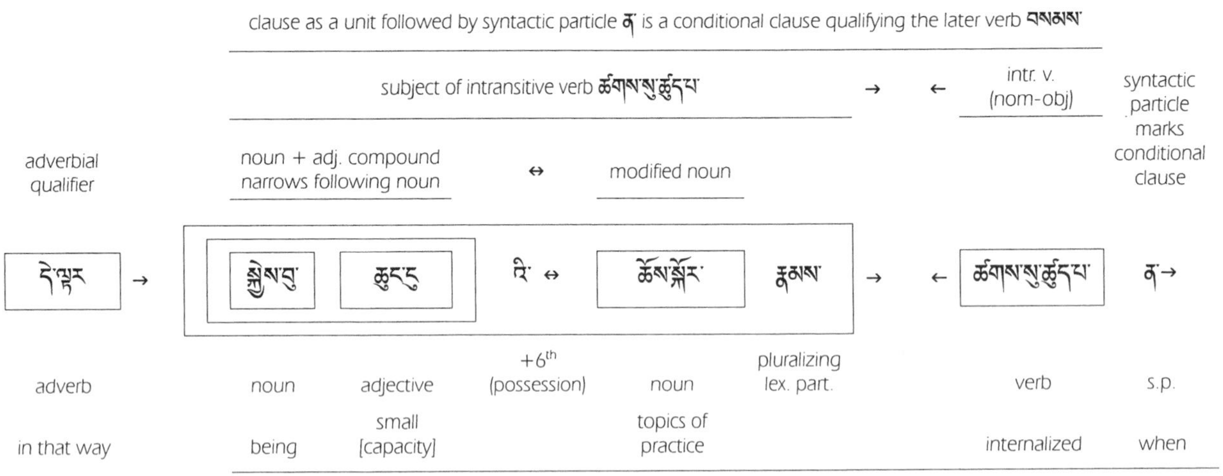

When in that way the topics of practice for a being of small capacity have been internalized, ...

Glossary for Part 1

དེ་ལྟར་	adv. pronoun., *such, thus (in that way)*
སྐྱེས་	intr. v. (nom-obj), *be produced, be generated, be born, arise*
	སྐྱེ་སྐྱེས་སྐྱེ། ཐ་མི་དད།
བསྐྱེད་	trans. v. (ag-nom), *create, produce, generate, give birth to*
	སྐྱེད་བསྐྱེད་བསྐྱེད་སྐྱེད། ཐ་དད།
སྐྱེས་བུ་	n., *being*
ཆུང་ངུ་	adj., *small*
སྐྱེས་བུ་ཆུང་ངུ་	noun phrase (n. + adj.), *a being of small [capacity]*
སྐྱེས་བུ་ཆུང་ངུའི་	noun phrase + 6th case particle fused to suffixless final syllable
འི་	particle fused to suffixless final syllable; either 1) a syntactic particle following a verb or verb phrase signifying conjunction or disjunction, or 2) a 6th case particle following nouns, pronouns, postpositions, and adjectives
ཆོས་སྐོར་	noun phrase, *topics of practice*
རྣམས་	lexical pluralizing particle
ཚགས་སུ་ཆུད་པ་	intr. phrasal verb (nom-obj), *be included, be involved, be internalized*
	ཚུད་ཚུད་ཚུད། ཐ་མི་དད།
ཚགས་སུ་ཆུད་པ་ན་	verb + conditional syntactic particle marking a conditional clause
ན་	particle; either 1) a rhetorical syntactic particle marking a conditional clause following a verb or verb phrase, or 2) a case particle following nouns, pronouns, postpositions, and adjectives marking the 2nd, 4th and 7th cases

Grammar review • Recasting the intransitive conditional clause into a transitive translation

དེ་ལྟར་སྐྱེས་བུ་ཆུང་ངུའི་ཆོས་སྐོར་རྣམས་ཚགས་སུ་ཚུད་པ་ན — This is an intransitive conditional clause: "when the topics of practice by a being of small capacity **are internalized**..." Because English favors transitive active voice constructions, you may consider recasting the clause into the more commonly seen transitive active voice construction: "when **you have internalized** the topics of practice by a being of small capacity..."

ཚགས་སུ་ཚུད་པ་ — intr. phrasal verb (nom-obj), *be included, be involved, be internalized*

Part 2 • འཁོར་བ་སྤྱི་དང་བྱེ་བྲག་གི་ཉེས་དམིགས་མང་དུ་བསམས་ལ

The thought begun with the conditional clause in Part 1 is completed in Part 2

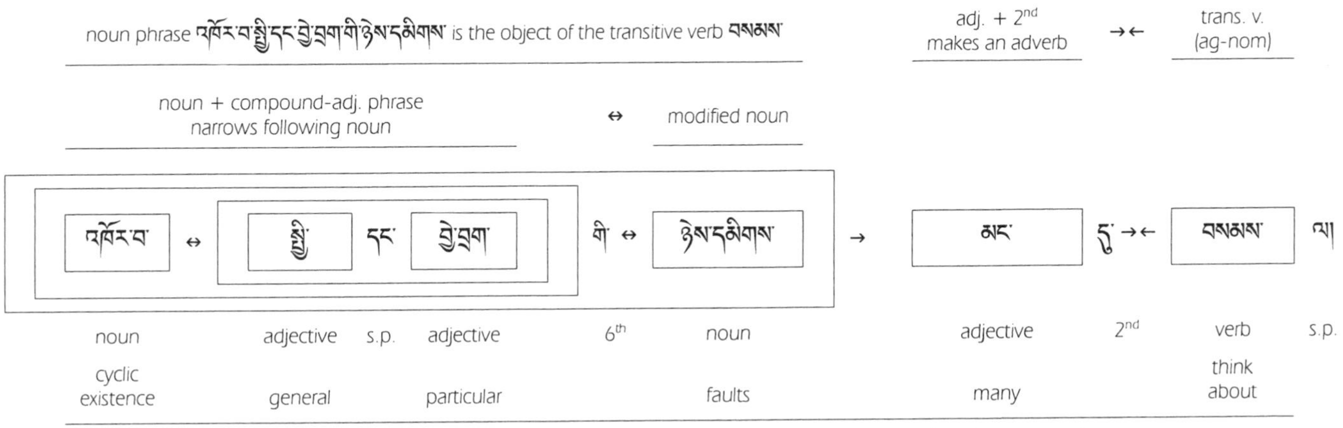

You should frequently contemplate the faults of cyclic existence in general and in particular.

Glossary for Part 2

འཁོར་ — intr. v. (nom-obj), *be turned* — འཁོར་འཁོར་འཁོར། ཐ་མི་དད།

སྐོར་ — trans. v. (ag-nom), *turn* — སྐོར་སྐོར་སྐོར་སྐོར། ཐ་དད།

འཁོར་བ་ — n., *cyclic existence*

སྤྱི་ — n., *generality;* adj., *general;* here: adj.

འཁོར་བ་སྤྱི་ — noun phrase, *cyclic existence in general*

དང་ — particle, used three ways: 1) continuative syntactic particle used following nouns and noun phrases (*and,* or with negative verb, *or*); 2) syntactic particle marking the qualifier of an intr. nom-s.p. v. of conjunction, as in ང་རང་མི་སྡུག་པ་དང་ཕྲད་ན *if we meet with unpleasantness;* and 3) syntactic particle marking the qualifier of an intr. nom-s.p. v. of disjunction, as in རྟོག་པ་དང་བྲལ་ *free from conceptuality*

བྱེ་བྲག — n., *instance, particularity;* adj., *particular;* here: adj.

འཁོར་བ་སྤྱི་དང་བྱེ་བྲག — noun phrase (noun + compound adjective), *cyclic existence in general and in particular*

འཁོར་བ་སྤྱི་དང་བྱེ་བྲག་གི་ — noun phrase + 6th case particle

གི་ — particle; either 1) a syntactic particle following a verb or verb phrase signifying conjunction or disjunction, or 2) a 6th case

	particle following nouns, pronouns, postpositions, and adjectives
ཉེས་དམིགས་	n., *faults*
མང་	adj., *many, much,* abbreviation of མང་པོ་
མང་པོ་	adj., *many, much*
མང་དུ་	adj. + 2nd case particle followed by a verb = adverb, *frequently*
དུ་	particle; either 1) a verb-modifying syntactic particle within a verb phrase, or 2) a case particle following nouns, pronouns, postpositions, and adjectives marking the 2nd, 4th and 7th cases
བསམས་	trans. v. (ag-nom), *think about, consider* སེམས་བསམས་བསམ་སོམས། ཐ་དད།
བསམས་ལ།	trans. v. + syntactic particle signifying conjunction or disjunction; here: conjunctive syntactic particle, *and*
ལ་	particle; either 1) a syntactic particle following a verb or verb phrase signifying conjunction or disjunction, or 2) a case particle following nouns, pronouns, postpositions, and adjectives marking the 2nd, 4th and 7th cases

Grammar review • Adjectives + 2nd case particle followed by a verb can create an adverbial qualifier

མང་དུ་བསམས་	verb clause (adverb + verb), *consider frequently*
མང་དུ་	adj. + 2nd case particle followed by a verb can create an adverbial qualifier. The adj. *many* becomes the adverb *frequently.*

Grammar review • The syntactic particle ལ་ following a verb is not a case particle, but rather a syntactic particle functioning as punctuation

བསམས་ལ།	The particle following a verb is not a case particle, but rather a syntactic particle following a verb or verb phrase signifying conjunction or disjunction between two sentences. Context will determine whether it should be translated conjunctively as **and**, or disjunctively as **but**.

Part 3 • འཁོར་བ་སྤྱི་ལས་བློ་ཅི་ལྡོག་བྱ།

You may recast this intransitive construction as a transitive English sentence

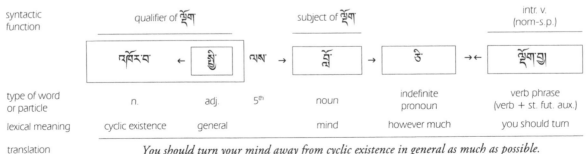

syntactic function	qualifier of ལྡོག་			subject of ལྡོག་		intr. v. (nom-s.p.)
	འཁོར་བ་ ←	སྤྱི་	ལས་ →	བློ་ →	ཅི་ →←	ལྡོག་བྱ།
type of word or particle	n.	adj.	5th	noun	indefinite pronoun	verb phrase (verb + st. fut. aux.)
lexical meaning	cyclic existence	general		mind	however much	you should turn
translation	*You should turn your mind away from cyclic existence in general as much as possible.*					

Glossary for Part 3

འཁོར་བ n., *cyclic existence*

སྤྱི n., *generality;* adj., *general;* here: adj.

འཁོར་བ་སྤྱི noun phrase, *cyclic existence in general*

འཁོར་བ་སྤྱི་ལས noun phrase + 5th case particle

ལས particle; either 1) syntactic particle marking adverbs, participles or disjunction, or 2) a case particle marking the 5th case

བློ n., *mind, awareness*

ཅི interrogative pronoun, *what, which, however much,* used here as an indefinite adverbial pronoun qualifying the verb by showing **to what extent** you should turn your mind from cyclic existence

ལྡོག intr. v. (nom-s.p.), *be isolated from, be reversed* ལྡོག་ལྡོག་ལྡོག ཐ་མི་དད།

ལྡོག་བྱ ལྡོག་པར་བྱ

ལྡོག་པར་བྱ verb phrase (verbal infinitive + strong future auxiliary), *[I] will turn, [you] should turn...*

ལྡོག་པར verbal infinitive; here, the fused ར is a syntactic particle modifying a verb to create an infinitive within the verb phrase འབད་པར་བྱ *[you] should turn;* it is **not** a case particle marking the 2nd, 4th or 7th cases because it does not follow a noun—it is within a verb phrase

བྱ trans. v. (ag-nom) (future tense), *do, make, perform, take;* also strong auxiliary verb. བྱེད་བྱས་བྱ་བྱོས། ཐ་དད།

སུ་རུ་ཏུ་དུ་ར are the five syntactic particles used to modify verbs to create infinitives within verb phrases

ལོག intr. v., *be reversed, be turned* ལོག་ལོག་ལོག ཐ་མི་དད།

Grammar review • One of the six uses of the 5th case is marking the qualifier of a verb of separation: that from which a subject is separated

The fifth case is used to mark qualifiers of transitive and intransitive verbs indicating source, instrument, separation, comparison, inclusion, and logical sequence.

འཁོར་བ་ལས་ལྡོག The noun འཁོར་བ is declined with the 5th case particle ལས signifying འཁོར་བ *cyclic existence* is qualifying the verb ལྡོག by showing that from which the subject is separated, *[unstated subject] is turned away from cyclic existence.*

འཁོར་བ་ལས n. + 5th case particle. The 5th case here is marking separation: that from which the subject is separated.

Grammar review • Intransitive verbs of separation have qualifiers marked with the 5th case

ལྡོག intr. v. (nom-s.p.), *be isolated, be reversed.* Wilson classifies this intransitive **verb of separation** as a nominative-syntactic particle verb together with **verbs of absence, conjunction,** and **disjunction.** However its qualifier, that from which the subject is separated, is marked with a true 5th case particle, not a syntactic particle as the name of the class suggests. It may be more helpful to think of this class of intransitive verbs of separation as nominative-originative.

ལྡོག་བྱ abbreviation for ལྡོག་པར་བྱ *[I] will reverse* or *[you] should reverse*

ལྡོག་པར་བྱ verb phrase (verbal infinitive + strong future auxiliary), *[I] will turn, [you] should turn...*

ལྡོག་པར verbal infinitive; here, the fused ར is a syntactic particle modifying a verb to create an infinitive within the verb phrase ལྡོག་པར་བྱ *[you] should turn;* it is **not** a case particle marking the 2nd, 4th or 7th cases because it does not follow a noun—it is within a verb phrase

བྱ trans. v. (ag-nom) (future tense), *do, make, perform, take;* also strong auxiliary verb བྱེད་བྱས་བྱ་བྱོས། ཐ་དད།

Parts 4 and 5 • དེ་ནས་འཁོར་བ་གང་ལས་འབྱུང་བའི་རྒྱུ་ལས་དང་ཉོན་མོངས་པའི་ངོ་བོ་ངོས་བཟུང་ནས་དེ་སྤོང་འདོད་བཅོས་མ་མིན་པ་བསྐྱེད།

Parts 4 and 5 form a complete sentence composed of two clauses, each anchored by a transitive verb

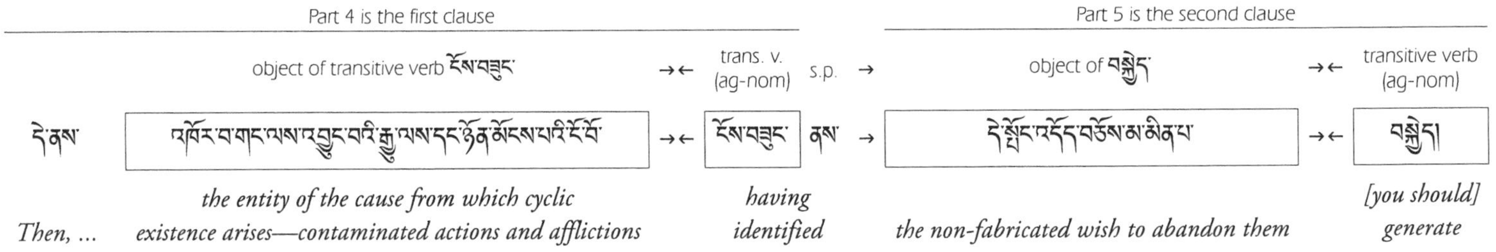

Parts 4 and 5 in full form

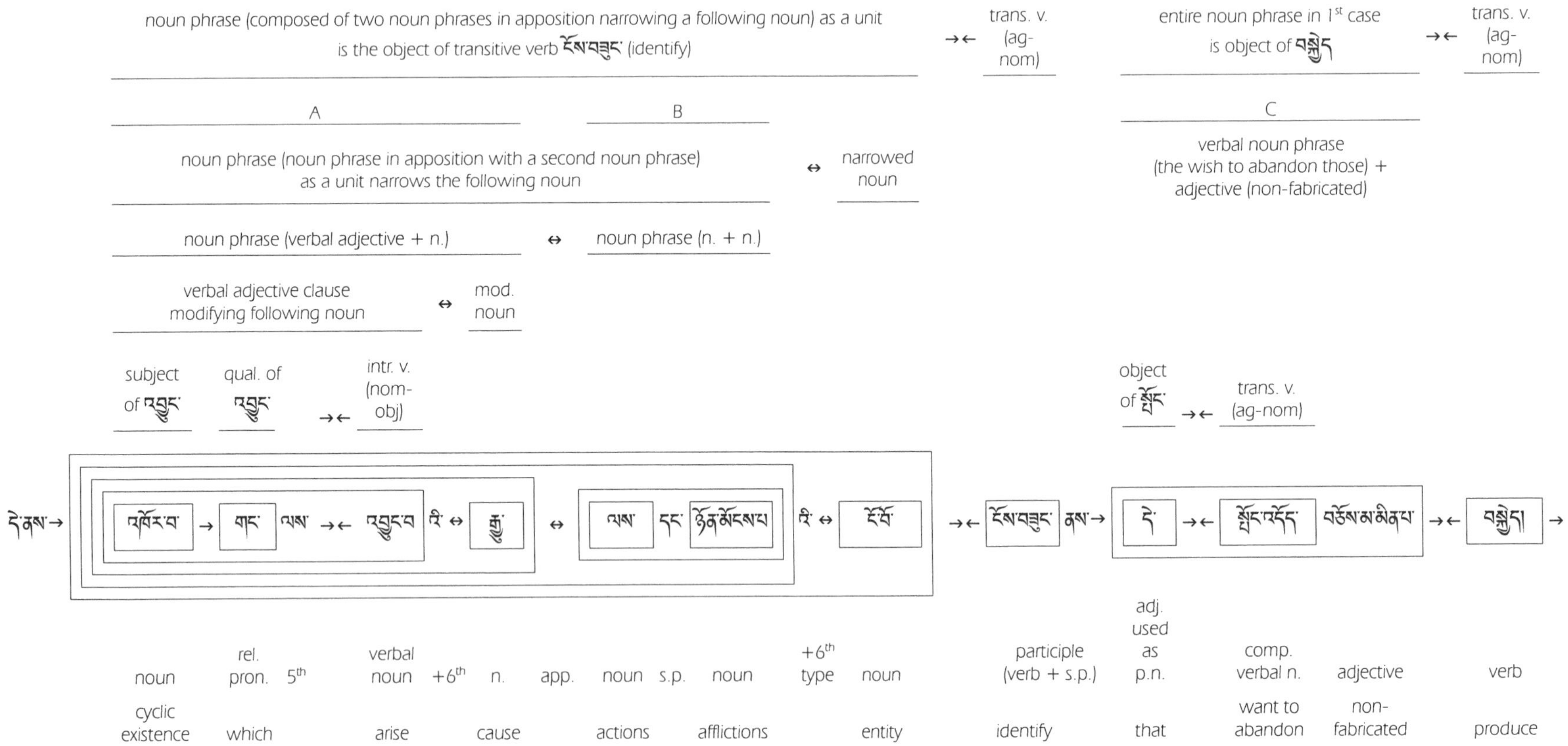

Then, identifying the entity which is [contaminated] actions and afflictions as the causes from which cyclic existence arises, generate a non-simulated wish to abandon them.

Glossary for Parts 4 and 5

དེ་ནས་ a syntactic particle translated *then;* literally, *after that*

འཁོར་བ་ n., *cyclic existence*

གང་ relative pronoun, *which*

གང་ལས་ relative pronoun + 5th case particle

ལས་ particle; either 1) syntactic particle marking adverbs, participles or disjunction, or 2) a case particle marking the 5th case

འབྱུང་ intr. v. (nom-obj), *arise, come forth, emerge, occur, appear*

འབྱུང་བྱུང་འབྱུང་། ཐ་མི་དད།

འབྱུང་བ་ verbal noun; *arising, occurrence*

འབྱུང་བའི་ verbal noun + 6th case particle fused to suffixless final syllable

འི་ particle fused to suffixless final syllable; either 1) a syntactic particle following a verb or verb phrase signifying conjunction or disjunction, or 2) a 6th case particle following nouns, pronouns, postpositions, and adjectives

རྒྱུ་ n., *cause*

ལས་ n., action (*karma*)

ལས་ particle; either 1) syntactic particle marking adverbs, participles or disjunction, or 2) a case particle marking the 5th case

དང་ particle, used three ways: 1) continuative syntactic particle used following nouns and noun phrases (*and,* or with negative verb, *or*); 2) syntactic particle marking the qualifier of an intr. nom-s.p. v. of conjunction, as in ང་རང་མི་སྐྱུག་པ་དང་ཕྲད་ན་ *if we meet with unpleasantness;* and 3) syntactic particle marking the qualifier of an intr. nom-s.p. v. of disjunction, as in རྟོག་པ་དང་བྲལ་ *free from conceptuality*

ཉོན་མོངས་ n., *affliction*

ཉོན་མོངས་པའི་ n. + 6th case particle fused to suffixless final syllable

འི་ particle fused to suffixless final syllable; either 1) a syntactic particle following a verb or verb phrase signifying conjunction or disjunction, or 2) a 6th case particle following nouns, pronouns, postpositions, and adjectives

ངོ་བོ་ n., *entity*

ངོས་བཟུང་ trans. v. (ag-nom) (past tense), *identify*

ངོས་འཛིན། ངོས་བཟུང་། ངོས་གཟུང་། ངོས་ཟུང་། ཐ་དད།

ངོས་བཟུང་ནས་ trans. v. + verb-modifying s.p., *having identified*

ནས་ particle; either 1) a syntactic particle following verbs and verb phrases marking adverbs, participles or disjunction, or 2) a case particle marking the 5th case

དེ་ adj. and pronoun, *that, those*

སྤོང་ trans. v. (ag-nom), *abandon* སྤོང་སྤངས་སྤང་སྤོངས། ཐ་དད།

འདོད་ trans. v. (ag-nom), *want, wish, assert.* This verb is listed in the *Great Word Treasury* as ཐ་མི་དད། but I think it is a transitive ag-nom verb. འདོད་འདོད་འདོད། ཐ་མི་དད།

སྤོང་འདོད་ verb phrase, *want to abandon;* abbreviation for སྤོང་བར་འདོད་

སྤོང་བར་འདོད་ verb phrase, *want to abandon*

སྤོང་བར་ verbal infinitive; here, the fused ར་ is a syntactic particle modifying a verb to create an infinitive within the verb phrases སྤོང་བར་འདོད་ *[you] want to abandon;* it is **not** a case particle marking the 2nd, 4th or 7th cases because it does not follow a noun—it is within a verb phrase

བཅོས་མ་མིན་པ་ adj., *non-fabricated, non-simulated*

བཅོས་མིན་ adj., *non-fabricated, non-simulated*

བསྐྱེད་ trans. v. (ag-nom), *create, produce, generate, give birth to*

སྐྱེད་བསྐྱེད་བསྐྱེད་སྐྱེད། ཐ་དད།

སྐྱེས་ intr. v. (nom-obj), *be produced, be generated, be born, arise*

སྐྱེ་སྐྱེས་སྐྱེ། ཐ་མི་དད།

Notes on Parts 4 and 5

Parts 4 and 5 are composed of two clauses anchored by transitive verbs. This sentence begins with the introductory syntactic particle དེ་ནས་ *then...* indicating sequence. In each clause, the objects of the transitive verbs are complex noun phrases. In translation, the sentence has the following form:
Having identified the entity as AB, generate C.

In the first clause of Part 4, the object of the participle formed from the verb ངོས་བཟུང་ is a noun phrase containing within it two noun phrases in apposition acting as a unit to narrow the meaning of the following noun. This typical construction contains two elements of special interest for the Tibetan language student.

- The contrasting uses of the particles ལས་ and ནས་ illustrate how particles used to mark cases may also be used in other ways as syntactic particles.
- The first of the two noun phrases in apposition contains a verbal adjective. The way verbal adjectives modify nouns requires some detailed exposition.

Grammar review • 19 particles are used both to mark case relationships and as syntactic particles.

Part 4 contains the particles ལས་ and ནས་. A total of 19 particles are used both to mark case relationships and also to mark unrelated syntactic use. Accordingly, the meaning indicated by any given instance of one of these particles can vary widely depending on whether it is serving as a case particle or as a syntactic particle. In general, case relationships are signified for nouns and noun phrases. Syntactic functions such as punctuation, conjunction and disjunction, and the modification of verbs within verb phrases are additional syntactic functions that these particles may indicate. In the following charts, I have arranged groups of equivalent case particles and how these particles are used also as syntactic particles.

7 equivalent particles used to mark 2nd, 4th and 7th cases, and their additional syntactic uses

སུ་རུ་ཏུ་དུ་ན་ར་ལ་	members of this group of 7 equivalent case particles follow nouns, pronouns, postpositions, and adjectives marking the 2nd, 4th and 7th cases.
སུ་རུ་ཏུ་དུ་ར་	these five can also be syntactic particles, modifying verbs to create infinitives within verb phrases
ན་	following a verb or verb phrase, this particle is a syntactic particle, marking a conditional clause, often translated *when...*, and *if...*,
ལ་	following a verb or verb phrase, this particle is a syntactic particle marking conjunction or disjunction. Sometimes it will be translated as *and* or *but,* while sometimes it is sufficient to end a sentence in translation at that point.

5 equivalent particles used to mark the 6th case, and their additional syntactic uses

གི་ཀྱི་གྱི་འི་ཡི་	equivalent particles; either 1) a syntactic particle following a verb or verb phrase signifying conjunction or disjunction, or 2) a 6th case particle following nouns, pronouns, postpositions, and adjectives

5 equivalent particles used to mark the 3rd case, and their additional syntactic uses

གིས་ཀྱིས་གྱིས་འིས་ཡིས་	equivalent particles; either 1) syntactic particle creating an adverbial construction, 2) syntactic particle marking the qualifier of an intransitive nom-s.p. verb of absence, or 3) case particle marking the 3rd case

2 equivalent particles used to mark the 5th case, and the particles' additional syntactic uses

ནས་ and ལས་	equivalent particles; either 1) a syntactic particle following verbs and verb phrases marking adverbs, participles or disjunction, or 2) a case particle marking the 5th case

Grammar review • Participles are formed from verbs + syntactic particle ནས་

Notice that the first clause ends with the transitive verb ངོས་བཟུང་ *identify* transformed into a participle with the addition of the syntactic particle ནས་

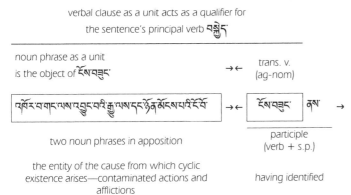

verbal clause as a unit acts as a qualifier for
the sentence's principal verb བསྐྱེད་

noun phrase as a unit
is the object of ངོས་བཟུང་ →← trans. v. (ag-nom)

འཁོར་བ་གང་ལས་འབྱུང་བའི་རྒྱུ་ལས་དང་ཉོན་མོངས་པའི་ངོ་བོ་	→←	ངོས་བཟུང་	ནས་	→
two noun phrases in apposition		participle (verb + s.p.)		
the entity of the cause from which cyclic existence arises—contaminated actions and afflictions		having identified		

having identified the entity of the cause from which cyclic existence arises—contaminated actions and afflictions

ནས་ is not a case marking particle here because it follows a verb, not a noun or noun phrase. The particle ནས་ following a verb turns the verb into a participle. A participle is a hybrid with some verb-like characteristics and some noun-like characteristics.

The participle acts like a verb (here ངོས་བཟུང་) by taking an object.

It acts like a noun in that the entire construction qualifies the action expressed by the sentence's principal verb བསྐྱེད་ *produce* by showing that having identified the causes of cyclic existence, you should generate the wish to abandon them.

Grammar review • A verbal adjective precedes the noun it modifies

The object of ངོས་བཟུང་ is a unit composed of two noun phrases in apposition; the first noun phrase contains a verbal adjective qualified by a general relative pronoun

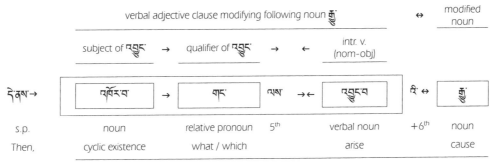

verbal adjective clause modifying following noun རྒྱུ་ ↔ modified noun

	subject of འབྱུང་	→	qualifier of འབྱུང་		→ ←	intr. v. (nom-obj)		
དེ་ནས་→	འཁོར་བ་	→	གང་	ལས་	→←	འབྱུང་བ	འི་ ↔	རྒྱུ་
s.p.	noun		relative pronoun	5th		verbal noun	+6th	noun
Then,	cyclic existence		what / which			arise		cause

the causes from which cyclic existence arises

འཁོར་བ་གང་ལས་འབྱུང་བའི་ — This is a verbal adjective modifying the following noun རྒྱུ་ the causes *from which cyclic existence arises.*

ནས་ and ལས་ — equivalent particles; either 1) syntactic particle marking adverbs, participles or disjunction, or 2) a case particle marking the 5th case

འཁོར་བ་ — noun, *cyclic existence.* This is the subject of the intransitive nominative action verb འབྱུང་

གང་ལས་ — relative pronoun + 5th case particle (source). This noun is qualifying the action expressed by the verb འབྱུང་ by showing the source of the action.

The 5th case is used to mark qualifiers signifying **source, instrument, separation, comparison, inclusion,** and **logical sequence.** From among these six relationships, the 5th case is here showing the **source** of the action indicated by the verb.

Grammar review • Determining the relationship implied between the modified noun and modifying verbal adjective clause

The key to correct translation of verbal adjective clauses is understanding the relationship implied between the modified noun and modifying verbal clause. The verbal adjective is connected to the modified noun with a 6th case particle. The noun thus modified is often the **understood** subject, agent, object, qualifier, or complement of the verbal clause. In order to translate the verbal adjective correctly, you must understand **which implied relationship is signified.**

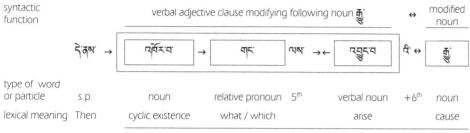

syntactic function		verbal adjective clause modifying following noun རྒྱུ་				↔	modified noun
	དེ་ནས་ →	འཁོར་བ →	གང་	ལས་ →←	འབྱུང་བ	འི་ ↔	རྒྱུ་
type of word or particle	s.p.	noun	relative pronoun	5th	verbal noun	+6th	noun
lexical meaning	Then	cyclic existence	what / which		arise		cause
translation		*the cause from which cyclic existence arises*					

Nouns and noun phrases are often modified by a preceding verbal clause acting as an adjective. Here the noun རྒྱུ་ *cause* is being modified by the verbal clause འཁོར་བ་གང་ལས་འབྱུང་བའི་ *from which cyclic existence arises.* If རྒྱུ་ were to occur prior to the verb it would be declined in the 5th case and be a qualifier showing the source from which cyclic existence arises.

Grammar review • Simple adjectives and verbal adjectives compared

Simple adjectives are words. When they precede the noun they modify they are connected to that noun with a 6th case particle.

	དམ་པ	འི་	ཆོས་
type of word or particle	adjective	+6th	noun
lexical meaning	excellent		Dharma, doctrine
translation	*the excellent Dharma*		

Like a simple adjective, a verbal adjective also precedes the noun it modifies and is also connected to it with a sixth case particle. Unlike a simple adjective, a verbal adjective is a verbal clause.

syntactic function	agent of བསྟན་		trans. v. (ag-nom)		implied object of བསྟན་
	སངས་རྒྱས་	གྱིས་ ↔	བསྟན་པ	འི་ ↔	ཆོས་
type of word or particle	noun	3rd	verb	+6th	noun
lexical meaning	Buddha		taught		Dharma, the doctrine
translation	*the doctrine Buddha taught*				

སངས་རྒྱས་གྱིས་བསྟན་ verbal clause, *taught by Buddha*

སངས་རྒྱས་གྱིས་བསྟན་པའི་ verbal adjective clause + 6th case particle, *[the doctrine] taught by Buddha*

Grammar review • The eight basic units of Classical Tibetan syntax

I present Tibetan grammar in terms of **eight basic building blocks of Tibetan syntax**. On the most basic level of syntactic function, Classical Tibetan has eight elements: **agents of transitive verbs, objects of transitive verbs, complements of objects, subjects of intransitive verbs, complements of subjects, qualifiers of verbs, transitive verbs,** and **intransitive verbs.** These syntactic functions may be filled by a single word, or phrases and clauses made up of words and particles. The following chart illustrates the typical order in which these elements may be found in a Classical Tibetan sentence, together with cases in which the declined elements may be found.

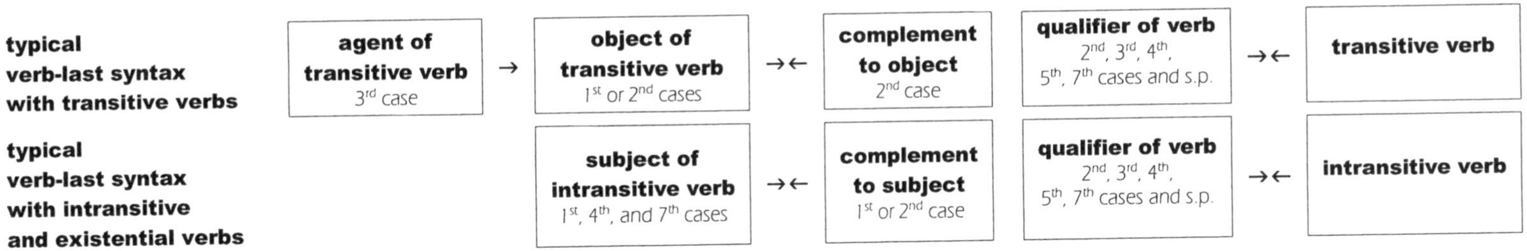

A series of four examples to help you understand how to tell which relationship is implied by verbal adjectives

In order to help you learn to identify which relationship a verbal adjective may imply through modifying a noun, it may be useful to see in a generalized way four of the possible relationships that one finds in the Tibetan sentence. In a series of examples I will use the parts of a simple sentence to create verbal adjectives, each implying a different relationship. The first example is a sentence composed of a transitive verb, an agent in the 3rd case, an object in the 1st case, and a qualifier in the 2nd case. The following three examples are verbal adjectives modifying the noun that is its implied agent, implied object, and implied qualifier.

1. The basic sentence has four elements: an agent in the 3rd case, an object in the 1st case, a qualifier in the 2nd case, and a transitive verb

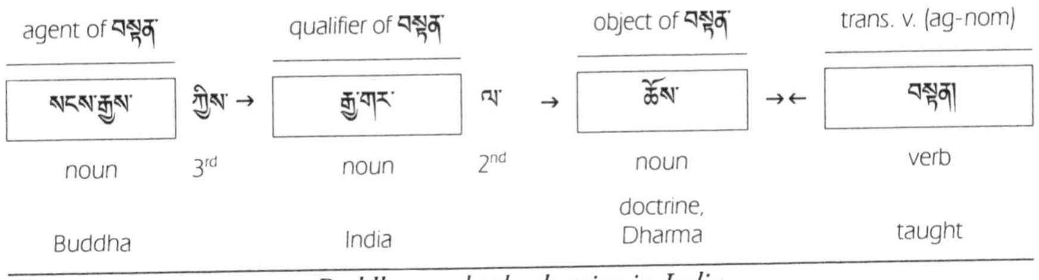

Buddha taught the doctrine in India.

སངས་རྒྱས་ཀྱིས་ the noun སངས་རྒྱས་ *Buddha* is declined in the 3rd case with the particle ཀྱིས་ to indicate it is the **agent** of the transitive verb བསྟན་ *teach*

རྒྱ་གར་ལ་ the noun རྒྱ་གར་ *India* is declined in the 2nd case with the particle ལ་ to indicate it is a qualifier showing the **place of activity**

ཆོས་ the noun ཆོས་ *doctrine* is in the 1st case to indicate it is the **object** of the transitive verb བསྟན་ *teach*

བསྟན་ the transitive, agentive-nominative verb བསྟན་ takes a 3rd case agent སངས་རྒྱས་ཀྱིས་ and a 1st case object ཆོས་

2. **The elements rearranged as a noun phrase composed of a verbal adjective modifying a noun that is its implied agent**

verbal clause རྒྱ་གར་ལ་ཆོས་བསྟན་པའི་ is adj. modifying the noun སངས་རྒྱས་					↔	modified noun
qualifier of བསྟན་		object of བསྟན་	→←	trans. v. (ag-nom)		understood agent of བསྟན་
རྒྱ་གར་	ལ་ →	ཆོས་	→←	བསྟན་པ	འི་ ↔	སངས་རྒྱས་
noun	2nd	noun		verbal noun	+6th	noun
India		the doctrine		taught		Buddha

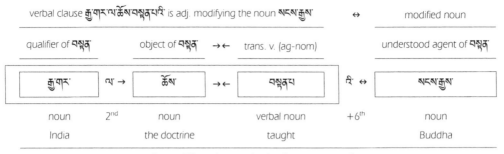

the Buddha who taught the doctrine in India...

3. **The elements rearranged as a noun phrase composed of a verbal adjective modifying a noun that is its implied object**

verbal clause སངས་རྒྱས་ཀྱིས་རྒྱ་གར་ལ་བསྟན་པའི་ is adj. modifying the following noun ཆོས་					↔	modified noun
agent of བསྟན་		qualifier of བསྟན་	→←	trans. v. (ag-nom)		implied object of བསྟན་
སངས་རྒྱས་	ཀྱིས་ →	རྒྱ་གར་	ལ་ →←	བསྟན་པ	འི་ ↔	ཆོས་
noun	3rd	noun	2nd	verb	+6th	noun
Buddha		India		taught		the doctrine

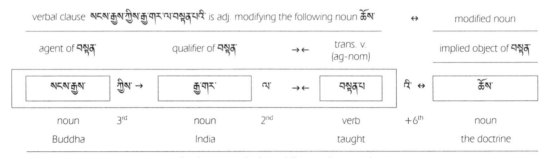

the doctrine which Buddha taught in India...

4. **The elements rearranged as a noun phrase composed of a verbal adjective modifying a noun that is its implied qualifier**

verbal clause སངས་རྒྱས་ཀྱིས་ཆོས་བསྟན་པའི་ is adj. modifying the noun ཡུལ་						modified noun
agent of བསྟན་		object of བསྟན་	→←	trans. v. (ag-nom)		implied qualifier of བསྟན་
སངས་རྒྱས་	ཀྱིས་ →	ཆོས་	→←	བསྟན་པ	འི་ ↔	ཡུལ་
noun	3rd	noun		verb	+6th	noun
Buddha		the doctrine		taught		place

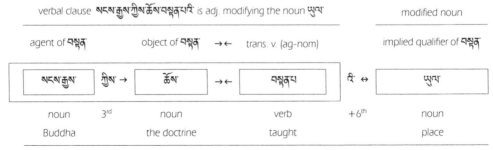

the place where Buddha taught the doctrine

Back to Part 4: the verbal adjective phrase འཁོར་བ་གང་ལས་འབྱུང་བའི་རྒྱུ་

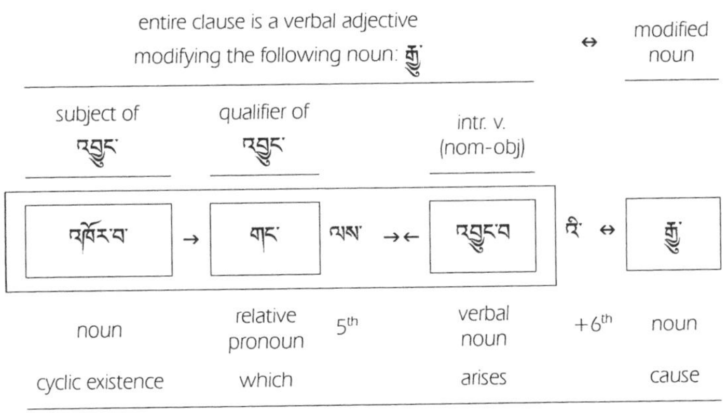

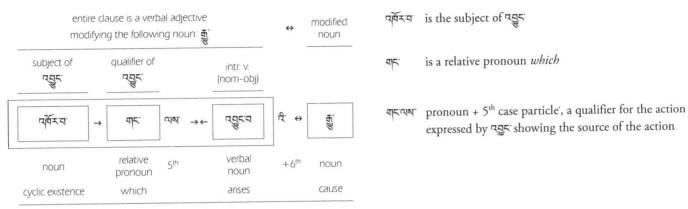

the cause from which cyclic existence arises

འཁོར་བ་ is the subject of འབྱུང་

གང་ is a relative pronoun *which*

གང་ལས་ pronoun + 5th case particle, a qualifier for the action expressed by འབྱུང་ showing the source of the action

Here the noun རྒྱུ་ is being modified adjectivally by the verbal adjective which precedes it. Put another way, *from which cyclic existence arises* is a verbal adjective clause modifying the noun *cause*. The fused 6th case ending འི་ connects the verbal adjective to the noun it modifies. Wilson calls this use of the 6th case a **clause connective to the qualifier** because it connects a verbal adjective clause to the noun that would **qualify** the verb (by showing the source from which the subject arises).

Recasting the elements in the verb-last syntax of a complete sentence

Recasting the entire phrase འཁོར་བ་གང་ལས་འབྱུང་བའི་རྒྱུ་ as a sentence with verb-last syntax requires two steps: 1. Replace the relative pronoun with its referent noun: the relative pronoun གང་ (*which*) would be replaced by the noun it stands for: རྒྱུ་ (*cause*). 2. The referent noun now qualifies the action expressed by the terminal verb by showing source of the action expressed by the verb.

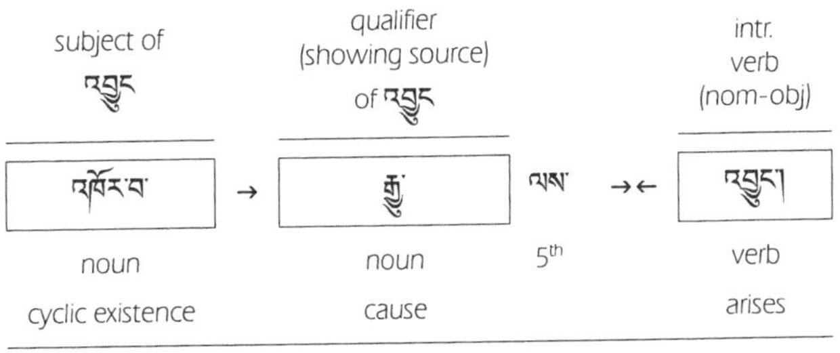

Cyclic existence arises from causes.

འབྱུང་ intr. v. (nom-obj), *arise, come forth, emerge, occur, appear.* Notice that while the verb belongs to the class of nom-obj verbs, in this sentence there is no 2nd case qualifier (such as would show **place of activity**). Instead, there is a 5th case qualifier showing source. Saying that the verb is a member of the class of nom-obj verbs means that this verb will most likely have a 2nd case qualifier, not that one is required.

Part 6 • འཁོར་བ་ལས་གྲོལ་བའི་ལམ་བསླབ་པ་གསུམ་སྤྱི་ལ་ངེས་པ་དྲང་ཞིང་

Parts 6 and 7 are a compound sentence: "Strive at A and B." The auxiliary to the final verb in Part 7 distributes also to the verb ending Part 6. The agent of both Parts 6 and 7 is an implied "you." The object in Part 6 is a long verbal clause with an intransitive verb qualified by two noun phrases in apposition.

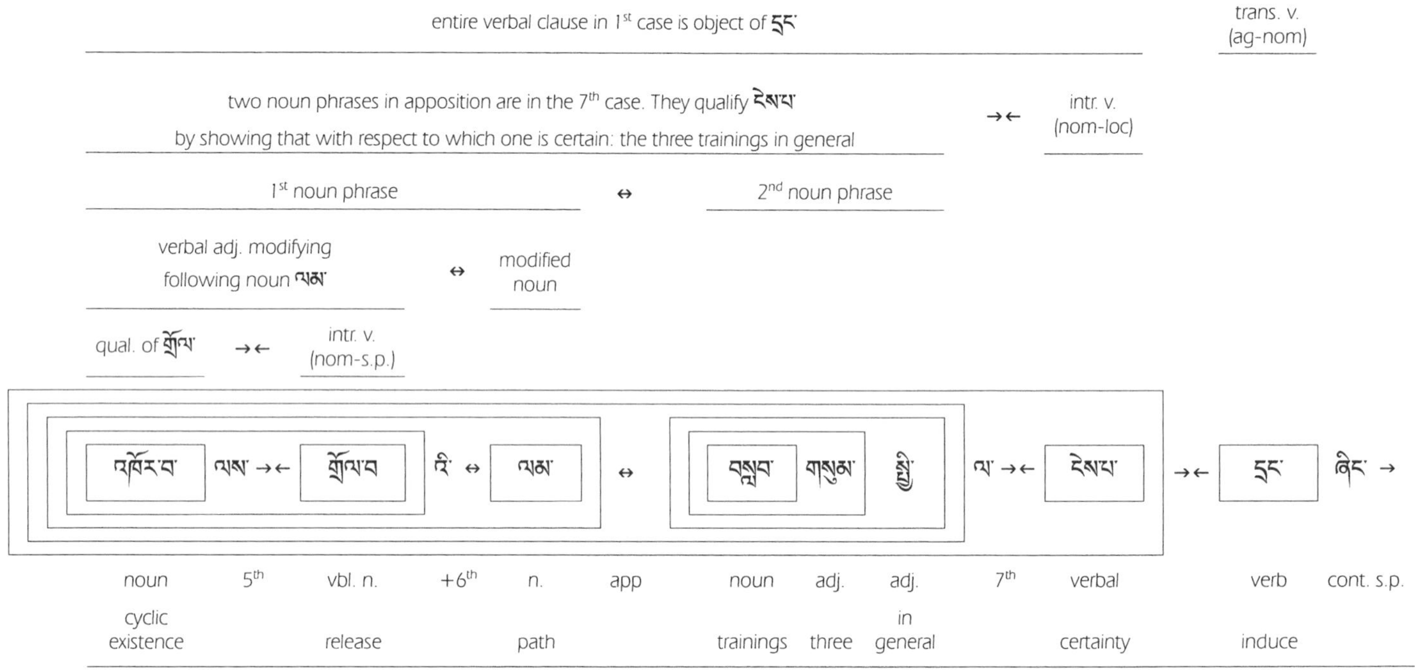

You should strive at inducing certainty regarding the paths by which you are released from cyclic existence: the three trainings in general.

Glossary for Part 6

འཁོར་བ — n., *cyclic existence*

འཁོར་བ་ལས་ — noun + 5th case particle marking that from which the subject is separated

ལས་ — particle; either syntactic particle or 5th case particle

གྲོལ་ — intr. v. (nom-s.p.), *be released [from something].* This **verb of separation** is classified as a nom-s.p. verb together with verbs of absence, conjunction and disjunction, but its qualifier, that from which the subject is separated, is marked with a true 5th case particle.

གྲོལ་བའི་ — verbal noun + 6th case particle fused to suffixless final syllable

འི་ — particle fused to suffixless final syllable; either 1) a syntactic particle following a verb or verb phrase signifying conjunction or disjunction, or 2) a 6th case particle following nouns, pronouns, postpositions, and adjectives

ལམ་ — n., *path*

བསླབ་ — trans. v. (ag-obj) (future tense), *will train in*

སློབ་བསླབས་བསླབ་སློབས། ཐ་དད།

བསླབ་པ་	verbal noun, *training*
གསུམ་	n. or adj., *three;* here: adj.
བསླབ་པ་གསུམ་	noun phrase (verbal noun + adj.), *the three trainings*
སྤྱི་	n., *generality;* adj., *general*
བསླབ་པ་གསུམ་སྤྱི་	noun phrase (verbal noun + adj.), *the three trainings in general*
བསླབ་པ་གསུམ་སྤྱི་ལ་	noun phrase + 7th case particle marking qualifier of intransitive nom-loc verb ངེས་ *be certain, ascertain*
ལ་	particle; either 1) a syntactic particle following a verb or verb phrase signifying conjunction or disjunction, or 2) a case particle following nouns, pronouns, postpositions, and adjectives marking the 2nd, 4th and 7th cases

ངེས་	intr. v. (nom-loc), *be certain* ངེས་ངེས་ངེས། ཐ་མི་དད།
ངེས་པ་	verbal n., *certainty, ascertainment*
དྲང་	trans. v. (ag-nom), *induce*
	འདྲེན་དྲངས་དྲང་དྲོངས། ཐ་དད།
འདྲོང་	intr. v. (nom-loc), *be induced*
	འདྲོང་འདྲོངས་འདྲོང་། ཐ་མི་དད།
ཞིང་	conjunctive syntactic particle following verbs and verb phrases: *and*

The qualifier of the intransitive verb ངེས་ *be certain* is two noun phrases in apposition

འཁོར་བ་ལས་གྲོལ་བའི་ལམ་ and བསླབ་པ་གསུམ་སྤྱི་ are two noun phrases in apposition.

འཁོར་བ་ལས་གྲོལ་བའི་ལམ་བསླབ་པ་གསུམ་སྤྱི་ as a unit, these two phrases in apposition are the qualifier of the intransitive verb ངེས་ *be certain;* the qualifier shows that with respect to which one is certain.

Grammar review • ཅིང་ཞིང་ཤིང་ follow verbs and verb phrases, དང་ follows nouns and noun phrases

ཅིང་ཞིང་ཤིང་ three equivalent continuative syntactic particles used following verbs and verb phrases, *and,* or left untranslated where it ends a sentence.

- ཅིང་ follows words ending with the letters གདབ་ and with the secondary suffix ད་ (which is invisible)
- ཞིང་ follows words ending with the letters ངནམའརལ་ and with suffixless final syllables
- ཤིང་ follows words ending with ས་ and with the secondary suffix ས་

Compare the three uses for དང་ when it follows nouns and noun phrases

དང་ particle following nouns and noun phrases used in three ways

1) continuative syntactic particle used following nouns and noun phrases *(and,* or with negative verb, *or);*
2) syntactic particle marking the qualifier of an intransitive nom-s.p. v. of conjunction, as in ང་རང་མི་སྡུག་པ་དང་ཕྲད་ན་ *if we meet with unpleasantness;* or
3) syntactic particle marking the qualifier of an intransitive nom-s.p. v. of disjunction, as in རྟོག་པ་དང་བྲལ་ *free from conceptuality*

Part 7 completes the compound sentence begun in Part 6

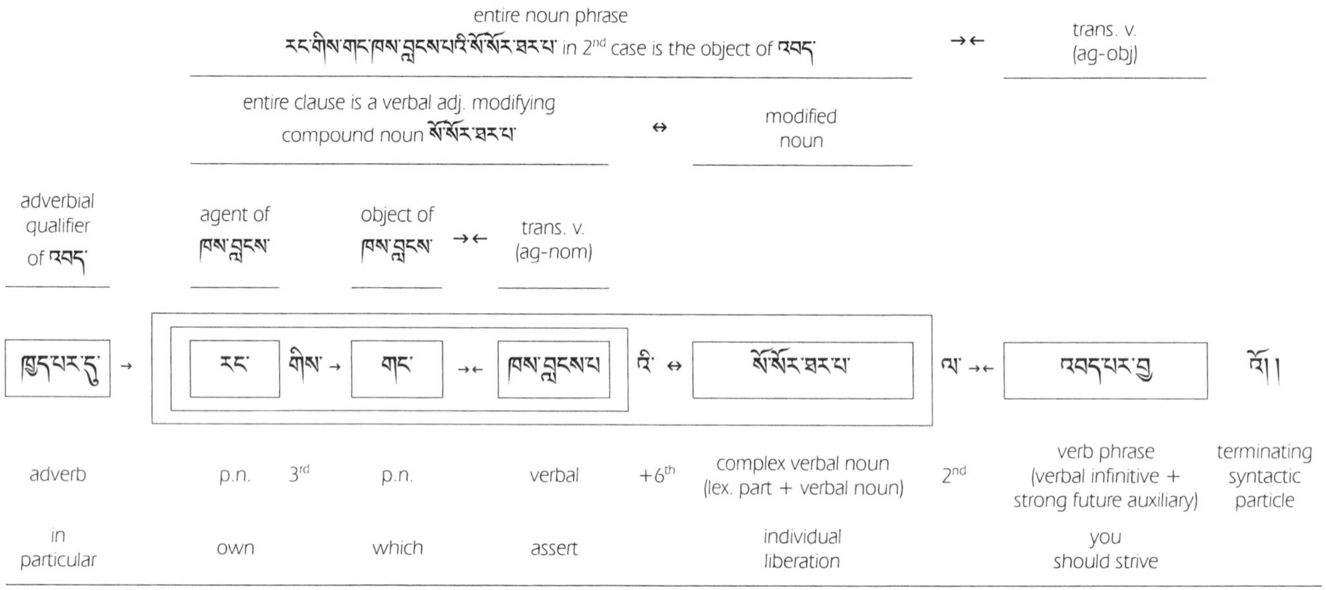

In particular, you should strive at the [vow of] individual liberation which you have taken.

Glossary for Part 7

ཁྱད་པར་ — n. and adv.; as noun, *attribute, feature, qualification, difference;* as adverb, *in particular, especially*

ཁྱད་པར་དུ་ — noun + 2nd case particle creating adverbial construction

དུ་ — particle; either 1) a verb-modifying syntactic particle within a verb phrase, or 2) a case particle following nouns, pronouns, postpositions, and adjectives marking the 2nd, 4th and 7th cases

རང་ — reflexive pronoun, *itself, oneself*

རང་གིས་ — reflexive pronoun + 3rd case particle; here: 3rd case (agent)

གིས་ — particle; either 1) syntactic particle creating an adverbial construction, 2) syntactic particle marking the qualifier of an intransitive nom-s.p. verb of absence, or 3) case particle marking the 3rd case

གང་ — interrogative pronoun, *what, which*

ཁས་བླངས་ — trans. v. (ag-nom), *assert* (literally *hold by the mouth*)

ཁས་ལེན། ཁས་བླངས། ཁས་བླང་། ཁས་ལོངས། ཐ་དད།

ཁས་བླངས་པ་ — verbal n., *assertion*

ཁས་བླངས་པའི་ — verbal noun + 6th case particle fused to suffixless final syllable

འི་ — particle fused to suffixless final syllable; either 1) a syntactic particle following a verb or verb phrase signifying conjunction or disjunction, or 2) a 6th case particle following nouns, pronouns, postpositions, and adjectives

སོ་སོར་ཐར་པ་ — verbal n., *[vow of] individual liberation*

སོ་སོར་ lexical prefix particle translating the Sanskrit *prati-, individual*

སོ་སོར་ཐར་པ་ལ་ n. + 2nd case particle marking the noun as the object of the transitive verb འབད་ *work at, strive at*

ལ་ particle; either 1) a syntactic particle following a verb or verb phrase signifying conjunction or disjunction, or 2) a case particle following nouns, pronouns, postpositions, and adjectives marking the 2nd, 4th and 7th cases

འབད་ trans. v. (ag-obj), *strive*

འབད་འབད་འབད་འབོད། ཐ་དད།

འབད་པར་བྱ་ verb phrase (verbal infinitive + strong future auxiliary), *[I] will strive, [you] should strive*

འབད་པར་ verbal infinitive; here, the fused ར་ is a syntactic particle modifying a verb to create a verbal infinitive within the verb phrase འབད་པར་བྱ་ *[I] will strive, [you] should strive;* it is **not** a case particle marking the 2nd, 4th or 7th cases because it does not follow a noun—it is within a verb phrase

བྱ་ trans. v. (ag-nom) (future tense), *do, make, perform, take;* also strong future auxiliary བྱེད་བྱས་བྱ་བྱོས། ཐ་དད།

སུ་རུ་ཏུ་དུ་ར་ are the five syntactic particles used to modify verbs to create infinitives within verb phrases

འབད་པར་བྱའོ།། final verb + terminating syntactic particle འོ་ fused to suffixless final syllable

འོ་ terminating syntactic particle འོ་ fused to suffixless final syllable

Understanding the precise meaning signified by the verbal adjective in Part 6

A frequently seen (this is the fifth time in our text so far) method of modifying a noun adjectivally is with a verbal clause which precedes it and is joined to it with a 6th case particle. The noun following a clause ending in a verbal noun or adjective, and connected to it by a 6th case particle, is often **the understood subject, agent, object, qualifier, or complement of that clause.**

1. In this noun phrase, the noun ལམ་ path is modified by a verbal adjective འཁོར་བ་ལས་གྲོལ་བ་ which precedes it

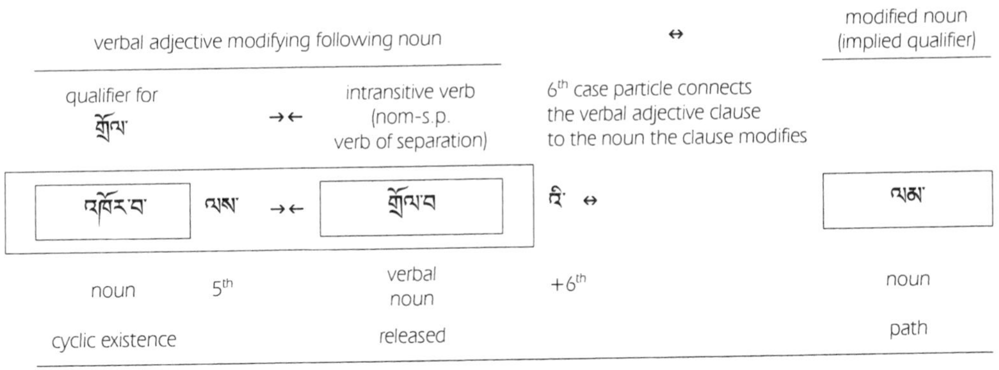

the path by which one is released from cyclic existence

2. The elements of the noun phrase rearranged with the verbal adjective and modified noun recast in verb-last syntax

Here is how the implied qualifier would look if the elements were rearranged into a sentence. Some unstated subject (1st case) is released **from** (5th case) cyclic existence ***by means of*** (3rd case) *the path.*

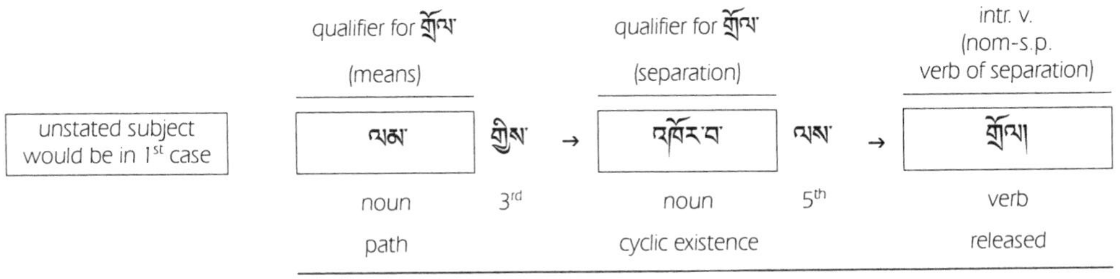

One is released from cyclic existence by means of paths.

Grammar review • For the subclass of verbs of separation, the class name "nom-s.p. verbs" is a misnomer

An additional oddity is the verb གྲོལ་ *be released* from something. Wilson classifies this intransitive **verb of separation** as a nominative-syntactic particle verb together with **verbs of absence, conjunction,** and **disjunction.** However its qualifier, that from which the subject is separated, is marked with a true 5th case particle, not a syntactic particle as the name of the class suggests. It may be more helpful to think of this class of intransitive verbs of separation as nominative-originative. They are like nom-obj verbs of motion, except the verb is not qualified by where the subject is going (2nd case destination), but rather by that from which the subject is separating (5th case separation).

Understanding the precise meaning signified by a verbal adjective in Part 7

1. The noun སོ་སོར་ཐར་པ་ is modified by the verbal adjective རང་གིས་གང་ཁས་བླངས་པའི་ which precedes it

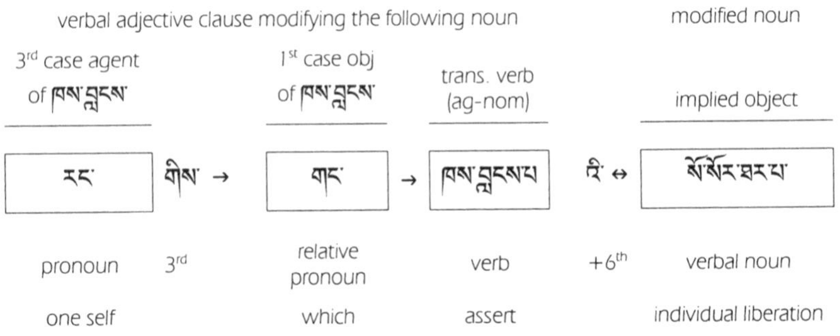

[the vow of] individual liberation which you have assumed

2. The elements rearranged with the verbal adjective and modified noun recast in verb-last syntax

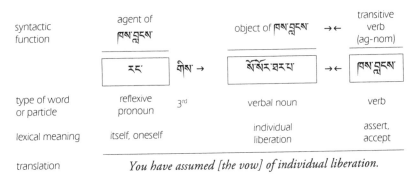

syntactic function	agent of ཁས་བླངས་		object of ཁས་བླངས་	→←	transitive verb (ag-nom)
	རང་	གིས་ →	སོ་སོར་ཐར་པ་	→←	ཁས་བླངས་
type of word or particle	reflexive pronoun	3rd	verbal noun		verb
lexical meaning	itself, oneself		individual liberation		assert, accept
translation	*You have assumed [the vow] of individual liberation.*				

Parts 6 and 7 together

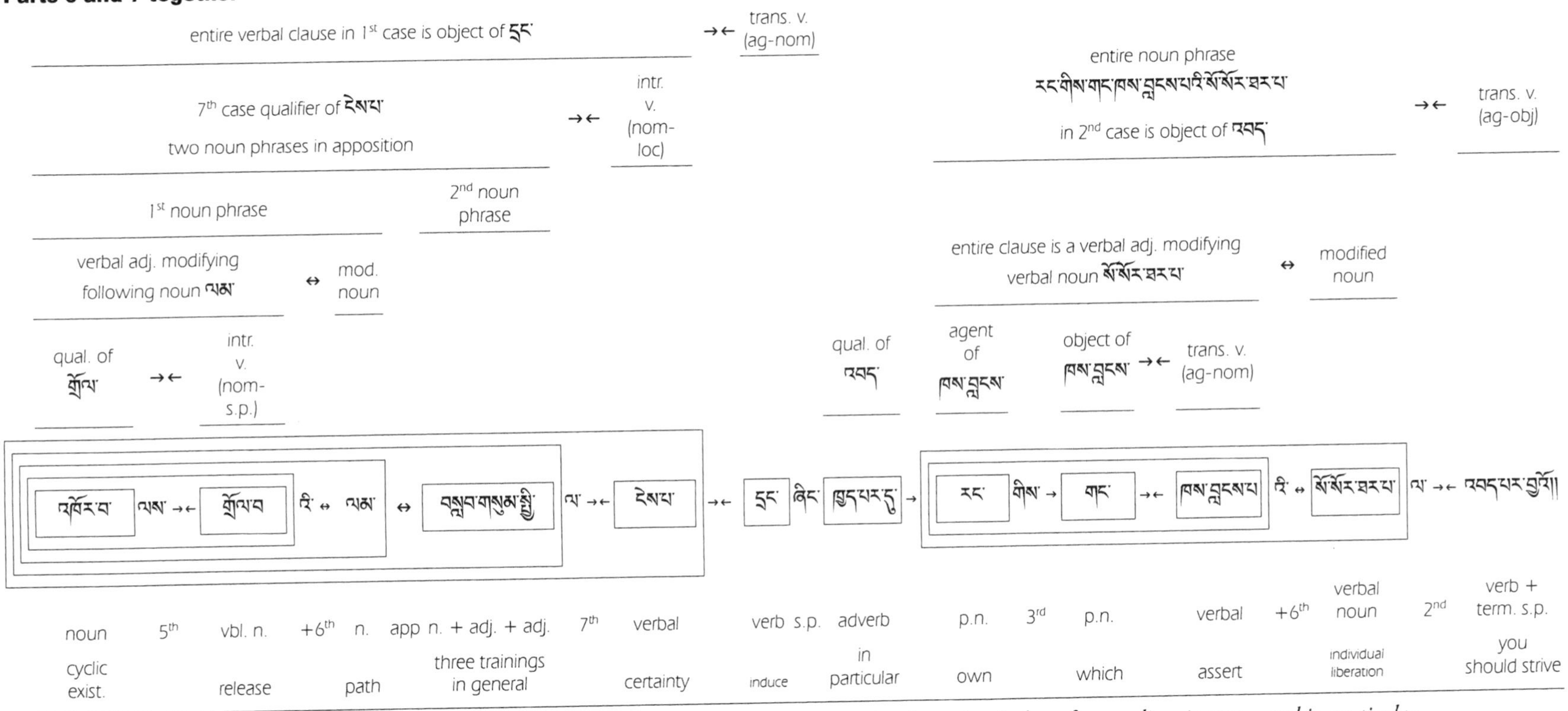

You should strive at inducing certainty regarding the three trainings in general—the paths of release from cyclic existence—and in particular at the [vow of] individual emancipation which you have taken.

Chapter Four Self Test

Write out the passage, boxing and identifying every syntactic element.

དེ་ལྟར་སྐྱེས་བུ་ཆུང་ངུའི་ཆོས་སྐོར་རྣམས་ཚགས་སུ་ཚུད་པ་ན་འཁོར་བ་སྤྱི་དང་བྱེ་བྲག་གི་ཉེས་དམིགས་མང་དུ་བསམས་ལ། འཁོར་བ་སྤྱི་ལས་བློ་ཅི་ལྡོག་བྱ། དེ་ནས་འཁོར་བ་གང་ལས་འབྱུང་བའི་རྒྱུ་ལས་དང་ཉོན་མོངས་པའི་ངོ་བོ་ངོས་བཟུང་ནས་དེ་སྤོང་འདོད་བཅོས་མ་མིན་པ་བསྐྱེད། འཁོར་བ་ལས་གྲོལ་བའི་ལམ་བསླབ་པ་གསུམ་སྤྱི་ལ་ངེས་པ་དྲང་ཞིང་ཁྱད་པར་དུ་རང་གིས་གང་ཁས་བླངས་པའི་སོ་སོར་ཐར་པ་ལ་འབད་པར་བྱའོ།།

Vocabulary

For each word, can you identify what part of speech it is (noun, pronoun, adjective, verb, adverb, postposition) and what it means?
For each syntactic particle, can you identify what class of syntactic particle it belongs to and how it is used?

སྐོར་	གྲོལ་	འབྱུང་	བསླབ་	ཆུང་ངུ་
སྤྱི་	བྱེ་བྲག་	འབད་པར་བྱ་	བསམས་	ཅིང་
སྐྱེས་བུ་ཆུང་ངུ་	བྱ་	འབད་	བཅོས་མིན་	ཅི་
སྐྱེས་བུ་	ཁྱད་པར་	འདོད་	བཅོས་མ་མིན་པ་	ངོ་བོ་
སྐྱེས་	སོ་སོར་ཐར་པ་	འཁོར་བ་	ནས་	ངོས་བཟུང་
སྤོང་འདོད་	སོ་སོར་	འཁོར་	ན་	ངེས་པ་
སྤོང་	ཞིང་	ཞིང་	དུ་	ངེས་
ལྡོག་པར་བྱ་	ལོག་	ཚགས་སུ་ཚུད་པ་	དེ་ལྟར་	གིས་
ལྡོག་	ལམ་	མང་པོ་	དེ་	གི་
རྒྱུ་	ལ་	མང་དུ་	དང་	གསུམ་
རྣམས་	རང་	མང་	ཉོན་མོངས་	གང་
བློ་	འི་	བསྐྱེད་	ཉེས་དམིགས་	ཁས་བླངས་པ་
ངང་	འབྱུང་བ་	བསླབ་པ་	ཆོས་སྐོར་	

Translation of Tsong-kha-pa's text

དེ་ལྟར་སྐྱེས་བུ་ཆུང་ངུའི་ཆོས་སྐོར་རྣམས་ཚགས་སུ་ཚུད་པ་ན་འཁོར་བ་སྤྱི་དང་བྱེ་བྲག་གི་ཉེས་དམིགས་མང་དུ་བསམས་ལ། འཁོར་བ་སྤྱི་ལས་བློ་ཅི་ལྡོག་བྱ། དེ་ནས་འཁོར་བ་གང་ལས་འབྱུང་བའི་རྒྱུ་ལས་དང་ཉོན་མོངས་པའི་ངོ་བོ་ངོས་བཟུང་ནས་དེ་སྤོང་འདོད་བཅོས་མ་མིན་པ་བསྐྱེད། འཁོར་བ་ལས་གྲོལ་བའི་ལམ་བསླབ་པ་གསུམ་སྤྱི་ལ་ངེས་པ་དྲང་ཞིང་ཁྱད་པར་དུ་རང་གིས་གང་ཁས་བླངས་པའི་སོ་སོར་ཐར་པ་ལ་འབད་པར་བྱའོ། །

When, in that way, the topics of practice by a being of small capacity have been internalized, you should contemplate frequently the faults of cyclic existence in general and in particular, thereby turning your mind away from cyclic existence in general as much as possible. Then, having identified contaminated actions and afflictions as the causes from which cyclic existence arises, generate a non-simulated wish to abandon them. You should strive at inducing certainty regarding the paths by which you are released from cyclic existence: the three trainings in general. Work hard in particular at the [vow of] individual emancipation which you have taken.

Annotations for Tsong-kha-pa's text in Chapter Four

Here is Tsong-kha-pa's text as supplemented by *The Four Interwoven Annotations*, 829.5–830.3

། ཚུལ་ དེ་ལྟར་ བྱས་ཏེ་ སྐྱེས་བུ་ཆུང་ངུའི་ཆོས་སྐོར་རྣམས་ ལེགས་པར་བྱང་ནས་ ཚགས་སུ་ཚུད་ ཅིང་གཞི་ཐེབས་ པ་ན་ དེའི་རྗེས་སུ་བློ་དེས་དྲང་ཏེ་མཐོན་མཐོ་ན་ཡང་ བདེ་བ་མེད་ཚུལ་སོགས་ཀྱི་སྒོ་ནས་སྲིད་རྩེ་ནས་མནར་མེད་ཀྱི་བར་གྱི་ འཁོར་བ་སྤྱི་དང་བྱེ་བྲག་གི་ཉེས་དམིགས་ ཏེ་སྐྱོན་སྡུག་བསྔལ་རྣམས་ཞིབ་པར་ མང་དུ་བསམས་ལ། སྐྱོ་བ་བསྐྱེད་དེ་ འཁོར་བ་སྤྱི་ལས་བློ་ཅི་ལྡོག་ ལ་འབད་པར་ བྱ། དེ་ལྟར་བྱས་པའི་རྗེས་ དེ་ནས་ འཁོར་བ་མི་འདོད་ན་འཁོར་བའི་རྒྱུ་སྤོང་དགོས་པས་ འཁོར་བ་ དེ་ཉིད་ གང་ལས་འབྱུང་བའི་རྒྱུ་ རྒྱུད་བཅད་དེ་དེ་འདྲའི་རྒྱུ་ ལས་དང་ཉོན་མོངས་ པ་ལ་ཐུག་པར་ངེས་པར་བྱས་ནས་ལས་དང་ཉོན་མོངས་ པའི་ངོ་བོ་ ཅི་ནས་ ངོས་བཟུང་ ནས་ ལས་ཉོན་ དེ་ ཉིད་ སྤོང་ བར་ འདོད་ པའི་བློ་ བཅོས་མ་མིན་པ་བསྐྱེད་ པར་བྱས་ཏེ། དེ་འདྲའི་བློ་ངེས་དྲངས་ནས་ འཁོར་བ་ལས་གྲོལ་ བར་འདོད་ན་དེ་ ལས་གྲོལ་ བའི་ ཐབས་ནི་ ལམ་བསླབ་པ་གསུམ་སྤྱི་ལ་ རག་ལས་པར་ ངེས་པ་ སྐྱེད་ནས་ དྲང་ པར་བྱ་ ཞིང་ བསླབ་པ་གསུམ་གྱི་ནང་ནས་ཀྱང་བསླབ་པ་ཐམས་ཅད་ཀྱི་ གཞིམ་ ཁྱད་པར་དུ་ གལ་ཆེ་བ་ནི་ རང་གིས་གང་ཁས་བླངས་པའི་སོ་སོར་ཐར་པ འི་ཚུལ་ཁྲིམས་འདི་ཉིད་ཡིན་པས་ན་དེ་ཉིད་ ལ་འབད་པར་བྱའོ། །

When you have done that properly [i.e., motivated by the faith of conviction in causes and their effects, you engage in virtuous actions and disengage from non-virtuous actions, together with engaging the four powers of confession and so forth to purify the effects of non-virtuous actions done earlier—all done with the motivation of avoiding bad migrations in future lifetimes]. When you have thus internalized and settled into the topics of practice for a being of small capacity through purifying them well, then after that, induced by those practices, you should contemplate in frequent detail the faults of [all of] cyclic existence—from the peak of cyclic existence [the most subtle formless absorption] to the lowest hell. Think about the faults in general and in particular, its defects and sufferings, through considering how even if you do attain high status, there is no happiness, and so forth. After you have contemplated in that way, you should strive at generating an attitude of sadness [about all of cyclic existence, i.e., that even high status is not happiness], and thereby turn your mind from cyclic existence in general as much as you can.

Then, after you have done that, if you do not want cyclic existence, you must abandon the causes of cyclic existence. Therefore, research the causes from which cyclic existence arises. When you have recognized that the causes [of cyclic existence] meet back to [contaminated] actions and afflictions, having identified the entity of [contaminated] actions and afflictions you must generate the non-simulated attitude [i.e., a now pervasive attitude which was developed after much intentional reflection] of wanting to abandon them [i.e., contaminated actions and afflictions].

When, induced by that attitude [of wanting to abandon contaminated actions and afflictions], you want to be released from cyclic existence, you need to induce certainty from the depths that the method for release from cyclic existence depends on the three trainings in general. The most important from within all three trainings, the foundation of all the trainings, is the ethics of whichever [vow] of individual liberation you have taken in particular. Therefore you must strive at that [vow of individual liberation].

Chapter Five

དེ་ལྟར་སྐྱེས་བུ་འབྲིང་གི་ཆོས་སྐོར་རྣམས་ཚགས་སུ་ཚུད་པ་ན། རང་ཉིད་སྲིད་མཚོར་ལྷུང་བ་ཇི་འདྲ་བ་དེ་བཞིན་དུ། མ་རྣམས་ཀྱང་དེ་འདྲ་བར་སོང་བ་ཡིན་ལ་བྱས་ཏེ། བྱམས་པ་དང་སྙིང་རྗེའི་རྩ་བ་ཅན་གྱི་བྱང་ཆུབ་ཀྱི་སེམས་སྦྱངས་ལ་ཅི་སྐྱེ་ལ་འབད་དགོས་ཏེ། དེ་མེད་ན་སྤྱོད་པ་ཕྱིན་དྲུག་དང་རིམ་གཉིས་སོགས་རྨང་མེད་པའི་ཐོག་བྱེད་པ་དང་འདྲ་བར་འགྱུར་བ་ཡིན་ནོ། །དེ་ལ་སྦྱོང་བའི་རྣམ་པ་ཐན་ཐུན་རྒྱུད་ལ་སྐྱེས་ན་ཚོགས་བཟུང་ལ། དེའི་བསླབ་བྱ་ལ་འབད་ནས་སློན་པ་ཅི་བརྟན་བྱ།

Division of the passage into units to facilitate the analysis of the syntax

I have subdivided Chapter Five into six parts to facilitate the discussion of its grammar and syntax. I have also used grammatical structures that come up as points of departure for more generalized observations useful for those learning to read Classical Tibetan.

1

དེ་ལྟར་སྐྱེས་བུ་འབྲིང་གི་ཆོས་སྐོར་རྣམས་ཚགས་སུ་ཚུད་པ་ན

2

རང་ཉིད་སྲིད་མཚོར་ལྷུང་བ་ཇི་འདྲ་བ་དེ་བཞིན་དུ་མ་རྣམས་ཀྱང་དེ་འདྲ་བར་སོང་བ་ཡིན་ལ་བྱས་ཏེ།

3

བྱམས་པ་དང་སྙིང་རྗེའི་རྩ་བ་ཅན་གྱི་བྱང་ཆུབ་ཀྱི་སེམས་སྦྱངས་ལ་ཅི་སྐྱེ་ལ་འབད་དགོས་ཏེ།

4

དེ་མེད་ན་སྤྱོད་པ་ཕྱིན་དྲུག་དང་རིམ་གཉིས་སོགས་རྨང་མེད་པའི་ཐོག་བྱེད་པ་དང་འདྲ་བར་འགྱུར་བ་ཡིན་ནོ། །

5

དེ་ལ་སྦྱོང་བའི་རྣམ་པ་ཐན་ཐུན་རྒྱུད་ལ་སྐྱེས་ན་ཚོགས་བཟུང་ལ།

6

དེའི་བསླབ་བྱ་ལ་འབད་ནས་སློན་པ་ཅི་བརྟན་བྱ།

Part 1 • དེ་ལྟར་སྐྱེས་བུ་འབྲིང་གི་ཆོས་སྐོར་རྣམས་ཚགས་སུ་ཚུད་པ་ན།

Part 1 is a conditional clause; the thought begun in Part 1 is completed in Part 2

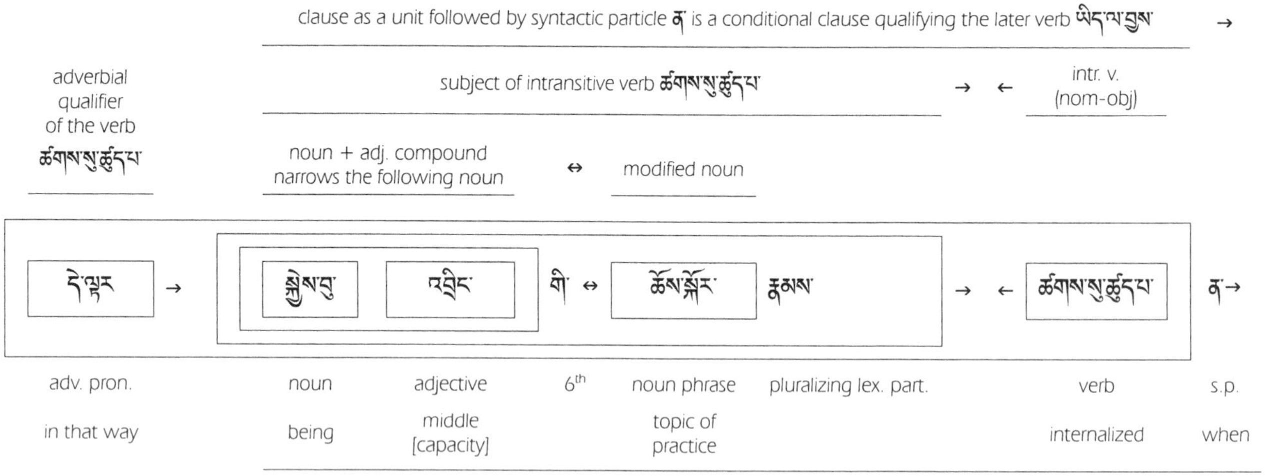

When in that way the topics of practice by a being of middle capacity have been internalized,

Glossary for Part 1

དེ་ལྟར་ adverbial pronoun, *in that way, thus*

སྐྱེས་བུ་ n., *being*

འབྲིང་ adj., *middle*

སྐྱེས་བུ་འབྲིང་ noun + adj. compound, *being of middle [capacity].* The beings of the three capacities are distinguished by way of what an individual seeks through practice: high status within cyclic existence for a being of small capacity, release from cyclic existence for a being of middle capacity, and the enlightenment of a Buddha so as to be able to lead all sentient beings to their own enlightenment for a being of great capacity.

སྐྱེས་བུ་འབྲིང་གི་ noun phrase + 6th case particle marking possession

གི་ particle; either 1) a syntactic particle following a verb or verb phrase signifying conjunction or disjunction, or 2) a 6th case particle following nouns, pronouns, postpositions, and adjectives

ཆོས་ n., Sanskrit, *dharma, phenomena, religion* (what Buddha taught)

སྐོར་ trans. v. (ag-nom), *turn* སྐོར་སྐོར་སྐོར་སྐོར། ཐ་དད།

འཁོར་ intr. v. (nom-obj), *turn* འཁོར་འཁོར་འཁོར། ཐ་མི་དད།

ཆོས་སྐོར་ noun phrase, *topics of practice*

རྣམས་ pluralizing suffix particle following nouns and noun phrases

ཚགས་སུ་ཚུད་པ་ intr. phrasal v. (nom-obj), *be included, be involved, be internalized* ཚུད་ཚུད་ཚུད། ཐ་མི་དད།

ཚགས་སུ་ཚུད་པ་ན་ verb + conditional syntactic particle marking a conditional clause, *when [those topics of practice] are understood, ...*

ན་ particle; either 1) a rhetorical syntactic particle following a verb or verb phrase marking a conditional clause, or 2) a case particle following nouns, pronouns, postpositions, and adjectives marking the 2nd, 4th and 7th cases

Grammar review • Sometimes an intransitive Tibetan construction may be recast as a transitive construction in English

སྐྱེས་བུ་འབྲིང་གི་ཆོས་སྐོར་རྣམས་ཚགས་སུ་ཚུད་ན conditional clause (intransitive verb ཚགས་སུ་ཚུད་ + 1st case subject སྐྱེས་བུ་འབྲིང་གི་ཆོས་སྐོར་རྣམས་) + conditional syntactic particle.

This is an intransitive conditional clause "when the topics of practice by a being of middle capacity **are internalized**..." Because English favors transitive constructions, you may consider recasting the clause in the more commonly seen transitive construction: "when **you have internalized** the topics of practice by a being of middle capacity..." In effect, we are recasting the subject as an object and adding the indefinite pronoun "you" as an agent, making the construction transitive.

ཚགས་སུ་ཚུད་ intr. phrasal v. (nom-obj), *be included, be involved, be internalized* ཚུད་ཚུད་ཚུད། ཐ་མི་དད།

Grammar review • 6th case here marks possession

སྐྱེས་བུ་འབྲིང་གི་ཆོས་སྐོར་རྣམས་ noun-adjective compound + 6th case + noun and a pluralizing lexical particle རྣམས་, *topics of practice by a being of middle capacity.*
This is a use of the 6th case marking possession by a person, here a being of middle capacity.
Tibetan nouns are ambiguous as to number unless some explicit element indicates plurality, in this case the particle རྣམས་

Part 2 • དེ་ལྟར་སྐྱེས་བུ་འབྲིང་གི་ཆོས་སྐོར་རྣམས་ཚགས་སུ་ཚུད་པ་ན།

Part 2 is a simile

In essential form, this construction is an ag-nom verb with an implied agent (you) and a 1st case (nominative) object in the form "just as A, so too B."

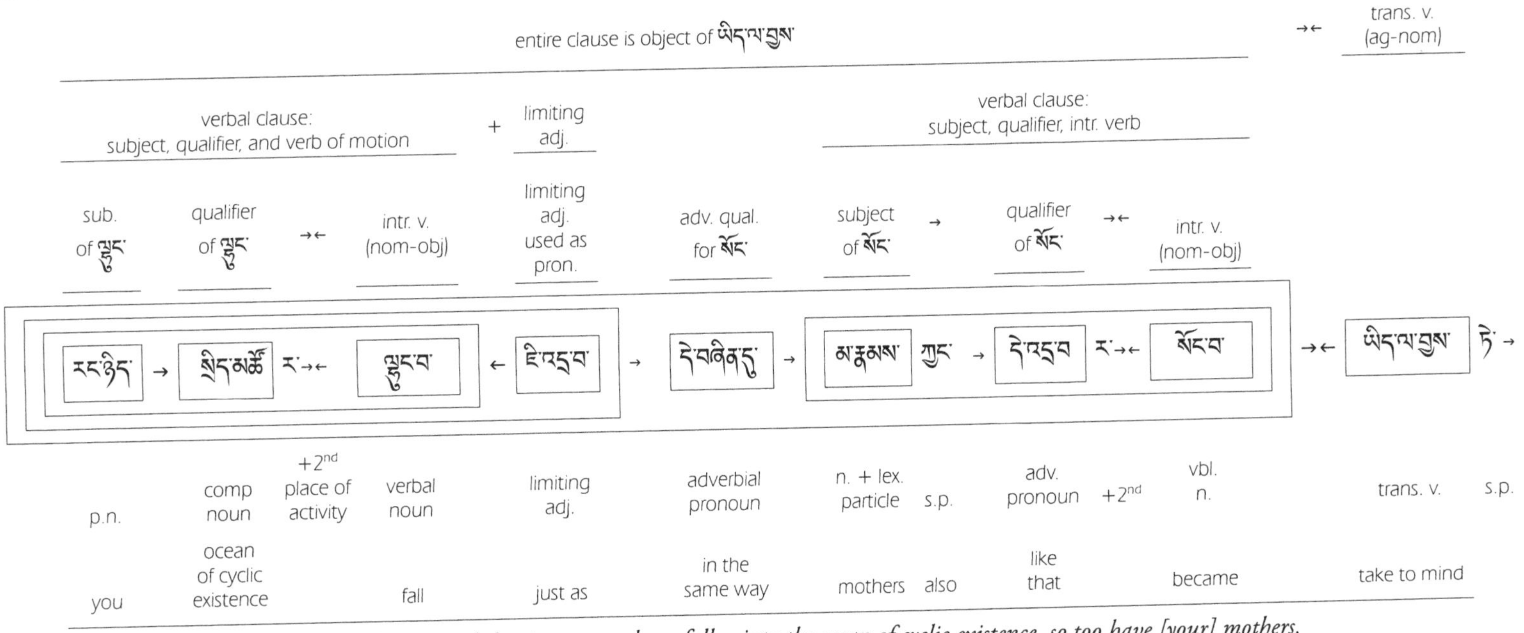

You should take to mind that just as you have fallen into the ocean of cyclic existence, so too have [your] mothers.

Glossary for Part 2

རང་ཉིད་ — reflexive pronoun, *yourself, itself, oneself*

སྲིད་ — n., *existence, cyclic existence*

མཚོ་ — n., *ocean*

རྒྱ་མཚོ་ — n., *ocean*

མཚོར་ — n. + fused 2nd 4th or 7th case particle; here: 2nd place of activity, i.e., where the wandering is happening

ར་ — particle fused to suffixless final syllable; either 1) a verb-modifying syntactic particle within a verb phrase, or 2) a case particle following nouns, pronouns, postpositions, and adjectives marking the 2nd, 4th and 7th cases

ལྟུང་ — intr. v. (nom-obj), *fall*

ལྟུང་ལྟུང་ལྟུང་ལྟུངས། ཐ་མི་དད།

ལྟུང་བ་ — verbal noun, *fall*

ཇི་ལྟ་བ་ — adverbial pronoun, *just like*

དེ་བཞིན་དུ་ — adverbial pronoun, *thus, so, in that way*

མ་ — n., *mother*

མ་ — negative lexical prefix particle

རྣམས་ — optional pluralizing suffix particle

ཀྱང་ — conjunctive and disjunctive syntactic particle used after nouns, pronouns, adjectives, verbs, and verb phrases, *but, even, also*

ཀྱང་ཡང་འང་ — are equivalent conjunctive and disjunctive syntactic particles used after nouns, pronouns, adjectives, verbs, and verb phrases, *but, even, also*

ཀྱང་ — follows words ending with the letters གདབས་

ཡང་ — follows words ending with the letters ངནམའརལ་ and after suffixless words

འང་ — follows suffixless words

དེ་འདྲ་ — limiting adj. here used as pronoun, *such;* also an adverbial pronoun

དེ་ལྟ་བ་ — adverbial pronoun, *like that*

དེ་ལྟ་བར་ — adverbial pron. + 2nd case particle fused to suffixless final syllable

ར་ — particle fused to suffixless final syllable; either 1) a verb-modifying syntactic particle within a verb phrase, or 2) a case particle following nouns, pronouns, postpositions, and adjectives marking the 2nd, 4th and 7th cases

སོང་ — intr. v. (nom-obj) (alternate past tense), *went;* often used metaphorically in the sense of *turn into* or *become*

འགྲོ་ཕྱིན་འགྲོ་སོང་། ཐ་མི་དད། སོང་ is also an alternate past form

སོང་བ་ — verbal noun (formed from past tense), *became*

ཡིད་ལ་བྱས་ — trans. phrasal v. (ag-nom) (past tense), *taken to mind;* literally, a verb phrase: *take to mind*

ཡིད་ — n., *mind*

ལ་ — particle; either 1) a syntactic particle following a verb or verb phrase signifying conjunction or disjunction, or 2) a case particle following nouns, pronouns, postpositions, and adjectives marking the 2nd, 4th and 7th cases

བྱས་ — trans. v. (past tense) (ag-nom), *do, make, perform, take*

བྱེད་བྱས་བྱ་བྱོས། ཐ་དད།

ཡིད་ལ་བྱས་ཏེ། — verb phrase + continuative syntactic particle showing sequence by indicating that more relevant information will follow.

ཏེ་ སྟེ་ and དེ་ — are equivalent syntactic particles; either 1) continuative syntactic particles following verbs and verb phrases showing sequence, or 2) punctuational syntactic particles following words or phrases marking appositives

ཏེ་ — follows words ending with suffix letters ནརལས་

སྟེ་ — follows suffixless words and words ending with suffix letters གངབམའ་

དེ་ — follows words ending with suffix letter ད་

Notice how the pair of adverbial pronouns relate the two parts of the simile in Part 2

ཇི་འདྲ་བ་ is acting as an adverb by setting up the first part of the simile: *just as you have fallen, ...*

དེ་བཞིན་དུ་ an adverbial pronoun, completes the simile: *so too, ...*

Part 3 • བྱམས་པ་དང་སྙིང་རྗེའི་རྩ་བ་ཅན་གྱི་བྱང་ཆུབ་ཀྱི་སེམས་སྦྱངས་ལ་ཅི་སྐྱེ་ལ་འབད་དགོས་ཏེ།

Part 3 is a compound sentence: "You must train in A, and strive at generating B."

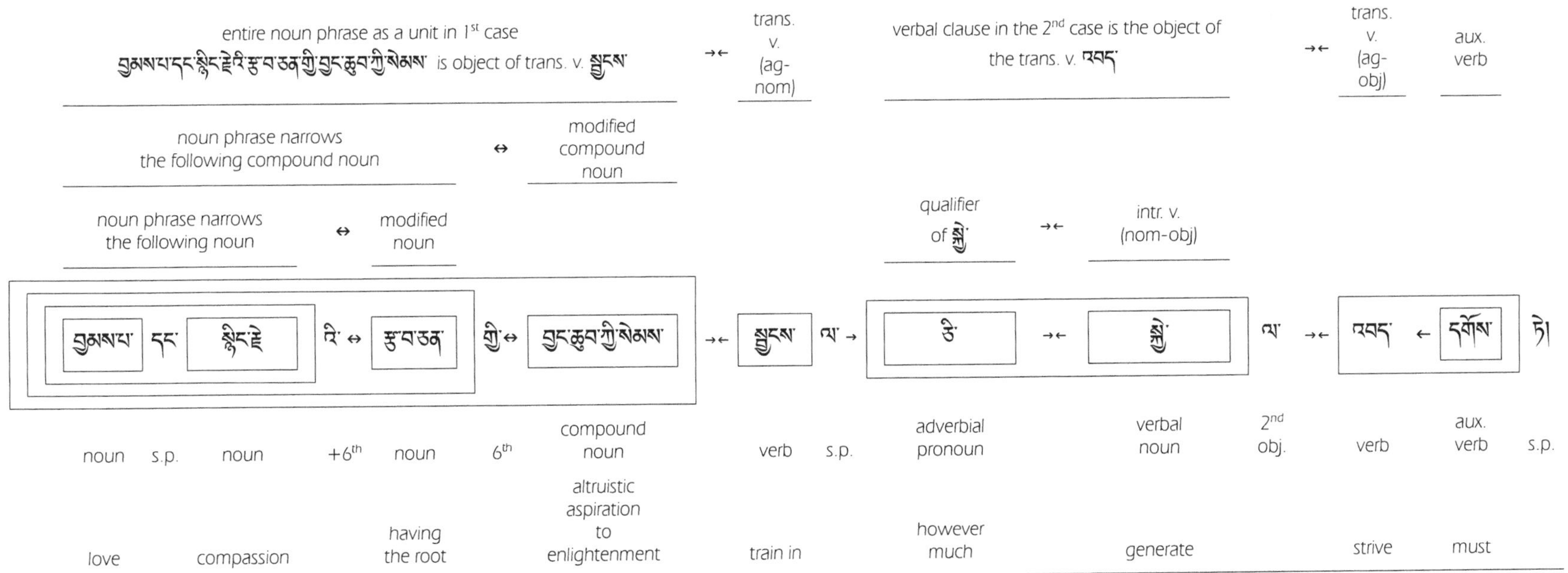

You must train in the altruistic aspiration to enlightenment that has love and compassion as its root and strive at generating [it] as much you can.

Glossary for Part 3

བྱམས་པ་ n., *love;* love is understood as the wish that others have happiness and the causes of happiness.

དང་ syntactic particle, used as a continuative following nouns and noun phrases (*and,* or with negative verb, *or*), here: *and*

སྙིང་རྗེ་ n., *compassion;* compassion is understood as the wish that others be separated from suffering and the causes of suffering.

སྙིང་རྗེའི་ noun + 6th case particle fused to suffixless final syllable

འི་ particle fused to suffixless final syllable; either 1) a syntactic particle following a verb or verb phrase signifying conjunction or disjunction, or 2) a 6th case particle following nouns, pronouns, postpositions, and adjectives

རྩ་བ་ n., adj., *root, main, principal*

ཅན། lexical suffix particle indicating possession

རྩ་བ་ཅན། n., *having the root*

རྩ་བ་ཅན་གྱི། noun + 6th case particle

གྱི། particle used following words ending with the suffix letters ན་མ་ར་ and ལ་; either 1) a syntactic particle following a verb or verb phrase signifying conjunction or disjunction, or 2) a 6th case particle following nouns, pronouns, postpositions, and adjectives

བྱང་ཆུབ་ n., *enlightenment*

བྱང་ཆུབ་ཀྱི། n. + 6th case particle

ཀྱི། particle used following words ending with the suffix letters ད་བ་ and ས་; either 1) a syntactic particle following a verb or verb phrase signifying conjunction or disjunction, or 2) a 6th case particle following nouns, pronouns, postpositions, and adjectives

བྱང་ཆུབ་ཀྱི་སེམས་ noun phrase, *the altruistic aspiration to enlightenment*

སྦྱངས་ trans. v. (ag-nom), *train in;* སྦྱོང་སྦྱངས་སྦྱང་སྦྱོངས། ཐ་དད།

སྦྱངས་ལ་ verb + conjunctive syntactic particle

ལ་ particle; either 1) a syntactic particle following a verb or verb phrase signifying conjunction or disjunction, or 2) a case particle following nouns, pronouns, postpositions, and adjectives marking the 2nd, 4th and 7th cases

ཅི་ indefinite and general relative pronoun, and interrogative pronoun, *what, which, however, whatever*

སྐྱེ་ intr. v. (nom-obj), *be produced, be generated, be born, arise*

སྐྱེ་སྐྱེས་སྐྱེ། ཐ་མི་དད།

བསྐྱེད་ trans. v. (ag-nom), *create, produce, generate, give birth to*

སྐྱེད་བསྐྱེད་བསྐྱེད་སྐྱེད། ཐ་དད།

ཅི་སྐྱེས་ verbal clause, *generate as much as [you] can*

ཅི་སྐྱེས་ལ་ verbal clause + 2nd case particle marking the object of the transitive verb འབད་ *work at, strive*

ལ་ particle; either 1) a syntactic particle following a verb or verb phrase signifying conjunction or disjunction, or 2) a case particle following nouns, pronouns, postpositions, and adjectives marking the 2nd, 4th and 7th cases

འབད་ trans. v. (ag-obj), *strive*

འབད་འབད་འབད་འབོད། ཐ་དད།

དགོས་ intr. v. (b/p-nom), *be necessary, need, require*

དགོས་དགོས་དགོས། ཐ་མི་དད།

འབད་དགོས་ verb phrase (verb + auxiliary verb), *[you] must strive*

འབད་དགོས་ཏེ། verb phrase + continuative syntactic particle showing sequence by indicating that more relevant information will follow

---

Notes on Part 3

The agent of the transitive verb སྦྱངས་ is implied

བྱང་ཆུབ་ཀྱི་སེམས་སྦྱངས་ལ་ verbal clause (object + verb + conjunctive syntactic particle) *[you should] train in the altruistic aspiration to enlightenment, and, ...*

སྦྱངས་ལ་ verb + conjunctive syntactic particle. When the particle ལ་ follows a verb or verb phrase, it is a **syntactic particle** used to show conjunction or disjunction; it is **not a case marking particle** because it does not follow a noun or noun-equivalent.

The second clause of Part 3 has two interesting features

The object of the transitive verb is a verbal clause, and the auxiliary verb དགོས་ operates only on the principal verb འབད་

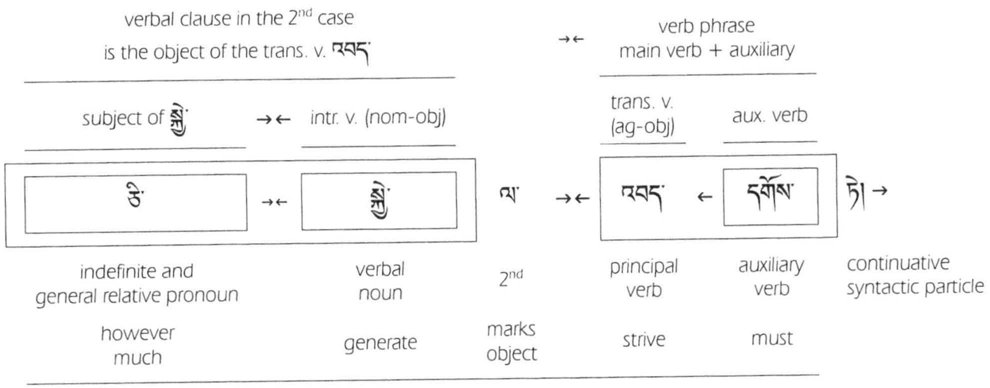

[You] must strive at however much [you can] generate

1. The object of the transitive verb is a verbal clause

ཅི་ pronoun; either 1) indefinite and general relative pronoun, or 2) interrogative pronoun, *what, which, however, whatever*

ཅི་སྐྱེ་ verb phrase (subject/indefinite relative pronoun + intransitive verb), *however much is generated.* This intransitive construction can be recast in the transitive: *however much you can generate.*

ཅི་སྐྱེ་ལ་ the ལ་ following the སྐྱེ་ is a case particle indicating the 2nd case object of the compound verb འབད་དགོས་ *must strive*

2. Notice that the auxiliary verb དགོས་ operates only on the principal verb འབད་

འབད་དགོས་ compound verb wherein the second verb དགོས་ *must* is an auxiliary, acting only on the first verb འབད་ *strive*

འབད་ trans. v. (ag-obj), *strive*

འབད་འབད་འབད་འབོད། ཐ་དད།

དགོས་ intr. v. (b/p-nom), *be necessary, need, require*

དགོས་དགོས་དགོས། ཐ་མི་དད།

འབད་དགོས་ཏེ། the continuative syntactic particle ཏེ་ (one of three similar particles དེ་ ཏེ་ སྟེ་) follows core verbs and auxiliary verb phrases signifying that something more relevant to what has been said will follow.

Note on བྱང་ཆུབ་ཀྱི་སེམས་ *the altruistic aspiration to enlightenment*

The altruistic aspiration to enlightenment has two components

Following Hopkins, I translate བྱང་ཆུབ་ཀྱི་སེམས་ as *the altruistic aspiration to enlightenment.* The Lamrim Chenmo Translation Committee translates the term as *the spirit of enlightenment.* བྱང་ཆུབ་ཀྱི་སེམས་ is the altruistic motivation of the practitioner who seeks to become a Buddha. As such, it is **the central theme of Mahayana Buddhism.** In brief, a Great Vehicle practitioner seeks to transforms her motivation from selfish aims—her own temporary welfare, to altruism—concern for others' welfare induced by love and compassion. Motivated by altruism, she aspires to Buddhahood so as to be able to affect the welfare of **all** sentient beings. In dependence on this aspiration to Buddhahood, she trains her mind in the methods which are the causes of becoming a Buddha, the Bodhisattva deeds.

In དགོངས་པ་རབ་གསལ་, *Illumination of the Thought,* Tsong-kha-pa comments on the two elements of the altruistic aspiration to enlightenment, saying the following:

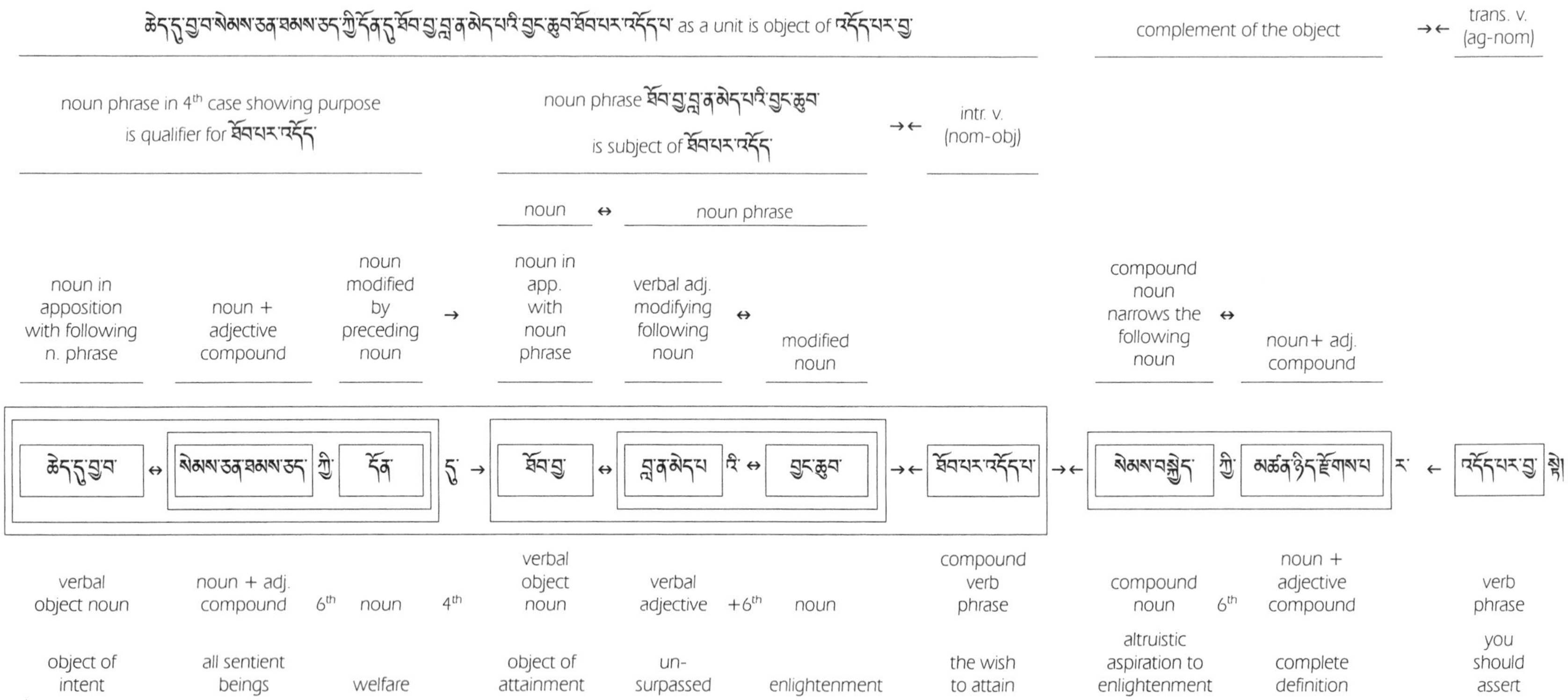

You should assert that the wish to attain unsurpassed enlightenment—the object of attainment, for the welfare of all sentient beings—the objects of intent, is the complete definition of the altruistic aspiration to enlightenment.

Further clarification of the two elements of the altruistic aspiration to enlightenment

ཆེད་དུ་བྱ་བ་ verbal object noun, *object of intent*

སེམས་ཅན་ཐམས་ཅད་ཀྱི་དོན་དུ་ noun phrase, *welfare of all sentient beings.* དོན་ here means *welfare;* it is marked with a 4th case particle signifying **recipient** of the benefit

ཐོབ་བྱ་ verbal object noun, *object of attainment*

བླ་ན་མེད་པའི་བྱང་ཆུབ་ verbal adjective + noun compound, *highest enlightenment, unsurpassed enlightenment;* literally, *enlightenment for which a higher does not exist;* this means Buddhahood.

ཐོབ་པར་འདོད་པ་ verb noun phrase (verbal infinitive + auxiliary verb), *the wish to attain*

ཐོབ་ intr. v. (nom-obj) (past tense), *attain, obtain, get.* This is an intransitive verb, taking བླ་ན་མེད་པའི་བྱང་ཆུབ་, *unsurpassed enlightenment,* as its subject. Because English favors transitive constructions, I have recast the **subject** of the intransitive construction as the **object** of the transitive construction: *the wish that unsurpassed enlightenment be attained* becomes *the wish to attain unsurpassed enlightenment.*

སེམས་བསྐྱེད་ཀྱི་མཚན་ཉིད་རྫོགས་པར་ noun phrase, *the complete defining characteristic of having generated the altruistic aspiration to enlightenment* + 2nd case particle fused to suffixless final syllable. Syntactically, this is a 2nd case complement within a transitive construction, telling us more about the object in that the object is the complement.

འདོད་པར་བྱ་ verb phrase (verbal infinitive + strong future auxiliary), *[I] will assert, [you] should assert*

New vocabulary • The sevenfold cause and effect precepts for the generation of the altruistic aspiration to enlightenment

A well-known method for the generation of the altruistic aspiration to enlightenment is a seven-step procedure called the seven cause and effect instructions:
These are the stages of reflection by which one develops great compassion (read from bottom of the list to the top).

7. བྱང་ཆུབ་ཀྱི་སེམས་ *altruistic aspiration to enlightenment*

   At this point, all sharp trainees and most dull trainees learn to meditate on emptiness. Through deep personal experience with emptiness in meditation, these practitioners vividly understand that the afflictions are not part of the mind itself, are adventitious, and can be removed. Thus, attaining the state of a completely perfect Buddha is possible.

6. ལྷག་བསམ་ *the unusual attitude [personally assuming the burden of freeing all sentient being from suffering and establishing all in the happiness of their own Buddhahood]*

5. སྙིང་རྗེ་ *compassion [the wish they be separated from suffering and the causes of suffering]*

4. བྱམས་པ་ *love [the wish that they have happiness and the causes of happiness]*

3. དྲིན་གཟོ་ *the intention to repay [their] kindness*

2. དྲིན་དྲན་ *remembering [their] kindness*

1. སེམས་ཅན་ཐམས་ཅད་མར་ཤེས། *know all sentient being as [you former] mothers*

Part 4 • དེ་མེད་ན་སྤྱོད་པ་ཕྱིན་དྲུག་དང་རིམ་གཉིས་སོགས་རྨང་མེད་པའི་ཐོག་བྲེད་པ་དང་འདྲ་བར་འགྱུར་བ་ཡིན་ནོ། །

Part 4 is a conditional clause followed by a simile: "If you don't have A, B would be like C."

conditional clause qualifying འདྲ་བར་འགྱུར་				B compound subject of འདྲ་					C s.p. དང་ marks qualifier of འདྲ་					→←	intr. v. of conjunction (nom-s.p.) + weak auxiliary
									verbal adj. modifying following noun		↔	modified noun			
implied antecedent	A object of མེད་	→← trans. v. of possession (loc-nom)		this noun phrase is a list of nouns: the bodhisattva deeds, the six perfections, the two stages of Highest Yoga Tantra					sub. of མེད་	→← negative intr. v. of existence (nom-loc)					
[སེམས་བསྐྱེད་]	དེ་ →←	མེད་	ན་ →	སྤྱོད་པ་ ↔	ཕྱིན་ དྲུག་	དང་	རིམ་གཉིས་	སོགས་ →	རྨང་ →←	མེད་པ	འི་ ↔	ཐོག་བྲེད་པ་		དང་ →←	འདྲ་བར་འགྱུར་བ་ཡིན་ནོ། ।
noun	pronoun	verb	s.p.	noun	n. + adj.	s.p.	n. + adj.	lex. p.	noun	verbal noun	+6th	verbal noun		s.p.	intransitive verb + weak auxiliary
altruistic aspiration generation	that	do not have		deeds	six perfections		two stages	and so forth	foundation	without		roof			[it] would be like

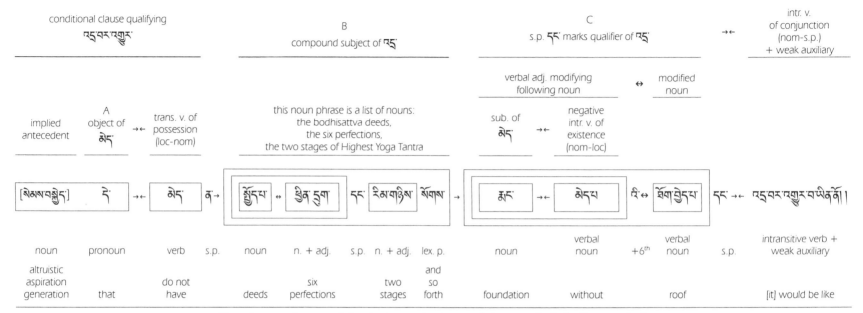

If you have not [generated the altruistic aspiration to enlightenment], the bodhisattva deeds, the six perfections, the two stages [of Highest Yoga Tantra], and so forth would be like a roof without a supporting foundation.

Glossary for Part 4

དེ་	adj. and p.n., *that, those*
མེད་	intr. v. (nom-loc), *not exist* trans. v. (loc-nom), *not have*
དེ་མེད་	verbal clause, *that does not exist, [you] do not have that*
དེ་མེད་ན་	verbal clause + conditional syntactic particle marking a conditional clause: *if that doesn't exist, if [you] don't have that*
ན་	particle; either 1) a rhetorical syntactic particle marking a conditional clause following a verb or verb phrase, or 2) a case particle following nouns, pronouns, postpositions, and adjectives marking the 2nd, 4th and 7th cases
སྤྱོད་	trans. v. (ag-nom), *use* སྤྱོད་སྤྱད་སྤྱད་སྤྱོད། ཐདད།
སྤྱོད་པ་	n., *deeds*
ཕྱིན་	here, an abbreviation for the verbal noun phrase ཕ་རོལ་ཏུ་ཕྱིན་པ་
ཕ་རོལ་ཏུ་ཕྱིན་པ་	n., *perfection,* literally a verbal noun phrase, *gone to the other side*
ཕྱིན་	intr. v. (nom-obj) (past tense), *went,* often used metaphorically in the sense of *turned into* or *became* འགྲོ་ཕྱིན་འགྲོ་སོང་། ཐམིདད། སོང་ is also an alternate past form
དྲུག་	n. or adj., *six;* here: adj.

ཕྱིན་དྲུག་ noun phrase (n. + adj.), *the six perfections*

སྦྱིན་པ་ n., *generosity*

ཚུལ་ཁྲིམས་ n., *ethics*

བཟོད་པ་ n., *patience*

བརྩོན་འགྲུས་ n., *effort*

བསམ་གཏན་ n., *concentration*

ཤེས་རབ་ n., *wisdom*

དང་ syntactic particle; used as a continuative following nouns and noun phrases (*and,* or with negative verb. *or*), or used to mark the qualifier of intr. v. of separation (*from*) and intr. v. of conjunction (*with*); here: *and*

རིམ་ n., *stage*

གཉིས་ n. or adj., *two;* here: adj.

རིམ་གཉིས་ noun phrase (n. + adj.), *the two stages.* In this context the two stages refer to the two stages of Highest Yoga Tantra: stage of generation and stage of completion.

བསྐྱེད་རིམ་ comp. n., *stage of generation*

རྫོགས་རིམ་ comp. n., *stage of completion*

སོགས་ s.p., optional generalizing syllable, *and so forth*

རྨང་ n., *foundation*

རྨང་མེད་པ་ verbal clause, *without a foundation*

མེད་ negative verbal suffix particle

རྨང་མེད་པའི་ verbal clause + 6th case particle fused to suffixless syllable

འི་ particle fused to suffixless final syllable; either 1) a syntactic particle following a verb or verb phrase signifying conjunction or disjunction, or 2) a 6th case particle following nouns, pronouns, postpositions, and adjectives

ཐོག་བྱེད་པ་ n., *roof*

བྱེད་ trans. v. (ag-nom), *do, make, perform, take* བྱེད་བྱས་བྱ་བྱོས། ཐ་དད།

ཐོག་བྱེད་པ་དང་ n. + syntactic particle marking the qualifier of a nom-s.p. verb of conjunction འདྲ་ *be similar to* (i.e., the དང་ marks that to which is subject is similar)

འདྲ་ intr. v. (nom-s.p. verb: qualifier marked with དང་), *be similar to*

འདྲ་དྲས་དྲ་དྲོས། ཐ་དད།

འདྲ་བར་འགྱུར་བ་ཡིན་ནོ། ། syntactically irregular but frequently seen alternate form of a sentence ending construction, *is a case of being like, are like...*

འདྲ་བར་འགྱུར་ verb phrase (verbal infinitive + weak present/future auxiliary, *[it] would be like, [it] will be like*

འདྲ་བར་ verbal infinitive; here, the fused ར་ is a syntactic particle modifying a verb to create a verbal infinitive within the verb phrase འདྲ་བར་འགྱུར་ *would be similar, will be similar;* it is **not** a case particle marking the 2nd, 4th or 7th cases because it does not follow a noun—it is within a verb phrase

སུ་རུ་ཏུ་དུ་ར་ are the five syntactic particles used to modify verbs to create infinitives within verb phrases

གྱུར་ intr. v. (nom-obj), *become;* also the weak auxiliary

འགྱུར་གྱུར་འགྱུར། ཐ་མི་དད།

བྱེད་ trans. v. (ag-nom), *do, make, perform, take;* also strong auxiliary

བྱེད་བྱས་བྱ་བྱོས། ཐ་དད།

ཡིན་ intr. v. (nom-nom) linking verb, *is, are* ཡིན་ཡིན་ཡིན་ཡིན། ཐ་མི་དད།

ཡིན་ནོ། ། linking verb + sentence-ending terminating syntactic particle

ནོ། ། a sentence-terminating syntactic particle following words ending with a ན་ suffix.

The basic structure of Part 4

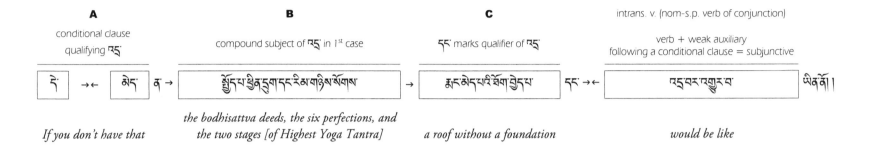

A		B		C		intrans. v. (nom-s.p. verb of conjunction)	
conditional clause qualifying འདྲ་		compound subject of འདྲ་ in 1st case		དང་ marks qualifier of འདྲ་		verb + weak auxiliary following a conditional clause = subjunctive	
དེ་ →← མེད་	ན་ →	སྤྱོད་པ་ཕྱིན་དྲུག་དང་རིམ་གཉིས་སོགས་	→	རྨང་མེད་པའི་ཐོག་བྲེད་པ་	དང་ →←	འདྲ་བར་འགྱུར་བ་	ཡིན་ནོ།
If you don't have that		*the bodhisattva deeds, the six perfections, and the two stages [of Highest Yoga Tantra]*		*a roof without a foundation*		*would be like*	

The simile: If you don't have A, B would be like C

Tsong-kha-pa is introducing a simile here: **B is like** C. But rather than stating it in the present tense indicative mood (B is like C), the construction is in what in English is called the subjunctive following a conditional clause. **If A is the case, B would be like** C.

མེད་ You need to keep in mind that མེད་ can mean either ***not exist*** (nom-loc) or ***not have*** (loc-nom). The context tells us that Tsong-kha-pa is intending the verb ***not have***. He is telling us that **we** must train in the altruistic aspiration to enlightenment བྱང་ཆུབ་ཀྱི་སེམས་ because if **we don't have** it, our practice of the perfections and so forth **would be like** a roof without a foundation.

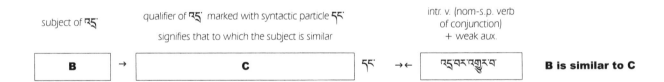

subject of འདྲ་		qualifier of འདྲ་ marked with syntactic particle དང་ signifies that to which the subject is similar		intr. v. (nom-s.p. verb of conjunction) + weak aux.	
B	→	**C**	དང་ →←	འདྲ་བར་འགྱུར་བ་	**B is similar to C**

འདྲ་ intr. v. (nom-s.p. verb of conjunction) meaning *be similar:* B *is similar to* C. Its subject is in the 1st case (nominative) and its qualifier—that to which the subject is conjoined—is marked with the syntactic particle དང་

འདྲ་བར་འགྱུར་ verb phrase (verbal infinitive + weak present/future auxiliary), *[it] would be like, [it] will be like*

འདྲ་བར་ verbal infinitive; here, the fused ར་ is a syntactic particle modifying a verb to create a verbal infinitive within the verb phrase འདྲ་བར་འགྱུར་ *would be similar, will be similar;* it is **not** a case particle marking the 2nd, 4th or 7th cases because it does not follow a noun—it is within a verb phrase

གྱུར་ intr. v. (nom-obj), *become;* also the weak auxiliary འགྱུར་གྱུར་འགྱུར། ཐ་མི་དད།

Part 5 • དེ་ལ་སྦྱོང་བའི་རྣམ་པ་ཐན་ཐུན་རྒྱུད་ལ་སྐྱེས་ན་ཆོ་གས་བཟུང་ལ།

Part 5 begins with a conditional clause: in generalized form, "when you have generated A in terms of B..."

entire verbal clause is a conditional qualifier, marked with the conditional syntactic particle ན་

noun phrase དེ་ལ་སྦྱོང་བའི་རྣམ་པ་ཐན་ཐུན་ as a unit is the subject of སྐྱེས → ← intrans. v. (nom-obj)

noun phrase modified by following adjective ↔ simple adjective

verbal adj. modifying following noun ↔ modified noun

implied antecedent for དེ་ | implied noun-adj. compound | qualifier of སྦྱོང་ →← intr. v. (nom-loc) | 2nd case qualifier: place of activity

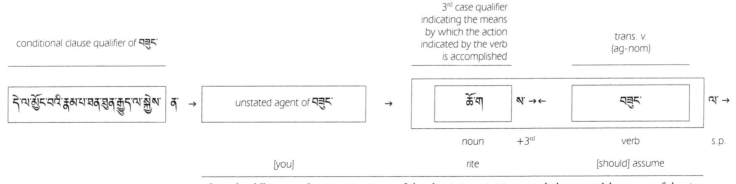

[སེམས་བསྐྱེད་] ↔ དེ་ ལ་ →← སྦྱོང་བ འི་ ↔ རྣམ་པ་ ↔ ཐན་ཐུན་ | རྒྱུད་ ལ་ →← སྐྱེས་ ན། →

[སེམས་བསྐྱེད་]	དེ་	ལ་	སྦྱོང་བ	འི་	རྣམ་པ་	ཐན་ཐུན་	རྒྱུད་	ལ་	སྐྱེས་	ན།
verbal noun phrase	limiting adjective used as a pronoun	7th	verbal noun	+6th	noun	adjective	noun	2nd case place of activity	verb	conditional s.p.
[generation of the altruistic aspiration to enlightenment]	that		experience		form, aspect	some	continuum		is generated	

When you have generated in your continuum some form of experience with respect to it [the generation of altruistic aspiration to enlightenment],

Part 5 concludes with a transitive construction

conditional clause qualifier of བཟུང་ | 3rd case qualifier indicating the means by which the action indicated by the verb is accomplished | trans. v. (ag-nom)

དེ་ལ་སྦྱོང་བའི་རྣམ་པ་ཐན་ཐུན་རྒྱུད་ལ་སྐྱེས་ ན་ → unstated agent of བཟུང་ → ཆོ་ག ས་ →← བཟུང་ ལ་ →

དེ་ལ་སྦྱོང་བའི་རྣམ་པ་ཐན་ཐུན་རྒྱུད་ལ་སྐྱེས་ ན་	unstated agent of བཟུང་	ཆོ་ག	ས་	བཟུང་	ལ་
		noun	+3rd	verb	s.p.
	[you]	rite		[should] assume	

[you should] assume [it, i.e., generation of the altruistic aspiration to enlightenment] by means of the rite

Glossary for Part 5

དེ་ adj. and pronoun, *that, those*

དེ་ལ་ limiting adjective used as a pronoun + 7th case particle, *with respect to that, in terms of that.* The 7th case signifies the general referential context of the action expressed by the verb མྱོང་ The unstated antecedent of the adjective is སེམས་བསྐྱེད་ *the generation of the altruistic aspiration to enlightenment*

ལ་ particle; either 1) a syntactic particle following a verb or verb phrase signifying conjunction or disjunction, or 2) a case particle following nouns, pronouns, postpositions, and adjectives marking the 2nd, 4th and 7th cases

དེ་ལ་མྱོང་ verb clause (qualifier marked with the 7th case + nom-loc verb expressing attitude or cognitive state), *experience with respect to that*

མྱོང་ intr. v. (nom-loc), *be experienced*

མྱོང་མྱོང་མྱོང་། ཐ་མི་དད།

མྱོང་བ་ verbal noun, *experienced, experience*

མྱོང་བའི་ verbal n. + 6th case particle fused to suffixless syllable

འི་ particle fused to suffixless final syllable; either 1) a syntactic particle following a verb or verb phrase signifying conjunction or disjunction, or 2) a 6th case particle following nouns, pronouns, postpositions, and adjectives

རྣམ་པ་ n., *aspect*

ཕན་ཐུན adj., *a little, some*

རྒྱུད་ n., *stream, continuum*

རྒྱུད་ལ་ n. + 2nd case particle marking place of activity

ལ་ particle; either 1) a syntactic particle following a verb or verb phrase signifying conjunction or disjunction, or 2) a case particle following nouns, pronouns, postpositions, and adjectives marking the 2nd, 4th and 7th cases

སྐྱེས་ intr. v. (nom-obj) (past tense), *be born, arise, be created, be produced*

སྐྱེ་སྐྱེས་སྐྱེ། ཐ་མི་དད།

བསྐྱེད་ trans. v. (ag-nom), *produce, generate, create, give birth to*

སྐྱེད་བསྐྱེད་བསྐྱེད་སྐྱེད། ཐ་དད།

སྐྱེས་ན་ past tense intransitive verb + conditional syntactic particle marking a conditional clause, *when [experience] has been generated*

ན་ particle; either 1) a rhetorical syntactic particle marking a conditional clause following a verb or verb phrase, or 2) a case particle following nouns, pronouns, postpositions, and adjectives marking the 2nd, 4th and 7th cases

ཆོ་ག་ n., *rite*

ཆོ་གས་ noun + 3rd case particle fused to suffixless final syllable

ས་ abbreviation of the particle ཡིས་ (when ཡིས་ is fused to a suffixless final syllable, the ཡི goes away and all that's left is a fused ས་); either 1) syntactic particle creating an adverbial construction, 2) syntactic particle marking the qualifier of an intransitive nom-s.p. verb of absence, or 3) case particle marking the 3rd case

བཟུང་ trans. v. (ag-nom) (past tense), *grasp,* used metaphorically: *apprehend, assume*

འཛིན་བཟུང་གཟུང་ཟུང་། ཐ་དད།

བཟུང་ལ། sentence-ending final verb + conjunctive syntactic particle acting as punctuation

ལ་ particle; either 1) a syntactic particle following a verb or verb phrase signifying conjunction or disjunction, or 2) a case particle following nouns, pronouns, postpositions, and adjectives marking the 2nd, 4th and 7th cases

Translation tips • Sometimes an intransitive Tibetan sentence may be translated into English with a transitive construction

།དེ་ལ་སྦྱོང་བའི་ཉམས་པ་ཐན་ཐུན་སྐྱེས་ན — སྐྱེས is an intransitive verb, thus this clause literally says *when some form of experience with that has been generated...* Because Tsong-kha-pa clearly intends his reader to take the advice personally, we might choose to translate the clause as if the transitive verb བསྐྱེད་ had been used and implying the pronoun "you" as the agent: *when you have generated some form of experience with the altruistic aspiration...*

After the conditional, a qualifier showing the means by which the verb's action is accomplished qualifies the verb

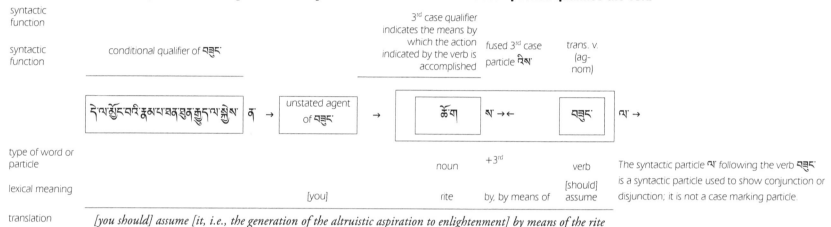

syntactic function						
syntactic function	conditional qualifier of བཟུང་		3rd case qualifier indicates the means by which the action indicated by the verb is accomplished	fused 3rd case particle རིས་	trans. v. (ag-nom)	
	དེ་ལ་སྦྱོང་བའི་ཉམས་པ་ཐན་ཐུན་རྒྱུད་ལ་སྐྱེས་ ན་ →	unstated agent of བཟུང་ →	ཆོ་ག	ས་ →←	བཟུང་	ལ་ →
type of word or particle			noun	+3rd	verb	The syntactic particle ལ་ following the verb བཟུང་ is a syntactic particle used to show conjunction or disjunction; it is not a case marking particle.
lexical meaning		[you]	rite	by, by means of	[should] assume	
translation	*[you should] assume [it, i.e., the generation of the altruistic aspiration to enlightenment] by means of the rite*					

Grammar review • Note regarding 3rd case qualifiers occurring with transitive verbs

The third case is used to mark agents of transitive verbs and qualifiers of verbs indicating the **means** by which some action is accomplished or the **reason** for some action. Students learning to read Tibetan tend to assume that a noun (or noun phrase) in the third case preceding a transitive verb is the verb's agent, but more often than not this is not so. Sentences with transitive verbs are often about the object, not the agent, in the sense that the new information isn't introducing a new agent, but rather newly telling **what** that agent is doing. In Part 5 neither the agent, nor the object of the transitive verb བཟུང་ is explicitly stated; both are clear from the context.

ཆོ་གས་ — noun *rite* + 3rd case particle fused to suffixless final syllable

ས་ — abbreviation of the particle རིས་ (when རིས་ is fused to a suffixless final syllable, the རི goes away and all that's left is a fused ས་); either 1) syntactic particle creating an adverbial construction, 2) syntactic particle marking the qualifier of an intransitive nom-s.p. verb of absence, or 3) case particle marking the 3rd case

གིས་ཀྱིས་གྱིས་རིས་ཡིས་ — five equivalent particles, marking the 3rd case and also marking syntactic and adverbial relationships.

བཟུང་ — trans. v. (ag-nom) (past tense), *grasp,* used metaphorically: *apprehend, assume* འཛིན་བཟུང་གཟུང་ཟུངས། ཐ་དད།

བཟུང་ལ། — final verb + syntactic particle. The particle ལ་ following the verb བཟུང་ is a syntactic particle used to show conjunction or disjunction; it is not a case marking particle.

Part 6 • དེའི་བསླབ་བྱ་ལ་འབད་ནས་སྨོན་པ་ཅི་བརྟན་བྱ།

verbal clause དེའི་བསླབ་བྱ་ལ་འབད་ནས་ qualifies བརྟན་བྱ་

object of འབད་				→←	trans. v. (ag-obj)		object of བརྟན་		adverbial qualifier	→←	trans. v. (ag-nom)
དེ	འི་	བསླབ་བྱ་	ལ་	→←	འབད་	ནས་ →	སྨོན་པ་	→	ཅི་	→←	བརྟན་བྱ།
pronoun	+6th	verbal object noun	2nd		verb	s.p. with verb makes participle	noun		rel. p.n.		verb + st. future aux.
that		objects of training			strive	through striving	aspirational [mind]		as much as		you should make stable

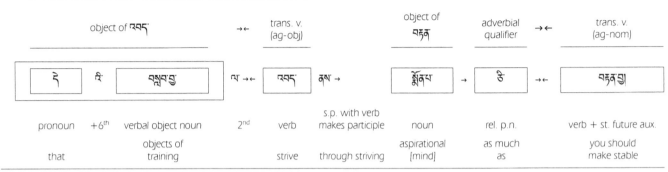

[You] should make the aspirational [altruistic intention] as stable as you can through striving at its points of training.

Glossary for Part 6

དེ་ — limiting adjective here used as a pronoun, *that*

དེའི་ — limiting adjective used as a pronoun + 6th case particle fused to suffixless final syllable

འི་ — particle fused to suffixless final syllable; either 1) a syntactic particle following a verb or verb phrase signifying conjunction or disjunction, or 2) a 6th case particle following nouns, pronouns, postpositions, and adjectives

བསླབ་ — trans. v. (ag-obj) (future tense), *train [in something]*
སློབ་བསླབས་བསླབ་སློབས། ཐ་དད།

བསླབ་བྱ་ — verbal object noun; *object(s) of training;* verbal object nouns are formed using the future form of the core verb + the strong future auxiliary བྱ་

བསླབ་བྱ་ལ་ — verbal object noun + 2nd case particle marking the object of the transitive verb འབད་ *strive at, work at*

ལ་ — particle; either syntactic particle (following verb) signifying conjunction or disjunction, or case particle (following noun) marking the 2nd, 4th and 7th cases; here: 2nd case object of the transitive verb

འབད་ — trans. v. (ag-obj), *strive* འབད་འབད་འབད་འབོད། ཐ་དད།

འབད་ནས་ — verb + continuative syntactic particle

ནས་ — particle; either 1) a syntactic particle following verbs and verb phrases marking adverbs, participles or disjunction, or 2) a case particle marking the 5th case

སྨོན་པ་ — n., *aspirational [altruistic intention];* abbreviation for སྨོན་སེམས་

ཅི་ — general relative pronoun and interrogative pronoun, *what, which, however, whatever*

བརྟན་ — trans. v. (ag-nom), *make stable* རྟོན་བརྟན་བརྟན་རྟོན། ཐ་དད།

བརྟན་བྱ་ — abbreviation for བརྟན་པར་བྱ་

བརྟན་པར་བྱ་ — verb phrase (verbal infinitive + strong future auxiliary), *[I] will make [it] stable, [you] should make [it] stable*

བརྟན་པར་ — verbal infinitive; here, the fused ར་ is a syntactic particle modifying a verb to create a verbal infinitive within the verb phrase བརྟན་པར་བྱ་ *[I] will make [it] stable, [you] should make [it] stable;* it is **not** a case particle marking the 2nd, 4th or 7th cases because it does not follow a noun—it is within a verb phrase.

བྱ་ — here, this is the strong future auxiliary བྱེད་བྱས་བྱ་བྱོས། ཐ་དད།

Grammar review • Verbs and their derivative nouns

There are four classes of nouns which have their origins in verbs. We will look at them using the transitive verb ཤེས་ *know, understand* and སློབ་ *train [in something]* as our root verbs.

Here is the root verb ཤེས་

ཤེས་ trans. v., (ag-nom), *know, understand.* This verb is listed in the *Great Word Treasury* as ཐ་མི་དད། but I think it is a transitive verb (ag-nom).

ཤེས་ཤེས་ཤེས། ཐ་མི་དད།

Here are the derivative nouns

ཤེས་པ་ verbal noun, *consciousness*

ཤེས་བྱེད་ verbal agent noun (present tense of core verb + present strong auxiliary), *source*

ཤེས་བྱ་ verbal object noun (future form of the core verb and the strong future auxiliary), *object of knowledge*

Here is the root verb སློབ་

བསླབ་ trans. v. (ag-obj) (future tense), *train [in something]*

སློབ་བསླབས་བསླབ་སློབས། ཐ་དད།

Here are the derivative nouns

སློབ་པ་ verbal noun, *learner*

བསླབ་བྱ་ verbal object noun (future form of the core verb and the strong future auxiliary), *object of training*

Note on deciphering the sentence-ending construction བརྟན་བྱ།

Sometimes a sentence-ending verbal phrase such as བརྟན་པར་བྱ་ *[I] will make [it] stable, [you] should make [it] stable* is abbreviated to བརྟན་བྱ་, so that it looks like the verbal object noun. The way you can tell that བརྟན་བྱ་ in this context is an abbreviation for བརྟན་པར་བྱ་ is that the verbal object noun will not end a sentence. Verbs end sentences, thus here བརྟན་བྱ་ is an abbreviation for བརྟན་པར་བྱ་

Grammar review • Participles are formed from verbs + the syntactic particle ནས་

object of འབད་			→←	participle formed from trans. v. (ag-obj) + syntactic particle ནས་ *striving*		
དེ	འི་	བསླབ་བྱ་	ལ་ →←	འབད་	ནས་	→
pronoun	+6th	verbal object noun	2nd	verb	s.p.	
that		objects of training		strive		

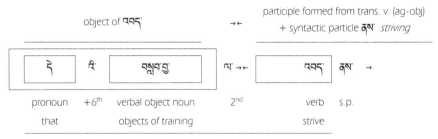

striving at their objects of training

དེའི་བསླབ་བྱ་ལ་འབད་ verbal clause (object in 2nd case + transitive ag-obj verb), *strive at their objects of training.*

དེའི་བསླབ་བྱ་ noun phrase (pronoun + 6th case particle + verbal object noun), *their objects of training.*

དེའི་བསླབ་བྱ་ལ་ the ལ་ particle after the verbal object noun བསླབ་བྱ་ signifies that it is the 2nd case object of the transitive verb འབད་

དེའི་བསླབ་བྱ་ལ་འབད་ནས་ verbal clause + continuative syntactic particle. འབད་ནས་ is a verb + syntactic particle, not a noun declined in the 5th case

ནས་ particle; either 1) a syntactic particle following verbs and verb phrases marking adverbs, participles or disjunction, or 2) a case particle marking the 5th case

Grammar review • Many particles are used as syntactic particles following verbs and as case particles following nouns and noun phrases

The following chart illustrates how frequently-seen particles function as syntactic particles following verbs, but are case particles following nouns.

verb or verb phrase + syntactic particle			**noun or noun phrase + case particle or syntactic particle**		
verb or verb phrase +	ནས་	syntactic particle creates a **participle** with the tense determined by the verb	noun or noun phrase +	ནས་	case particle marking **the 5th case**
verb or verb phrase +	ལ་	syntactic particle signifying **conjunction** or **disjunction**	noun or noun phrase +	ལ་	case particle marking **the 2nd, 4th or 7th cases**
verb or verb phrase +	གི་ཀྱི་གྱི་འི་ཡི་	syntactic particles signifying **conjunction** or **disjunction**	noun or noun phrase +	གི་ཀྱི་གྱི་འི་ཡི་	case particles marking **the 6th case**
verb or verb phrase +	ཏེ་སྟེ་དེ་	continuative syntactic particles show **sequence**	noun or noun phrase +	ཏེ་སྟེ་དེ་	**punctuational syntactic particles** signifies **apposition** with noun or noun phrase that follows

Chapter Five Self Test

Write out the passage, boxing and identifying every syntactic element.

དེ་ལྟར་སྐྱེས་བུ་འབྲིང་གི་ཆོས་སྐོར་རྣམས་ཚགས་སུ་ཚུད་པ་ན། རང་ཉིད་སྲིད་མཚོར་ལྷུང་བ་ཇི་འདྲ་བ་དེ་བཞིན་དུ། མ་རྣམས་ཀྱང་དེ་འདྲ་བར་སོང་བ་ཡིད་ལ་བྱས་ཏེ། བྱམས་པ་དང་སྙིང་རྗེའི་རྩ་བ་ཅན་གྱི་བྱང་ཆུབ་ཀྱི་སེམས་སྦྱངས་ལ་ཅི་སྐྱེ་ལ་འབད་དགོས་ཏེ། དེ་མེད་ན་སྤྱོད་པ་ཕྱིན་དྲུག་དང་རིམ་གཉིས་སོགས་རྐང་མེད་པའི་ཐོག་བྱེད་པ་དང་འདྲ་བར་འགྱུར་བ་ཡིན་ནོ། །དེ་ལ་སྦྱོང་བའི་རྣམ་པ་ཐ་ན་ཐུན་རྒྱུད་ལ་སྐྱེས་ན་ཆོགས་བཟུང་ལ། དེའི་བསླབ་བྱ་ལ་འབད་ནས་སྨོན་པ་ཅི་བརྟན་བྱ།

Vocabulary

For each word, can you identify what part of speech it is (noun, pronoun, adjective, verb, adverb, postposition) and what it means?
For each syntactic particle, can you identify what class of syntactic particle it belongs to and how it is used?

སྐོར་	ལྷུང་	བྱང་ཆུབ་ཀྱི་སེམས་	རིམ་གཉིས་
རྩ་བ་ཅན་	རྒྱུད་	བྱང་ཆུབ་	རིམ་
རྩ་བ་	རྒྱ་མཚོ་	བྱ་	རང་ཉིད་
སྦྱངས་	རྫོགས་རིམ་	ཕྱིན་དྲུག་	ཡིན་
སྤྱོད་པ་	རྐང་མེད་པ་	ཕྱིན་	ཡིད་
སྤྱོད་	རྐང་	འགྱུར་	ཡང་
སྦྱིན་པ་	རྣམས་	གྱི་	འི་
སྐྱེས་བུ་འབྲིང་	རྣམ་པ་	ཀྱི་	འབྲིང་
སྐྱེས་བུ་	སྲིད་	ཀྱང་ཡང་འང་	འདྲ་བར་འགྱུར་
སྐྱེས་	དྲུག་	སོང་བ་	འདྲ་
སྐྱེ་	སྦྱོང་བ་	སོང་	འབད་
སྨོན་པ་	སྦྱོང་	སོགས་	འང་
སྲེ་	བྱེད་	ས་	འཁོར་
སྙིང་རྗེ་	བྱས་	ཤེས་རབ་	ཚུལ་ཁྲིམས་
ལྷུང་བ་	བྱམས་པ་	ལ་	ཚགས་སུ་ཚུད་པ་

མེད་	བསླབ་བྱ་	དེ་ལྟར་	ཆོས་སྐོར་
མཚོ་	བསླབ་	དེ་འདྲ་	ཆོས་
མ་	བསམ་གཏན་	དེ་བཞིན་དུ་	ཆོ་ག་
བརྟོན་འགྲུས་	བཟོད་པ་	དེ་	ཅི་
བསྐྱེད་རིམ་	བཟུང་	དང་	ཅན་
བསྐྱེད་	ཕ་རོལ་ཏུ་ཕྱིན་པ་	དགོས་	གི་
བརྟན་བྱ་	ནོ་	ཐན་ཐུན་	གཉིས་
བརྟན་པར་བྱ་	ནས་	ཏེ་ སྟེ་ and དེ་	
བརྟན་	ན་	ཇི་འདྲ་བ་	

Translation of Tsong-kha-pa's text

དེ་ལྟར་སྐྱེས་བུ་འབྲིང་གི་ཆོས་སྐོར་རྣམས་ཚགས་སུ་ཚུད་པ་ན། རང་ཉིད་སྲིད་མཚོར་ལྷུང་བ་ཇི་འདྲ་བ་དེ་བཞིན་དུ། མ་རྣམས་ཀྱང་དེ་འདྲ་བར་སོང་བ་ཡིད་ལ་བྱས་ཏེ། བྱམས་པ་དང་སྙིང་རྗེའི་རྩ་བ་ཅན་གྱི་བྱང་ཆུབ་ཀྱི་སེམས་སྦྱངས་ལ་ཅི་སྐྱེ་ལ་འབད་དགོས་ཏེ། དེ་མེད་ན་སྤྱོད་པ་ཕྱིན་དྲུག་དང་རིམ་གཉིས་སོགས་རྨང་མེད་པའི་ཐོག་བྱེད་པ་དང་འདྲ་བར་འགྱུར་བ་ཡིན་ནོ། །དེ་ལ་མྱོང་བའི་རྣམ་པ་ཐན་ཐུན་རྒྱུད་ལ་སྐྱེས་ན་ཆོ་གས་བཟུང་ལ། དེའི་བསླབ་བྱ་ལ་འབད་ནས་སྨོན་པ་ཅི་བརྟན་བྱ།

When, in that way, the topics of practice of a being of middle capacity have been internalized, you should take to mind [your] mothers who have fallen into the ocean of cyclic existence just as you have. [Motivated by concern for their welfare], you should train in the altruistic aspiration to enlightenment which has love and compassion as its root, and you must strive to generate [it] however much you can. If you do not have that [i.e., generation of the altruistic aspiration to enlightenment], the bodhisattva deeds, the six perfections, the two stages [of Highest Yoga Tantra], and so forth are like a roof without a foundation. When you have generated some form of experience with respect to it, assume it through the rite. Through striving at its points of training, you should make the aspirational mind as stable as you can.

Annotations for Tsong-kha-pa's text in Chapter Five

Here is Tsong-kha-pa's text as supplemented by *The Four Interwoven Annotations,* 830.3-831.3

།ཚུལ་ དེ་ལྟར་ བྱས་ནས་ སྐྱེས་བུ་འབྲིང་གི་ཆོས་སྐོར་རྣམས་ ལེགས་པར་བྱང་སྟེ་ ཚགས་སུ་ཚུད་ ཅིང་གཞི་ཚུགས་ པ་ན། དེའི་རྗེས་སུ་བློ་དེ་ཉིད་ཀྱིས་དྲངས་ཏེ་ རང་ཉིད་སྲིད་ པ་འཁོར་བའི་རྒྱ་ མཚོར་ལྟུང་ ནས་སྡུག་བསྔལ་མཐའ་མེད་པར་མྱོང་ བ་ཇི་འདྲ་བ་དེ་བཞིན་དུ། དྲིན་ཅན་གྱི་ མ ར་གྱུར་པའི་འགྲོ་བ་ རྣམས་ཀྱང་ སྲིད་པར་འཁྱམས་ཤིང་སྡུག་བསྔལ་མྱོང་ཚུལ་ དེ་ དང་ འདྲ་བར་སོང་བ འི་ཚུལ་གྱི་གནས་སྐབས་དེ་འདྲ་ ཡིད་ལ་བྱས་ཏེ། མར་ཤེས་དྲིན་དྲན་དྲིན་གཟོ་གསུམ་གྱིས་དྲངས་པའི་གཅེས་ཤིང་འཕངས་པའི་རྣམ་པ་ཅན་གྱི་ཡིད་འོང་གི་ བྱམས་པ་ བསྐྱེད་པ་ དང་ བྱམས་པ་དེའི་ཤུགས་ཀྱིས་དྲངས་པའི་སྙིང་རྗེ་ཆེན་པོ་བསྐྱེད་ནས་ སྙིང་རྗེ་ དེས་གཞན་དོན་རང་ཉིད་ཀྱི་ཁུར་དུ་འཁྱེར་བ འི་ ལྷག་བསམ་གྱི་ རྩ་བ་ཅན་བྱང་ཆུབ་ཀྱི་སེམས་ གཞན་དོན་དུ་རྫོགས་པའི་བྱང་ཆུབ་ཐོབ་པར་འདོད་པའི་རྣམ་པ་ཅན་དེ་ཉིད་ལ་བློ་ སྦྱངས་ལ་ བྱང་ཆུབ་ཀྱི་སེམས་ འདི་ཅི་སྐྱེ་ལ་འབད་དགོས་ པ་ཡིན་ ཏེ། སེམས་བསྐྱེད་ དེ་མེད་ན་ བྱང་སེམས་ཀྱི་ སྤྱོད་པ་ཕྱིན་དྲུག་དང་ སྔགས་ཀྱི་བསྐྱེད་རིམ་དང་རྫོགས་པའི་ རིམ་ པ་གཉིས་སོགས་ གང་ལ་སྦྱངས་ཀྱང་རྩིག་ རྨང་མེད་པའི་ ཁང་པ་ལ་ ཐོག་ མང་པོ་རྩིག་པར་ བྱེད་པ་དང་འདྲ་བར་ བརྟེན་པའི་གཞི་མེད་པར་ འགྱུར་བ་ཡིན་ནོ། །དེ་འདྲ་བའི་སེམས་བསྐྱེད་ལ་ནི་སྨོན་པའི་སེམས་བསྐྱེད་ཅེས་བྱ་ཞིང་སེམས་བསྐྱེད་ དེ་ལ་ གོམས་ནས་ མྱོང་བའི་རྣམ་པ་ཐན་ཐུན་ ཅུང་ཟད་ རྒྱུད་ལ་སྐྱེས་ པ་བྱུང་ ན་ སེམས་བསྐྱེད་དེ་གོང་དུ་བཤད་པའི་སྨོན་སེམས་ཀྱི་ ཆོ་ག འི་སྒོ་ན ས་བཟུང་ལ། སྨོན་སེམས་ དེ་ མི་གཏོང་ཞིང་འཕེལ་བ འི་བསླབ་བྱ་ གོང་དུ་བཤད་པ་དེ་རྣམས་ ལ་འབད་ནས་ བསླབ་ཅིང་ སྨོན་པ འི་སེམས་དེ་ཉིད་ཅི་འཕེལ་དང་ ཅི་བརྟན་བྱ།

When having done that properly [i.e., taking the vow of individual liberation as your foundation, you strive at the three trainings because they are the path to liberation from cyclic existence], you have purified well and thereby internalized and taken as your basis the topics of practice of a being of middle capacity, then induced by that attitude, consider the following: just as you will experience limitless sufferings through having fallen into the ocean of cyclic existence, so too migrators who have been your kind mothers have a similar status in that they wander in cyclic existence and experience suffering.

You should train in the attitude of wishing to attain the complete enlightenment [of a Buddha] in order to bring about others' welfare, [called] the altruistic aspiration to enlightenment. This is based on the unusual attitude of bearing the burden of others' welfare due to love—which is a pleasant sense of cherishing others which was induced by recognizing all these migrators as having been your mothers, remembering their kindness [in caring for you], and wishing to repay their kindness, and due to compassion—through love inducing the generation of great compassion [i.e., wishing to separate all your mothers from suffering].

You must strive at generating this altruistic aspiration to enlightenment to whatever extent you can because, if you do not have the altruistic aspiration to enlightenment, then although you may train in the Bodhisattva deeds, the six perfections, or the two stages [of Highest Yoga Tantra—the stages of generation and completion] and so forth, you would be without the basic support, as you would be if in a house you were trying to build ceiling joists without walls to support them.

This sort of altruistic aspiration to enlightenment is called the aspirational altruistic intention. When you have generated some slight experience through cultivating that altruistic intention in your mental continuum, assume that aspirational altruistic intention to enlightenment through the rite of the aspirational altruistic intention which I explained above. Train through striving at the precepts, whereby you do not forsake that aspirational mind as I explained earlier, and extend it. You must make that aspirational altruistic intention as extensive and stable as possible.

Chapter Six

དེ་ནས་བྱང་སེམས་ཀྱི་སྤྱོད་པ་རླབས་ཆེ་བ་རྣམས་མཉན་ལ། ལྡོག་འཇུག་གི་མཚམས་རྣམས་ཞེས་པ་དང་དེ་ལ་སློབ་འདོད་དྲག་པོ་བསྐྱེད། བློ་དེ་དག་སྐྱེས་པ་ན་འཇུག་པའི་སྡོམ་པ་ཆོགས་བཟུང་ལ། རང་རྒྱུད་སྨིན་པར་བྱེད་པའི་ཕྱིན་དྲུག་དང་གཞན་རྒྱུད་སྨིན་བྱེད་ཀྱི་བསྡུ་བཞི་སོགས་ལ་བསླབ། ཁྱད་པར་དུ་རྩ་ལྟུང་ལ་འབད་པ་དྲག་པོས་སྲོག་བསྡོས་བྱ། ཟག་པ་ཆུང་འབྲིང་དང་ཉེས་བྱས་རྣམས་ཀྱིས་མ་གོས་པ་ལ་འབད་ཅིང་གོས་ན་འང་ཕྱིར་འཆོས་པ་ལ་འབད་དོ། །

Division of the passage into units to facilitate the analysis of the syntax

This chapter is composed of three two-part sentences. The division into meaning-units which I diagram individually in the following pages is shown below.

1

དེ་ནས་བྱང་སེམས་ཀྱི་སྤྱོད་པ་རླབས་ཆེ་བ་རྣམས་མཉན་ལ།

2

ལྡོག་འཇུག་གི་མཚམས་རྣམས་ཞེས་པ་དང་དེ་ལ་སློབ་འདོད་དྲག་པོ་བསྐྱེད།

3

བློ་དེ་དག་སྐྱེས་པ་ན་འཇུག་པའི་སྡོམ་པ་ཆོགས་བཟུང་ལ།

4

རང་རྒྱུད་སྨིན་པར་བྱེད་པའི་ཕྱིན་དྲུག་དང་གཞན་རྒྱུད་སྨིན་བྱེད་ཀྱི་བསྡུ་བཞི་སོགས་ལ་བསླབ།

5

ཁྱད་པར་དུ་རྩ་ལྟུང་ལ་འབད་པ་དྲག་པོས་སྲོག་བསྡོས་བྱ།

6

ཟག་པ་ཆུང་འབྲིང་དང་ཉེས་བྱས་རྣམས་ཀྱིས་མ་གོས་པ་ལ་འབད་ཅིང་གོས་ན་འང་ཕྱིར་འཆོས་པ་ལ་འབད་དོ། །

Parts 1 and 2 form a compound sentence: "Listen to X, and generate Y and Z."

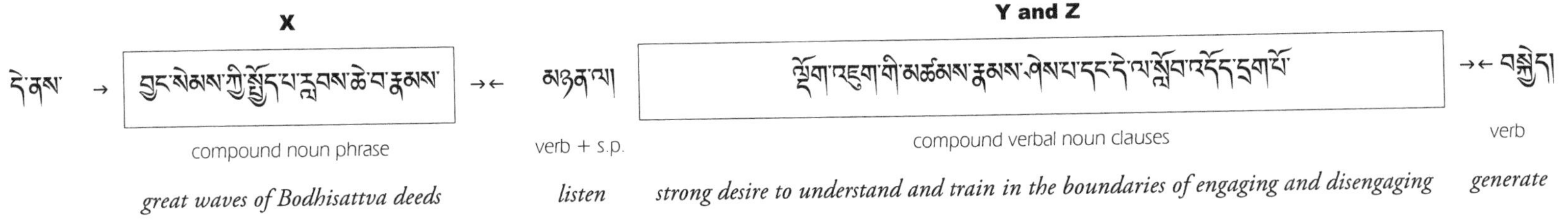

Part 1 in detail

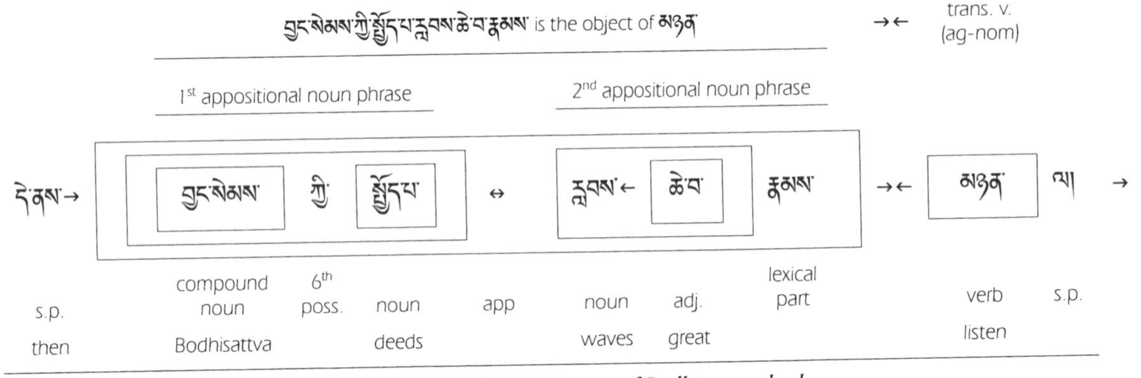

After that, listen to the great waves of Bodhisattva deeds.

Glossary for Part 1

དེ་ནས་ — an introductory syntactic particle translated *then;* (literally, pronoun + 5th case: *after that*).

བྱང་སེམས་ — abbreviation for བྱང་ཆུབ་སེམས་དཔའ་ *Bodhisattva*

བྱང་ཆུབ་ཀྱི་སེམས་ — n. phrase, *the altruistic aspiration to enlightenment*

བྱང་སེམས་ཀྱི་ — n. + 6th case particle

ཀྱི་ — particle; either 1) a syntactic particle following a verb or verb phrase signifying conjunction or disjunction, or 2) a 6th case particle following nouns, pronouns, postpositions, and adjectives

སྤྱོད་པ་ — n., *deed;* here: the Bodhisattva deeds of training in the perfections, generosity and so forth

རླབས་ — n., *wave*

ཆེ་བ་ — adj., *great*

རླབས་ཆེ་བ་ — noun phrase (n. + adj.), *great waves*

རླབས་ཆེ་བ་རྣམས་ — noun phrase (n. + adj. + pluralizing particle), *great waves*

རྣམས་ — optional pluralizing suffix particle

མཉན་ — trans. v. (ag-nom), *listen to* ཉན་མཉན་མཉན་ཉོན། ཐ་དད།

མཉན་ལ། — verb + conjunctive syntactic particle

ལ་ — particle; either 1) a syntactic particle following a verb or verb phrase signifying conjunction or disjunction, or 2) a case particle following nouns, pronouns, postpositions, and adjectives marking the 2nd, 4th and 7th cases

Note on the great waves of Bodhisattva deeds

བྱང་སེམས་ཀྱི་སྤྱོད་པ་རླབས་ཆེ་བ་རྣམས་ — *the great waves of the Bodhisattva deeds,* taken as a unit, the object of the verb མཉན་ *listen.*

སྟོན་པའི་མདོ་དང་དགོངས་འགྲེལ་མན་ངག་སོགས་ — What are the Bodhisattva deeds? The Four Interwoven Annotations identifies བྱང་སེམས་ཀྱི་སྤྱོད་པ་རླབས་ཆེ་བ་རྣམས་ as The Teacher's sutras, commentaries on his thought, quintessential instructions, and so forth.

སྟོན་པའི་མདོ་ — noun phrase (n. + 6th case particle + n.), *the Teacher's (i.e., Buddha's) sutras*

དགོངས་འགྲེལ་ — noun phrase (n. + understood 6th case particle + n.), *commentaries on [Buddha's] thought*

མན་ངག་ — n., *quintessential instructions*

Part 2 • ལྡོག་འཇུག་གི་མཚམས་རྣམས་ཤེས་པ་དང་དེ་ལ་སློབ་འདོད་དྲག་པོ་བསྐྱེད།

This sentence has an agentive verb and a compound object composed of two verbal clauses. In reduction, it is in the form "generate understanding of the boundaries of A and B, and the wish to train in C."

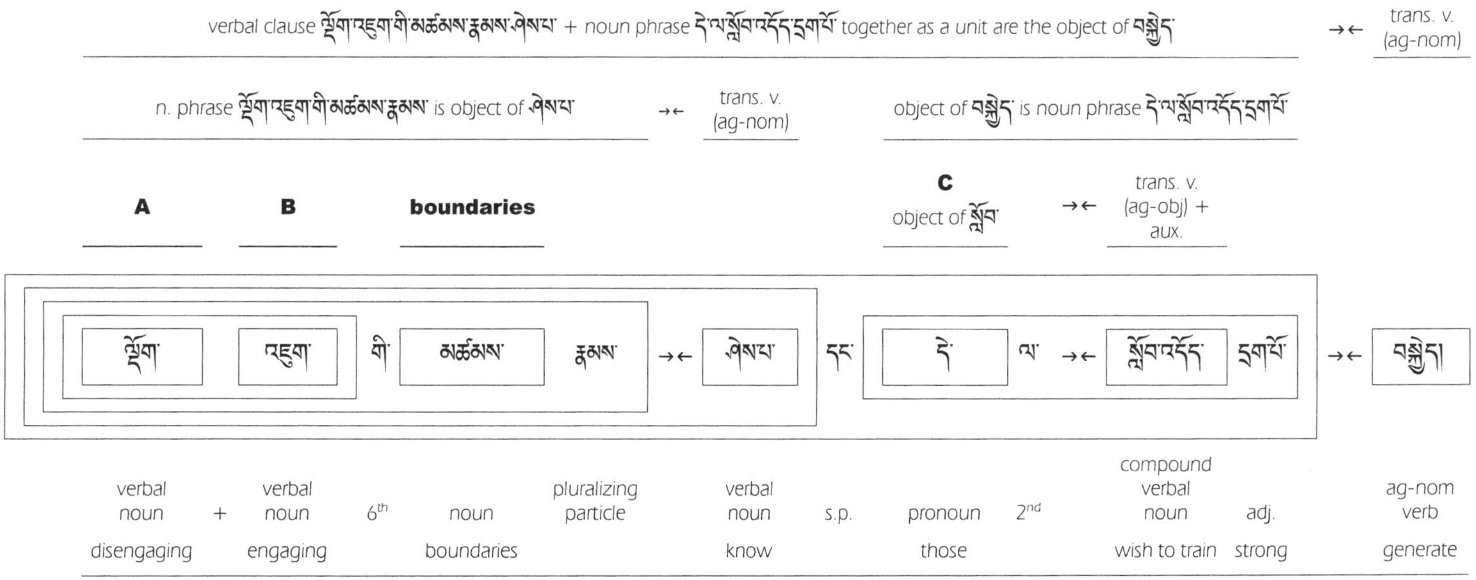

Generate [both] the understanding of the boundaries of disengaging from [actions to be abandoned] and entering into [actions to be adopted] and the strong wish to train in them.

Glossary for Part 2

ལྡོག་	intr. v. (nom-s.p.), *be isolated, be reversed* ལྡོག་ལྡོག་ལྡོག ཐ་མི་དད།
ལོག་	intr. v. (nom-s.p.), *be reversed, be turned* ལོག་ལོག་ལོག ཐ་མི་དད།
འཇུག་	intr. v. (nom-obj), *enter, engage, apply* འཇུག་བཙུག་གཞུག་ཚུག ཐ་མི་དད།
འཇུག་	trans. v. (ag-obj), causative in sense of *make something happen* འཇུག་ཞུགས་འཇུག་ཞུགས། ཐ་དད།
ལྡོག་འཇུག་	noun phrase (verbal n. + verbal n.), *disengaging and engaging*
ལྡོག་འཇུག་གི་	noun phrase + 6th case particle
གི་	particle; either 1) a syntactic particle following a verb or verb phrase signifying conjunction or disjunction, or 2) a 6th case particle following nouns, pronouns, postpositions, and adjectives
མཚམས་	n., *boundary*
ལྡོག་འཇུག་གི་མཚམས་	noun phrase (n. phrase + 6th case particle + n.), *the boundaries of disengaging and engaging*
ལྡོག་འཇུག་གི་མཚམས་རྣམས་	noun phrase (n. phrase + 6th case particle + n. + pluralizing particle), *the boundaries of disengaging and engaging*
རྣམས་	optional pluralizing suffix particle
ཤེས་	trans. v., (ag-nom), *know, understand.* This verb is listed in the *Great Word Treasury* as ཐ་མི་དད།, but I think it is a transitive ag-nom verb. ཤེས་ཤེས་ཤེས། ཐ་མི་དད།
ཤེས་པ་	verbal noun, *consciousness, knowledge*
དང་	particle, used three ways: 1) continuative syntactic particle used following nouns and noun phrases (*and,* or with negative verb, *or*); 2) syntactic particle marking the qualifier of an intr. nom-s.p. v. of conjunction, as in ང་རང་མི་སྡུག་པ་དང་ཕྲད་ན་ *if we meet **with** unpleasantness;* and 3) syntactic particle marking the qualifier of an intr. nom-s.p. v. of disjunction, as in རྟོག་པ་དང་བྲལ་ *free **from** conceptuality*
དེ་	adj. and pronoun, *that, those*
དེ་ལ་	pronoun + 2nd case particle marking the object of the transitive verb སློབ་ *train in*
ལ་	particle; either 1) a syntactic particle following a verb or verb phrase signifying conjunction or disjunction, or 2) a case particle following nouns, pronouns, postpositions, and adjectives marking the 2nd, 4th and 7th cases
སློབ་	trans. v. (ag-obj), *train in* སློབ་བསླབས་བསླབ་སློབས། ཐ་དད།
འདོད་	trans. v. (ag-nom), *want, wish, assert.* This verb is listed in the *Great Word Treasury* as ཐ་མི་དད།, but I think it is a transitive ag-nom verb. འདོད་འདོད་འདོད། ཐ་མི་དད།
སློབ་འདོད་	verb phrase (verb + auxiliary verb), *want to train, wish to train;* abbreviation for སློབ་པར་འདོད་
སློབ་པར་འདོད་	verb phrase (verbal infinitive + auxiliary verb), *want to train, wish to train*
སློབ་པར་	verbal infinitive; here, the fused ར་ is a syntactic particle modifying a verb to create a verbal infinitive within the verb phrases སློབ་པར་འདོད་ *[you] want to train;* it is **not** a case particle marking the 2nd, 4th or 7th cases because it does not follow a noun—it is within a verb phrase
འདོད་	an auxiliary verb acting only on the verbal infinitive it follows, *[you] want [to train in ...]*
དྲག་པོ་	adj., *strong*
སློབ་འདོད་དྲག་པོ་	noun phrase (verbal noun + adj.), *the strong wish to train*
བསྐྱེད་	trans. v. (ag-nom), *produce, generate* སྐྱེད་བསྐྱེད་བསྐྱེད་སྐྱེད། ཐ་དད།
སྐྱེས་	intr. v. (nom-obj), *be born, arise, be created* སྐྱེ་སྐྱེས་སྐྱེ། ཐ་མི་དད།

Understanding the meaning signified by the construction ལྡོག་འཇུག་གི་མཚམས་རྣམས་

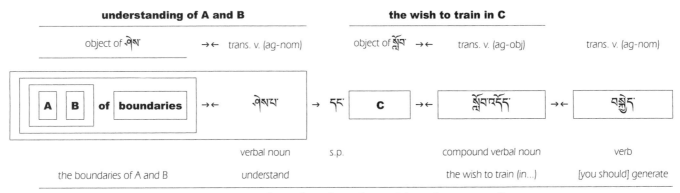

understanding of A and B				the wish to train in C			
object of ཤེས་	→←	trans. v. (ag-nom)		object of སློབ་	→←	trans. v. (ag-obj)	trans. v. (ag-nom)
[[[A] [B] of [boundaries]]	→←	ཤེས་པ་]	→ དང་	C	→←	སློབ་འདོད་	→← བསྐྱེད་
		verbal noun	s.p.			compound verbal noun	verb
the boundaries of A and B		understand				the wish to train (in...)	[you should] generate

generate understanding of A and B, and the wish to train in C.

Understanding the implied terms of "A" and "B"

To make sense of ལྡོག་འཇུག་གི་མཚམས་རྣམས་ one needs to understand the implied objects of the verbal nouns ལྡོག་ and འཇུག་
The implied elements indicated in brackets are taken from *The Four Interwoven Annotations.*

noun phrase ལྡོག་འཇུག་གི་མཚམས་རྣམས་ taken as a unit is the object of the transitive verb ཤེས་								→←	trans. v. (ag-nom)
verbal noun compound narrowing the following noun མཚམས་							modified noun		
understood subject of ལྡོག་	→←	intr. v. (nom-s.p.)		understood subject of འཇུག་	→←	intr. v. (nom-obj)			
[བྱང་སེམས་ཀྱི་སྤྱོད་པའི་སྐབས་ཀྱི་སྤང་བྱ་]	→←	ལྡོག་	དང་	[བྱང་སེམས་ཀྱི་སྤྱོད་པའི་སྐབས་ཀྱི་བླང་བྱ་]	→←	འཇུག་	གི་ མཚམས་རྣམས་	→←	ཤེས་པ་
adjectival construction modifying a verbal object noun		verbal noun	s.p.	adjectival construction modifying a verbal object noun		verbal noun	6th noun + pluralizing lexical particle		verbal noun
objects to be abandoned in the context of the Bodhisattva deeds		disengaging		objects to be adopted in the context of the Bodhisattva deeds		engaging	boundaries		understanding

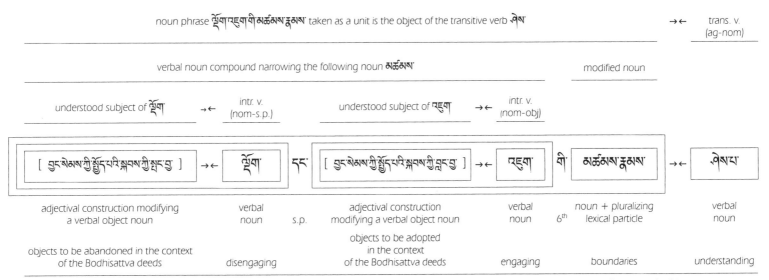

the understanding of the boundaries of disengaging from [actions to be abandoned in the context of the Bodhisattva deeds] and engaging in [actions to be adopted on the occasion of the Bodhisattva deeds]

Additional Glossary for "A" and "B"

བྱང་ཆུབ་སེམས་དཔའ་ n., *Bodhisattva*

སྤྱོད་པ་ n., *deed;* here: the Bodhisattva deeds of training in the six perfections

སྤྱོད་པའི་ either syntactic or case particle fused to suffixless final syllable པ་

འི་ particle fused to suffixless final syllable; either 1) a syntactic particle following a verb or verb phrase signifying conjunction or disjunction, or 2) a 6th case particle following nouns, pronouns, postpositions, and adjectives

སྐབས་ n., *occasion, context;* by extension, *chapter*

སྤང་བྱ་ / བླང་བྱ་ verbal object nouns, *objects to be abandoned* and *objects to be taken up.* These are verbal object nouns., i.e., nouns formed by adding the strong future auxiliary བྱ་ *the thing that is done* to the future form of the verb

བྱ་ trans. v. (ag-nom) (future tense), *do, make, perform.* This is the strong auxiliary. བྱེད་བྱས་བྱ་བྱོས། ཐ་དད།

སྤང་ trans. v. (ag-nom) (future), *abandon;* སྤོང་སྤང་སྤང་སྤོངས། ཐ་དད།

སྤང་བྱ་ verbal object noun derived from the verb སྤོང་ *abandon: object of abandonment, object to be abandoned*

ལྡོག་ intr. v. (nom-s.p.), *be isolated, be reversed* ལྡོག་ལྡོག་ལྡོག་ ཐ་མི་དད།

བྱང་སེམས་ཀྱི་སྤྱོད་པའི་སྐབས་ཀྱི་བླང་བྱ་ noun phrase, *objects to be taken up in the context of [training] in the bodhisattva deeds*

བླང་ trans. v. (ag-nom) (future), *take, obtain, grasp, seize, take up, obtain, appropriate;* ལེན་བླངས་བླང་ལོངས། ཐ་དད།

བླང་བྱ་ verbal object noun derived from the verb ལེན་ *take, obtain, grasp, seize, take up, obtain, appropriate abandon: object to be taken up*

The syntax of བྱང་སེམས་ཀྱི་སྤྱོད་པའི་སྐབས་ཀྱི་སྤང་བྱ་ ལྡོག་

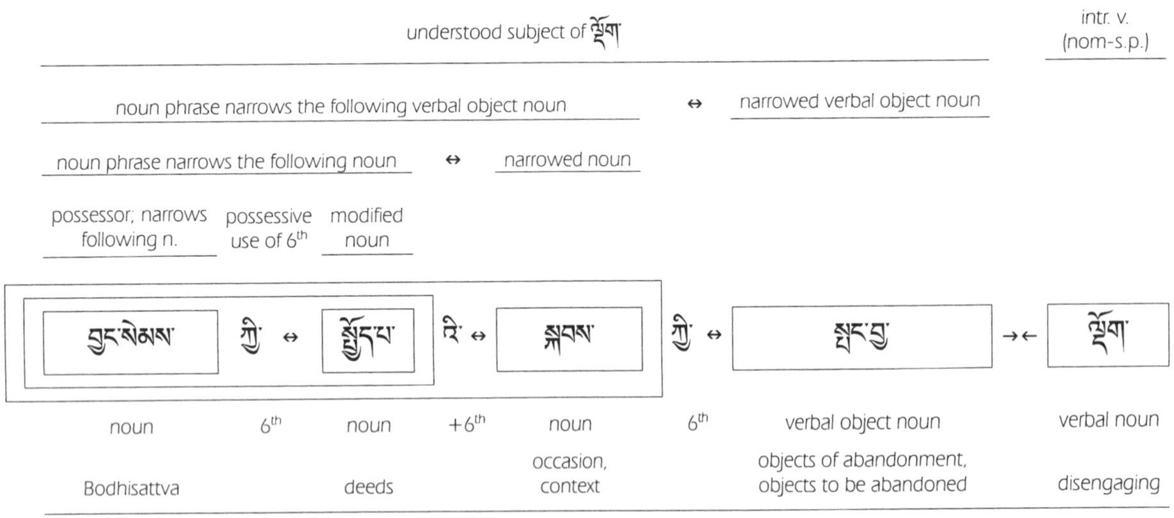

disengaging from objects of abandonment within the context of the Bodhisattva deeds

The syntax of བྱང་སེམས་ཀྱི་སྤྱོད་པའི་སྐབས་ཀྱི་བླང་བྱ་འཇུག

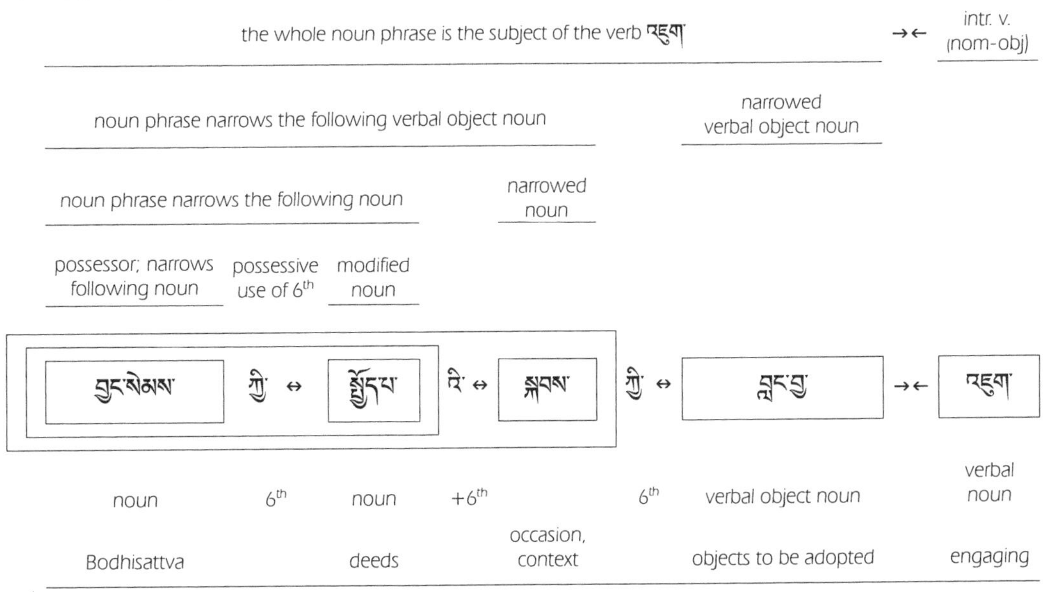

engaging in the objects to be adopted within the context of the Bodhisattva deeds

Understanding the implied terms of "C"

Here we have a pair of compound verbs. In compound verb phrases, the syntax of the sentence is governed by the first verb, not the second verb that acts as an auxiliary. The additional material (which I needed to make sense of this) comes from *The Four Interwoven Annotations.*

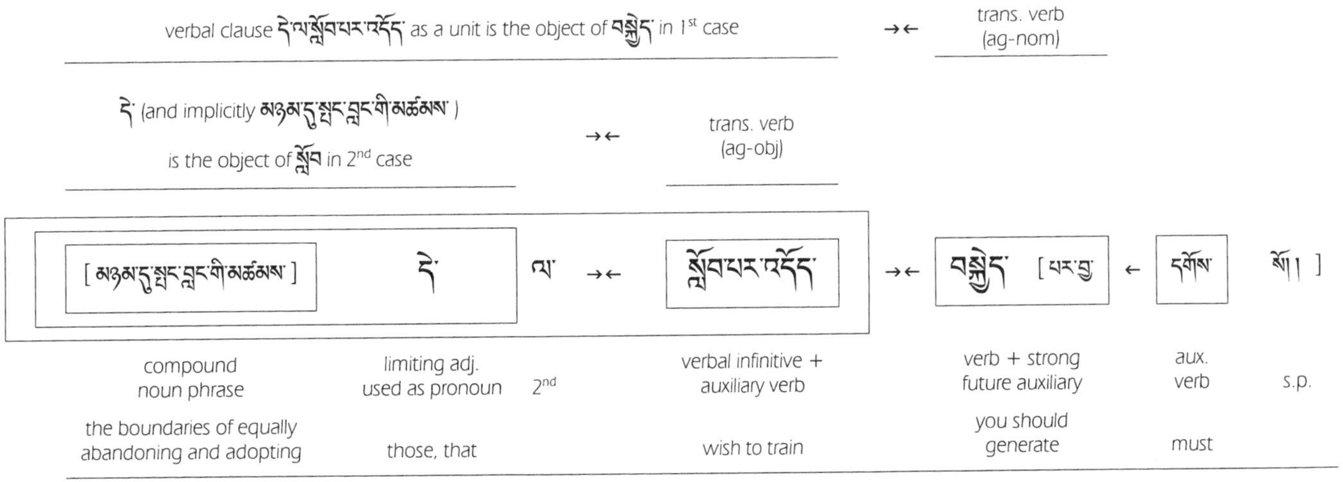

You must generate the wish to train in those [limits of abandonment and adoption equally].

Additional Glossary for "C"

[མཉམ་དུ་སྤང་བྱ་བླང་བྱ་གི་མཚམས་]དེ་ལ་	pronoun + 2nd case particle. དེ་ by itself here is a pronoun, but it is an adjective when used with the bracketed noun phrase. The antecedent of the relative pronoun དེ་ is མཉམ་དུ་སྤང་བྱ་བླང་བྱ་གི་མཚམས་
མཉམ་	adj., *equal, alike, similar, same*
མཉམ་དུ་	adj. + 2nd case particle creating an adverbial construction, *equally, together*
སྤང་བླང་	abbreviation for སྤང་བྱ་དང་བླང་བྱ་ *objects to be abandoned and objects to be taken up.*
སྤང་བྱ་ and བླང་བྱ་	verbal object nouns, *objects to be abandoned* and *objects to be taken up*. These are verbal object nouns., i.e., nouns formed by adding the strong future auxiliary to the future form of the verb. བྱ་ carries the sense of *the thing that is done*
སློབ་འདོད་	verb phrase (verbal infinitive + auxiliary); abbreviation for སློབ་པར་འདོད་ *the wish to train*
སློབ་པར་	verbal infinitive; here, the fused ར་ is a syntactic particle modifying a verb to create a verbal infinitive within the verb phrase སློབ་པར་འདོད་ *wish to train;* it is **not** a case particle marking the 2nd, 4th or 7th cases because it does not follow a noun—it is within a verb phrase
འདོད་	trans. v. (ag-nom), *wish, assert;* here, used as an auxiliary verb in a compound verb construction, it operates only on the first verb སློབ, and has no effect of the syntax of the preceding sentence
བསྐྱེད་པར་བྱ་དགོས།	verb phrase + auxiliary verb, *you must generate*
བསྐྱེད་པར་བྱ་	verb phrase (verbal infinitive + strong future auxiliary), *[you] should generate*
བསྐྱེད་པར་	verbal infinitive; here, the fused ར་ is a syntactic particle modifying a verb to create a verbal infinitive within the verb phrase བསྐྱེད་པར་བྱ་ *[I] will generate* or *[you] should generate;* it is **not** a case particle marking the 2nd, 4th or 7th cases because it does not follow a noun—it is within a verb phrase
སུ་རུ་ཏུ་དུ་ར་	are the five syntactic particles used to modify verbs to create infinitives within verb phrases
བྱ་	trans. v. (ag-nom) (future tense), *do, make, perform, take;* also, strong future auxiliary བྱེད་བྱས་བྱ་བྱོས། ཐ་དད།
དགོས་	intr. v. (b/p-nom), *be necessary, need, require.* In this construction དགོས་ is operating as an auxiliary verb དགོས་དགོས་དགོས། ཐ་མི་དད།

Part 3 • བློ་དེ་དག་སྐྱེས་པ་ན་འཇུག་པའི་སྡོམ་པ་ཆོ་གས་བཟུང་ལ།

Part 3 is a complete thought ending with a transitive verb and a continuative syntactic particle as punctuation. The basic syntax begins with a conditional clause, continues with the object of the transitive verb, and, immediately before the verb, a qualifier showing the means by which the action expressed by the verb is undertaken.

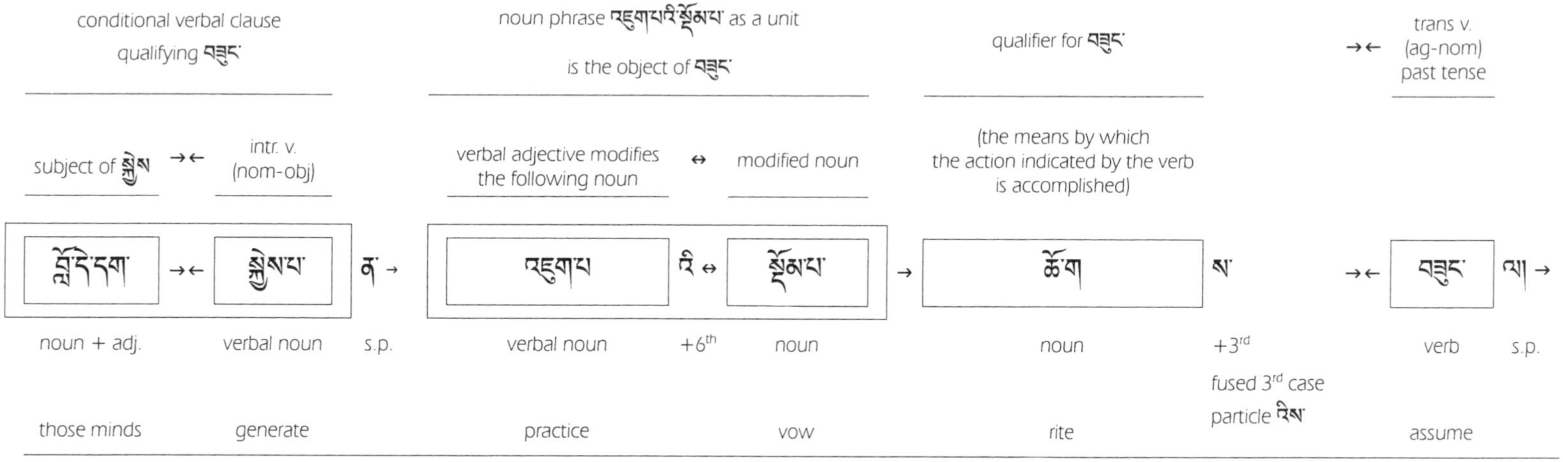

When you have generated those minds, take the vow of practice through the rite.

Glossary for Part 3

བློ་ n., *mind, awareness*

དེ་དག plural limiting adj. often used as pronoun, *those*

དག lexical pluralizing particle

སྐྱེས་ intr. v. (nom-obj) (past tense), *was born, arose, was created*

སྐྱེ་སྐྱེས་སྐྱེ། ཐ་མི་དད།

སྐྱེས་པ་ verbal noun derived from intransitive verb, *be produced*

སྐྱེས་པ་ན་ verbal noun + conditional syntactic particle marking a conditional clause

ན་ particle; either 1) a rhetorical syntactic particle marking a conditional clause following a verb or verb phrase, or 2) a case particle following nouns, pronouns, postpositions, and adjectives marking the 2nd, 4th and 7th cases

འཇུག intr. v. (nom-obj), *take (of a vow), enter, engage, apply*

འཇུག་འཚུག་གཞུག་ཚུག ཐ་མི་དད།

འཇུག trans. v. (ag-obj), causative in sense of *make something happen*

འཇུག་ཞུགས་འཇུག་ཞུགས། ཐ་དད།

འཇུག་པ་ verbal noun, *engaging, practice*

འཇུག་པའི་ verbal noun + 6th case particle fused to suffixless syllable

འི་ particle fused to suffixless final syllable; either 1) a syntactic particle following a verb or verb phrase signifying conjunction or disjunction, or 2) a 6th case particle following nouns, pronouns, postpositions, and adjectives

སྡོམ་ trans. v. (ag-nom), *vow* སྡོམ་བསྡམས་བསྡམ་སྡོམས། ཐ་དད།

སྡོམ་པ་ n., *vow*

འཇུག་སྡོམ་ compound n., *vow of practice*

ཆོ་ག། n., *rite*

ཆོ་གས་ n. + 3rd case particle fused to suffixless final syllable

ས་ abbreviation of the particle འིས་ (when འིས་ is fused to a suffixless final syllable, the འི goes away and all that's left is a fused ས་); either 1) syntactic particle creating an adverbial construction, 2) syntactic particle marking the qualifier of an intransitive nom-s.p. verb of absence, or 3) case particle marking the 3rd case

གིས་ཀྱིས་གྱིས་འིས་ཡིས་ five equivalent particles, marking the 3rd case and also marking syntactic adverbial relationships.

བཟུང་ trans. v. (ag-nom) (past tense), *grasp, apprehend, assume* འཛིན་བཟུང་གཟུང་ཟུངས། ཐ་དད།

བཟུང་ལ། verb + conjunctive syntactic particle ending what, in translation, is a sentence

ལ་ particle; either 1) a syntactic particle following a verb or verb phrase signifying conjunction or disjunction, or 2) a case particle following nouns, pronouns, postpositions, and adjectives marking the 2nd, 4th and 7th cases

Notes on Part 3

བློ་དེ་དག་སྐྱེས་པ་ན་ a conditional clause ending with the conditional syntactic particle ན་, *when those have been generated.* The construction is noteworthy because the verb སྐྱེས་ is appearing in the nominalized form སྐྱེས་པ་ This is unusual. Normally, སྐྱེས་ན་ is a verbal construction and སྐྱེས་པ་ན་ is a verbal noun + 2nd, 4th, or 7th case particle

སྐྱེས་ན་ intr. verb + conditional syntactic particle, *when you have generated ...*

སྐྱེས་པ་ན་ verbal noun + 2nd, 4th, or 7th case particle *at the time of generation*

འཇུག་པའི་སྡོམ་པ་ noun phrase (verbal adjective + 6th case particle + noun) *the vow of practice;* this noun phrase as a unit is the object of the transitive verb བཟུང་

ཆོ་གས་བཟུང་ verb phrase (qualifier showing the means by which some action is undertaken + fused 3rd case particle + verb), *assume [it] by means of the rite.*,

ཆོ་གས་ noun ཆོ་ག་ plus the 3rd case particle འིས་ abbreviated to ས་ when fused to the suffixless syllable ག།

ས་ abbreviation of the particle འིས་ (when འིས་ is fused to a suffixless final syllable, the འི goes away and all that's left is a fused ས་); either 1) syntactic particle creating an adverbial construction, 2) syntactic particle marking the qualifier of an intransitive nom-s.p. verb of absence, or 3) case particle marking the 3rd case

གིས་ཀྱིས་གྱིས་འིས་ཡིས་ five equivalent particles, marking the 3rd case, qualifiers of verbs of absence, and also marking syntactic adverbial relationships.

བློ་དེ་དག་སྐྱེས་པ་ན་འཇུག་པའི་སྡོམ་པ་ཆོ་གས་བཟུང་ལ། this sentence ends with the syntactic particle ལ་ following the main verb of the sentence བཟུང་ *assume*

ལ་ particle; either 1) a syntactic particle following a verb or verb phrase signifying conjunction or disjunction, or 2) a case particle following nouns, pronouns, postpositions, and adjectives marking the 2nd, 4th and 7th cases

Part 4 • རང་རྒྱུད་སྨིན་པར་བྱེད་པའི་ཕྱིན་དྲུག་དང་གཞན་རྒྱུད་སྨིན་བྱེད་ཀྱི་བསྡུ་བ་བཞི་སོགས་ལ་བསླབ།

Part 4 is essentially "Train in A, B and so forth."

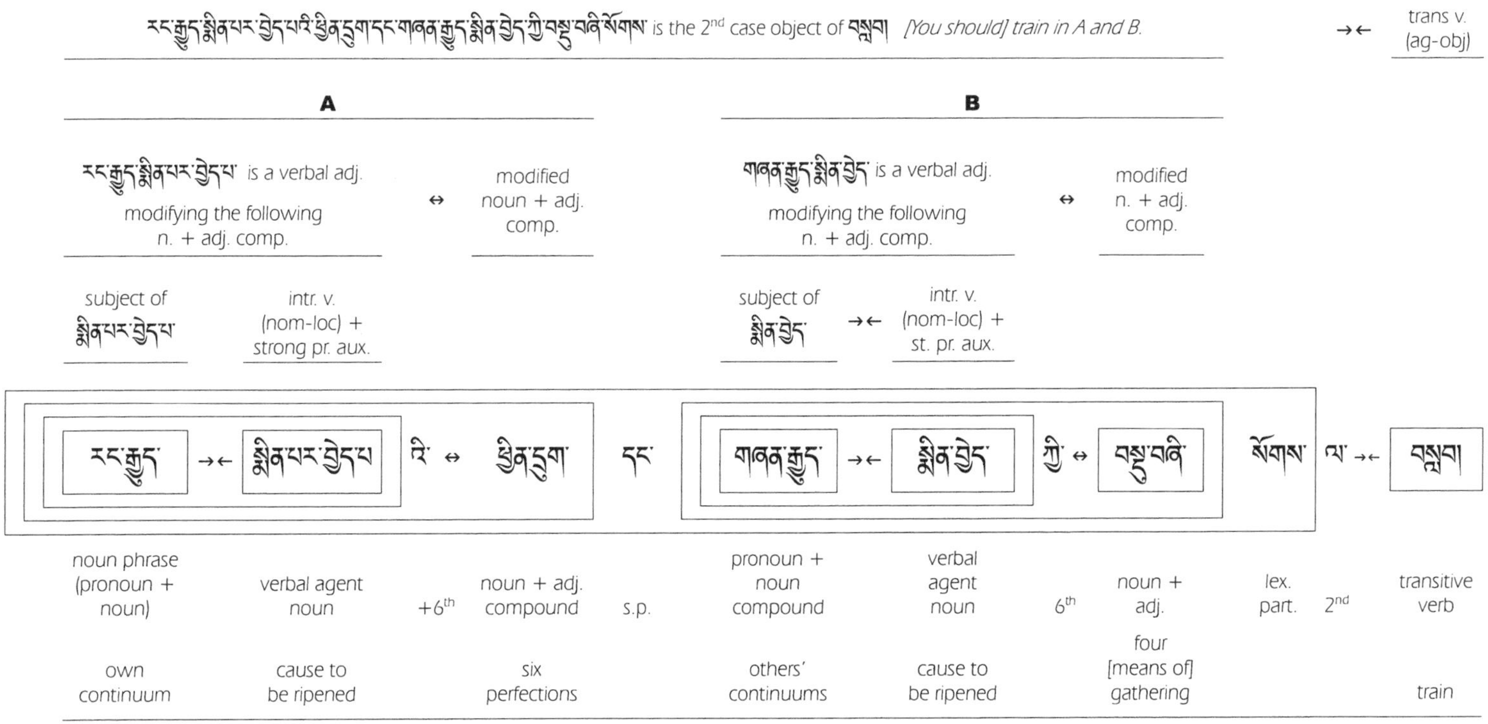

[You should] train in the six perfections which ripen your own continuum and in the four [means of] gathering [trainees] and so forth which ripen others' continuums.

Glossary for Part 4

རང་	reflexive pronoun, *itself, oneself, yourself*
རྒྱུད་	n., *continuum*
རང་རྒྱུད་	noun phrase, abbreviation for རང་གི་རྒྱུད་
རང་གི་	pronoun + 6th case particle here indicating possession
གི་	particle; either 1) a syntactic particle following a verb or verb phrase signifying conjunction or disjunction, or 2) a 6th case particle following nouns, pronouns, postpositions, and adjectives
རང་གི་རྒྱུད་	noun phrase (pronoun + 6th case particle + noun), *one's own continuum*
སྨིན་	intr. v. (nom-loc), *be ripened* སྨིན་སྨིན་སྨིན། ཐ་མི་དད།
སྨིན་པ་	verbal noun, *ripen*
སྨིན་པར་བྱེད་	verb phrase (verbal infinitive + strong present auxiliary), *ripener.* When the strong auxiliary is used with an intransitive verb, it conveys a causative sense, i.e., *causes [others' continuums] to be ripened*

སྨིན་པར་	verbal infinitive; here, the fused ར་ is a syntactic particle modifying a verb to create a verbal infinitive within the verb phrase སྨིན་པར་བྱེད་ *ripener;* it is **not** a case particle marking the 2nd, 4th or 7th cases because it does not follow a noun—it is within a verb phrase
བྱེད་	trans. v. (ag-nom) (present tense), *do, make, perform, take;* also strong present auxiliary བྱེད་བྱས་བྱ་བྱོས། ཐ་དད།
སྨིན་པར་བྱེད་པ་	verbal agent noun, *ripener;* abbreviated as སྨིན་བྱེད་
སྨིན་པར་བྱེད་པའི་	verbal + 6th case particle is here a verbal adjective
འི་	particle fused to suffixless final syllable; either 1) a syntactic particle following a verb or verb phrase signifying conjunction or disjunction, or 2) a 6th case particle following nouns, pronouns, postpositions, and adjectives
ཕྱིན་	intr. v. (nom-obj) (past tense), *went* འགྲོ་ཕྱིན་འགྲོ་སོང་། ཐ་མི་དད། སོང་ is also an alternate past form
ཕྱིན་དྲུག་	n. + adj. compound: *the six perfections*
དང་	particle; used three ways: 1) continuative syntactic particle used following nouns and noun phrases (*and,* or with negative verb, *or*); 2) syntactic particle marking the qualifier of an intr. nom-s.p. v. of conjunction, as in ང་རང་མི་སྡུག་པ་དང་ཕྲད་ན་ *if we meet with unpleasantness;* and 3) syntactic particle marking the qualifier of an intr. nom-s.p. v. of disjunction, as in རྟོག་པ་དང་བྲལ་ *free from conceptuality*
གཞན་	n., adj., *other, the other one*
རྒྱུད་	n., *continuum*
གཞན་རྒྱུད་	noun phrase (n. + implied 6th case particle + n.), *others' continuums*
གཞན་གྱི་རྒྱུད་	noun phrase (n. + 6th case particle + n.), *others' continuums*
སྨིན་	intr. v. (nom-loc), *be ripened* སྨིན་སྨིན་སྨིན། ཐ་མི་དད།
སྨིན་བྱེད་	verb phrase (v. + aux), *cause to be ripened;* abbreviation for སྨིན་པར་བྱེད་པ་
སྨིན་པར་བྱེད་	verb phrase (verbal infinitive + strong present auxiliary), *ripener*
སྨིན་པར་	verbal infinitive; here, the fused ར་ is a syntactic particle modifying a verb to create a verbal infinitive within the verb phrase སྨིན་པར་བྱེད་ *ripener;* it is **not** a case particle marking the 2nd, 4th or 7th cases because it does not follow a noun—it is within a verb phrase
བྱེད་	trans. v. (ag-nom) (present tense), *do, make, perform, take;* also strong present auxiliary
སྨིན་བྱེད་ཀྱི་	verbal noun + 6th case particle. The 4-syllable verbal noun སྨིན་པར་བྱེད་པ་ is abbreviated by eliminating the 2nd and 4th syllables
ཀྱི་	particle; either 1) a syntactic particle following a verb or verb phrase signifying conjunction or disjunction, or 2) a 6th case particle following nouns, pronouns, postpositions, and adjectives
བསྡུ་	trans. v. (ag-nom), *gather, collect* སྡུད་བསྡུས་བསྡུ་སྡུས། ཐ་དད།
འདུས་	intr. v. (nom-obj), *be gathered, be included* འདུད་འདུས་འདུ་འདུས། ཐ་མི་དད།
བསྡུ་བ་	n., *collection*
བསྡུ་བཞི་	noun phrase (n. + adj.), *the four means of gathering [students]:*
བསྡུ་བཞི་སོགས་	noun phrase + generalizing suffix particle, *the four means of gathering [students] and so forth*
སོགས་	s.p., generalizing suffix particle, *and so forth, etc.*
སོགས་	this particle indicates absent members of a known list, as in the phrase "the presidents of the United States, Washington, Jefferson, and so forth." Whereas in English "and so forth" often is used when we can't think of anything else but want to cover ourselves against a later criticism of underinclusion, སོགས་ refers to a specific list with specific members.
བསྡུ་བཞི་སོགས་ལ་	noun phrase (n. + adj.) + 2nd case particle
ལ་	particle; either 1) a syntactic particle following a verb or verb phrase signifying conjunction or disjunction, or 2) a case particle following nouns, pronouns, postpositions, and adjectives marking the 2nd, 4th and 7th cases
བསླབ་	trans. v. (ag-obj), *train* སློབ་བསླབས་བསླབ་སློབས། ཐ་དད།

Grammar review • Use of strong auxiliaries with intransitive verbs

སྨིན་ intr. v. (nom-loc), *be ripened* སྨིན་སྨིན་སྨིན། ཐ་མི་དད།

སྨིན་པར་བྱེད་ verb phrase (verbal infinitive + strong present auxiliary), *causes to ripen, brings about ripening.* When the strong auxiliaries བྱེད་, བྱས་ and བྱ་ are used with an intransitive verb, they convey a causative sense. Used here with the present tense, the four means of gathering trainees *causes others' continuums to be ripened*

སྨིན་པར་བྱས་ verb phrase (verbal infinitive + strong past auxiliary), *caused to ripened, brought about ripening*

སྨིན་པར་བྱ་ verb phrase (verbal infinitive + strong future auxiliary), *will cause to be ripened, should cause to be ripened*

Additional vocabulary for Part 4: the six perfections and the four means of gathering students

ཕྱིན་དྲུག n. + adj., *the six perfections:*

སྦྱིན་པ་ n., *generosity*

ཚུལ་ཁྲིམས་ n., *ethics*

བཟོད་པ་ n., *patience*

བརྩོན་འགྲུས་ n., *effort*

བསམ་གཏན་ n., *concentration*

ཤེས་རབ་ n., *wisdom*

བསྡུ་བཞི་སོགས་ noun phrase, *the four methods for gathering [students] and so forth*

བསྡུ་བའི་དངོས་པོ་བཞི་ noun phrase, *the four methods for gathering students*

མཁོ་བ་སྦྱིན་པ། *giving whatever is necessary;*

སྙན་པར་སྨྲ་བ། *speaking pleasantly* (this means speaking about the paths leading to high status and definite goodness);

དོན་མཐུན་པ། *purposeful behavior* (this means causing others to practice what is beneficial) and

དོན་སྤྱོད་པ། *concordant behavior* (this means to oneself practice what you recommend to others).

Grammar review • Verb, verbal noun, verbal agent noun, and verbal object noun forms contrasted using the transitive verb བསྐྱེད་

བསྐྱེད་ trans. v. (ag-nom), *produce, generate, create, give birth to*

སྐྱེད་བསྐྱེད་བསྐྱེད་སྐྱེད། ཐ་དད།

བསྐྱེད་པ་ verbal noun, *production, product*

སྐྱེད་བྱེད་ verbal agent noun, *producer*

བསྐྱེད་བྱ་ verbal object noun, *object produced*

Part 5 is supplemented with additions from *The Four Interwoven Annotations.*

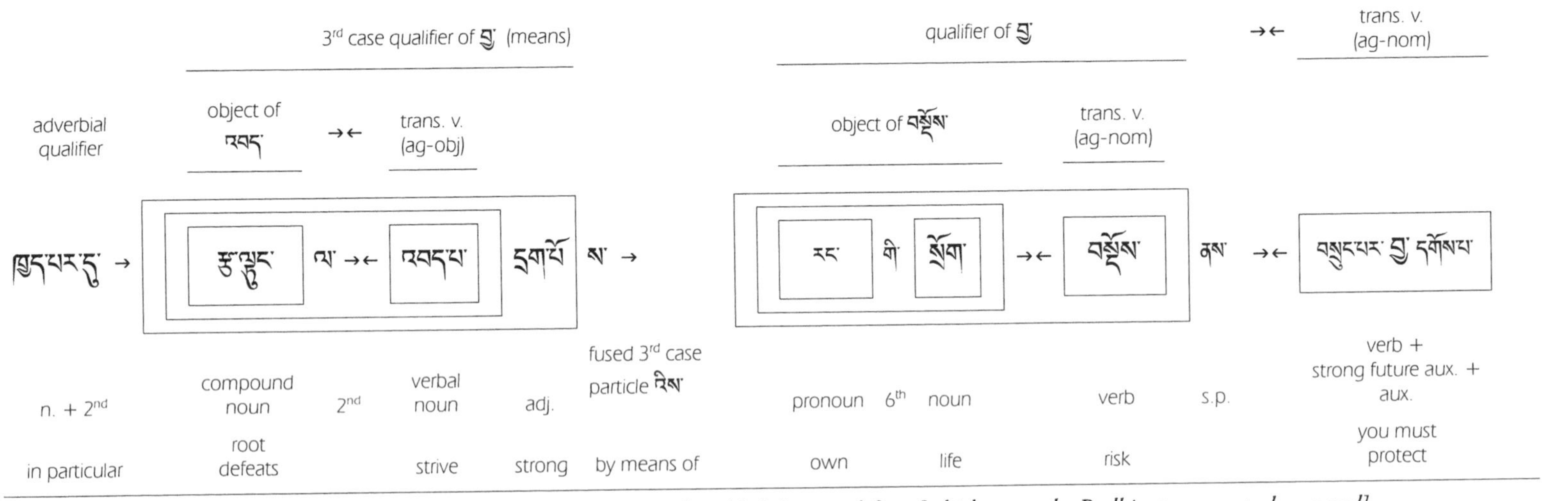

In particular, through strong striving at [not being polluted by] the root defeats [which cause the Bodhisattva vow to be severed], you should [protect your vows] through risking [even] your life.

Glossary for Part 5

ཁྱད་པར་ — n. and adv.; as noun, *attribute, feature, qualification, difference;* as adverb, *in particular, especially*

ཁྱད་པར་དུ་ — n. + 2nd case particle here creates an adverb, *in particular*

རྩ་བ་ — n., adj., *root, main, principal*

ལྟུང་ — intr. v. (nom-obj), *fall*

ལྟུང་ལྟུངས་ལྟུང་། ཐ་མི་དད།

རྩ་ལྟུང་ — compound n., *root downfalls*

རྩ་ལྟུང་བཅོ་བརྒྱད་ལ་ — noun phrase + 2nd case particle (marking the object of the transitive verb འབད་ *strive at, work at), the eighteen root downfalls*

ལ་ — particle; either 1) a syntactic particle following a verb or verb phrase signifying conjunction or disjunction, or 2) a case particle following nouns, pronouns, postpositions, and adjectives marking the 2nd, 4th and 7th cases

འབད་ — trans. v. (ag-obj), *strive*

འབད་འབད་འབད་འབོད། ཐ་དད།

འབད་པ་ — verbal noun, *striving*

དྲག་པོ་ — adj., *strong*

དྲག་པོས་ — adj. + 3rd case particle fused to suffixless final syllable

སྲོག་ — n., *life*

བསྐྱོས་ trans. v. (ag-nom), *risk*

སྐྱོ་བསྐྱོས་བསྐྱོ་སྐྱོས། ཐ་དད།

བསྐྱོས་བྱ་ verb phrase, *[I] will risk* or *[you] should risk;* abbreviation for སྐྱོས་པར་བྱ་

བསྐྱོས་པར་བྱ་ verb phrase (verbal infinitive + strong future auxiliary), *[I] will risk* or *[you] should risk*

བསྐྱོས་པར་ verbal infinitive; here, the fused ར་ is a syntactic particle modifying a verb to create a verbal infinitive within the verb phrase བསྐྱོས་པར་བྱ་ *[I] will risk* or *[you] should risk;* it is **not** a case particle marking the 2nd, 4th or 7th cases because it does not follow a noun—it is within a verb phrase

སུ་རུ་ཏུ་དུ་ར་ are the five syntactic particles used to modify verbs to create infinitives within verb phrases

བྱ་ trans. v. (ag-nom) (future), *do, make, perform, take;* also the strong future auxiliary

བྱེད་བྱས་བྱ་བྱོས། ཐ་དད།

བསྲུང་ trans. v. (ag-nom) (future tense), *protect, safeguard, maintain*

སྲུང་བསྲུངས་བསྲུང་སྲུངས། ཐ་དད།

བསྲུང་བར་བྱ་ verb phrase (verbal infinitive + strong future auxiliary), *you should protect, you should safeguard*

བསྲུང་བར་བྱ་དགོས་པ་ verb phrase (verbal infinitive + strong future auxiliary + auxiliary), *you must protect.* This is a very strong verb form.

Notes on Part 5

རྩ་ལྟུང་ལ་འབད་ འབད་ is a transitive agentive-objective verb; its object is the noun phrase རྩ་ལྟུང་ *root downfalls,* marked with the 2nd case particle

རྩ་ལྟུང་ལ་འབད་པ་དྲག་པོས་ the verbal noun + adj. compound རྩ་ལྟུང་ལ་འབད་པ་དྲག་པོ་ is declined as a unit in the 3rd case.

དྲག་པོས་ is the adjective དྲག་པོ་ plus the 3rd case ending ཡིས་, abbreviated to ས་ when fused to the suffixless syllable པོ་

ས་ abbreviation of the particle ཡིས་ (when ཡིས་ is fused to a suffixless final syllable, the ཡི goes away and all that's left is a fused ས་); either 1) syntactic particle creating an adverbial construction, 2) syntactic particle marking the qualifier of an intransitive nom-s.p. verb of absence, or 3) case particle marking the 3rd case

སྲོག་བསྐྱོས་བྱ། སྲོག་ is the object of བསྐྱོས་བྱ། བསྐྱོས་བྱ་ is an abbreviation for བསྐྱོས་པར་བྱ

བསྐྱོས་པར་བྱ་ verb phrase (verbal infinitive + strong future auxiliary), *[I] will isk* or *[you] should risk*

བསྐྱོས་པར་ verbal infinitive; here, the fused ར་ is a syntactic particle modifying a verb to create a verbal infinitive within the verb phrase བསྐྱོས་པར་བྱ་ *[I] will protect* or *[you] should risk;* it is **not** a case particle marking the 2nd, 4th or 7th cases because it does not follow a noun—it is within a verb phrase

སུ་རུ་ཏུ་དུ་ར་ are the five syntactic particles used to modify verbs to create infinitives within verb phrases

བྱ་ trans. v. (ag-nom) (future), *do, make, perform, take;* also the strong future auxiliary

Part 6 • ཟག་པ་ཆུང་འབྲིང་དང་ཉེས་བྱས་རྣམས་ཀྱིས་མ་གོས་པ་ལ་འབད་ཅིང་གོས་ན་འང་ཕྱིར་འཆོས་པ་ལ་འབད་དོ།

Part 6 is a compound sentence: "Strive at not being polluted by X, but if you are polluted by X, strive at Y."

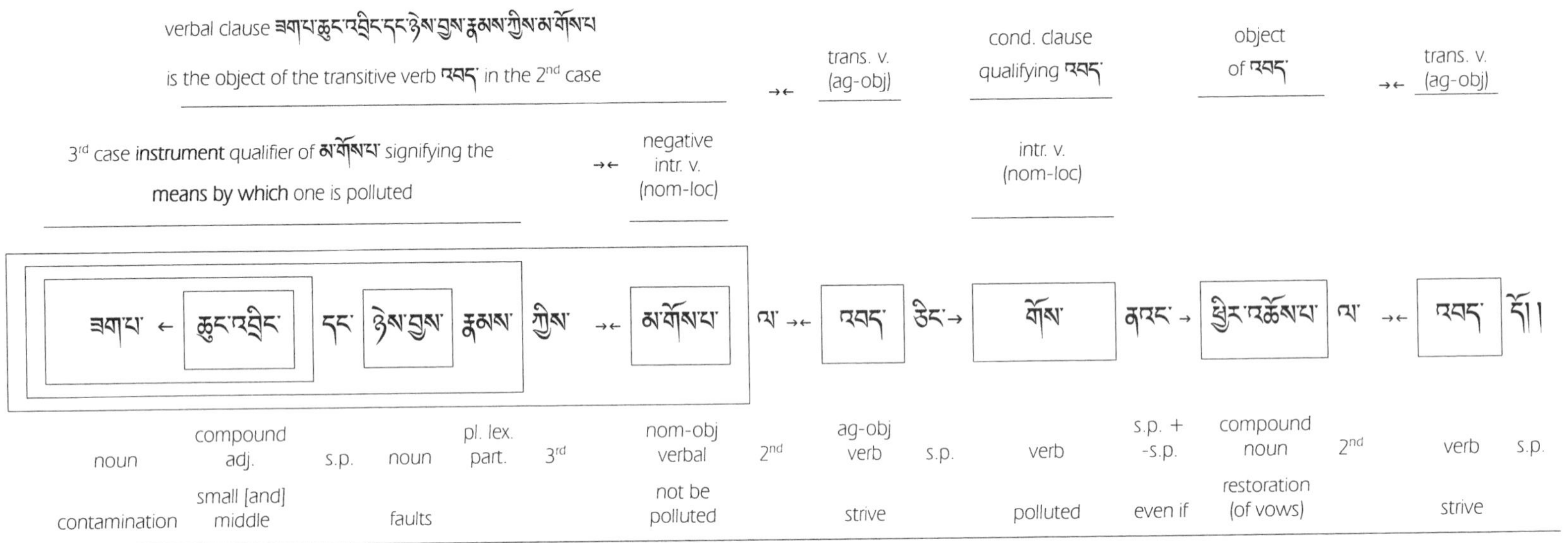

Strive at not being polluted by the lesser and middle contaminations or faults; even if polluted by such, work at restoration.

Glossary for Part 6

ཟག་པ་ n., *contamination*

ཆུང་དུ་ n. and adj., *small*

འབྲིང་ n. and adj., *middle*

དང་ particle; used three ways: 1) continuative syntactic particle used following nouns and noun phrases (*and*, or with negative verb, *or*); 2) syntactic particle marking the qualifier of an intr. nom-s.p. v. of conjunction, as in ང་རང་མི་སྡུག་པ་དང་ཕྲད་ན་ *if we meet with unpleasantness;* and 3) syntactic particle marking the qualifier of an intr. nom-s.p. v. of disjunction, as in རྟོག་པ་དང་བྲལ་ *free from conceptuality*

ཉེས་བྱས་ comp. n., the [46] *secondary faults*

ཉེས་བྱས་བཞི་བཅུ་ཞེ་དྲུག comp. n. + adj., *forty-six secondary faults*

བཞི་ n., adj., *four*

བཅུ་ n., adj., *ten*

བཞི་བཅུ་ཞེ་དྲུག n., adj., *forty-six*

དྲུག n., adj., *six*

ཉེས་བྱས་རྣམས་ comp. n. + pluralizing lexical particle

རྣམས་ optional pluralizing suffix particle

ཉེས་བྱས་རྣམས་ཀྱིས་ comp. n. + pluralizing lexical particle + 3rd case particle

ཟག་པ་ཆུང་འབྲིང་དང་ཉེས་བྱས་རྣམས་ཀྱིས་ — 3rd case **instrument** qualifier of མ་གོས་པ་ signifying the **means by which** one is polluted. It is not the agent of མ་གོས་པ་ because མ་གོས་པ་ is an intransitive verb.

ཀྱིས་ — either a syntactic particle creating an adverbial construction, 2) a syntactic particle marking the qualifier of an intransitive nom- s.p. verb of absence, or 3) case particle marking the 3rd case

མ་གོས་ — negative intr. v. (nom-loc), *not be polluted*

མ་ — negative lexical prefix particle

མ་མི་ — negative lexical prefix particles that precede the word they negate

མིན་མེད་ — negative lexical suffix particles that follow the word they negate

གོས་ — intr. v. (nom-loc), *be polluted*

གོས་གོས་གོས། ཐ་མི་དད་

གོས་པ་ — n., *pollution*

གོས་པ་ལ་ — verbal noun + 2nd case particle marking the object of the transitive verb འབད་ *strive at, work at*

ལ་ — particle; either 1) a syntactic particle following a verb or verb phrase signifying conjunction or disjunction, or 2) a case particle following nouns, pronouns, postpositions, and adjectives marking the 2nd, 4th and 7th cases

འབད་ — trans. v. (ag-obj), *strive to, strive at, make effort in*

འབད་འབད་འབད་འབོད། ཐ་དད།

འབད་ཅིང་ — verb + continuative syntactic particle

མ་གོས་པ་ལ་འབད་ཅིང་ — the syntactic particle ཅིང་ marks the end of the first clause of this compound sentence.

ཅིང་ — follows words ending with the letters ག་ད་བ་ and with the secondary suffix ད་ (which is invisible)

ཞིང་ — follows words ending with the letters ང་ན་མ་འ་ར་ལ་ and with suffixless final syllables

ཤིང་ — follows words with ས་ and with the secondary suffix ས་

གོས་པ་ — verbal noun, *polluted, pollution*

གོས་པ་ནའང་ — verbal noun + conditional syntactic particle + a second syntactic particle fused to a suffixless syllable

ནའང་ — 2 fused s.p. = ན་ + འང་ *even if...*

ན་ — particle; either syntactic particle (following a verb) or case particle (following a noun) marking the 2nd, 4th and 7th cases; here: conditional s.p., *if*

ཀྱང་ཡང་འང་ — are equivalent conjunctive and disjunctive syntactic particles used after nouns, pronouns, adjectives, verbs, and verb phrases, *but, even, also*

ཀྱང་ — follows words ending with the letters ག་ད་བ་ས་

ཡང་ — follows words ending with the letters ང་ན་མ་འ་ར་ལ་ and after suffixless words

འང་ — follows suffixless words

ཕྱིར་ — adverb, *again, back*

ཕྱིར་ — postposition indicating intention, *for the sake of, for the purpose of, because*

ཕྱིར་འཆོས་པ་ — noun (internally, a verbal noun phrase), *restoration [of vows through confession of transgressed vows ceremony]*

འཆོས་ — trans. v. (ag-nom), *fabricate, make up* འཆོས་བཅོས་བཅོས་ཆོས། ཐ་དད།

ཕྱིར་འཆོས་པ་ལ་ — verbal noun + 2nd case particle marking the object of the transitive verb འབད་ *work at, strive at*

འབད་ — trans. v. (ag-obj), *strive to, strive at, make effort in*

འབད་འབད་འབད་འབོད། ཐ་དད།

འབད་དོ།། — final verb + terminating s.p. དོ་ following word ending with the suffix letter ད་

དོ་ — terminating s.p. དོ་ following word ending with the suffix letter ད་

Chapter Six Self Test

Write out the passage, boxing and identifying every syntactic element.

དེ་ནས་བྱང་སེམས་ཀྱི་སྤྱོད་པ་རླབས་ཆེ་བ་རྣམས་མཉན་ལ། ལྡོག་འཇུག་གི་མཚམས་རྣམས་ཤེས་པ་དང་དེ་ལ་སློབ་འདོད་དྲག་པོ་བསྐྱེད། བློ་དེ་དག་སྐྱེས་པ་ན་འཇུག་པའི་སྡོམ་པ་ཆོ་གས་བཟུང་ལ། རང་རྒྱུད་སྨིན་པར་བྱེད་པའི་ཕྱིན་དྲུག་དང་གཞན་རྒྱུད་སྨིན་བྱེད་ཀྱི་བསྡུ་བཞི་སོགས་ལ་བསླབ། ཁྱད་པར་དུ་རྩ་ལྟུང་ལ་འབད་པ་དྲག་པོས་སྲོག་བསྔོས་བྱ། ཟག་པ་ཆུང་འབྲིང་དང་ཉེས་བྱས་རྣམས་ཀྱིས་མ་གོས་པ་ལ་འབད་ཅིང་གོས་ན་འང་ཕྱིར་འཆོས་པ་ལ་འབད་དོ། །

Vocabulary

For each word, can you identify what part of speech it is (noun, pronoun, adjective, verb, adverb, postposition) and what it means?
For each syntactic particle, can you identify what class of syntactic particle it belongs to and how it is used?

རྩ་ལྟུང་བཅོ་བརྒྱད་	ལྟུང་	བྱང་ཆུབ་ཀྱི་སེམས་	རང་རྒྱུད་
རྩ་ལྟུང་	རྒྱུད་	བྱ་	རང་གི་རྒྱུད་
རྩ་བ་	རྣམས་	ཕྱིར་འཆོས་པ་	རང་གི་
སྤྱོད་པ་	སློབ་འདོད་དྲག་པོ་	ཕྱིན་དྲུག་	རང་
སྦྱིན་པ་	སློབ་འདོད་	ཁྱད་པར་	ཡང་
སྐྱེས་པ་	སློབ་པར་འདོད་	ཀྱིས་	འི་
སྐྱེས་	སློབ་	ཀྱི་	འབྲིང་
སྨིན་བྱེད་	རླབས་ཆེ་བ་	ཀྱང་ཡང་འང་	འབད་པ་
སྨིན་པར་བྱེད་པ་	རླབས་	སོགས་	འབད་
སྨིན་པ་	བློ་	ས་	འདུས་
སྨིན་	སྲོག་	ཤེས་རབ་	འདོད་
སྡོམ་པ་	དྲུག་	ཤེས་པ་	འཇུག་སྡོམ་
སྡོམ་	དྲག་པོ་	ཤིང་	འཇུག་པ་
ལྡོག་འཇུག་	བྱེད་	ཞིག་	འཆོས་
ལྡོག་	བྱང་སེམས་	ལ་	འང་

ཟག་པ་	བསྔོས་པར་བྱ་	བཅོ་བརྒྱད་	ཆུང་ངུ་
ཞིང་	བསྔོས་	བཅུ་	ཅིང་
ཚུལ་ཁྲིམས་	བསྡུ་བའི་	ནའང་	གོས་པ་
མེད་	བསྡུ་བ་	ན་	གོས་
མིན་	བསྡུ་	དོ་	གི་
མཚམས་	བསླབ་	དེ་དག་	གཞན་རྒྱུད་
མཉན་	བསམ་གཏན་	དེ་	གཞན་གྱི་རྒྱུད་
མཁོ་པ་སྦྱིན་པ།	བཟོད་པ་	དང་	གཞན་
བརྩོན་འགྲུས་	བཟུང་	ཉེས་བྱས་	དེ་ནས་
བསྐྱེད་	བཞི་བཅུ་ཞེ་དྲུག་	ཚོག་	
བསྔོས་བྱ་	བཞི་	ཆེ་བ་	

Translation of Tsong-kha-pa's text

དེ་ནས་བྱང་སེམས་ཀྱི་སྤྱོད་པ་རླབས་ཆེ་བ་རྣམས་མཉན་ལ། ལྡོག་འཇུག་གི་མཚམས་རྣམས་ཤེས་པ་དང་དེ་ལ་སློབ་འདོད་དྲག་པོ་བསྐྱེད། བློ་དེ་དག་སྐྱེས་པ་ན་འཇུག་པའི་སྡོམ་པ་ཆོ་གས་བཟུང་ལ། རང་རྒྱུད་སྨིན་པར་བྱེད་པའི་ཕྱིན་དྲུག་དང་གཞན་རྒྱུད་སྨིན་བྱེད་ཀྱི་བསྡུ་བཞི་སོགས་ལ་བསླབ། ཁྱད་པར་དུ་རྩ་ལྟུང་ལ་འབད་པ་དགོས་སྲོག་བསྔོས་བྱ། ཟག་པ་ཆུང་འབྲིང་དང་ཉེས་བྱས་རྣམས་ཀྱིས་མ་གོས་པ་ལ་འབད་ཅིང་གོས་ནའང་ཕྱིར་འཆོས་པ་ལ་འབད་དོ། །

Then, hear about the great waves of Bodhisattva deeds and generate understanding of the boundaries of engagement and disengagement as well as a wish to train in them. When that mind is generated, take the vow of practice through the rite. Train in the six perfections which ripen your own continuum and in the four means of gathering [trainees] and so forth which ripen others' continuums. In particular, risk even your life [to keep] from the root infractions. Strive at not being polluted by the lesser and middle contaminations or faults; even if polluted by such, work at restoration.

Annotations for Tsong-kha-pa's text in Chapter Six

Here is Tsong-kha-pa's text as supplemented by *The Four Interwoven Annotations,* 831.3-832.2

སྨོན་སེམས་བརྟན་པར་བྱས་པ་ དེ་ནས་ དེའི་རྗེས་སུ་ བྱང་སེམས་ཀྱི་སྤྱོད་པ་རླབས་ཆེ་བ་རྣམས་ སྟོན་པའི་མདོ་དང་དགོངས་འགྲེལ་མན་ངག་སོགས་རང་གིས་ མཉན་པར་བྱས་ ལ། བྱང་སེམས་ཀྱི་སྤྱོད་པའི་སྐབས་ཀྱི་སྤང་བྱ་ ལྡོག་ པ་དང་བླང་བྱ་ འཇུག་ པའི་ཚུལ་དག་ གི་མཚམས་རྣམས་ མ་འདྲེས་པར་ཚུལ་བཞིན་དུ་ཤེས་པར་བྱས་ནས་ དེ་དག་ལེགས་པར་ ཤེས་པ་དང་ མཉམ་དུ་སྤང་བླང་གི་མཚམས་ དེ་ དག་ ལ་སློབ་འདོད་དྲག་པོ་བསྐྱེད་ པར་བྱ་དགོས་སོ། །བླང་དོར་གྱི་ བློ་དེ་དག་ ལེགས་པར་སྐྱེས་པ་ འི་ཚེ་ ན་ རྒྱལ་སྲས་ཀྱི་སྤྱོད་པ་ལ་འཇུག་པའི་ འཇུག་ སེམས་བསྐྱེད་ པའི་སྡོམ་པ་ཆོ་ག འི་སྒོ་ན་ ས་བཟུང་ པར་བྱས་ ལ། རང་རྒྱུད་སྨིན་པར་བྱེད་པའི་ཕ་རོལ་ཏུ་ ཕྱིན་ པ་ དྲུག་ གི་སྤྱོད་པ་ དང་གཞན་རྒྱུད་སྨིན་བྱེད་ཀྱི་བསྡུ་ བའི་དངོས་པོ་ བཞི་སོགས་ བྱང་སེམས་ཀྱི་འཇུག་སྡོམ་གྱི་བསླབ་བྱའི་གནས་ཐམས་ཅད་ ལ་བསླབ་ པར་བྱ་དགོས་ཤིང་། ཁྱད་པར་དུ་ ཡང་བྱང་སེམས་ཀྱི་སྡོམ་པ་གཏོང་བའི་ རྩ་ལྟུང་ལ་ སྒོ་ཐམས་ཅད་ནས་ འབད་པ་དྲག་པོས་ རང་གི་ སྲོག་ དང་ བསྡོས་ནས་བསྲུང་བར་ བྱ་ དགོས་པ་ཡིན། རྩ་ལྟུང་གི་འོག་མ་ ཟག་པ་ཆུང་འབྲིང་ རྣམས་ དང་ཉེས་བྱས་ གཞན་ རྣམས་ཀྱིས་ ཀྱང་ཅི་ནས་ མ་གོས་པ་ལ་འབད་ཅིང་གལ་ཏེ་ཉོན་མོངས་མང་བ་སོགས་ཀྱིས་རང་དབང་མེད་པར་ གོས་ན་འང་། ཡུ་ཚོམ་དུ་མི་འཇུག་པར་ ཕྱིར་འཆོས་པ་ལ་ ཅི་ནས་ཀྱང་ འབད་དོ། །

Translation of Tsong-kha-pa's text with annotations, 831.3-832.2

After you have made that aspirational altruistic intention stable, you should listen to [i.e., study] the great waves of the deeds of Bodhisattvas: the Teacher's sutras, commentaries on his thought, and quintessential instructions, etc. You need to understand properly, without mixing them up, what are the boundaries of what is to be discarded and what is to be adopted in the context of the Bodhisattva deeds, and you need to generate the strong wish to train equally in those boundaries of abandoning and adopting.

When you have properly generated those attitudes of adopting and discarding, you should take by the rite the practical altruistic intention vow of practice to engage in the deeds of Conqueror's children. You must train in all the precepts of the practical altruistic intention to enlightenment: the deeds of the six perfections which ripen your own continuum and the four methods for gathering students which ripen others' continuums, and so forth—for all the precepts of the Bodhisattva practice vow. You should risk even your life [to protect them]. In particular, you must safeguard [the Bodhisattva vow], through strong striving [at not being polluted at all] from all points of view by the root defeats that cut the Bodhisattva vow. You should strive at not being polluted at all by less than root defeats: small and middle contaminations and other secondary faults. Even if you are polluted powerlessly by the many afflictions and so forth, without hurrying, you should work at restoration as much as you can.

Chapter Seven

དེ་ནས་ཕར་ཕྱིན་ཕ་མ་གཉིས་ལ་ཁྱད་པར་དུ་བསླབ་དགོས་པས་བསམ་གཏན་སྐྱོང་ལུགས་ལ་མཁས་པར་བྱས་ལ་ཏིང་ངེ་འཛིན་བསྒྲུབ། བདག་མེད་པ་གཉིས་ཀྱི་ལྟ་བ་རྟག་ཆད་དང་བྲལ་བའི་རྣམ་དག་ཅིག་རྒྱུད་ལ་ཅི་སྐྱེ་བྱས་ཏེ། རྙེད་པ་དང་ལྟ་ཐོག་དེར་བཞག་ནས་སྐྱོང་བའི་སྐྱོང་ཚུལ་རྣམ་དག་ཤེས་པར་བྱས་ལ་བསྐྱང་ངོ་། །དེ་འདྲ་བའི་བསམ་གཏན་དང་ཤེས་རབ་གཉིས་ལ་ཞི་ལྷག་གི་མིང་བཏགས་པ་ཡིན་གྱི། ཕར་ཕྱིན་ཕ་མ་གཉིས་ལས་ཟུར་པ་ཞིག་མེད་པས་བྱང་སེམས་ཀྱི་སྡོམ་པ་བཟུང་ནས་དེའི་བསླབ་བྱ་ལ་སློབ་པའི་གསེབ་ནས་འོང་བ་ཡིན་ནོ། །

Division of the passage into units to facilitate the analysis of the syntax

Chapter Seven is three sentences divided into six principal meaning units.

1

དེ་ནས་ཕར་ཕྱིན་ཕ་མ་གཉིས་ལ་ཁྱད་པར་དུ་བསླབ་དགོས་པས

2

བསམ་གཏན་སྐྱོང་ལུགས་ལ་མཁས་པར་བྱས་ལ་ཏིང་ངེ་འཛིན་བསྒྲུབ།

3

བདག་མེད་པ་གཉིས་ཀྱི་ལྟ་བ་རྟག་ཆད་དང་བྲལ་བའི་རྣམ་དག་ཅིག་རྒྱུད་ལ་ཅི་སྐྱེ་བྱས་ཏེ།

4

རྙེད་པ་དང་ལྟ་ཐོག་དེར་བཞག་ནས་སྐྱོང་བའི་སྐྱོང་ཚུལ་རྣམ་དག་ཤེས་པར་བྱས་ལ་བསྐྱང་ངོ་། །

5

དེ་འདྲ་བའི་བསམ་གཏན་དང་ཤེས་རབ་གཉིས་ལ་ཞི་ལྷག་གི་མིང་བཏགས་པ་ཡིན་གྱི།

6

ཕར་ཕྱིན་ཕ་མ་གཉིས་ལས་ཟུར་པ་ཞིག་མེད་པས་བྱང་སེམས་ཀྱི་སྡོམ་པ་བཟུང་ནས་དེའི་བསླབ་བྱ་ལ་སློབ་པའི་གསེབ་ནས་འོང་བ་ཡིན་ནོ། །

Part 1 • དེ་ནས་ཕར་ཕྱིན་ཐ་མ་གཉིས་ལ་ཁྱད་པར་དུ་བསླབ་དགོས་པས་

Part 1 illustrates a 3rd case qualifier stating a reason qualifying Part 2. While Part 1 naturally translates into a single English sentence, in Tibetan it is a verbal clause declined as a whole in the third case, indicating that the entire verbal clause is a reason qualifying a principal verb later in the sentence.

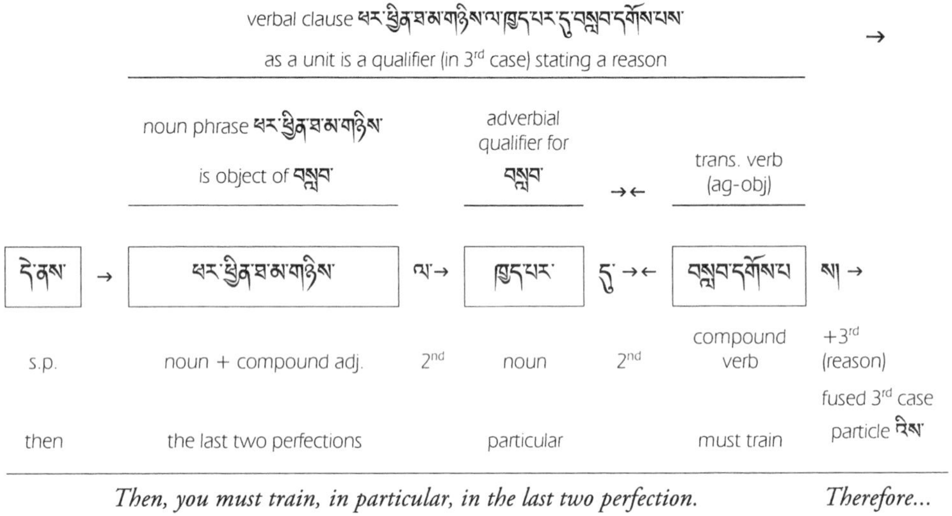

Glossary for Part 1

དེ་ནས་	an introductory syntactic particle translated *then;* (literally, pronoun + 5th case particle: *after that*)
ཕར་ཕྱིན་	n., *perfection;* literally, verbal clause *gone to the [other] side,* contraction for ཕ་རོལ་ཏུ་ཕྱིན་པ་
ཕ་རོལ་ཏུ་ཕྱིན་པ་	n., *perfection* (literally, a verbal clause meaning *gone to the other side)*
ཕྱིན་	intr. v. (nom-obj) (past tense), *went*
	འགྲོ་ཕྱིན་འགྲོ་སོང་། ཐ་མི་དད། སོང་ is an alternate past form
ཐ་མ་	adj., *last*
གཉིས་	n., and adj., *two;* here, adjective
ཕར་ཕྱིན་ཐ་མ་གཉིས་	noun phrase (noun + adj. + adj.), *the last two perfections [concentration and wisdom]*
ཕར་ཕྱིན་ཐ་མ་གཉིས་ལ་	noun phrase + 2nd case particle marking the object of the transitive verb འབད་ *work at, strive at*
ལ་	particle; either 1) a syntactic particle following a verb or verb phrase signifying conjunction or disjunction, or 2) a case particle following nouns, pronouns, postpositions, and adjectives marking the 2nd, 4th and 7th cases
ཁྱད་པར་	n. and adv.; as noun, *attribute, feature, qualification, difference;* as adverb, *in particular, especially*
ཁྱད་པར་དུ་	n. + 2nd, 4th or 7th case; here: 2nd case adv., *in particular*

དུ་ — particle; either 1) a verb-modifying syntactic particle within a verb phrase, or 2) a case particle following nouns, pronouns, postpositions, and adjectives marking the 2nd, 4th and 7th cases

བསླབ་ — trans. v. (ag-obj) (future), *train*

སློབ་བསླབས་བསླབ་སློབས། ཐ་དད།

དགོས་ — intr. v. (b/p-nom), *be necessary, need, require*
དགོས་དགོས་དགོས། ཐ་མི་དད།

བསླབ་དགོས — compound verb (trans. v. + aux.), *[you] must train.* As is the rule with compound verb constructions, the syntax is governed by the initial verb. Here the transitive, agentive-objective verb བསླབ་ takes an object, *the last two perfections*, in the second case.

དགོས་པ་ — verbal noun, *need, requirement*

དགོས་པས་ — verbal noun + 3rd case particle fused to suffixless final syllable

ས་ — abbreviation of the particle འིས་ (when འིས་ is fused to a suffixless final syllable, the འི goes away and all that's left is a fused ས་); either 1) syntactic particle creating an adverbial construction, 2) syntactic particle marking the qualifier of an intransitive nom-s.p. verb of absence, or 3) case particle marking the 3rd case

གིས་ཀྱིས་གྱིས་འིས་ཡིས་ — are equivalent particles, marking the 3rd case and also marking syntactic adverbial relationships.

How the word for perfection ཕར་ཕྱིན་ is derived from the verb of motion འགྲོ་ *go*

ཕར་ཕྱིན་ is a contraction for ཕ་རོལ་དུ་ཕྱིན་པ་; literally, a verbal clause employing the past tense of the verb *go*

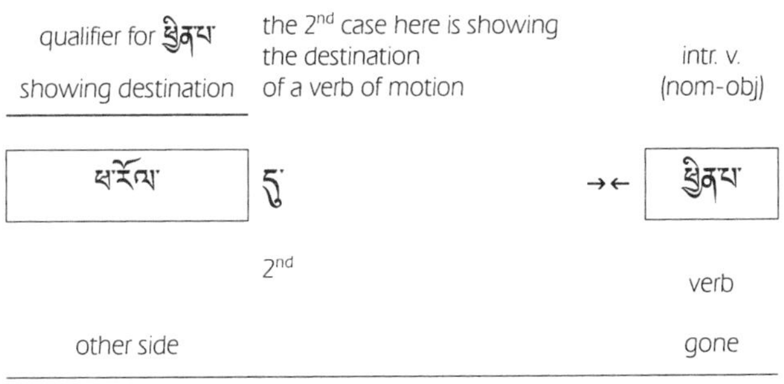

gone to the other side

Glossary

ཕར་ཕྱིན་ — n., *perfection;* contraction for ཕ་རོལ་དུ་ཕྱིན་པ་; literally, a verbal clause employing the past tense of the verb *go, gone to the [other] side*

ཕྱིན་ — intr. v. (nom-obj) (past tense), *went*

འགྲོ་ཕྱིན་འགྲོ་སོང་། ཐ་མི་དད། སོང་ is an alternate past form

ཕ་རོལ་དུ་ — the 2nd case is used to signify the destination of a verb of motion: *to the other side*

Part 2 • བསམ་གཏན་སྐྱོང་ལུགས་ལ་མཁས་པར་བྱས་ལ་ཏིང་ངེ་འཛིན་བསྒྲུབ།

In the verb phrase མཁས་པར་བྱས་ the strong past auxiliary with the intransitive verb *be skilled* conveys a causative sense: *you have caused yourself to have become skillful.*

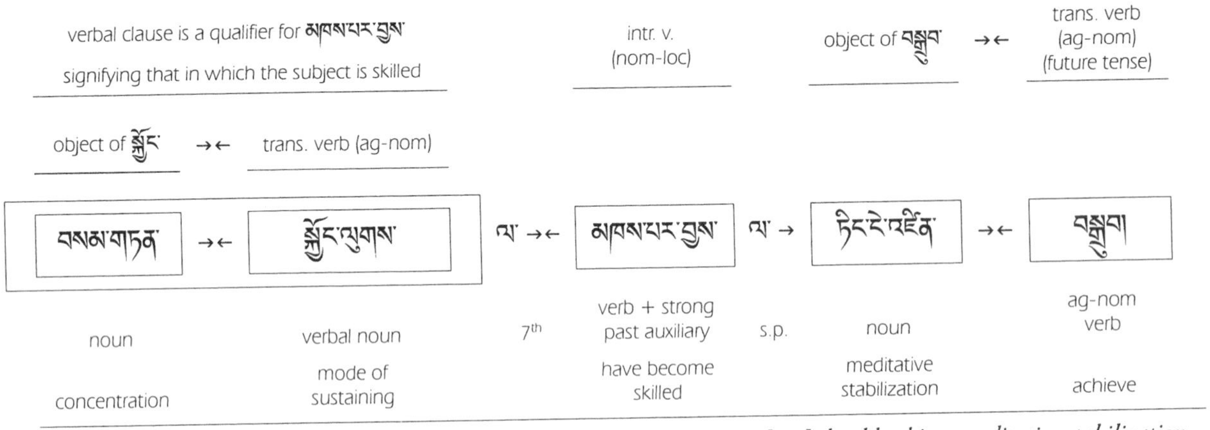

Having become skilled in the mode of sustaining meditative concentration, [you] should achieve meditative stabilization.

Glossary for Part 2

བསམ་གཏན་ n., *concentration*

བསམ་པ་ verbal noun, *mind*

གཏན་པ་ verbal noun, *stable*

སྐྱོང་ trans. v. (ag-nom), *sustain* སྐྱོང་བསྐྱངས་བསྐྱང་སྐྱོངས། ཐ་དད།

ལུགས་ n., *system*

སྐྱོང་ལུགས་ compound noun, *mode of sustaining*

སྐྱོང་ལུགས་ལ་ compound noun + 7th case particle marking qualifier of intr. v. (nom-loc), མཁས་ *be skilled*

ལ་ particle; either 1) a syntactic particle following a verb or verb phrase signifying conjunction or disjunction, or 2) a case particle following nouns, pronouns, postpositions, and adjectives marking the 2nd, 4th and 7th cases

མཁས་ intr. v. (nom-loc), *be skilled* མཁས་མཁས་མཁས། ཐ་མི་དད།

མཁས་པར་བྱས་ verb phrase (verbal infinitive + strong past auxiliary) *[I, you] have become skilled*

མཁས་པར་ verbal infinitive; here, the fused ར་ is a syntactic particle modifying a verb to create a verbal infinitive within the verb phrase མཁས་པར་བྱ་ *[I, you] have become skilled;* it is **not** a case particle marking the 2nd, 4th or 7th cases because it does not follow a noun—it is within a verb phrase

སུ་རུ་ཏུ་དུ་ར་ are the five syntactic particles used to modify verbs to create infinitives within verb phrases

བྱས་ trans. v. (ag-nom)(past tense), *did, made, performed, took;* here: the strong past auxiliary within a verb phrase བྱེད་བྱས་བྱ་བྱོས། ཐ་དད།

མཁས་པར་བྱས་ལ་ verb phrase + conjunctive syntactic particle

ལ་ particle; either 1) a syntactic particle following a verb or verb phrase signifying conjunction or disjunction, or 2) a case particle following nouns, pronouns, postpositions, and adjectives marking the 2nd, 4th and 7th cases

ཏིང་ངེ་འཛིན་ n., *meditative stabilization*

བསྒྲུབ་ trans. v. (ag-nom) (future tense), *achieve, attain, accomplish, complete; prove*

སྒྲུབ་བསྒྲུབས་བསྒྲུབ་སྒྲུབས། ཐ་དད།

གྲུབ་ intr. v. (nom-obj) (past tense), *be established, be proven, exists*

འགྲུབ་གྲུབ་འགྲུབ། ཐ་མི་དད།

Notes on Part 2

བསམ་གཏན་སྐྱོང་ལུགས་ noun phrase, *the mode of sustaining concentration.* བསམ་གཏན་སྐྱོང་ is a verbal clause: བསམ་གཏན་ is the object of the transitive (ag-nom) verb སྐྱོང་ *sustain*

སྐྱོང་ trans. verb (ag-nom), *sustain* སྐྱོང་བསྐྱངས་བསྐྱང་སྐྱོངས། ཐ་དད།

བསམ་གཏན་ n., *concentration;* 5th of the six perfections

སྐྱོང་ལུགས་ n., *mode of sustaining, the system for sustaining*

བསམ་གཏན་སྐྱོང་ལུགས་ལ་མཁས་ བསམ་གཏན་སྐྱོང་ལུགས་ལ་ is the 7th case qualifier of the intransitive (nom-loc) verb མཁས་ *be skilled in.* It signifies that with respect to which one is skilled.

ཏིང་ངེ་འཛིན་བསྒྲུབ། ཏིང་ངེ་འཛིན་ is the 1st case object of the transitive (ag-nom) verb བསྒྲུབ།

Grammar review • Remember to distinguish the transitive verb (ag-nom) སྒྲུབ་ and the related intransitive verb (nom-obj) འགྲུབ་

སྒྲུབ་ transitive verb (ag-nom), *achieve, attain, accomplish, complete; prove.* This verb takes an object in the 1st case.

སྒྲུབ་བསྒྲུབས་བསྒྲུབ་སྒྲུབས། ཐ་དད།

འགྲུབ་ intransitive verb (nom-obj), *be established, be proven, exists.* This verb is intransitive, meaning it does not take an object. Remember also that the verb འགྲུབ་ sometimes just means *exist,* like ཡོད་

འགྲུབ་གྲུབ་འགྲུབ། ཐ་མི་དད།

Part 3 • བདག་མེད་པ་གཉིས་ཀྱི་ལྟ་བ་རྟག་ཆད་དང་བྲལ་བའི་རྣམ་དག་ཅིག་རྒྱུད་ལ་ཅི་སྐྱེ་བྱས་ཏེ།

Part 3 starts with a verbal clause using the intransitive nom-s.p. verb of disjunction བྲལ་

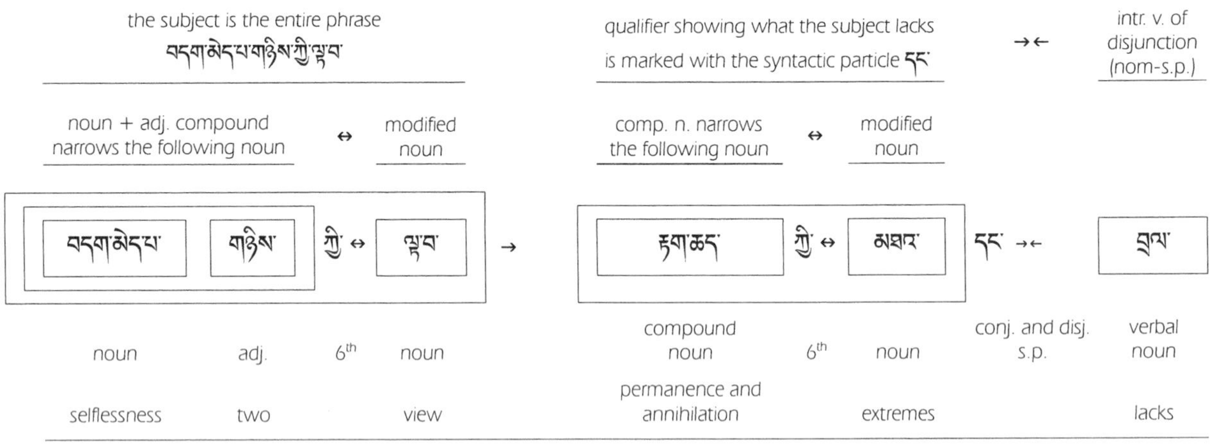

The view of the two selflessnesses lacks the extremes of permanence and annihilation.

Partial Glossary for Part 3

བདག་མེད་པ་ n., *selfless, selflessness;* often abbreviated as བདག་མེད་

གཉིས་ n., and adj., *two;* here: adjective

བདག་མེད་པ་གཉིས་ noun phrase (noun + adjective), *the two selflessnesses*

གང་ཟག་གི་བདག་མེད་ noun phrase, *selflessness of persons*

ཆོས་ཀྱི་བདག་མེད་ noun phrase, *selflessness of phenomena*

བདག་མེད་པ་གཉིས་ཀྱི་ noun + adj. compound + 6th case particle

ཀྱི་ particle; either 1) a syntactic particle following a verb or verb phrase signifying conjunction or disjunction, or 2) a 6th case particle following nouns, pronouns, postpositions, and adjectives

ལྟ་ trans. v. (ag-obj), *look at, regard* ལྟ་བ་བལྟས་བལྟ་ལྟོས། ཐ་དད།

ལྟོས་ intr. v. (nom-loc), *depend, be contingent on, be within the context [of something].* ལྟོས་བལྟོས་ལྟོས། ཐ་མི་དད།

ལྟ་བ་ n., *view*

བདག་མེད་པ་གཉིས་ཀྱི་ལྟ་བ་ this noun phrase as a unit is the subject in the 1st case of the intransitive nom-s.p. verb of disjunction བྲལ་, *lack, be free of*

རྟག་ abbreviation for རྟག་པ་, permanent, permanent phenomena

རྟག་པ་ n. or adj., *permanent phenomena, permanence*

ཆད་ intr. v. (nom-obj) (past tense), *be severed, be cut*

འཆད་ཆད་འཆད། ཐ་མི་དད།

རྟག་ཆད་ཀྱི་མཐའ་ this noun phrase means རྟག་གི་མཐའ་ *the extreme of permanence,* and ཆད་ཀྱི་མཐའ་ *the extreme of annihilation*

རྟག་མཐའ་ noun phrase (n. + implied 6th case particle + n.), *extreme of permanence;* abbreviation of རྟག་གི་མཐའ་ *the extreme of permanence*

ཆད་མཐའ་ noun phrase (n. + implied 6th case particle + n.), *extreme of annihilation;* abbreviation of ཆད་ཀྱི་མཐའ་ *the extreme of annihilation*

རྟག་ཆད་དང་བྲལ་ verbal clause (qualifier + verb), *free from the extremes of permanence and annihilation;* here the syntactic particle དང་ marks the qualifier of the intr. v. of conjunction བྲལ་ *lack, be free of, be devoid of*

རྟག་ཆད་དང་ noun phrase + syntactic particle marking the qualifier for the verb of disjunction བྲལ་ *lack, be free of, be devoid of*

དང་ particle used in three ways: 1) continuative syntactic particle used following nouns and noun phrases (*and,* or with negative verb, *or*); 2) syntactic particle marking the qualifier of an intr. nom-s.p. v. of conjunction, as in ང་རང་མི་སྡུག་པ་དང་ཕྲད་ན་ *if we meet with unpleasantness;* and 3) syntactic particle marking the qualifier of an intr. nom-s.p. v. of disjunction, as in རྟོག་པ་དང་བྲལ་ *free from conceptuality*

བྲལ་ intr. v. (nom-s.p. verb of disjunction) (past tense), *lack, be free of, be devoid of ;* the syntactic particle དང་ marks the qualifier of this intr. v. of disjunction. འབྲལ་བྲལ་འབྲལ། ཐ་མི་དད།

Part 3's opening clause is now seen to be a verbal adjective modifying a following noun

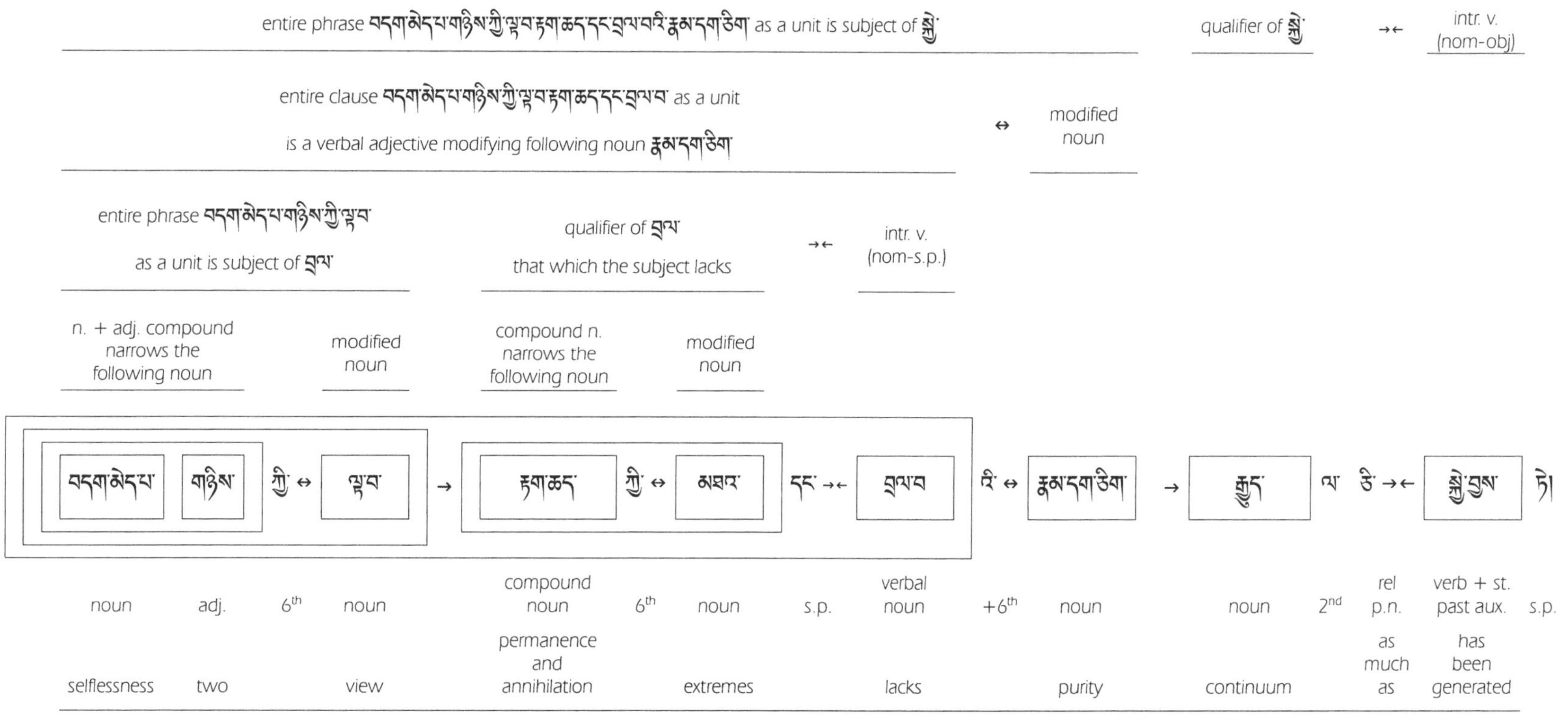

Cause the purity which is the view of two selflessnesses free from the extremes of permanence and annihilation to be generated in [your] continuum as much as you can.

Recast as an active voice, transitive sentence:

As much as you can, generate in your continuum the pure view of the two selflessnesses free from the extremes of permanence and annihilation.

Partial Glossary for Part 3

བྲལ་ intr. v. (nom-s.p. verb of disjunction) (past tense), *lack, be free of, be devoid of*; the syntactic particle དང་ marks the qualifier of this intr. v. of disjunction
འབྲལ་བྲལ་འབྲལ། ཐ་མི་དད།

བྲལ་བ་ verbal noun, *lacking, devoid of*

བྲལ་བའི་ verbal noun + 6th case particle fused to suffixless final syllable

འི་ particle fused to suffixless final syllable; either 1) a syntactic particle following a verb or verb phrase signifying conjunction or disjunction, or 2) a 6th case particle following nouns, pronouns, postpositions, and adjectives

རྣམ་དག་ adj., *pure, very pure, complete;* abbreviation for རྣམ་པར་དག་པ་

རྣམ་པར་དག་པ་ adj., *pure, very pure, complete*

ཅིག་ pronoun or adj. (following nouns), *one, a, some, a little;* modified form of གཅིག་

ཅིག་ imperative marking syntactic particle (following verbs)

ཞིག་ pronoun or adj. (following nouns), *one, a, some, a little;* modified form of གཅིག་

ཞིག་ syntactic particle turning an adj. into an adverb

ཞིག་ following verbs, an imperative marking syntactic particle

རྒྱུད་ n., *continuum*

རྒྱུད་ལ་ n. + 2nd case particle marking place of activity

ལ་ particle; either 1) a syntactic particle following a verb or verb phrase signifying conjunction or disjunction, or 2) a case particle following nouns, pronouns, postpositions, and adjectives marking the 2nd, 4th and 7th cases

ཇི་ relative pronoun, *as much as*

སྐྱེ་ intr. v. (nom-obj), *be born, arise, be created*
སྐྱེ་སྐྱེས་སྐྱེ། ཐ་མི་དད།

བསྐྱེད་ trans. v. (ag-nom), *produce, generate, create, give birth to*
སྐྱེད་བསྐྱེད་བསྐྱེད་སྐྱེད། ཐ་དད།

སྐྱེ་བྱས་ verbal phrase (past tense), *has been produced;* abbreviation for སྐྱེ་པར་བྱས་

སྐྱེ་པར་བྱས་ verb phrase *has been produced.* The use of the strong auxiliary with an intransitive verb conveys a causative sense: *however much you have caused to be produced in your continuum*

སྐྱེ་པར་ verbal infinitive; here, the fused ར་ is a syntactic particle modifying a verb to create a verbal infinitive within the verb phrase སྐྱེ་པར་བྱས་ *[it] has been produced;* it is **not** a case particle marking the 2nd, 4th or 7th cases because it does not follow a noun—it is within a verb phrase

བྱས་ trans. v. (ag-nom) (past tense), *do, make, perform, take;* here: used as the strong past auxiliary
བྱེད་བྱས་བྱ་བྱོས། ཐ་དད།

སྐྱེ་བྱས་སྟེ། verb phrase + continuative syntactic particle showing sequence by indicating that more relevant information will follow.

ཏེ་ སྟེ་ and དེ་ are equivalent syntactic particles; either 1) continuative syntactic particles following verbs and verb phrases showing sequence, or 2) punctuational syntactic particles following words or phrases marking appositives

ཏེ་ follows words ending with suffix letters ན་ར་ལ་ས་

སྟེ་ follows suffixless words and words ending with suffix letters ག་ང་བ་མ་འ་

དེ་ follows words ending with suffix letter ད་

Part 4 • རྙེད་པ་དང་ལྟ་ཐོག་དེར་བཞག་ནས་སྐྱོང་བའི་སྐྱོང་ཚུལ་རྣམ་དག་ཤེས་པར་བྱས་ལ་བསྐྱང་ངོ།

In simplified form: "Having come to understand the mode of sustaining within A and B, sustain it."

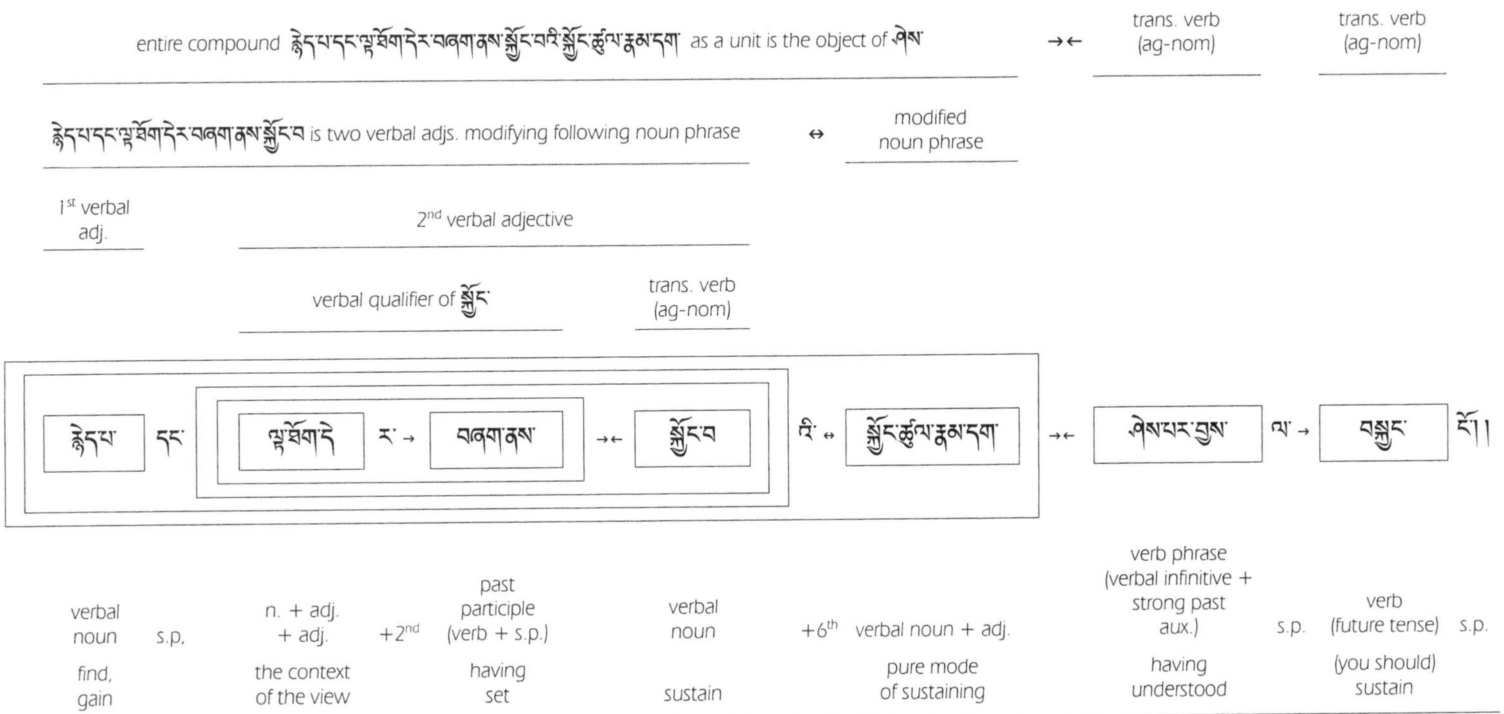

Having understood how to gain [the view] and how to sustain [it] within setting [the mind] in the context of the view, sustain [that continuum of that mind].

Alternate translation with more bracketed material:

Once you have understood the pure way to sustain [the view] through finding [the view free from the two extremes] and sustaining it through setting [the mind] in the context of the view, [you should] sustain [that continuum of that mind].

Glossary for Part 4

རྙེད་ intr. v. (nom-obj), *be found* རྙེད་རྙེད་རྙེད། ཐ་མི་དད།

རྙེད་པ་ n., *found*

རྙེད་པ་ the understood object of རྙེད་ is ལྟ་བ་, *the view [of selflessness]*. The fused 6th case particle འི་ is distributed to རྙེད་པ་ and སྐྱོང་བ་

དང་ particle; used three ways: 1) continuative syntactic particle used following nouns and noun phrases (*and*, or with negative verb, *or*); 2) syntactic particle marking the qualifier of an intr. nom-s.p. v. of conjunction, as in ང་རང་མི་སྡུག་པ་དང་ཕྲད་ན་ *if we meet with unpleasantness;* and 3) syntactic particle marking the qualifier of an intr. nom-s.p. v. of disjunction, as in རྟོག་པ་དང་བྲལ་ *free from conceptuality*

ལྟ་ n., *view;* abbreviation for ལྟ་བ་

ཐོག་ n., *top;* by extension: *context*

དེ་ limiting adj. used as pronoun, *that*

དེར་ limiting adj. used as pronoun + fused 2nd, 4th or 7th case particle; here: 2nd case

ར་ particle fused to suffixless final syllable; either 1) a verb-modifying syntactic particle within a verb phrase, or 2) a case particle following nouns, pronouns, postpositions, and adjectives marking the 2nd, 4th and 7th cases

བཞག་ trans. v. (ag-nom) (future), *posit, put, set, designate*

འཇོག་བཞག་གཞག་ཞོག ཐ་དད།

བཞག་ནས་ verb + continuative syntactic particle, *having posited*

ནས་ particle; either 1) a syntactic particle following verbs and verb phrases marking adverbs, participles or disjunction, or 2) a case particle marking the 5th case. Here ནས་ is a continuative syntactic particle modifying the verb བཞག་ making a past participle. The whole clause is a verbal qualifier of སྐྱོང་ *sustain.* How should you sustain? *Sustain it within setting [the mind] in the context of the view.*

སྐྱོང་ trans. v. (ag-nom), *sustain* སྐྱོང་བསྐྱངས་བསྐྱང་སྐྱོངས། ཐ་དད།

སྐྱོང་བ་ verbal noun, *sustain*

སྐྱོང་བའི་ n. + 6th case particle fused to suffixless final syllable

འི་ particle fused to suffixless final syllable; either 1) a syntactic particle following a verb or verb phrase signifying conjunction or disjunction, or 2) a 6th case particle following nouns, pronouns, postpositions, and adjectives

སྐྱོང་ཚུལ་ n., *mode of sustaining*

རྣམ་དག adj., *pure*

ཤེས་ trans. v. (ag-nom), *know, understand.* This verb is listed in the *Great Word Treasury* as ཐ་མི་དད།, but I think it is a transitive ag-nom verb. ཤེས་ཤེས་ཤེས། ཐ་མི་དད།

ཤེས་པར་བྱས་ verb phrase (verbal infinitive + strong past auxiliary), *having understood*

ཤེས་པར་ verbal infinitive; here, the fused ར་ is a syntactic particle modifying a verb to create an infinitive within the verb phrase ཤེས་པར་བྱས་ *having understood [something];* it is **not** a case particle marking the 2nd, 4th or 7th cases because it does not follow a noun—it is within a verb phrase

བྱས་ trans. v. (ag-nom) (past), *did, made, performed, taken;* here: the strong past auxiliary

བྱེད་བྱས་བྱ་བྱོས། ཐ་དད།

ཤེས་པར་བྱས་ལ་ verb phrase + conjunctive syntactic particle

ལ་ particle; either 1) a syntactic particle following a verb or verb phrase signifying conjunction or disjunction, or 2) a case particle following nouns, pronouns, postpositions, and adjectives marking the 2nd, 4th and 7th cases

བསྐྱང་ trans. v. (ag-nom), *will sustain;* future form of སྐྱོང་

སྐྱོང་བསྐྱངས་བསྐྱང་སྐྱོངས། ཐ་དད།

བསྐྱང་ངོ། final verb + sentence-terminating syntactic particle

ངོ། terminating s.p. ending the sentence where suffix letter of final word is ང་

Part 5 • དེ་འདྲ་བའི་བསམ་གཏན་དང་ཤེས་རབ་གཉིས་ལ་ཞི་ལྷག་གི་མིང་བཏགས་པ་ཡིན་གྱི།

Overview of Part 5

In Part 5 an unstated agent designates a name (the object) to the point of reference (qualifier in 7th case).

	qualifier in 7th case		object in 1st case	verb
unstated agent →	དེ་འདྲ་བའི་བསམ་གཏན་དང་ཤེས་རབ་གཉིས་	ལ་ →	ཞི་ལྷག་གི་མིང་	→← བཏགས་པ་ཡིན་གྱི།
	noun phrase	7th	comp. n.	verb
	the two, concentration and wisdom like that		*the names calm abiding and special insight*	*are designated*

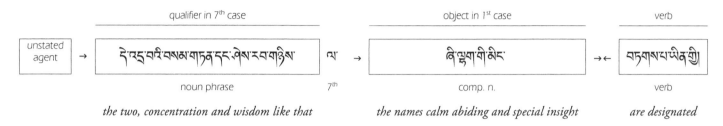

Part 5 in full form

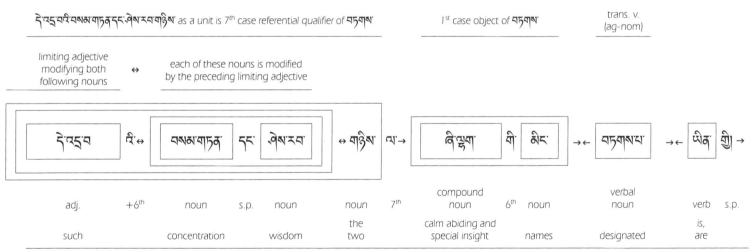

དེ་འདྲ་བའི་བསམ་གཏན་དང་ཤེས་རབ་གཉིས་ as a unit is 7th case referential qualifier of བཏགས་

1st case object of བཏགས་

trans. v. (ag-nom)

limiting adjective modifying both following nouns ↔ each of these nouns is modified by the preceding limiting adjective

དེ་འདྲ་བ	འི་↔	བསམ་གཏན་	དང་	ཤེས་རབ་	↔ གཉིས་	ལ་→	ཞི་ལྷག་	གི་	མིང་	→← བཏགས་པ་	→← ཡིན་	གྱི། →
adj.	+6th	noun	s.p.	noun	noun	7th	compound noun	6th	noun	verbal noun	verb	s.p.
such		concentration		wisdom	the two		calm abiding and special insight		names	designated	is, are	

the names calm abiding and special insight are designated to the two, such concentration and wisdom.

Glossary for Part 5

དེ་འདྲ་བ་ limiting adjective, pronoun, *such, like that;* here: limiting adjective

འདྲ་ intr. v. (nom-s.p. verb: qualifier marked with དང་), *be similar to*

དེ་འདྲ་བའི་ limiting adjective + 6th case particle fused to suffixless final syllable

འི་ particle fused to suffixless final syllable; either 1) a syntactic particle following a verb or verb phrase signifying conjunction or disjunction, or 2) a 6th case particle following nouns, pronouns, postpositions, and adjectives

བསམ་གཏན་ n., *concentration*

དང་ particle; used three ways: 1) continuative syntactic particle used following nouns and noun phrases (*and,* or with negative verb, *or*); 2) syntactic particle marking the qualifier of an intr. nom-s.p. v. of conjunction, as in ང་རང་མི་སྡུག་པ་དང་ཕྲད་ན་ *if we meet with unpleasantness;* and 3) syntactic particle marking the qualifier of an intr. nom-s.p. v. of disjunction, as in རྟོག་པ་དང་བྲལ་ *free from conceptuality*

ཤེས་རབ་ n., *wisdom*

གཉིས་ n., and adj., *two;* here, pronoun

བསམ་གཏན་དང་ཤེས་རབ་གཉིས་ noun phrase (noun phrase (n. + s.p. + n.) in apposition with pronoun), *the two—concentration and wisdom*

བསམ་གཏན་དང་ཤེས་རབ་གཉིས་ལ་ noun phrase + 2nd case particle

ལ་ particle; either syntactic particle (following verb) signifying conjunction or disjunction, or case particle (following noun) marking the 2nd, 4th and 7th cases; here: 2nd case

ཞི་ལྷག་ ཞི་གནས་དང་ལྷག་མཐོང་

ཞི་ལྷག་ abbreviated comp. n. *calm abiding and special insight*

ཞི་གནས་ comp. n., *calm abiding*

ཞི་ intr. v. (nom-loc), *be peaceful, be calm* ཞི་ཞི་ཞི། ཐ་མི་དད།

གནས་ intr. v. (nom-loc), *abide, dwell* གནས་གནས་གནས་གནས། ཐ་མི་དད།

གནས་ n., *place, abode, location,* and by extension: *status, state, situation, source, object, topic,* and *basis*

གནས་པ་ verbal n., *dwelling, remaining, one who dwells or remains*

ལྷག་མཐོང་ n., *special insight*

ལྷག་ lexical prefix particle, *special, intense*

མཐོང་ trans. v. (ag-nom), *see, preceive.* This verb is listed in the *Great Word Treasury* as ཐ་མི་དད།, but I think it is a transitive verb (ag-nom).
མཐོང་མཐོང་མཐོང་། ཐ་མི་དད།

ཞི་ལྷག་གི་ compound noun + 6th case particle

གི་ particle; either 1) a syntactic particle following a verb or verb phrase signifying conjunction or disjunction, or 2) a 6th case particle following nouns, pronouns, postpositions, and adjectives

མིང་ n., *name*

བཏགས་ trans. v. (ag-nom) (past tense), *designated, imputed*

འདོགས་བཏགས་གདགས་ཐོགས། ཐ་དད།

གཉིས་ལ་ཞི་ལྷག་གི་མིང་བཏགས་ an unstated 3rd case agent *designated* བཏགས་ a 1st case object ཞི་ལྷག་གི་མིང་ to a 7th case qualifier གཉིས་ལ་

ཡིན་ intr. v. (nom-nom), *be, is, are*

ཡིན་ཡིན་ཡིན་ཡིན། ཐ་མི་དད།

བཏགས་པ་ཡིན་གྱི། this is a syntactically irregular but frequently seen use of the linking verb ཡིན་ to create the overall rhetorical tone of the sentence: *It is the case that* [the names ཞི་ལྷག] *are designated to* [such concentration and wisdom].

ཡིན་གྱི་ final verb + conjunctive or disjunctive syntactic particle, *[subject] is [complement], but...*

གྱི་ particle; either 1) a syntactic particle following a verb or verb phrase signifying conjunction or disjunction, or 2) a 6th case particle following nouns, pronouns, postpositions, and adjectives

Part 6 • པར་ཕྱིན་ཐ་མ་གཉིས་ལས་ཟུར་པ་ཞིག་མེད་པས་བྱང་སེམས་ཀྱི་སྡོམ་པ་བཟུང་ནས་དེའི་བསླབ་བྱ་ལ་སློབ་པའི་གསེབ་ནས་འོང་བ་ཡིན་ནོ། །

Part 6 begins with a 3rd case reason qualifying the principal verb

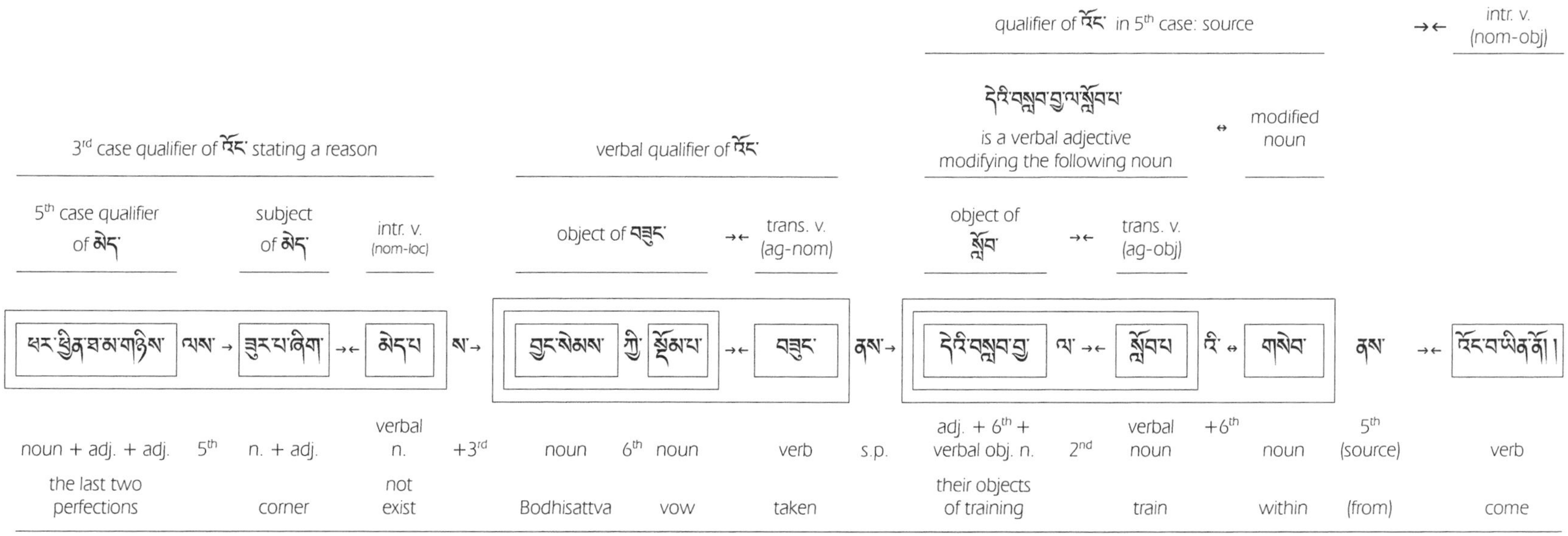

Because not even a portion of [calm abiding and special insight] is apart from [inclusion within] the last two perfections, [training in calm abiding and special insight] come within the points of training of the Bodhisattva vow once it has been taken.

Glossary for Part 6

པར་ཕྱིན་ n., *perfection;* contraction for ཕ་རོལ་ཏུ་ཕྱིན་པ་ literally, a verbal clause employing the past tense of the verb go *gone to the [other] side*

འགྲོ་ intr. v. (nom-obj), *go*; often used by extension in the metaphorical sense of *turns into* or *becomes*
འགྲོ་ཕྱིན་འགྲོ་སོང་། ཐ་མི་དད། སོང་ is an alternate past form

ཕ་རོལ་ཏུ་ཕྱིན་པ་ n., *perfection*, literally a verbal clause *gone to the other side*

ཐ་མ་ n., adj., *last*

གཉིས་ n., adj., *two*

ཐ་མ་གཉིས་ noun phrase (noun + adj.), *the last two*

པར་ཕྱིན་ཐ་མ་གཉིས་ལས་ noun phrase (n. + adj. + adj.) + 5th case particle; here, a qualifier for the verb of existence མེད་ *does not exist.*

The 5th case is used to mark qualifiers signifying **source, instrument, separation, comparison, inclusion,** and **logical sequence.**
From among the six, the particle ལས་ here indicates separation with the adverbial sense of མ་གཏོགས་ *except for, other than*

ལས་ particle; either 1) syntactic particle marking adverbs, participles or disjunction, or 2) case particle marking the 5th case

ཟུར་པ་ n., *corner, portion*

ཞིག་ pronoun or adj. (following nouns), *one, a, some, a little;* modified form of གཅིག་

ཞིག་ adv . s.p., makes preceding word, phrase or clause into an adverbial construction

མེད་ intr. v. (nom-loc), *not exist* མེད་མེད་མེད་མེད། ཐ་མི་དད།
trans. v. (loc-nom), *not have*

མེད་པ་ verbal noun, *non-existent*

མེད་པས་ verbal n. + 3rd case particle fused to suffixless final syllable; here marking a 3rd case reason qualifier

ས་ abbreviation of the particle འིས་ (when འིས་ is fused to a suffixless final syllable, the འི goes away and all that's left is a fused ས་); either 1) syntactic particle creating an adverbial construction, 2) syntactic particle marking the qualifier of an intransitive nom-s.p. verb of absence, or 3) case particle marking the 3rd case

གིས་ཀྱིས་གྱིས་འིས་ཡིས་ are equivalent particles

བྱང་སེམས་ n., *Bodhisattva;* abbreviation for བྱང་ཆུབ་སེམས་དཔའ་

བྱང་སེམས་ཀྱི་ n. + 6th case particle

ཀྱི་ particle; either 1) a syntactic particle following a verb or verb phrase signifying conjunction or disjunction, or 2) a 6th case particle following nouns, pronouns, postpositions, and adjectives

སྡོམ་ trans. v. (ag-nom), *vow, promise* སྡོམ་བསྡམས་བསྡམ་སྡོམས། ཐ་དད།

སྡོམ་པ་ n., *vow*

བཟུང་ trans. v. (ag-nom) (past tense), *grasp, apprehend, conceive*
འཛིན་བཟུང་གཟུང་ཟུང་། ཐ་དད།

བཟུང་ནས་ verb + continuative syntactic particle, *having taken*

ནས་ particle; either 1) a syntactic particle following verbs and verb phrases marking adverbs, participles or disjunction, or 2) a case particle marking the 5th case

དེ་ limiting adj. used as a pronoun, *that one*

དེའི adj. + 6th case particle fused to suffixless, single-syllable pronoun

འི་ particle fused to suffixless final syllable; either 1) a syntactic particle following a verb or verb phrase signifying conjunction or disjunction, or 2) a 6th case particle following nouns, pronouns, postpositions, and adjectives

བསླབ་བྱ་ verbal object noun, *object of training*

བསླབ་བྱ་ལ་ verbal object noun + 2nd case particle marking the object of the transitive verb སློབ་ *train in*

ལ་ particle; either 1) a syntactic particle following a verb or verb phrase signifying conjunction or disjunction, or 2) a case particle following nouns, pronouns, postpositions, and adjectives marking the 2nd, 4th and 7th cases

སློབ་ trans. v. (ag-obj), *train (in something)*
སློབ་བསླབས་བསླབ་སློབས། ཐ་དད།

སློབ་པ་ n., *training*

སློབ་པའི་ n. + 6th case particle fused to suffixless final syllable

འི་ particle fused to suffixless final syllable; either 1) a syntactic particle following a verb or verb phrase signifying conjunction or disjunction, or 2) a 6th case particle following nouns, pronouns, postpositions, and adjectives

གསེབ་ n., *the narrow interstices between things*

གསེབ་ནས་ n. + 5th case particle, *between, within*

ནས་ particle; either 1) a syntactic particle following verbs and verb phrases marking adverbs, participles or disjunction, or 2) a case particle marking the 5th case

འོང་ intr. v. (nom-obj), *come* འོང་འོངས་འོང་། ཐ་མི་དད།

འོང་བ་ཡིན་ syntactically irregular but frequently seen use of nom-nom linking verb ཡིན་ translated as: *it is the case that...*

ཡིན་ intr. v. (nom-nom), *is, are*

ཡིན་ནོ། ། final verb + sentence-terminating syntactic particle ending sentence where last word has suffix letter ན་

Grammar review • Two contrasting uses of the particle ནས་

One of the difficulties of learning to read Tibetan is that nineteen particles may be used both 1) as case particles marking declension following nouns, pronouns, postpositions, and adjectives and 2) as syntactic particles following verbs creating participles.

བཟུང་ནས་ past tense of the verb འཛིན་ + continuative syntactic particle creates a past participle expressing completed action, *having taken*

གསེབ་ནས་ n. + 5th case particle here shows the source of the action expressed by the verb, *from within*

ནས་ particle; either 1) a syntactic particle following verbs and verb phrases marking adverbs, participles or disjunction, or 2) a case particle marking the 5th case following nouns, pronouns, postpositions, and adjectives

དེའི་བསླབ་བྱ་ལ་སློབ་པའི་གསེབ་ནས་ verbal clause དེའི་བསླབ་བྱ་ལ་སློབ་པ plus the 6th case particle འི་ is a verbal adjective modifying the following noun གསེབ་ *within.* The entire clause is declined in the 5th case showing the source the requirement of training in calm abiding and special insight. It comes from within the need to train in the last two perfections once the Bodhisattva vow has been assumed.

Grammar review • Differentiating between syntactic particles and case particles

Because many particles signify different relationships depending on what sort of word they follow, I have repeated this chart for your review. Notice how the meaning signified shifts depending on whether the particle follows a verb or verb phrase, or a noun or noun phrase.

verb or verb phrase + syntactic particle		**noun or noun phrase + case particle or syntactic particle**	
verb or verb phrase + ནས་	syntactic particle creates a **participle** with the tense determined by the verb	noun or noun phrase + ནས་	case particle marking **the 5th case**
verb or verb phrase + ལ་	syntactic particle signifying **conjunction** or **disjunction**	noun or noun phrase + ལ་	case particle marking **the 2nd, 4th or 7th cases**
verb or verb phrase + གི་ཀྱི་གྱི་འི་ཡི་	syntactic particles signifying **conjunction** or **disjunction**	noun or noun phrase + གི་ཀྱི་གྱི་འི་ཡི་	case particles marking **the 6th case**
verb or verb phrase + ཏེ་སྟེ་དེ་	continuative syntactic particles show **sequence**	noun or noun phrase + ཏེ་སྟེ་དེ་	**punctuational syntactic particles** signifies **apposition** with noun or noun phrase that follows

Chapter Seven Self Test

Write out the passage, boxing and identifying every syntactic element.

དེ་ནས་ཕར་ཕྱིན་ཐ་མ་གཉིས་ལ་ཁྱད་པར་དུ་བསླབ་དགོས་པས་བསམ་གཏན་སྐྱོང་ལུགས་ལ་མཁས་པར་བྱས་ལ་ཏིང་ངེ་འཛིན་བསྒྲུབ། བདག་མེད་པ་གཉིས་ཀྱི་ལྟ་བ་རྟག་ཆད་དང་བྲལ་བའི་རྣམ་དག་ཅིག་རྒྱུད་ལ་ཅི་སྐྱེ་བྱས་ཏེ། རྙེད་པ་དང་ལྟ་ཐོག་དེར་བཞག་ནས་སྐྱོང་བའི་སྐྱོང་ཚུལ་རྣམ་དག་ཤེས་པར་བྱས་ལ་བསྐྱང་ངོ་། །དེ་འདྲ་བའི་བསམ་གཏན་དང་ཤེས་རབ་གཉིས་ལ་ཞི་ལྷག་གི་མིང་བཏགས་པ་ཡིན་གྱི། ཕར་ཕྱིན་ཐ་མ་གཉིས་ལས་ཟུར་པ་ཞིག་མེད་པས་བྱང་སེམས་ཀྱི་སྡོམ་པ་བཟུང་ནས་དེའི་བསླབ་བྱ་ལ་སློབ་པའི་གསེབ་ནས་འོང་བ་ཡིན་ནོ། །

Vocabulary

For each word, can you identify what part of speech it is (noun, pronoun, adjective, verb, adverb, postposition) and what it means?
For each syntactic particle, can you identify what class of syntactic particle it belongs to and how it is used?

ཕར་ཕྱིན་ཐ་མ་གཉིས་ལ་	དགོས་པ་	མཁས་པར་	གྲུབ་	ལྟ་བ་
དེ་ནས་	དགོས་པས་	མཁས་པར་བྱས་	བྲལ་	ལྟོས་
གཉིས་	ཕ་རོལ་ཏུ་ཕྱིན་པ་	མཁས་པར་བྱས་ལ་	བྲལ་བ་	སྐྱེ་
གཏན་པ་	ཕར་ཕྱིན་	འི་	བྲལ་བའི་	སྐྱེ་པར་
གང་ཟག་གི་བདག་མེད་	ཕར་ཕྱིན་ཐ་མ་གཉིས་	ལ་	རྟག་	སྐྱེ་པར་བྱས་
ཅི་	བདག་མེད་པ་	ལུགས་	རྟག་ཆད་དང་	སྐྱེ་བྱས་
ཅིག་	བདག་མེད་པ་གཉིས་ཀྱི་	ས་	རྟག་ཆད་དང་བྲལ་	སྐྱེ་བྱས་སྟེ།
ཆད་མཐར་	བདག་མེད་པ་གཉིས་	སུ་རུ་ཏུ་དུ་ར་	རྟག་པ་	སྐྱོང་
ཆོས་ཀྱི་བདག་མེད་	བསམ་གཏན་	ཀྱི་	རྟག་མཐར་	སྐྱོང་ལུགས་
ཏིང་ངེ་འཛིན་	བསམ་པ་	ཁྱད་པར་	རྣམ་དག་	སྐྱོང་ལུགས་ལ་
ཏེ་ སྟེ་ and དེ་	བསླབ་	ཁྱད་པར་དུ་	རྒྱུད་	སྒྲུབ་
ཐ་མ་	བསྐྱེད་	ཕྱིན་	རྒྱུད་ལ་	
དགོས་	མཁས་	བྱས་	ལྟ་	

Translation of Tsong-kha-pa's text

དེ་ནས་ཕར་ཕྱིན་ཐ་མ་གཉིས་ལ་ཁྱད་པར་དུ་བསླབ་དགོས་པས་བསམ་གཏན་སྒྲོང་ལུགས་ལ་མཁས་པར་བྱས་ལ་ཏིང་ངེ་འཛིན་བསྒྲུབ། བདག་མེད་པ་གཉིས་ཀྱི་ལྟ་བ་རྟག་ཆད་དང་བྲལ་བའི་རྣམ་དག་ཅིག་རྒྱུད་ལ་ཅི་སྐྱེ་བྱས་ཏེ། རྙེད་པ་དང་ལྟ་ཐོག་དེར་བཞག་ནས་སྐྱོང་བའི་སྐྱོང་ཚུལ་རྣམ་དག་ཤེས་པར་བྱས་ལ་བསྐྱང་ངོ་། །དེ་འདྲ་བའི་བསམ་གཏན་དང་ཤེས་རབ་གཉིས་ལ་ཞི་ལྷག་གི་མིང་བཏགས་པ་ཡིན་གྱི། ཕར་ཕྱིན་ཐ་མ་གཉིས་ལས་ཐུར་པ་ཞིག་མེད་པས་བྱང་སེམས་ཀྱི་སྡོམ་པ་བཟུང་ནས་དེའི་བསླབ་བྱ་ལ་སློབ་པའི་གསེབ་ནས་འོང་བ་ཡིན་ནོ། །

Then, since you must train in particular in the latter two perfections [concentration and wisdom], you should become skilled in how to sustain concentration [as explained earlier in the section on calm abiding] and how to achieve the meditative stabilization [of calm abiding]. As much as you can, generate in your continuum the pure [middle way] view of the two selflessnesses [the selflessness of persons and the selflessness of phenomena] free from the extremes of permanence and annihilation. Having understood how to find [the view] and how to sustain it within setting [the mind] in the context of the view, sustain [its continuum]. Such concentration and wisdom are designated with the names of calm abiding and special insight. Because not even a portion of [calm abiding and special insight] is apart from [inclusion within] the last two perfections, [training in calm abiding and special insight] come within the points of training of the Bodhisattva vow once it has been taken.

Annotations for Tsong-kha-pa's text in Chapter Seven

Here is Tsong-kha-pa's text as supplemented by *The Four Interwoven Annotations,* 832.2-833.1

དེ་ལྟར་སེམས་བསྐྱེད་པ་གཞིར་བྱས་ནས་ཕྱིན་དྲུག་སོགས་ལ་བསླབ་པ། དེ་ནས་ཕར་ཕྱིན་ཐ་མ་ བསམ་གཏན་དང་ཤེས་རབ་ཀྱི་ཕར་ཕྱིན་ནམ་ཞི་ལྷག་ གཉིས་ལ་ཁྱད་པར་དུ་ ཡང་དེས་པར་ བསླབ་ པར་བྱ་ དགོས་ པ་ཡིན་ པས་ ན། སྔར་ཞི་གནས་ཀྱི་སྐབས་སུ་བཤད་པ་ལྟར་ བསམ་གཏན་སྒྲོང་ལུགས་ལ་མཁས་པར་བྱས་ལ་ ཞི་གནས་ཀྱི་ ཏིང་ངེ་འཛིན་ རྣམ་དག་ བསྒྲུབ་ པ་དང་། དེའི་སྟེང་ནས་ཆོས་དང་གང་ཟག་གི་ བདག་མེད་ པ་ གཉིས་ཀྱི་ དབུ་མའི་ ལྟ་བ་རྟག་ཆད་ ཀྱི་མཐའ་གཉིས་ དང་བྲལ་བའི་རྣམ་དག་ཅིག་རྒྱུད་ལ་ཅི་སྐྱེ་ མེད་དུ་མི་རུང་བར་ བྱས་ཏེ། ལྟ་བ་དེ་འདྲ་ རྙེད་པ་དང་ མཉམ་དུ་ལྟ་ ཐོག་དེར་བཞག་ནས་ ལྟ་བ་དེ་ སྐྱོང་བའི་སྐྱོང་ཚུལ་ གོང་དུ་བཤད་པ་ལྟར་ རྣམ་ པར་ དག་ པ་ཞིག་ ཤེས་པར་བྱས་ལ་ ངེས་པར་ བསྐྱང་ངོ་། ། ཚུལ་དེ་ལྟར་བསྐྱང་རྒྱུ་ དེ་འདྲ་བའི་བསམ་གཏན་དང་ཤེས་རབ་གཉིས་པོ་དེ་ཉིད་ ལ་ཞི་ གནས་དང་ ལྷག་ མཐོང་ གི་མིང་བཏགས་པ་ཡིན་གྱི། ཕར་ཕྱིན་ཐ་མ་ བསམ་གཏན་དང་ཤེས་རབ་ཀྱི་ཕར་ཕྱིན་ གཉིས་ སུ་འདུས་པ་ ལས་

ཡོགས་སུ་ཞི་ལྷག་ཅེས་པའི་དོན་ ཟུར་བ་ཞིག་མེད་པས་ ན་ བྱང་སེམས་ཀྱི་ འཇུག་པའི་ སྡོམ་པ་བཟུང་ནས་ སྡོམ་པ་ དེའི་བསླབ་པའི་གསེབ་ནས་ ཞི་ལྷག་གཉིས་

ལ་སློབ་དགོས་པ་དེ་ཐོན་ འོང་བ་ཡིན་ནོ། །

Translation of Tsong-kha-pa's text with annotations, 832.2-833.1

Having taken the altruistic aspiration to enlightenment as your basis, you then train in the six perfections and so forth. In particular, you must definitely train in the latter two perfections—the perfections of concentration and wisdom, calm abiding and special insight. You should become skilled in how to sustain concentration as I explained earlier in the section on calm abiding. Then you should achieve the pure meditative stabilization of calm abiding. It is indispensable that—in connection with the calm abiding you have achieved—you generate in your continuum as much as you can the pure middle way view of the two selflessnesses—the selflessness of persons and the selflessness of phenomena—free from the extremes of permanence and annihilation. Then, you need to understand completely, as I explained earlier, the proper way to sustain [meditation on emptiness]: simultaneous with finding the view, you sustain it within setting the mind in the context of the view. [Having understood how to do this], you should definitely sustain [your mind within the context of the view].

The concentration and wisdom which are the causes of sustaining [the mind within the context of the view] are designated with the names of calm abiding and special insight. Because not even a portion of the meaning of calm abiding and special insight is separate from being included within the last two perfections—concentration and wisdom—the requirement of training in calm abiding and special insight comes about through its falling within the points of training of the Bodhisattva vow of practice once it has been taken.

Chapter Eight

འདི་ཡང་འོག་མ་འོག་མ་བསྒོམས་ཀྱིན་གོང་མ་གོང་མ་ལ་ཐོབ་འདོད་ཆེར་འགྲོ་བ་དང་གོང་མ་གོང་མ་མཚན་པ་ན་འོག་མ་འོག་མ་ལ་བསྐྱུབ་འདོད་
ཇེ་ཆེ་ཇེ་ཆེར་འགྲོ་བ་ཞིག་བྱུང་ན་གནད་དུ་སོང་བ་ཡིན་གྱི། སྔ་མ་རྣམས་ཅི་ཡང་མེད་པར་སེམས་ཀྱི་གནས་ཆ་རེ་ཙམ་དང་ལྟ་བའི་གོ་བ་ཙམ་རེ་ལ་
ནུས་པ་སྐྱུག་ལོ་བྱས་ཀྱང་གནད་དུ་འགྲོ་ཤིན་ཏུ་དཀའ་བས་ལམ་གྱི་ལུས་ཡོངས་སུ་རྫོགས་པ་ཞིག་ལ་ངེས་པ་འདྲོངས་དགོས་པ་ཡིན་ནོ། །

Division of the passage into units to facilitate the analysis of the syntax

Tsong-kha-pa does not provide any topical subheads within the "Summary of the General Path." Later commentators have explicitly identified the topical progression within Tsong-kha-pa's exposition by introducing subheadings along with further annotations. Chapter Eight begins a new topical subhead identified in *The Four Interwoven Annotations* as "the difference between successful and unsuccessful [cultivation of the path]." In Chapters One through Seven, Tsong-kha-pa presented the mode of procedure of the general path through summarizing the practices of beings of the three capacities. Now, Tsong-kha-pa identifies the important distinction between successful and unsuccessful cultivation of these practices.

I have divided the text of Chapter Eight into four principal meaning units.

1

འདི་ཡང་འོག་མ་འོག་མ་བསྒོམས་ཀྱིན་གོང་མ་གོང་མ་ལ་ཐོབ་འདོད་ཆེར་འགྲོ་བ་དང་

2

གོང་མ་གོང་མ་མཚན་པ་ན་འོག་མ་འོག་མ་ལ་བསྐྱུབ་འདོད་ཇེ་ཆེ་ཇེ་ཆེར་འགྲོ་བ་ཞིག་བྱུང་ན་ གནད་དུ་སོང་བ་ཡིན་གྱི།

3

སྔ་མ་རྣམས་ཅི་ཡང་མེད་པར་སེམས་ཀྱི་གནས་ཆ་རེ་ཙམ་དང་ལྟ་བའི་གོ་བ་ཙམ་རེ་ལ་ནུས་པ་སྐྱུག་ལོ་བྱས་ཀྱང་གནད་དུ་འགྲོ་ཤིན་ཏུ་དཀའ་བས་

4

ལམ་གྱི་ལུས་ཡོངས་སུ་རྫོགས་པ་ཞིག་ལ་ངེས་པ་འདྲོངས་དགོས་པ་ཡིན་ནོ། །

Parts 1 & 2

Parts 1 and 2, in most essential form: "When X, [cultivation of the path] is successful."

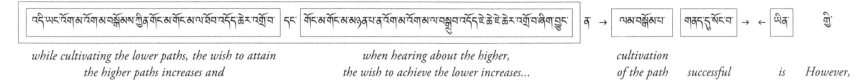

འདི་ཡང་འོག་མ་འོག་མ་བསྒོམས་ཀྱིན་གོང་མ་གོང་མ་ལ་ཐོབ་འདོད་ཆེར་འགྲོ་བ་	དང་	གོང་མ་གོང་མ་མཉན་པ་ན་འོག་མ་འོག་མ་ལ་བསྒྲུབ་འདོད་ཇེ་ཆེ་ཇེ་ཆེར་འགྲོ་བ་ཞིག་བྱུང་	ན	→	ལམ་བསྒོམ་པ་	གནད་དུ་སོང་བ་	→ ←	ཡིན་	ཀྱི་
while cultivating the lower paths, the wish to attain the higher paths increases and		*when hearing about the higher, the wish to achieve the lower increases...*			*cultivation of the path*	*successful*		*is*	*However,*

Metaphorical Extension of verbs of motion

In Part 1 the nom-obj verb of motion is used metaphorically: "When the lower [paths] are cultivated, the wish to attain the higher [paths] increases."

				verbal clause གོང་མ་གོང་མ་ལ་ཐོབ་འདོད་ is the subject of འགྲོ་			qualifier for འགྲོ་	→←	intr. v. (nom-obj)	
	object of བསྒོམས་ →←	trans. v. (ag-nom)		qualifier of ཐོབ་ →←		intr. v. (nom-obj)				
འདི་ཡང་ →	འོག་མ་འོག་མ་ →←	བསྒོམས་	ཀྱིན་ →	གོང་མ་གོང་མ་	ལ་ →←	ཐོབ་འདོད་ →	ཆེ་	ར་ →←	འགྲོ་བ་	དང་
s.p.	adj. used as pronoun	ag-nom verb	s.p.	adj. used as pronoun	2nd	comp v.	adj.	+2nd	verb of motion	s.p.
further-more	lower (paths)	while cultivating		higher		the wish to attain	great		becomes	

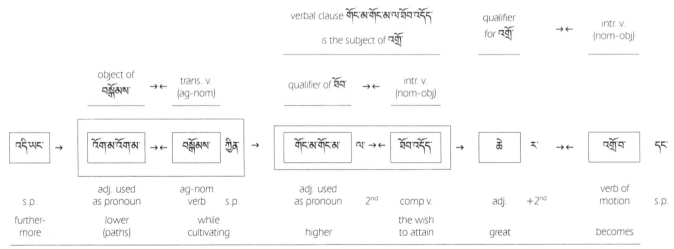

While you are cultivating the lower [paths], the wish to attain the higher [paths] increases and...

Glossary for Part 1

འདི་ limiting adj. used as a pronoun, *this one*

འདི་ཡང་ s.p., introductory particle, *furthermore*

འོག་མ་འོག་མ་ adj. and pronoun, *later, below, beneath, under*

བསྒོམས་ trans. v. (ag-nom) (past tense), *meditated on, cultivated*
སྒོམ་བསྒོམས་བསྒོམ་སྒོམས། ཐ་དད།

གོམས་ intr. v. (nom-loc), *be accustomed to* གོམས་གོམས་གོམས། ཐ་མི་དད།

བསྒོམས་ཀྱིན་ verb + syntactic particle signifying continuous action

ཀྱིན་གྱིན་གིན་ equivalent syntactic particles following verb signifying continuous action

གོང་མ་གོང་མ་ adj. and pronoun, *higher, the higher [ones]*

གོང་མ་གོང་མ་ལ་ pronoun + 2nd case particle

ལ་ particle; either 1) a syntactic particle following a verb or verb phrase signifying conjunction or disjunction, or 2) a case particle following nouns, pronouns, postpositions, and adjectives marking the 2nd, 4th and 7th cases

ཐོབ་ intr. v. (nom-obj) (past tense), *attain, obtain, get, arrive at*

འཐོབ་ཐོབ་འཐོབ། ཐ་མི་དད།

འདོད་ trans. v. (ag-nom), *want, wish, assert.* This verb is listed in the *Great Word Treasury* as ཐ་མི་དད།, but I think it is a transitive ag-nom verb.

འདོད་འདོད་འདོད། ཐ་མི་དད།

ཐོབ་འདོད་ verb phrase, abbreviation for ཐོབ་པར་འདོད་ *want to attain*

ཐོབ་པར་འདོད་ verb phrase (verbal infinitive + auxiliary verb)

ཐོབ་པར་ verbal infinitive; here, the fused ར་ is a syntactic particle modifying a verb to create a verbal infinitive within the verb phrases ཐོབ་པར་འདོད་ *[I, you] want to attain;* it is **not** a case particle marking the 2nd, 4th or 7th cases because it does not follow a noun—it is within a verb phrase

འདོད་ auxiliary verb, *want, wish*

ཆེ་ adj., *great, big*

ཆེར་ adj. + 2nd case particle fused to suffixless syllable

ར་ particle fused to suffixless final syllable; either 1) a verb-modifying syntactic particle within a verb phrase, or 2) a case particle following nouns, pronouns, postpositions, and adjectives marking the 2nd, 4th and 7th cases

འགྲོ་ intr. v. (nom-obj), *go;* by extension: often used metaphorically in the sense of *turns into* or *becomes*

འགྲོ་ཕྱིན་འགྲོ་སོང་། ཐ་མི་དད། སོང་ is also used as the past form

འགྲོ་བ་ verbal noun, *goer, migrator*

དང་ particle; used three ways: 1) continuative syntactic particle used following nouns and noun phrases (*and,* or with negative verb, *or*); 2) syntactic particle marking the qualifier of an intr. nom-s.p. v. of conjunction, as in ང་རང་མི་སྡུག་པ་དང་ཕྲད་ན་ *if we meet with unpleasantness;* and 3) syntactic particle marking the qualifier of an intr. nom-s.p. v. of disjunction, as in རྟོག་པ་དང་བྲལ་ *free from conceptuality*

The Four Interwoven Annotations begin this chapter with a new subheading

།སྒོམ་པ་གནད་དུ་སོང་དང་མ་སོང་གི་ཁྱད་པར། *the difference between successful and unsuccessful cultivation*

གནད་ n., *essential, essential point*

གནད་དུ་ n. + 2nd case particle

སོང་ intr. v. (nom-obj) (alternate past tense), *went;* often used by extension in the metaphorical sense of *turned into* or *became*

འགྲོ་ཕྱིན་འགྲོ་སོང་། ཐ་མི་དད། སོང་ is also an alternate past form

མ་སོང་ negative verb, *not gone, not turned into, not become*

མ་སོང་གི་ negative verbal noun + 6th case particle

ཁྱད་པར་ n. and adv.; as noun, *attribute, feature, qualification, difference;* as adverb, *in particular, especially*

Action verbs in a cognitive context: the metaphorical extension of the meaning of verbs

Tibetan metaphorically expands the meaning of some intransitive verbs of motion, and some transitive verbs expressing a physical action, to express cognitive relationships instead of physical relationships. འགྲོ་ *go* is often used by extension metaphorically in the sense of *turns into* or *becomes.* This construction follows the (nom-obj) paradigm of subject in the 1st case and qualifier in 2nd case for intransitive verbs of motion, but the construction no longer means physical going to a physical destination. Instead, the 1st case subject becomes something (marked with the 2nd case), as if the subject is going to a metaphorical destination.

1. Metaphorical extension of transitive verbs

འཛིན་ trans. v. (ag-nom), *grasp, hold;* by extension: *apprehend, conceive* འཛིན་བཟུང་གཟུང་ཟུང་། ཐ་དད།

བདག་འཛིན་ compound noun, *conception of a self.* Rather than translating བདག་འཛིན་ as *self-grasping,* a **physical relationship,** བདག་འཛིན་ is better understood as signifying a **cognitive relationship** translated as *conception of a self,* i.e., the superimposition of a mode of existence which, although strongly believed in, does not exist.

2. Metaphorical extension of intransitive verbs

འགྲོ་ intr. v. (nom-obj), *go;* used by extension metaphorically in the sense of *turns into* or *becomes.* འགྲོ་ཕྱིན་འགྲོ་སོང་། ཐ་མི་དད། སོང་ is also a past form

གོང་མ་གོང་མ་ལ་ཐོབ་འདོད་ཆེར་འགྲོ་ Here, འགྲོ་ is not signifying the physical activity of a verb of motion, but rather is being used metaphorically in the sense of a cognitive state being transformed into a deeper state of development: *the wish to attain the higher paths becomes greater, i.e., increases*

Just as the 2nd case marks the destination when འགྲོ་ is being used in the literal sense of *go to [somewhere],* the 2nd case marks the metaphorical destination when འགྲོ་ is being used in a non-literal, metaphorical sense. In these two examples the intransitive verb of motion is used to signify metaphorical transformation: "A becomes B."

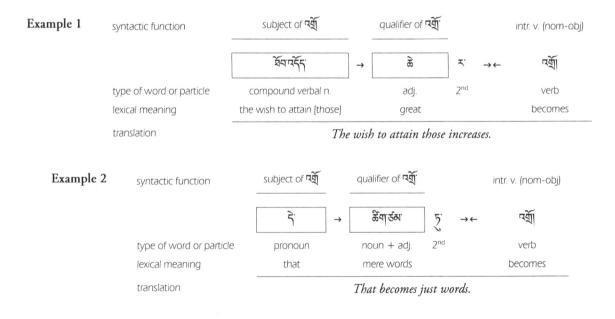

Example 1

syntactic function	subject of འགྲོ་	qualifier of འགྲོ་			intr. v. (nom-obj)
	ཐོབ་འདོད་ →	ཆེ	ར་	→←	འགྲོ།
type of word or particle	compound verbal n.	adj.	2nd		verb
lexical meaning	the wish to attain [those]	great			becomes
translation	*The wish to attain those increases.*				

Example 2

syntactic function	subject of འགྲོ་	qualifier of འགྲོ་			intr. v. (nom-obj)
	དེ་ →	ཚིག་ཙམ་	ཏུ་	→←	འགྲོ།
type of word or particle	pronoun	noun + adj.	2nd		verb
lexical meaning	that	mere words			becomes
translation	*That becomes just words.*				

Part 2 • གོང་མ་གོང་མ་མཉན་པ་ན་འོག་མ་འོག་མ་ལ་བསྒྲུབ་འདོད་ཇེ་ཆེ་ཇེ་ཆེར་འགྲོ་བ་ཞིག་བྱུང་ན་གནད་དུ་སོང་བ་ཡིན་གྱི།

Two sequential conditional clauses

The key to understanding this sentence lies in the two sequential conditional clauses: "When, upon hearing X, Y increases, [cultivation of the path] is successful."

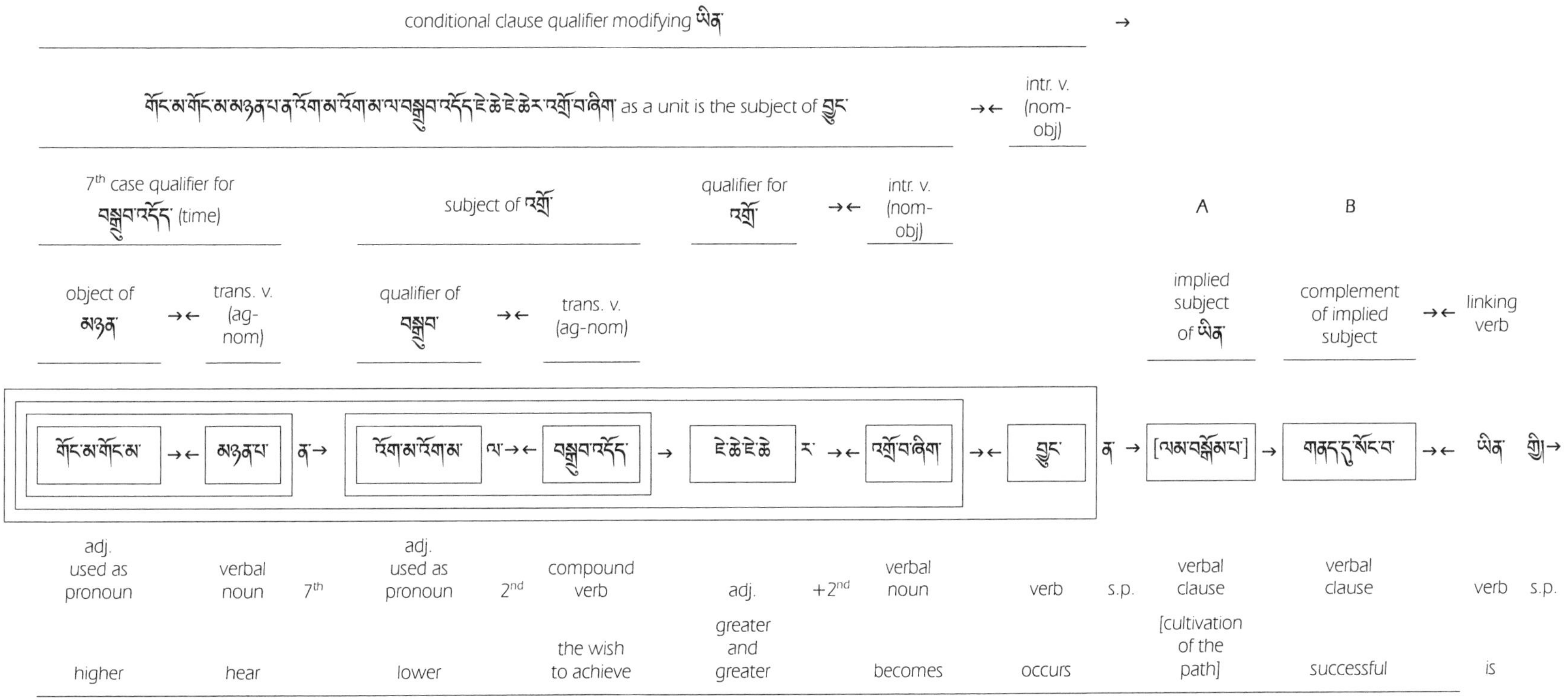

...and when upon hearing about the higher [paths], the wish to achieve the lower [paths] increases, [cultivation of the path] is successful.

Glossary for Part 2

གོང་མ་གོང་མ་ adjective and pronoun, *higher*

མཉན་ trans. v. (ag-nom) (past and future tenses), *listen to*

ཉན་མཉན་མཉན་ཉོན། བདད།

མཉན་པ་ verbal noun, *listening*

མཉན་པ་ན་ verb + syntactic particle marking conditional clause

ན་ particle; either 1) a rhetorical syntactic particle marking a conditional clause following a verb or verb phrase, or 2) a case particle following nouns, pronouns, postpositions, and adjectives marking the 2nd, 4th and 7th cases

མཉན་པ་ན་ Jam-yang-shay-ba glosses this as མཉན་པའི་ཚེ་ན་ *when, at the time of hearing* (ANN, 833.2)

འོག་མ་འོག་མ་ adj. and pronoun, *later, below, beneath, under, lower*

རོག་མ་རོག་མ་ལ་ pronoun + 2nd case particle marking the qualifier of the transitive verb བསྒྲུབ་ *achieve, establish* showing place of activity

ལ་ particle; either 1) a syntactic particle following a verb or verb phrase signifying conjunction or disjunction, or 2) a case particle following nouns, pronouns, postpositions, and adjectives marking the 2nd, 4th and 7th cases

བསྒྲུབ་ trans. v. (ag-nom), *achieve, establish*

སྒྲུབ་བསྒྲུབས་བསྒྲུབ་སྒྲུབས། ཐ་དད།

གྲུབ་ intr. v. (nom-obj), *be established, be proven, exists*

འགྲུབ་གྲུབ་འགྲུབ། ཐ་མི་དད།

འདོད་ trans. v. (ag-nom), *want, wish, assert*. This verb is listed in the *Great Word Treasury* as ཐ་མི་དད།, but I think it is a transitive ag-nom verb.

འདོད་འདོད་འདོད། ཐ་མི་དད།

ཇེ་ adv. particle, indicates comparative degree of adj. or adv., *increase* or *gradual increase.*

ཇེ་ཆེ་ comparative particle + adj., *bigger*

ཇེ་ཆེར་ adv. + adj. + 2nd case particle, *[something becomes] greater, increases*

ཇེ་ + adj. + 2nd case particle is an adverbial construction where ཇེ་ is an adverb modifying the adjective following it.

ར་ particle fused to suffixless final syllable; either 1) a verb-modifying syntactic particle within a verb phrase, or 2) a case particle following nouns, pronouns, postpositions, and adjectives marking the 2nd, 4th and 7th cases

ཇེ་ཆེ་ཇེ་ཆེ་ *larger and larger, greater and greater*

ཞིག་ adv. s.p., makes preceding word, phrase or clause into an adverbial construction

བྱུང་ intr. v. (nom-obj) (past tense), *arose, occurred, came forth*

འབྱུང་བྱུང་འབྱུང་། ཐ་མི་དད།

བྱུང་ན་ verb + syntactic particle marking conditional clause

ན་ particle; either 1) a rhetorical syntactic particle marking a conditional clause following a verb or verb phrase, or 2) a case particle following nouns, pronouns, postpositions, and adjectives marking the 2nd, 4th and 7th cases

གནད་ n., *essential, important point*

གནད་དུ་ noun + 2nd case particle marking the qualifier of the intransitive verb of motion སོང་ (used here metaphorically)

སོང་ intr. v. (nom-obj) (alternate past tense), *went;* by extension: *became*

འགྲོ་ཕྱིན་འགྲོ་སོང་། ཐ་མི་དད། སོང་ is also used as the past form

ཡིན་ intr. v. (nom-nom), *is, are*

ཡིན་གྱི་ linking verb + disjunctive syntactic particle, *[A] is [B], but...*

གྱི་ particle; either 1) a syntactic particle following a verb or verb phrase signifying conjunction or disjunction, or 2) a 6th case particle following nouns, pronouns, postpositions, and adjectives

Distinguish a declined noun མཉམ་པ་ན་ from a verb + syntactic particle བྱུང་ན་

གོང་མ་གོང་མ་མཉམ་པ་ན་	མཉམ་པ་ན་ is a noun + 2nd, 4th or 7th case particle. Here: 7th case to indicate **time**. It is a qualifier of the later compound verb བསྒྲུབ་འདོད་
བསྒྲུབ་འདོད་ཇེ་ཆེ་ཇེ་ཆེར་འགྲོ་བ་ཞིག་བྱུང་ན་	བྱུང་ན་ is a verb + a conditional syntactic particle, creating a conditional verbal clause: *when [that] happens, the wish to achieve [the higher paths] increases.*
གནད་དུ་སོང་བ་	*have become successful* (past tense); the forms of འགྲོ་ are འགྲོ་ཕྱིན་འགྲོ་སོང་།, but སོང་ is also seen as an alternate past form

Part 3 • སྔ་མ་རྣམས་ཅི་ཡང་མེད་པར་སེམས་ཀྱི་གནས་ཆ་རེ་ཙམ་དང་ལྟ་བའི་གོ་བ་ཙམ་རེ་ལ་ནུས་པ་སྒྲུག་ལོ་བྱས་ཀྱང་གནད་དུ་འགྲོ་ཤིན་ཏུ་དཀའ་བས

Part 3 begins with a qualifying construction employing a negative verbal, "without X, Y will not..."

verbal clause is an adverbial qualifier for later verb

སྔ་མ་རྣམས་	ཅི་ཡང་ →←	མེད་པ	ར་ →
	indefinite and general relative pronoun	negative verb	
noun + pluralizing lexical particle	indefinite and general negative relative pronoun		+2nd
the former [paths]	without any, not at all		2nd case here creates an adverbial sense

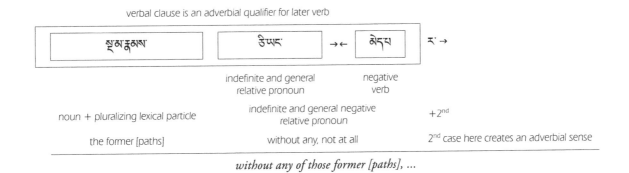

without any of those former [paths], ...

Part 3 continues

entire construction, declined in the 3rd case, is a qualifier of the later verb འཇོངས་དགོས་པ་ *must induce,* stating a reason

7th case qualifier for ནུས་ indicating that in which one has ability

intr. v. (nom-loc): ནུས་པ

trans. v. (ag-nom): བྱས་

subject of understood ཡིན: གནད་དུ་འགྲོ་

complement of གནད་དུ་འགྲོ་: ཤིན་ཏུ་དཀའ་བ

སེམས་	ཀྱི་	གནས་ཆ་	རེ་ཙམ་	དང་	ལྟ་བ	འི་	གོ་བ་ཙམ་	རེ་	ལ་ →←	ནུས་པ →	སྒྲུག་ལོ་ →←	བྱས་	ཀྱང་ →	གནད་དུ་འགྲོ་ →←	ཤིན་ཏུ་དཀའ་བ	ས་ →
noun	6th	compound noun	adj. + restrictive particle	s.p.	noun	+6th	vbl. n. + restrictive particle	adj.	7th	verbal noun		verb	s.p.	verbal noun	lex. prefix part. + adj.	+3rd
mind		factor of stability	a mere portion		the view		mere understanding	portion		capacity	stirred	work		becoming successful	very difficult	

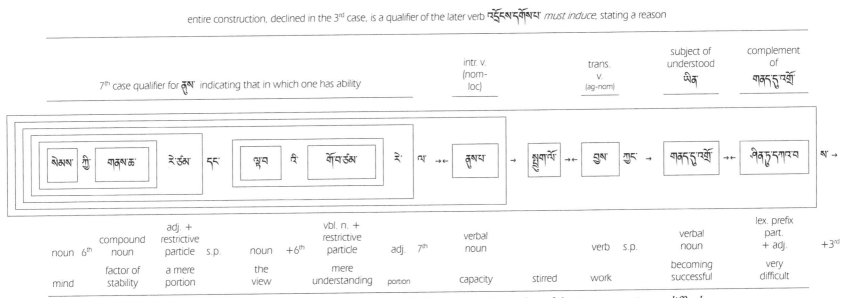

although one has gained a mere portion of the factor of stability and understanding of the view, success is very difficult.

Glossary for Part 3

སྔ་མ་ adj., *former*

རྣམས་ optional lexical pluralizing particle

ཅི་ཡང་ indefinite and general relative pronoun, *whatever, any, at all*

ཅི་ཡང་མེད་པར་ indefinite and general neg. relative pronoun + 2nd case particle fused to suffixless final syllable; *without any, not at all*

ར་ particle fused to suffixless final syllable; either 1) a verb-modifying syntactic particle within a verb phrase, or 2) a case particle following nouns, pronouns, postpositions, and adjectives marking the 2nd, 4th and 7th cases

སེམས་ n., *mind, awareness*

སེམས་ཀྱི་ noun + 6th case particle

ཀྱི་ particle; either 1) a syntactic particle following a verb or verb phrase signifying conjunction or disjunction, or 2) a 6th case particle following nouns, pronouns, postpositions, and adjectives

གནས་ཆ་ compound n., *factor of stability*

གནས་ intr. v. (nom-loc), *abide, dwell*

གནས་ n., *place, abode, location,* and also *status, state, situation, source, object, topic,* and *basis*

གནས་པ་ verbal n., *dwelling, remaining, one who dwells or remains*

ཆ་ n., *part, factor*

རེ་ limiting adj. used as a pronoun, *each*

ཙམ་ adj., and restrictive lexical suffix particle, *just, only, merely*

དང་ particle, used three ways: 1) continuative syntactic particle used following nouns and noun phrases (*and,* or with negative verb, *or*); 2) syntactic particle marking the qualifier of an intr. nom-s.p. v. of conjunction, as in ང་རང་མི་སྡུག་པ་དང་ཕྲད་ན་ *if we meet with unpleasantness;* and 3) syntactic particle marking the qualifier of an intr. nom-s.p. v. of disjunction, as in རྟོག་པ་དང་བྲལ་ *free from conceptuality*

ལྟ་ trans. v. (ag-obj), *look at, regard*

ལྟ་བལྟས་བལྟ་ལྟོས། ཐ་དད།

ལྟོས་ intr. v. (nom-loc), *depend; be contingent on, be within the context of*

ལྟོས་བལྟོས། ཐ་མི་དད།

ལྟ་བ་ n., *the view (of emptiness)*

ལྟ་བའི་ n. + 6th case particle fused to suffixless final syllable

འི་ particle fused to suffixless final syllable; either 1) a syntactic particle following a verb or verb phrase signifying conjunction or disjunction, or 2) a 6th case particle following nouns, pronouns, postpositions, and adjectives

གོ་ trans. v., (ag-nom), *know, understand.* This verb is listed in the *Great Word Treasury* as ཐ་མི་དད།, but I think it is a transitive verb (ag-nom).
གོ་གོ་གོ། ཐ་མི་དད།

གོ་བ་ n., *understanding*

གོ་བ་ཙམ་ noun phrase (n. + adj.), *mere understanding*

ཙམ་ adj. and restrictive lexical suffix particle, *just, only, merely*

རེ་ limiting adj. used as a pronoun, *each, every, a single, some*

རེ་ intr. v. (nom-loc), *expect, hope*

རེ་རེ་རེ། ཐ་མི་དད།

ལ་ particle; either syntactic particle (following verb) signifying conjunction or disjunction, or case particle (following noun) marking the 2nd, 4th and 7th cases; here: 7th case

ནུས་ intr. v. (nom-loc), *be able*

ནུ་ནུས་ནུ་ནུས། ཐ་དད།

ནུས་པ་ n., *capacity, ability*

སྤྲུག་ trans. v. (ag-nom), *shake off, shake, stir;* by extension: *purify*

སྤྲུག་སྤྲུགས་སྤྲུག་སྤྲུགས། ཐ་དད།

བྱས་	trans. v. (past tense), *do, make, perform, take;* here: used as the strong past auxiliary བྱེད་བྱས་བྱ་བྱོས། ཐ་དད།
ཀྱང་	conjunctive and disjunctive syntactic particle used after nouns, pronouns, adjectives, verbs, and verb phrases, *but, even, also*
ཀྱང་ཡང་འང་	are equivalent conjunctive and disjunctive syntactic particles used after nouns, pronouns, adjectives, verbs, and verb phrases, *but, even, also*
ཀྱང་	follows words ending with the letters ག་ད་བ་ས་
ཡང་	follows words ending with the letters ང་ན་མ་འ་ར་ལ་ and after suffixless words
འང་	follows suffixless words
གནད་དུ་འགྲོ་	intr. v. (nom-obj), *be successful* འགྲོ་ཕྱིན་འགྲོ་སོང་། ཐ་མི་དད། སོང་ is also an alternate past form
གནད་	n., *essential point, essential*
གནད་དུ་	n. + 2nd case particle followed by verb here creates an adverbial construction modifying the following verb འགྲོ་
འགྲོ་	intr. v. (nom-obj), *go;* often used metaphorically in the sense of *turns into* or *becomes*
གནད་དུ་འགྲོ་བ་	n., *success*
ཤིན་ཏུ་	adv., *very*
དཀའ་བ་	n., adj., *difficult*
དཀའ་བས་	n. + 3rd case particle fused to suffixless final syllable
ས་	abbreviation of the particle འིས་ (when འིས་ is fused to a suffixless final syllable, the འི goes away and all that's left is a fused ས་); either 1) syntactic particle creating an adverbial construction, 2) syntactic particle marking the qualifier of an intransitive nom-s.p. verb of absence, or 3) case particle marking the 3rd case
གིས་ཀྱིས་གྱིས་འིས་ཡིས་	are equivalent particles, marking the 3rd case and also marking syntactic adverbial relationships.

Note on the utility of annotations

The annotation in *The Four Interwoven Annotations* expands Tsong-kha-pa's brief remarks with commentary which I find particularly helpful in understanding Tsong-kha-pa's point here. Tsong-kha-pa is about to contrast the proper way to cultivate the path (cultivate the entire path) with the improper way (cultivate only parts). Here, he compares the progression of mutually reinforcing paths with a practice of paths imperfectly understood and incompletely practiced. Here is Tsong-kha-pa's text without annotations.

སྔ་མ་རྣམས་ཅི་ཡང་མེད་པར་སེམས་ཀྱི་གནས་ཆ་རེ་ཙམ་དང་ལྟ་བའི་གོ་བ་ཙམ་རེ་ལ་ནུས་པ་སྤྲུག་ལོ་བྱས་ཀྱང་གནད་དུ་འགྲོ་ཤིན་ཏུ་དཀའ་བས་

---

without any of those former [paths], although one has gained a mere portion of the factor of stability and understanding of the view, success is very difficult.

Here is Tsong-kha-pa's text clarified by the annotations

ལམ་གྱི་གཞི་མ་བཤེས་གཉེན་བསྟེན་པ་སོགས་ལམ་ སྔ་མ་རྣམས་ ངེས་པར་དགོས་པའི་མཐོང་དང་གཅེས་ ཅི་ཡང་མེད་པར་ དེ་དག་མི་བསྒོམ་པར་བཞག་

ནས་ སེམས་ཀྱི་གནས་ཆ་རེ་ཙམ་ རེ་འཚོལ་བ་ དང་ལྟ་བའི་གོ་བ་ཙམ་རེ་ འཚོལ་བ་ ལ་ རང་གི་རྩལ་ཅི་ཡོད་ཀྱི་ ནུས་པ་ བཏོན་ནས་ སྦྱུག་ལོ་ ཏེ་

ནུས་པ་གང་ཡོད་སྦྱུག་ཅིང་འདོན་ནོ་ཞེས་དེ་སྐད་ བྱས་ཀྱང་ ལམ་བསྒོམ་པ་ གནད་དུ་ གཏན་ནས་ འགྲོ་ བར་ ཤིན་ཏུ་དཀའ་བ་ ཡིན་པ་ ས་

Without seeing and valuing the definite need for the earlier paths such as the foundation of the path, and reliance on the spiritual guide, through not having cultivated those paths, instead you may strive at a mere portion of the factors of stability of the mind [i.e., not all those required to generate fully qualified calm abiding]. You may strive at a merely partial understanding of the view [of emptiness]. Although however much capacity as you have has been developed, and you say your ability [in stability and analysis] has been shaken and developed, it is extremely difficult to be completely successful in cultivating the path.

Notes

སྔ་མ་རྣམས་ the former; this is explained as ལམ་གྱི་གཞི་མ་བཤེས་གཉེན་བསྟེན་པ་སོགས་ལམ་ *[the former paths]—the foundation of the path, reliance on your spiritual guide, and so forth*

ཅི་ཡང་མེད་པར་ *without any* is explained as ངེས་པར་དགོས་པའི་མཐོང་ཅིང་གཅེས་ཅི་ཡང་མེད་པར་ *without seeing their definite need, and [without] valuing [them]*

དེ་དག་མི་བསྒོམ་པར་བཞག་ནས་ *posited without cultivating those;* this tells us what ཆ་རེ་ཙམ་ *a mere portion* means

སེམས་ཀྱི་གནས་ཆ་རེ་ཙམ་རེ་འཚོལ་བ་ *[you] strive at only a portion of the factor of stability*

ལྟ་བའི་གོ་བ་ཙམ་རེ་འཚོལ་བ་ *[you] strive at only partial understanding of the view [of emptiness]*

འཚོལ་བ་ལ་རང་གི་རྩལ་ཅི་ཡོད་ཀྱི་ནུས་པ་བཏོན་ནས་སྦྱུག་ལོ་ཏེ་ *the capacity of however much dexterity one has in terms of the [partial] striving, through being developed, is revealed*

ནུས་པ་བཏོན་ནས་སྦྱུག་ལོ་ཏེ་ནུས་པ་གང་ཡོད་སྦྱུག་ཅིང་འདོན་ནོ་ཞེས་དེ་སྐད་བྱས་ཀྱང་ *although one's capacity, through being developed, is revealed—whatever capacity you have is said to be revealed and developed*

འདོན་ trans. v. (ag-nom), *cause to come out, expel, recite* འདོན་བཏོན་གདོན་ཐོན། ཐ་དད།

འཚོལ་ trans. v. (ag-nom), *strive at, work at*

དེ་སྐད་ adverbial pronoun, *thus*

དེ་སྐད་བྱས་ adverbial phrase, *having done thus*

Part 3 employs a frequently seen implicit linking verb ཡིན་ linking the subject with its complement

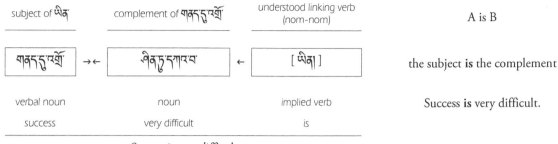

subject of ཡིན་		complement of གནད་དུ་འགྲོ་		understood linking verb (nom-nom)
གནད་དུ་འགྲོ་	→←	ཤིན་ཏུ་དཀའ་བ་	←	[ཡིན།]
verbal noun		noun		implied verb
success		very difficult		is

Success is very difficult.

A is B

the subject **is** the complement

Success **is** very difficult.

Grammar review • How a complement behaves as a syntactic unit

Complements are units of syntax that complete subjects or objects. Complements complete either the object (in a transitive sentence) or the subject (in an intransitive sentence) by **being** the subject or object, or **by appearing as** or **being perceived as** the subject or object.

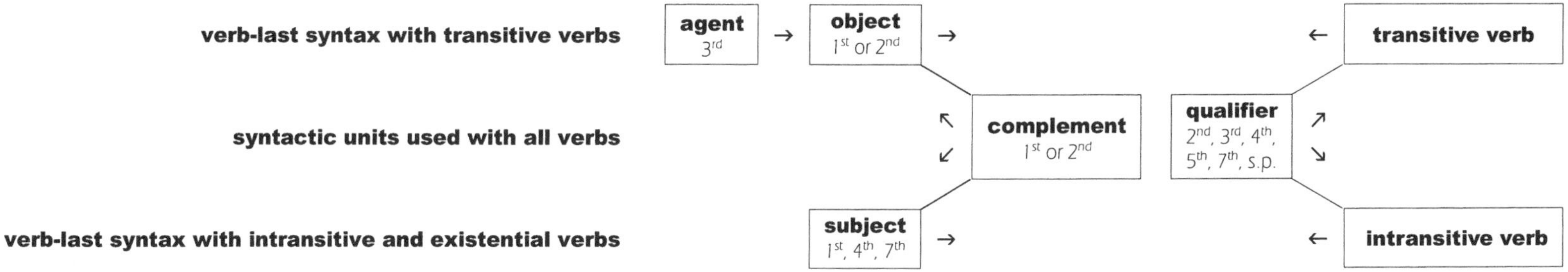

Grammar review • 1st case complements with linking verbs • The subject བུམ་པ་ is the complement མི་རྟག་པ་

In this example the complement completes the subject in the sense that the subject is the complement.

subject of linking verb ཡིན་		complement of subject བུམ་པ་		(nom-nom) linking verb
བུམ་པ་	→←	མི་རྟག་པ་	←	ཡིན།
noun		noun		linking verb
pot(s)		impermanent, impermanent phenomena		is/are

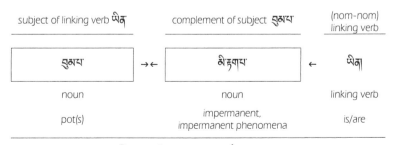

Pots are impermanent phenomena.

Grammar review • 2nd case complements with intransitive verbs • The subject གངས་རི་ is being perceived as being the complement སྔོན་པོ་

In this example the complement completes the subject in the sense that the subject is being perceived as the complement.

subject of སྣང་		qualifier: place of activity			complement of གངས་རི་			intransitive action verb (nom-obj)
གངས་རི་	→	མིག་ཤེས་	ལ་	→	སྔོན་པོ་	ར་	→←	སྣང་།
noun		noun	2nd		noun	+2nd		verb
snow mountain		eye consciousness			blue			appear

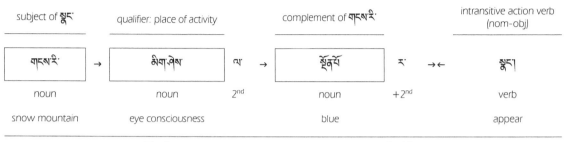

To the eye consciousness, snow mountains appear to be blue.

Grammar review • Complements with transitive verbs tell you more about the object • The object is the complement

In this example the complement completes the object in the sense that the object is being perceived as the complement.

agent of འདོད་		object of འདོད་		complement of སེམས་			transitive verb (ag-nom)
ཁ་ཅིག	གིས་ →	སེམས་	→	གང་ཟག་གི་མཚན་གཞི	ར་	→←	འདོད་དོ། །
noun	3rd	noun		noun phrase (n. + 6th case particle + n.)	+2nd		final verb + terminating syntactic particle
someone		mind		illustration of the person			assert

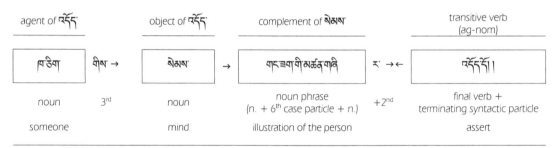

Some assert mind to be the illustration of the person.

Part 4 • ལམ་གྱི་ལུས་ཡོངས་སུ་རྫོགས་པ་ཞིག་ལ་ངེས་པ་འདྲོངས་དགོས་པ་ཡིན་ནོ། །

Part 4 states the conclusion

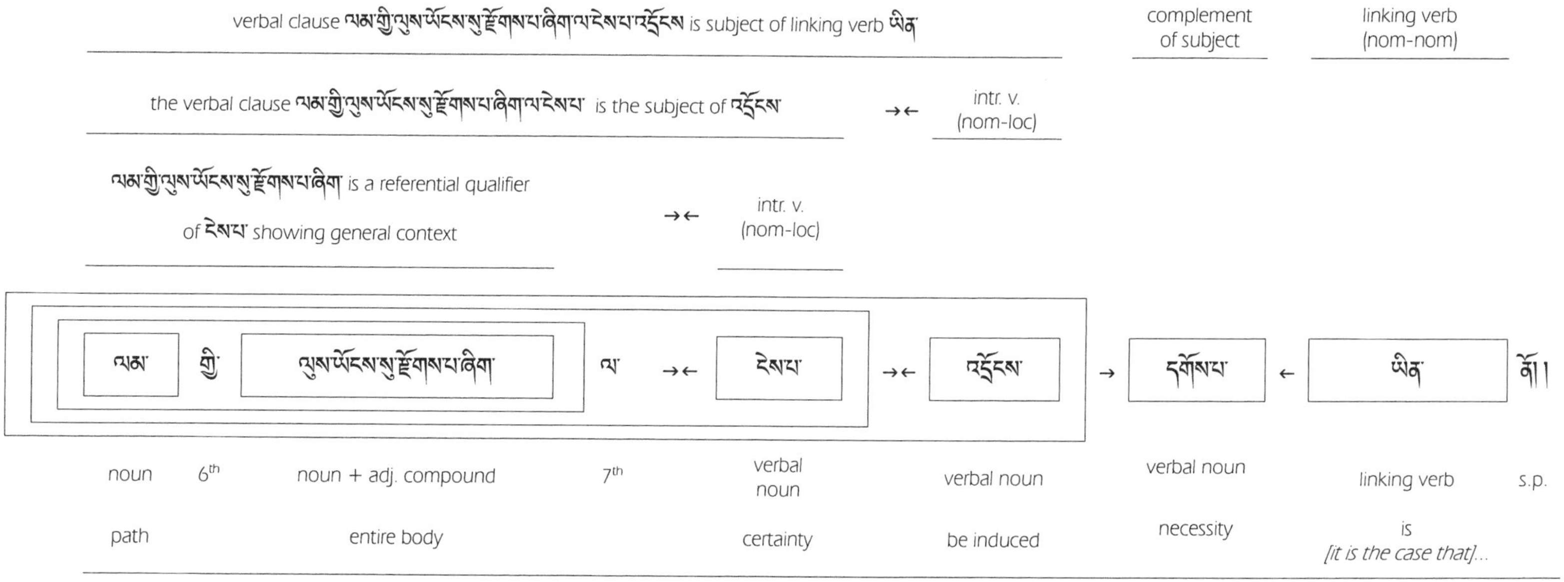

[Therefore,] inducing certainty regarding the entire body of the path [i.e., that in order to achieve Buddhahood, one must not stray from these paths] is a necessity.

Glossary for Part 4

ལམ་	n., *path*
ལམ་གྱི་	n. + 6th case particle
གྱི་	particle; either 1) a syntactic particle following a verb or verb phrase signifying conjunction or disjunction, or 2) a 6th case particle following nouns, pronouns, postpositions, and adjectives
ལུས་	n., *body, corpus*
ཡོངས་སུ་རྫོགས་པ་	n., *completely perfect*
ཡོངས་སུ་	lexical prefix particle, translates the Sanskrit prefix *pari-, completely, thoroughly*
རྫོགས་པ་	n., *completion*
ཡོངས་སུ་རྫོགས་པ་ཞིག་	n. + syntactic particle, *completely perfect*
ཞིག་	adv. s.p., makes preceding word, phrase or clause into an adverb

ཡོངས་སུ་རྫོགས་པ་ཞིག་ལ་ n. + 7th case particle

ལ་ particle; either 1) a syntactic particle following a verb or verb phrase signifying conjunction or disjunction, or 2) a case particle following nouns, pronouns, postpositions, and adjectives marking the 2nd, 4th and 7th cases

ངེས་ intr. v. (nom-loc), *be certain, ascertain*

ངེས་ངེས་ངེས། ཐ་མི་དད།

ངེས་པ་ n., *certainty, ascertainment*

འདྲོངས་ intr. v. (nom-loc), *be induced*

འདྲོང་འདྲོངས་འདྲོང་། ཐ་མི་དད།

འདྲེན་ trans. v. (ag-nom), *induce, lead, draw; cite*

འདྲེན་དྲངས་དྲང་དྲོངས། ཐ་དད།

དགོས་ intr. v. (b/p-nom), *be necessary, need, require*

དགོས་དགོས་དགོས། ཐ་མི་དད།

དགོས་པ་ n., *need, purpose, necessity*

ཡིན་ intr. v. (nom-nom), *is, are*

ཡིན་ནོ། verb + sentence-terminating syntactic particle following word with suffix letter ན་.

ནོ་ sentence-terminating syntactic particle following word with suffix letter ན་.

Notes on Part 4

ལམ་གྱི་ལུས་ཡོངས་སུ་རྫོགས་པ་ཞིག noun + adjective compound, *the complete body of the path.* Marked with a 7th case particle, this phrase is the qualifier of ངེས་པ་ *ascertain, be certain* showing general referential context

ལམ་གྱི་ལུས་ཡོངས་སུ་རྫོགས་པ་ཞིག་ལ་ངེས་པ་ verbal clause, *certainty regarding the entire body of the path,* is the subject of the intransitive verb (nom-loc) འདྲོངས་ *be induced*

ལམ་གྱི་ལུས་ཡོངས་སུ་རྫོགས་པ་ཞིག་ལ་ངེས་པ་འདྲོངས་ verbal clause, *the inducement of certainty regarding the entire body of the path* is the subject of the linking verb ཡིན་

ལམ་གྱི་ལུས་ཡོངས་སུ་རྫོགས་པ་ཞིག་ལ་ངེས་པ་འདྲོངས་དགོས་པ་ཡིན་ནོ། This sentence ending construction is syntactically irregular but frequently seen, conveying the sense "*it is the case that...*" In translating this sentence into English, we would more naturally not follow the Tibetan literally, *A is B,* but rather recast the sentence in an active voice: *[you] must induce certainty regarding the complete body of the path.*

Chapter Eight Self Test

Write out the passage, boxing and identifying every syntactic element.

འདི་ཡང་འོག་མ་འོག་མ་བསྒོམས་ཀྱིན་གོང་མ་གོང་མ་ལ་ཐོབ་འདོད་ཆེར་འགྲོ་བ་དང་གོང་མ་གོང་མ་མཉན་པ་ན་འོག་མ་འོག་མ་ལ་བསྒྲུབ་འདོད་ཧེ་ཆེ་ཧེ་ཆེར་འགྲོ་བ་ཞིག་བྱུང་ན་གཞན་དུ་སོང་བ་ཡིན་གྱི། སྔ་མ་རྣམས་ཅི་ཡང་མེད་པར་སེམས་ཀྱི་གནས་ཆ་རེ་ཙམ་དང་ལྟ་བའི་གོ་བ་ཙམ་རེ་ལ་ནུས་པ་སྤྲུག་ལོ་བྱས་ཀྱང་གནད་དུ་འགྲོ་ཤིན་ཏུ་དཀའ་བས་ལམ་གྱི་ལུས་ཡོངས་སུ་རྫོགས་པ་ཞིག་ལ་ངེས་པ་འདྲོངས་དགོས་པ་ཡིན་ནོ། །

Can you read this?

Tsong-kha-pa's *Middle Length Stages of the Path,* written later in his life, condenses the above passage to a single sentence. Can you read it?

འདི་ཡང་ལམ་འོག་མ་བསྒོམས་ཀྱིན་གོང་མ་ལ་ཐོབ་འདོད་ཆེར་འགྲོ་བ་དང༌། གོང་མ་མཉན་པ་ན་འོག་མ་ལ་བསྒྲུབ་འདོད་ཧེ་ཆེར་འགྲོ་བ་ཞིག་དགོས་སོ། །

Vocabulary

For each word, can you identify what part of speech it is (noun, pronoun, adjective, verb, adverb, postposition) and what it means?
For each syntactic particle, can you identify what class of syntactic particle it belongs to and how it is used?

གོང་མ་	ངེས་	ཐོབ་པར་འདོད་	ནུས་པ་
གཞན་	ངེས་པ་	ཐོབ་འདོད་	བསྒོམས་
གཞན་དུ་འགྲོ་	ཅི་ཡང་	དཀའ་བ་	ཀྱིན་
གནས་	ཅི་ཡང་མེད་	དགོས་	བསྒྲུབ་
གནས་ཆ་	ཆ་	དགོས་པ་	མཉན་
གནས་པ་	ཆེ་	དང་	མཉན་པ་
གོ་	ཧེ་	ན་	ཙམ་
གོ་བ་	ཧེ་ཆེ་	ནོ་	ཞིག་
གོམས་	ཐོབ་	ནུས་	འང་

འདི་	ཡིན་	སོང་	རྫོགས་པ་
འདི་ཡང་	ཡོངས་སུ་	ཀྱང་ཡང་འང་	ལྟ་
འདོད་	ཡོངས་སུ་རྫོགས་པ་	ཀྱི་	ལྟ་བ་
འགྲོ་	རེ་	ཀྱིན་	ལྟོས་
འགྲོ་བ་	ལ་	གྱི་	སྔ་མ་
འདྲེན་	ལམ་	བྱས་	སྤྲུག་
འདྲོངས་	ལུས་	བྱུང་	སྤྲུག་ལོ་
འི་	ལོ་	བྱུང་ན་	
འོག་མ་	ཤིན་ཏུ་	གྲུབ་	
ཡང་	སེམས་	རྣམས་	

Translations of Tsong-kha-pa's text

འདི་ཡང་འོག་མ་འོག་མ་བསྒོམས་ཀྱིན་གོང་མ་གོང་མ་ལ་ཐོབ་འདོད་ཆེར་འགྲོ་བ་དང་གོང་མ་གོང་མ་མཉན་པ་ན་འོག་མ་འོག་མ་ལ་བསྒྲུབ་འདོད་ཇེ་ཆེ་ཇེ་ཆེར་འགྲོ་བ་ཞིག་བྱུང་ན་གནད་དུ་སོང་བ་ཡིན་གྱི། སྔ་མ་རྣམས་ཅི་ཡང་མེད་པར་སེམས་ཀྱི་གནས་ཆ་རེ་ཙམ་དང་ལྟ་བའི་གོ་བ་ཙམ་རེ་ལ་ནུས་པ་སྤྲུག་ལོ་བྱས་ཀྱང་གནད་དུ་འགྲོ་ཤིན་ཏུ་དཀའ་བས་ལམ་གྱི་ལུས་ཡོངས་སུ་རྫོགས་པ་ཞིག་ལ་ངེས་པ་འདྲོངས་དགོས་པ་ཡིན་ནོ། །

[Cultivation of the paths] is successful if, when while cultivating the lower paths, the wish to attain the higher paths increases and when hearing about the higher [paths], the wish to achieve the lower [paths] increases. But, without any of the former [paths], though you have developed your capacity in terms of a mere portion of the factor of stability and a mere portion of understanding of the view [of emptiness], success is very difficult. Therefore, you must induce certainty regarding the entire body of the path.

Here is Tsong-kha-pa's text as supplemented by *The Four Interwoven Annotations,* 833.1-833.6

གཉིས་པ་གནད་དུ་སོང་མ་སོང་གི་ཁྱད་པར་ནི། དེ་ལྟར་བཤེས་གཉེན་བསྟེན་པ་ནས་ཞི་ལྷག་གི་བར་གྱི་ལམ་གྱི་ཉམས་སུ་ལེན་ཚུལ་ འདི་ཡང་ བཤེས་གཉེན་བསྟེན་པ་ལྟ་བུའི་ལམ་ འོག་མ་འོག་མ་བསྒོམས་ཀྱིན་གོང་མ་གོང་མ་ ལྷག་མཐོང་གི་བར་ ལ་ རང་གི་བློའི་ ཐོབ་འདོད་ རིམ་གྱིས་ཇེ་ ཆེར་འགྲོ་བ་དང་ ལྷག་མཐོང་ལྟ་བུའི་ལམ་ གོང་མ་གོང་མ འི་ཁྱེད་ལས་སོགས་གཞན་ལས་ མཉན་པ འི་ཚེ་ ན་འོག་མ་འོག་མ་ བཤེས་གཉེན་བསྟེན་པ་ལ་ཐུག་གི་བར་ ལ་བསླུབ་ པར་ འདོད་ པ་ ཇེ་ཆེ་ཇེ་ཆེར་འགྲོ་བ་ཞིག་བྱུང་ན་ ལམ་བསྒོམ་པ་ གནད་དུ་སོང་བ་ཡིན་གྱི། ལམ་གྱི་གཞི་མ་བཤེས་གཉེན་བསྟེན་པ་སོགས་ལམ་ སྔ་མ་རྣམས་ ངེས་པར་དགོས་པའི་མཐོང་དང་གཅིགས་ཅི་ཡང་མེད་པར་ དེ་དག་མི་བསྒོམ་པར་བཞག་ནས་ སེམས་ཀྱི་གནས་ཆ་རེ་ཙམ་ རེ་འཚོལ་བ་ དང་ལྟ་བའི་གོ་བ་ཙམ་རེ་ འཚོལ་བ་ ལ་ རང་གི་རྩལ་ཅི་ཡོད་ཀྱི་ ནུས་པ་ བཏོན་ནས་ སྒྲུག་ལོ་ ཏེ་ནུས་པ་གང་ཡོད་སྒྲུག་ཅིང་འདོན་ནོ་ཞེས་དེ་སྐད་ བྱས་ཀྱང་ ལམ་བསྒོམ་པ་ གནད་དུ་ གཏན་ནས་ འགྲོ་ བར་ ཤིན་ཏུ་དཀའ་བ་ ཡིན་པ་ ས་ལམ་གྱི་ རྩ་བ་ནས་བཟུང་སྟེ་མཐའི་བར་གྱི་ ལུས་ཡོངས་སུ་རྫོགས་ ཤིང་མ་ཚང་བ་མེད་ པ་ འབྲས་བུ་རྫོགས་པའི་སངས་རྒྱས་བསྒྲུབ་པ་ལ་རྒྱུ་འདི་ལས་མ་འདས་སྙམ་དུ་ཤེས་པའི་བསྒྲུབ་རྒྱུ་ ཞིག་ལ་ངེས་པ་ རྣམ་པར་དག་པ་ འདྲོངས་དགོས་པ་ཡིན་ནོ། །

Two: the difference between successful and unsuccessful [cultivation of these paths][1]

This way to practicing the path—from proper reliance on your spiritual guide through to calm abiding and special insight—is successful when the following occurs. While cultivating the lower paths such as reliance on your spiritual guide, your wish to attain the higher paths up to special insight increases gradually. When you hear from others [i.e., study] about the activities and so forth of the higher paths such as special insight, the wish to achieve the earlier paths— back to reliance on a spiritual guide—increases greater and greater.

However, you might not see the need for and value the earlier paths such as the foundation of the path—reliance on the spiritual guide. You might not cultivate those paths at all. Instead you may strive at a mere portion of the factors of stability of the mind [i.e., not all those required to generate fully qualified calm abiding]. You may strive at a merely partial understanding of the view [of emptiness]. Although however much capacity as you have has been developed, and you say your ability [in stability and analysis] has been shaken and developed, it is extremely difficult to be completely successful in cultivating the path. Therefore, you must induce the certainty wherein you think that the complete body of the path ranging from the root of the path to the end, without being incomplete, is the cause of achieving the effect, complete Buddhahood, and does not pass from this cause.

---

[1] *The four parts of the outline were identified on page 18:*

- the mode of procedure of the general path,
- the difference between successful and unsuccessful cultivation of the path,
- advice of earlier [lamas] to enhance your practice with fine discrimination, and
- advice to practice without becoming partial.

Chapter Nine

དེ་རྣམས་བསྒོམ་པའི་ཚེ་ཡང་རྟོག་པ་སྐྱུང་བར་བྱས་ནས་བློ་རྣམས་ཆ་མཉམ་དགོས་ཏེ། འདི་ལྟར་ལམ་ལ་འཁྲིད་པའི་བཤེས་གཉེན་ལ་གུས་པ་ཆུང་བར་སྣང་ན་ལེགས་ཚོགས་ཐམས་ཅད་ཀྱི་རྩ་བ་འཆད་པས་བསྟེན་ཚུལ་ལ་འབད། དེ་བཞིན་དུ་སྒྲུབ་པ་ལ་སྤྲོ་ཤུགས་ཆུངས་ན་དལ་འབྱོར་གྱི་སྐོར་དང་ཚེ་འདི་ལ་མངོན་ཞེན་ཆེ་བར་སོང་ན་མི་རྟག་པ་དང་ངན་འགྲོའི་ཉེས་དམིགས་སྒོམ་པ་ལ་གཙོ་བོར་བྱ་དགོས། ཁས་བླངས་པའི་བཅས་པ་རྣམས་ལ་གཡེལ་བར་སྣང་ན་ལས་འབྲས་ལ་ངེས་པ་ཆུང་བ་ཡིན་སྙམ་དུ་བསམས་ལ། ལས་འབྲས་སྒོམ་པ་ལ་གཙོ་བོར་བྱ། འཁོར་བ་མཐའ་དག་ལ་སྐྱོ་ཤས་ཆུངས་ན་ཐར་པ་དོན་གཉེར་གྱི་བློ་ཚིག་ཙམ་དུ་འགྲོ་བས་འཁོར་བའི་ཉེས་དམིགས་རྣམས་བསམ། ཅི་བྱེད་སེམས་ཅན་གྱི་དོན་དུ་བྱེད་པའི་བློ་ཤུགས་དྲག་མི་སྣང་ན་ཐེག་ཆེན་གྱི་རྩ་བ་འཆད་པས་སྨོན་སེམས་རྒྱུ་དང་བཅས་པ་ལ་མང་དུ་སྦྱང་།

Division of the passage into units to facilitate the analysis of the syntax

I have divided Chapter Nine into eighteen meaning units.

1
དེ་རྣམས་བསྒོམ་པའི་ཚེ་ཡང་རྟོག་པ་སྐྱུང་བར་བྱས་ནས་བློ་རྣམས་ཆ་མཉམ་དགོས་ཏེ།

2
འདི་ལྟར་ལམ་ལ་འཁྲིད་པའི་བཤེས་གཉེན་ལ་གུས་པ་ཆུང་བར་སྣང་ན

3
ལེགས་ཚོགས་ཐམས་ཅད་ཀྱི་རྩ་བ་འཆད་པས

4
བསྟེན་ཚུལ་ལ་འབད།

5
དེ་བཞིན་དུ་སྒྲུབ་པ་ལ་སྤྲོ་ཤུགས་ཆུངས་ན

6
དལ་འབྱོར་གྱི་སྐོར་དང

7
ཚེ་འདི་ལ་མངོན་ཞེན་ཆེ་བར་སོང་ན

8
མི་རྟག་པ་དང་ངན་འགྲོའི་ཉེས་དམིགས

9
སྒོམ་པ་ལ་གཙོ་བོར་བྱ་དགོས།

10
ཁས་བླངས་པའི་བཅས་པ་རྣམས་ལ་གཡེལ་བར་སྣང་ན

11
ལས་འབྲས་ལ་ངེས་པ་ཆུང་བ་ཡིན་སྙམ་དུ་བསམས་ལ།

12
ལས་འབྲས་སྒོམ་པ་ལ་གཙོ་བོར་བྱ།

13
འཁོར་བ་མཐའ་དག་ལ་སྐྱོ་ཤས་ཆུངས་ན

14
ཐར་པ་དོན་གཉེར་གྱི་བློ་ཚིག་ཙམ་དུ་འགྲོ་བས

15
འཁོར་བའི་ཉེས་དམིགས་རྣམས་བསམ།

16
ཅི་བྱེད་སེམས་ཅན་གྱི་དོན་དུ་བྱེད་པའི་བློ་ཤུགས་དྲག་མི་སྣང་ན

17
ཐེག་ཆེན་གྱི་རྩ་བ་འཆད་པས

18
སྨོན་སེམས་རྒྱུ་དང་བཅས་པ་ལ་མང་དུ་སྦྱང་།

Part 1 • དེ་རྣམས་བསྒོམ་པའི་ཚེ་ཡང་རྟོག་པ་སྦྱང་བར་བྱས་ནས་བློ་རྣམས་ཆ་མཉམ་དགོས་ཏེ།

Part 1 is the topic sentence

Part 1 is the topic sentence for the subsequent sequence identifying possible shortcomings in your practice and advice for how to correct them.

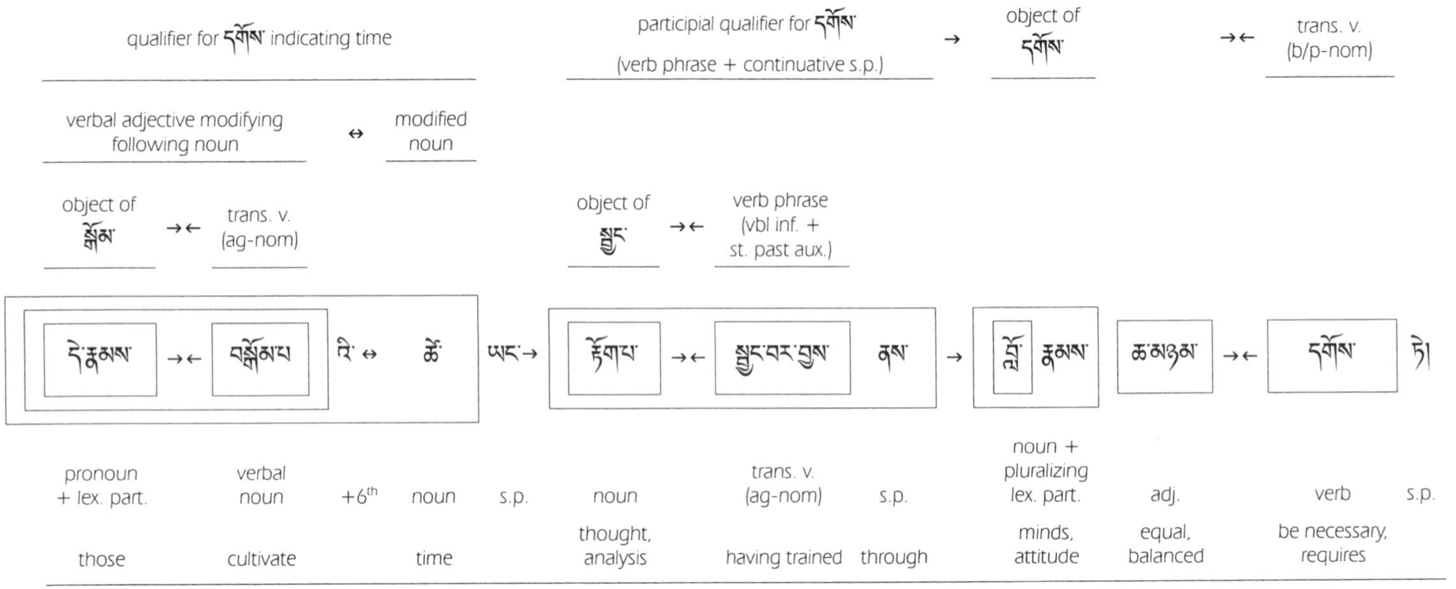

Also, when you meditate on these, a balanced attitude is required, having become skilled in analysis [of shortcomings in your practice].

Glossary for Part 1

དེ་	limiting adj. and pronoun, *that, those;* here: pronoun
དེ་རྣམས་	pronoun + pluralizing lexical particle
རྣམས་	optional lexical pluralizing suffix particle
བསྒོམ་	trans. v. (ag-nom) (future tense), *meditate on, cultivate*
	སྒོམ་བསྒོམས་བསྒོམ་སྒོམས། ཐ་དད།
གོམས་	intr. v. (nom-loc), *be accustomed to*
	གོམས་གོམས་གོམས། ཐ་མི་དད།
བསྒོམ་པ་	verbal noun, *contemplation, meditation*
བསྒོམ་པའི་	verbal noun + 6th case particle fused to suffixless final syllable
འི་	particle fused to suffixless final syllable; either 1) a syntactic particle following a verb or verb phrase signifying conjunction or disjunction, or 2) a 6th case particle following nouns, pronouns, postpositions, and adjectives
ཚེ་	n., *time, life, lifetime*
ཡང་	conjunctive syntactic particle occurring after nouns, pronouns, adverbs, and verbs; *but, even, also*
ཀྱང་ཡང་འང་	conjunctive and disjunctive syntactic particles used after declined nouns, pronouns, adjectives, and after verbs and verb phrases; conjunctively: *even, also;* disjunctively: *but, although*

ཀྱང་ after words ending with the letters གདབས་

ཡང་ after words ending with the letters ངནམའརལ་

འང་ after words with suffixless final syllables

རྟོག trans. v. (ag-nom), *think about, consider* རྟོག་བརྟགས་བརྟག་རྟོགས། ཐ་དད།

རྟོག་པ་ n., *thought, conceptual thought;* here *analysis*

རྟོག་པ་སྦྱང་ verbal compound: *skilled in analysis*

སྦྱང་ trans. v. (ag-nom), *wash, purify, train* སྦྱོང་སྦྱངས་སྦྱང་སྦྱོངས། ཐ་དད།

སྦྱང་བར་བྱས་ verb phrase (verbal infinitive + strong past auxiliary) *[I, you] have practiced purification*

སྦྱང་པར་ verbal infinitive; here, the fused ར་ is a syntactic particle modifying a verb to create an infinitive within the verb phrase སྦྱང་བར་བྱས་ *[I, you] have practiced purification;* it is **not** a case particle marking the 2nd, 4th or 7th cases because it does not follow a noun—it is within a verb phrase

བྱས་ trans. v. (ag-nom) (past tense), *did, made, performed, taken;* here: used as the strong past auxiliary within a verb phrase
བྱེད་བྱས་བྱ་བྱོས། ཐ་དད།

སྦྱང་བར་བྱས་ནས་ verb phrase + continuative syntactic particle, *having become skilled [in analysis]*

ནས་ particle; either 1) a syntactic particle following verbs and verb phrases marking adverbs, participles or disjunction, or 2) a case particle marking the 5th case; here, a continuative syntactic particle following verb; it's not a 5th case particle because it doesn't follow a noun

བློ་ n., *mind, awareness;* here *attitude*

རྣམས་ optional lexical pluralizing suffix particle

ཆ་ n., *part*

ཆ་མཉམ་ adj., *equal, balanced*

དགོས་ trans. v. (b/p-nom), *be necessary, need, require.* The *Great Word Treasury* lists this as an intransitive verb, but in English *require* is a transitive verb.
དགོས་དགོས་དགོས། ཐ་མི་དད།

དགོས་ཏེ་ verb phrase + continuative syntactic particle showing sequence by indicating that more relevant information will follow.

ཏེ་ སྟེ་ and དེ་ three equivalent syntactic particles; either 1) continuative syntactic particles following verbs and verb phrases showing sequence, or 2) punctuational syntactic particles following words or phrases marking appositives

ཏེ་ follows words ending with suffix letters ནརལས་

སྟེ་ follows suffixless words and words ending with suffix letters གངབམའ་

དེ་ follows words ending with suffix letter ད་

Notes on Part 1

དེ་རྣམས་བསྒོམ་པའི་ verbal adjective (transitive verb + its object) + 6th case particle connecting it to the following noun it modifies adjectivally: ཚེ་ *time.* What time? *the time when you meditate on those*

རྟོག་པ་སྦྱང་བར་བྱས་ནས་ verb clause (verbal phrase composed of verbal infinitive + strong past auxiliary) + continuative syntactic particle make a past participle. This construction is a qualifier of the later verb དགོས་

བློ་རྣམས་ཆ་མཉམ་དགོས་ཏེ། the syntactic particle ཏེ་ following the verb signifies that what follows relates to what has just been said. Immediately following, Parts 2, 3, 4, and 5 all show how one is to accomplish this equalized mind training. Each part is basically in the form: *If X, you should do Y.*

རྟོག་པ་ this noun means *thought* or *conceptuality*. This meaning is also extended sometimes, as it is here, to mean *analysis*

Part 2 • འདི་ལྟར་ལམ་ལ་འཁྲིད་པའི་བཤེས་གཉེན་ལ་གུས་པ་ཆུང་བར་སྣང་ན

Part 2 is a conditional clause, Part 3 is a reason qualifying Part 4, and Part 4 is the conclusion: "If it appears that X, because of Y, you should do Z."

2 is a conditional clause	3 states the reason qualifying the conclusion	4 states the conclusion
འདི་ལྟར་ལམ་ལ་འཁྲིད་པའི་བཤེས་གཉེན་ལ་གུས་པ་ཆུང་བར་སྣང་ན	ལེགས་ཚོགས་ཐམས་ཅད་ཀྱི་རྩ་བ་འཆད་པས་	བསྟེན་ཚུལ་ལ་འབད།

Part 2 is the conditional clause "if it appears that X"

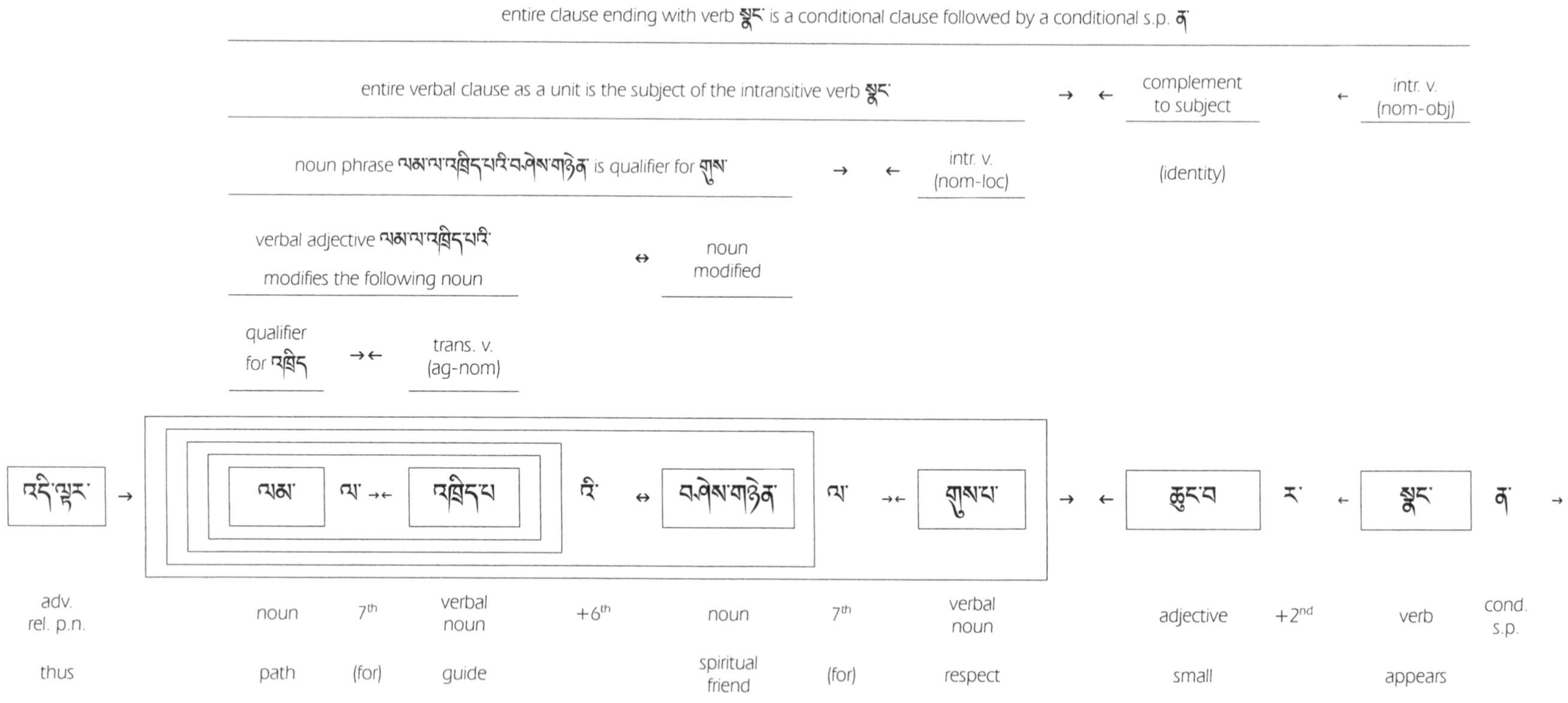

If respect for the spiritual guide leading you on the path appears to be small,...

Because English favors transitive constructions, you might want to recast this conditional clause as a transitive construction:
If it appears that you have little respect for the spiritual guide leading you on the path,...

Glossary for Part 2

འདི་ལྟར་ — adverbial relative pronoun, *such, thus*

ལམ་ — n., *path*

ལམ་ལ་ — n. + 7th case particle

ལ་ — particle; either 1) a syntactic particle following a verb or verb phrase signifying conjunction or disjunction, or 2) a case particle following nouns, pronouns, postpositions, and adjectives marking the 2nd, 4th and 7th cases

འཁྲིད་ — trans. v. (ag-nom), *guide [someone]*

འཁྲིད་ཁྲིད་འཁྲིད་ཁྲིད། ཐ་དད།

འཁྲིད་པ་ — n., *guide*

འཁྲིད་པའི་ — n. + 6th case particle fused to suffixless final syllable

འི་ — particle fused to suffixless final syllable; either 1) a syntactic particle following a verb or verb phrase signifying conjunction or disjunction, or 2) a 6th case particle following nouns, pronouns, postpositions, and adjectives

བཤེས་གཉེན་ — n., *Kalyānamitra, spiritual friend*

བཤེས་གཉེན་ལ་ — n. + 7th case particle

ལ་ — particle; either 1) a syntactic particle following a verb or verb phrase signifying conjunction or disjunction, or 2) a case particle following nouns, pronouns, postpositions, and adjectives marking the 2nd, 4th and 7th cases

གུས་ — intr. v. (nom-loc), *be respectful of*

གུས་གུས་གུས། ཐ་མི་དད།

གུས་པ་ — n., *respect*

ཆུང་བ་ — adj., *small, little*

ཆུང་བར་ — adj. + fused 2nd case particle

ར་ — particle fused to suffixless final syllable; either 1) a verb-modifying syntactic particle within a verb phrase, or 2) a case particle following nouns, pronouns, postpositions, and adjectives marking the 2nd, 4th and 7th cases

སྣང་ — intr. v. (nom-obj), *appear*

སྣང་སྣང་སྣང་། ཐ་མི་དད།

སྣང་ན་ — verb + conditional syntactic particle marking a conditional clause, *when [something]*

ན་ — particle; either 1) a rhetorical syntactic particle marking a conditional clause following a verb or verb phrase, or 2) a case particle following nouns, pronouns, postpositions, and adjectives marking the 2nd, 4th and 7th cases

Notes on Part 2

འདི་ལྟར་ལམ་ལ་འཁྲིད་པའི་བཤེས་གཉེན་ — verbal adjective clause (*who is the guide for the path*) + 6th case particle connecting the adjective to the following noun that it modifies, *the spiritual friend* ***who*** *is [your] guide to the path.* I'm taking the ལ་ particle in the verbal clause ལམ་ལ་འཁྲིད་ as 7th case referential: guide **for** the path

བཤེས་གཉེན་ལ་གུས་ — verbal clause (intransitive nom-loc attitude verb + qualifier in 7th case) *respect for the spiritual guide*

གུས་པ་ཆུང་བར་སྣང་ — verb clause (subject + 2nd case complement + verb). A second case complement in the context of an intransitive construction will tell you more about the subject: either **the subject is the complement** or **the subject is appearing as—or being perceived as—the complement**

Part 3 states the reason qualifying the conclusion and Part 4 states the conclusion

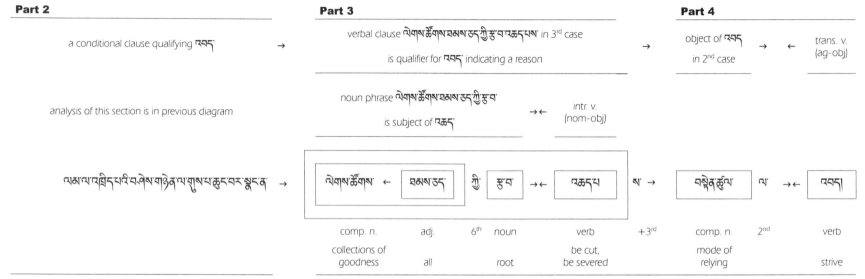

Part 2		Part 3								Part 4			
a conditional clause qualifying འབད་	→	verbal clause ལེགས་ཚོགས་ཐམས་ཅད་ཀྱི་རྩ་བ་འཆད་པས་ in 3rd case is qualifier for འབད་ indicating a reason							→	object of འབད་ in 2nd case		→ ←	trans. v. (ag-obj)
analysis of this section is in previous diagram		noun phrase ལེགས་ཚོགས་ཐམས་ཅད་ཀྱི་རྩ་བ་ is subject of འཆད་					→←	intr. v. (nom-obj)					
ལམ་ལ་འཁྲིད་པའི་བཤེས་གཉེན་ལ་གུས་པ་ཆུང་བར་སྣང་ན་	→	ལེགས་ཚོགས་	←	ཐམས་ཅད་	ཀྱི་	རྩ་བ་	→←	འཆད་པ	ས་ →	བསྟེན་ཚུལ་	ལ་	→←	འབད།
		comp. n.		adj.	6th	noun		verb	+3rd	comp. n.	2nd		verb
		collections of goodness		all		root		be cut, be severed		mode of relying			strive
If it appears that you have little respect for the spiritual guide leading you on the path,		*you should strive at the mode of reliance [on a spiritual guide] because the root of the collections of goodness is severed,*											

Glossary for Part 3

ལེགས་ཚོགས་	comp. n., *collection of goodness*
ལེགས་	n., *good*
ཚོགས་	n., *collection, gathering, group*
ཐམས་ཅད་	adj., *all*
ལེགས་ཚོགས་ཐམས་ཅད་ཀྱི་	n. + adj. compound + 6th case particle
ཀྱི་	particle; either 1) a syntactic particle following a verb or verb phrase signifying conjunction or disjunction, or 2) a 6th case particle following nouns, pronouns, postpositions, and adjectives
རྩ་བ་	n., adj., *root, main, principal*
འཆད་	intr. v. (nom-obj), *be cut, be severed* འཆད་ཆད་འཆད། ཐ་མི་དད།
འཆད་	trans. v. (ag-nom), *explain* འཆད་བཤད་བཤད་ཤོད། ཐ་དད།
འཆད་པ་	verbal n., *cut, severed*
འཆད་པས་	verbal n. + 3rd case particle fused to suffixless final syllable

ས་ — abbreviation of the particle རིས་ (when རིས་ is fused to a suffixless final syllable, the རི goes away and all that's left is a fused ས་); either 1) syntactic particle creating an adverbial construction, 2) syntactic particle marking the qualifier of an intransitive nom-s.p. verb of absence, or 3) case particle marking the 3rd case

གིས་ཀྱིས་གྱིས་འིས་ཡིས་ — are equivalent particles, marking the 3rd case and also marking syntactic adverbial relationships.

བསྟེན་ — trans. v. (ag-obj) (past and future tenses), *adhere to, rely on, stay close to*

སྟེན་བསྟེན་བསྟེན་བསྟེན། ཐ་དད།

རྟེན་ — intr. v. (nom-loc), *depend on, rely on*

རྟེན་བརྟེན་བརྟེན་རྟེན། ཐ་མི་དད།

ཚུལ་ — n., *mode*

བསྟེན་ཚུལ་ — compound noun, *mode of reliance*

བསྟེན་ཚུལ་ལ་ — comp. n. + 2nd case particle marking the object of the transitive verb འབད་ *work at, strive at*

ལ་ — particle; either 1) a syntactic particle following a verb or verb phrase signifying conjunction or disjunction, or 2) a case particle following nouns, pronouns, postpositions, and adjectives marking the 2nd, 4th and 7th cases

འབད་ — trans. v. (ag-obj), *strive*

འབད་འབད་འབད་འབོད། ཐ་དད།

Notes on Parts 3 and 4

ལེགས་ཚོགས་ཐམས་ཅད་ཀྱི་རྩ་བ་ — noun phrase ལེགས་ཚོགས་ཐམས་ཅད་ཀྱི་རྩ་བ་ *the root of the collections of goodness* is the **subject** of the intransitive verb འཆད་ *be cut*

ལེགས་ཚོགས་ཐམས་ཅད་ཀྱི་རྩ་བ་འཆད་པས་ — verbal clause ལེགས་ཚོགས་ཐམས་ཅད་ཀྱི་རྩ་བ་འཆད་ *the root of the collections of goodness is cut* + a fused 3rd case particle པས་ is transformed into a qualifier for འབད stating a reason. It can be translated in two ways:

1. *The root of all collections of goodness is cut. Therefore, ...*
2. *Because the root of all collections of goodness is cut, ...*

བསྟེན་ཚུལ་ — compound noun, *mode of reliance;* this also conveys the sense of *the proper way of relying, how properly to rely*

བསྟེན་ཚུལ་ལ་འབད། — 2nd case particle ལ་ here marks the object of the transitive verb འབད་ *work at, strive at*

Parts 5 and 6 • དེ་བཞིན་དུ་སྒྲུབ་པ་ལ་སྤྲོ་ཤུགས་ཆུང་ན་དལ་འབྱོར་གྱི་སྐོར་དང་

Parts 5-9 follow the pattern of conditional clause followed by conclusion, but this time two conditional clauses (5 and 7) are joined with two conclusions (6 and 8).

	5	6	7	8	9
དེ་བཞིན་དུ་	སྒྲུབ་པ་ལ་སྤྲོ་ཤུགས་ཆུང་ན་	དལ་འབྱོར་གྱི་སྐོར་དང་	ཚེ་འདི་ལ་མངོན་ཞེན་ཆེ་བར་སོང་ན་	མི་རྟག་པ་དང་ངན་འགྲོའི་ཉེས་དམིགས་	སྒོམ་པ་ལ་གཙོ་བོར་བྱ་དགོས།

In the previous sentence the form of Tsong-kha-pa's advice was *"If you lack A, because of B, you should do C."* This next sentence is introduced with the adverb དེ་བཞིན་དུ་ *similarly* alerting us that we will be seeing another *"If X, then you should do Y"* construction. Actually this part doubles the formula, so that Tsong-kha-pa's sentence is in the form *"If A, you should do B, and if C, you should do D."* Typical of the economy of Tibetan verb-last syntax, the *"you should meditate on"* part occurs only once at the end of the sentence and **distributes** to both preceding sections.

དེ་བཞིན་དུ་	སྒྲུབ་པ་ལ་སྤྲོ་ཤུགས་ཆུང་ན་དལ་འབྱོར་གྱི་སྐོར་དང་	ཚེ་འདི་ལ་མངོན་ཞེན་ཆེ་བར་སོང་ན་མི་རྟག་པ་དང་ངན་འགྲོའི་ཉེས་དམིགས་	སྒོམ་པ་ལ་གཙོ་བོར་བྱ་དགོས།
Similarly,	*if you have little force of enthusiasm for practice, [mainly work at meditating on] the topics of leisure and opportunity.*	*If you come to have great attachment to this life, [mainly work at meditating on] impermanence and the faults of bad migrations.*	*mainly work at meditating on*

To make the connection clear, I have diagrammed the first conditional clause and object directly to the final verb

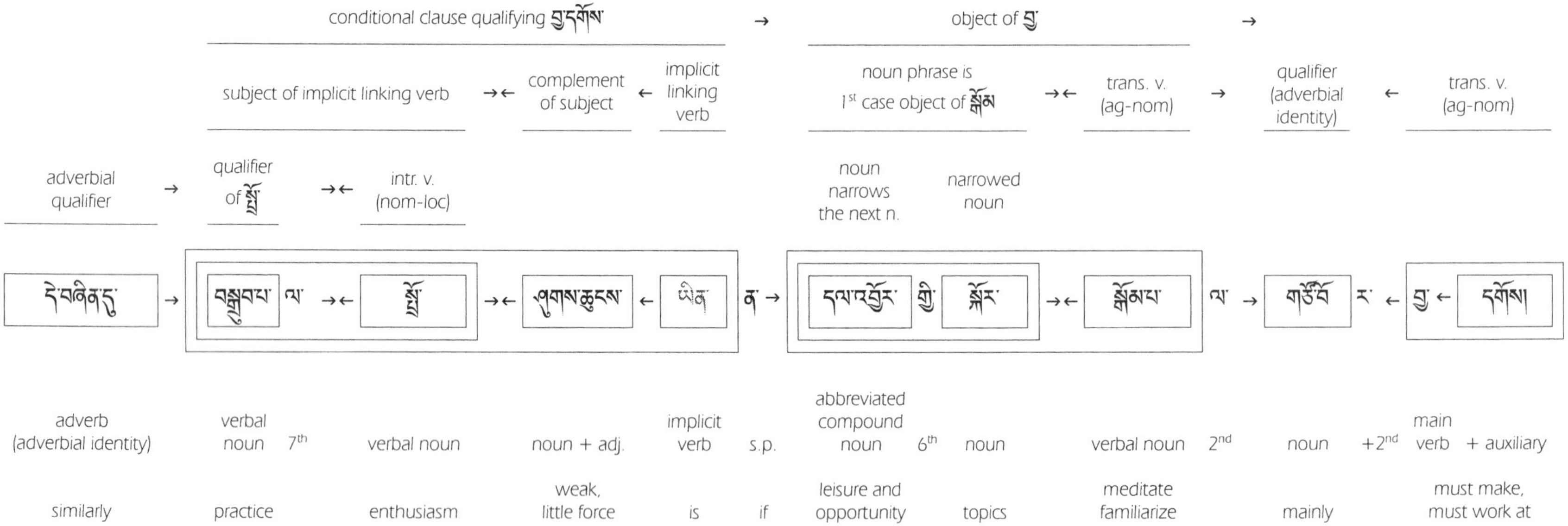

Similarly, if you have little force of enthusiasm for practice, you must mainly work at meditating on the topics of leisure and opportunity.

Glossary for Parts 5 and 6

དེ་བཞིན་དུ་ adverbial pronoun, *thus, so, in that way*

བསྒྲུབ་ trans. v. (ag-nom) (future), *achieve, accomplish*
སྒྲུབ་བསྒྲུབས་བསྒྲུབ་སྒྲུབས། ཐ་དད།

གྲུབ་ intr. v. (nom-obj), *be established, be proven, exists*
འགྲུབ་གྲུབ་འགྲུབ། ཐ་མི་དད།

སྒྲུབ་པ་ verbal n., *achievement, accomplishment*

སྒྲུབ་པ་ལ་ verbal n. + 2nd case particle

ལ་ particle; either 1) a syntactic particle following a verb or verb phrase signifying conjunction or disjunction, or 2) a case particle following nouns, pronouns, postpositions, and adjectives marking the 2nd, 4th and 7th cases

སྤྲོ་ trans. v. (ag-nom), *spread out, extend*
intr. v. (nom-obj), *be spread out, be enthusiastic (about something)*
སྤྲོ་སྤྲོ་སྤྲོ། ཐ་མི་དད།
སྤྲོ་སྤྲོས་སྤྲོ་སྤྲོས། ཐ་དད།

ཤུགས་ n., *force, strength, power*

ཆུངས་ adj., *small*

ཤུགས་ཆུངས་ noun phrase (n. + adj.), *small force*

ཤུགས་ཆུངས་ན་ noun phrase + conditional syntactic particle. I read this construction to be an abbreviation for ཤུགས་ཆུངས་ཡིན་ན་ with an implicit linking verb

ན་ particle; either 1) a rhetorical syntactic particle marking a conditional clause following a verb or verb phrase, or 2) a case particle following nouns, pronouns, postpositions, and adjectives marking the 2nd, 4th and 7th cases

དལ་འབྱོར་ compound n., *leisure and opportunity;*
abbreviation for དལ་བ་དང་འབྱོར་བ་

དལ་འབྱོར་གྱི་ n. + 6th case particle; here: 6th case type connective narrows the scope of the following noun སྐོར་

གྱི་ particle; either 1) a syntactic particle following a verb or verb phrase signifying conjunction or disjunction, or 2) a 6th case particle following nouns, pronouns, postpositions, and adjectives

སྐོར་ trans. v. (ag-nom), *turn* སྐོར་སྐོར་སྐོར་སྐོར། ཐ་དད།

འཁོར་ intr. v. (nom-obj), *be turned* འཁོར་འཁོར་འཁོར། ཐ་མི་དད།

སྐོར་ n., *topic*

དང་ particle, used three ways: 1) continuative syntactic particle used following nouns and noun phrases (*and,* or with negative verb, *or*); 2) syntactic particle marking the qualifier of an intr. nom-s.p. v. of conjunction, as in ང་རང་མི་སྡུག་པ་དང་ཕྲད་ན་ *if we meet with unpleasantness;* and 3) syntactic particle marking the qualifier of an intr. nom-s.p. v. of disjunction, as in རྟོག་པ་དང་བྲལ་ *free from conceptuality*

སྒོམ་ trans. v. (ag-nom), *meditate on, cultivate* སྒོམ་བསྒོམས་བསྒོམ་སྒོམས། ཐ་དད།

གོམས་ intr. v. (nom-loc), *be accustomed to* གོམས་གོམས་གོམས། ཐ་མི་དད།

སྒོམ་པ་ verbal n., *cultivation, meditation*

སྒོམ་པ་ལ་ verbal noun + 2nd case particle marking the object of the transitive verb བྱ་ *[you] should make*

ལ་ particle; either 1) a syntactic particle following a verb or verb phrase signifying conjunction or disjunction, or 2) a case particle following nouns, pronouns, postpositions, and adjectives marking the 2nd, 4th and 7th cases

གཙོ་བོ་ n. or adj., *main, principal;* here: noun

གཙོ་བོར་ n. + 2nd case particle fused to suffixless final syllable; here this creates an adverbial relationship with the following verb བྱ་ *[you] should make*

གཙོ་བོར་བྱ་ verb phrase (adverb + verb), *[you] should mainly make*

བྱ་ trans. v. (ag-nom), *do, make, perform, take* བྱེད་བྱས་བྱ་བྱོས། ཐ་དད།

དགོས་ intr. v. (b/p-nom), *be necessary, need, require* གོས་དགོས་དགོས། ཐ་མི་དད།

བྱ་དགོས་ verb phrase (verb + auxiliary) *must make, must take*

The first conditional clause has an implicit linking verb ཡིན་ linking the subject to the complement

Complements in linking-verb constructions tell you more about the subject in the sense that **the subject is the complement; A is B; enthusiasm for practice is weak.**

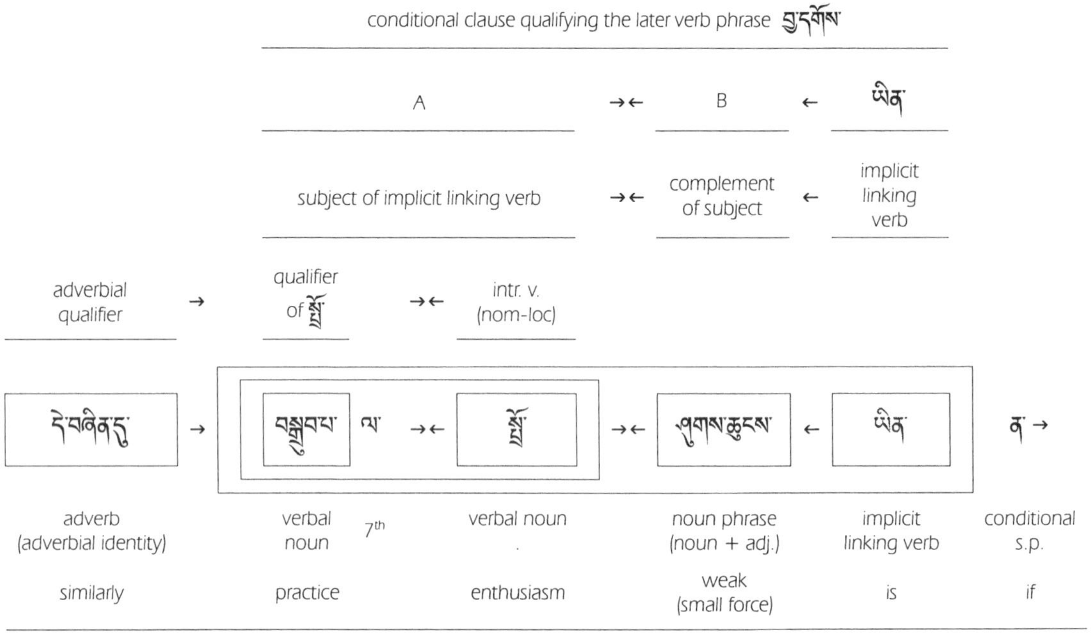

Similarly, if [your] enthusiasm for practice is weak, ...

Notes

དེ་བཞིན་དུ་ — This sentence is introduced with the adverbial construction, *similarly.* What is about to be said is similar to what has just been said.

In the previous sentence we were told, *"If it appears that you have little respect for the spiritual guide leading you on the path, you should strive at the mode of reliance [on a spiritual guide] because the root of the collections of goodness is severed."*

In the following sentence, we are told, *"If X, then you should do Y."*

To put it another way, just as contemplating the proper mode of relying on a spiritual guide is the antidote to the fault of having little respect for your spiritual teacher, so too meditating on the topics of leisure and opportunity is the antidote to the fault of having little enthusiasm for practice.

བསྒྲུབ་པ་ལ་སྤྲོ་ — Verb phrase (qualifier + 7th case particle + verb) is the subject of the understood linking verb ཡིན་ *is, are*

བསྒྲུབ་པ་ལ་སྤྲོ་ཤུགས་ཆུངས་ན་ — This conditional clause behaves as if there were an understood linking verb preceding the particle ན་

Parts 7, 8, and 9

7	8	9
ཚེ་འདི་ལ་མངོན་ཞེན་ཆེ་བར་སོང་ན་	མི་རྟག་པ་དང་ངན་འགྲོའི་ཉེས་དམིགས་	སྒོམ་པ་ལ་གཙོ་བོར་བྱ་དགོས།

1. "If A has become B, you should mainly meditate on C" **A** is ཚེ་འདི་ལ་མངོན་ཞེན་ **B** is ཆེ་བ་ **C** is མི་རྟག་པ་དང་ངན་འགྲོའི་ཉེས་དམིགས་

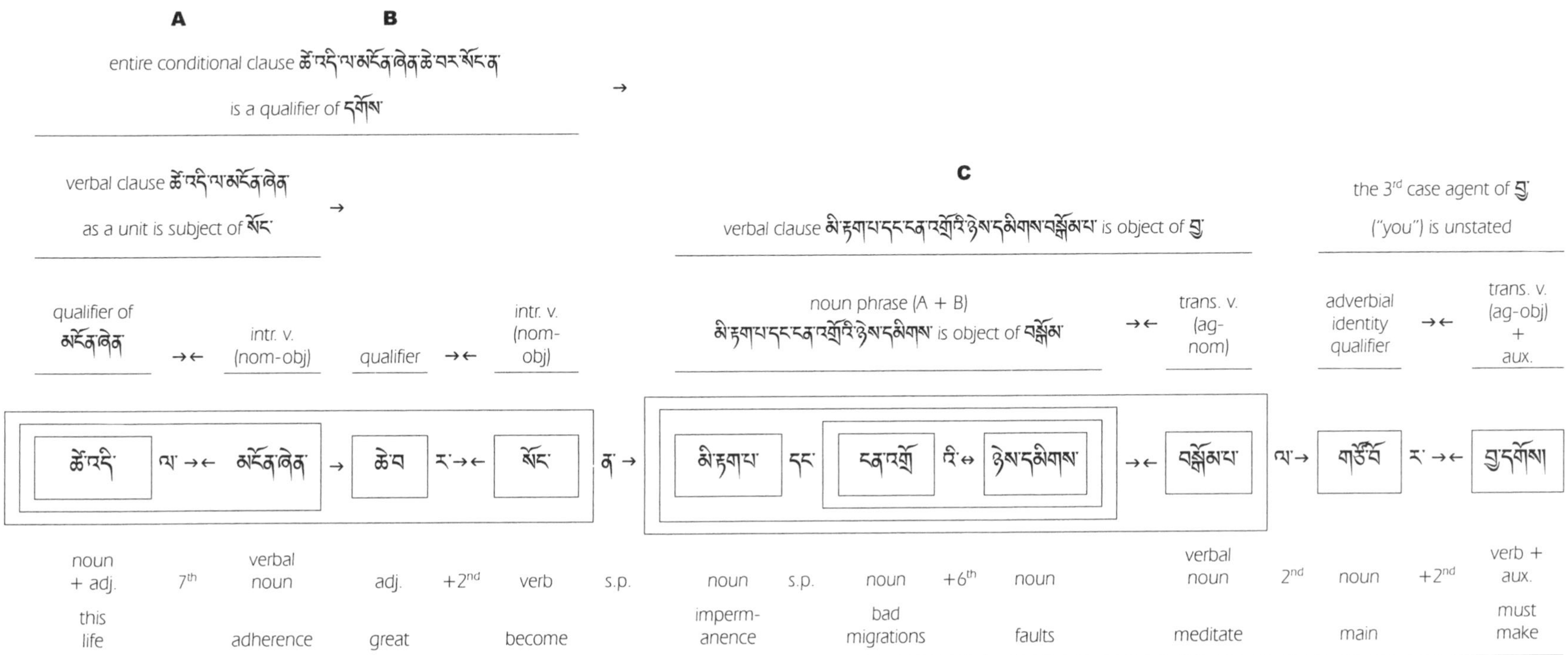

If you come to have great attachment to this life, mainly work at meditating on impermanence and the faults of bad migrations.

Glossary for Parts 7, 8, and 9

ཚེ་ n., *time, lifetime*

འདི་ limiting adj. used as a pronoun, *this one, this*

ཚེ་འདི་ noun phrase (n. + limiting adj.), *this lifetime*

ཚེ་འདི་ལ་ noun phrase + 7th case particle marking qualifier for following verb མངོན་ཞེན་ *adhere [to something]*, signifying referential locative

ལ་ particle; either 1) a syntactic particle following a verb or verb phrase signifying conjunction or disjunction, or 2) a case particle following nouns, pronouns, postpositions, and adjectives marking the 2nd, 4th and 7th cases

མངོན་ཞེན་ abbreviation for མངོན་པར་ཞེན་

མངོན་པར་ lexical prefix particle, trans. Sanskrit. *abhi-*, *exceptionally, extensively*

མངོན་པར་ཞེན་ intr. v. (nom-loc), *cling, adhere, strongly adhere*

ཞེན་ intr. v. (nom-loc), *cling, determine, conceive, adhere* ཞེན་ཞེན་ཞེན། ཐ་མི་དད།

ཆེ་བ་ adj., *great*

ཆེ་བར་ adj. + 2nd case particle fused to suffixless final syllable

ར་ particle fused to suffixless final syllable; either 1) a verb-modifying syntactic particle within a verb phrase, or 2) a case particle following nouns, pronouns, postpositions, and adjectives marking the 2nd, 4th and 7th cases

སོང་ intr. v. (alt. past), *went*, often used by extension in the sense of *turns into* or *becomes*
འགྲོ་ཕྱིན་འགྲོ་སོང་། ཐ་མི་དད།། སོང་ is also an alternate past tense form

ཆེ་བར་སོང་ verb clause (qualifier + verb), *become great;* here the verb of motion is being used by extension metaphorically in the sense of *turns into* or *becomes.* Because the verb of motion is being used metaphorically, the qualifier is a "metaphorical destination" instead of the actual physical destination. The qualifier is what the subject becomes, rather than where the subject is going.

སོང་ན་ verb + conditional syntactic particle, *if [the subject] has become [qualifier], ...*

ན་ particle; either 1) a rhetorical syntactic particle marking a conditional clause following a verb or verb phrase, or 2) a case particle following nouns, pronouns, postpositions, and adjectives marking the 2nd, 4th and 7th cases

མི་རྟག་པ་ n., *impermanence, impermanent phenomena*

དང་ particle, used three ways: 1) continuative syntactic particle used following nouns and noun phrases (*and,* or with negative verb, *or*); 2) syntactic particle marking the qualifier of an intr. nom-s.p. v. of conjunction, as in ང་རང་མི་སྡུག་པ་དང་ཕྲད་ན་ *if we meet with unpleasantness;* and 3) syntactic particle marking the qualifier of an intr. nom-s.p. v. of disjunction, as in རྟོག་པ་དང་བྲལ་ *free from conceptuality*

ངན་འགྲོ་ n., *[the three] bad migrations*

ངན་འགྲོའི་ n. + 6th case particle fused to suffixless final syllable

ཉེས་དམིགས་ n., *fault*

སྒོམ་ trans. v. (ag-nom), *meditate on, cultivate* སྒོམ་བསྒོམས་བསྒོམ་སྒོམས། ཐ་དད།

གོམས་ intr. v. (nom-loc), *be accustomed to* གོམས་གོམས་གོམས། ཐ་མི་དད།

སྒོམ་པ་ verbal n., *cultivation, meditation*

སྒོམ་པ་ལ་ verbal noun + 2nd case particle marking the object of the transitive verb བྱ་ *[you] should make*

ལ་ particle; either 1) a syntactic particle following a verb or verb phrase signifying conjunction or disjunction, or 2) a case particle following nouns, pronouns, postpositions, and adjectives marking the 2nd, 4th and 7th cases

གཙོ་བོ་ n. or adj., *main, principal;* here: noun

གཙོ་བོར་ n. + 2nd case particle fused to suffixless final syllable; here this creates an adverbial relationship with the following verb བྱ་ *[you] should make*

གཙོ་བོར་བྱ་ verb phrase (adverb + verb), *[you] should mainly make*

བྱ་ trans. v. (ag-nom), *do, make, perform, take*
བྱེད་བྱས་བྱ་བྱོས། ཐ་དད།

དགོས་ intr. v. (b/p-nom), *be necessary, need, require* དགོས་དགོས་དགོས། ཐ་མི་དད།

བྱ་དགོས་ verb phrase (verb + auxiliary), *must make*

Grammar review • Metaphorical use of verb of motion in a transformative sense of something becoming something else

འགྲོ་ intr. v., *go,* often used by extension in the sense of *turns into* or *becomes.* འགྲོ་ཕྱིན་འགྲོ་སོང་། ཐ་མི་དད། སོང་ is an alternate form of the past tense

མཐོང་ཞེན་ཆེ་བར་སོང་ verb clause (qualifier + verb), *come to have great attachment;* here the verb of motion is being used by extension metaphorically in the sense of *turns into* or *becomes.* Because the verb of motion is being used metaphorically, the qualifier is a "metaphorical destination" instead of the actual physical destination. The qualifier is what the subject becomes, rather than where the subject is going.

Parts 10 and 11

10
ཁས་བླངས་པའི་བཅས་པ་རྣམས་ལ་གཡེལ་བར་སྣང་ན

11
ལས་འབྲས་ལ་ངེས་པ་ཆུང་བ་ཡིན་སྙམ་དུ་བསམས་ལ།

Parts 10 and 11 form a complex sentence, with Part 10 being a conditional clause, and Part 11 stating the conclusion

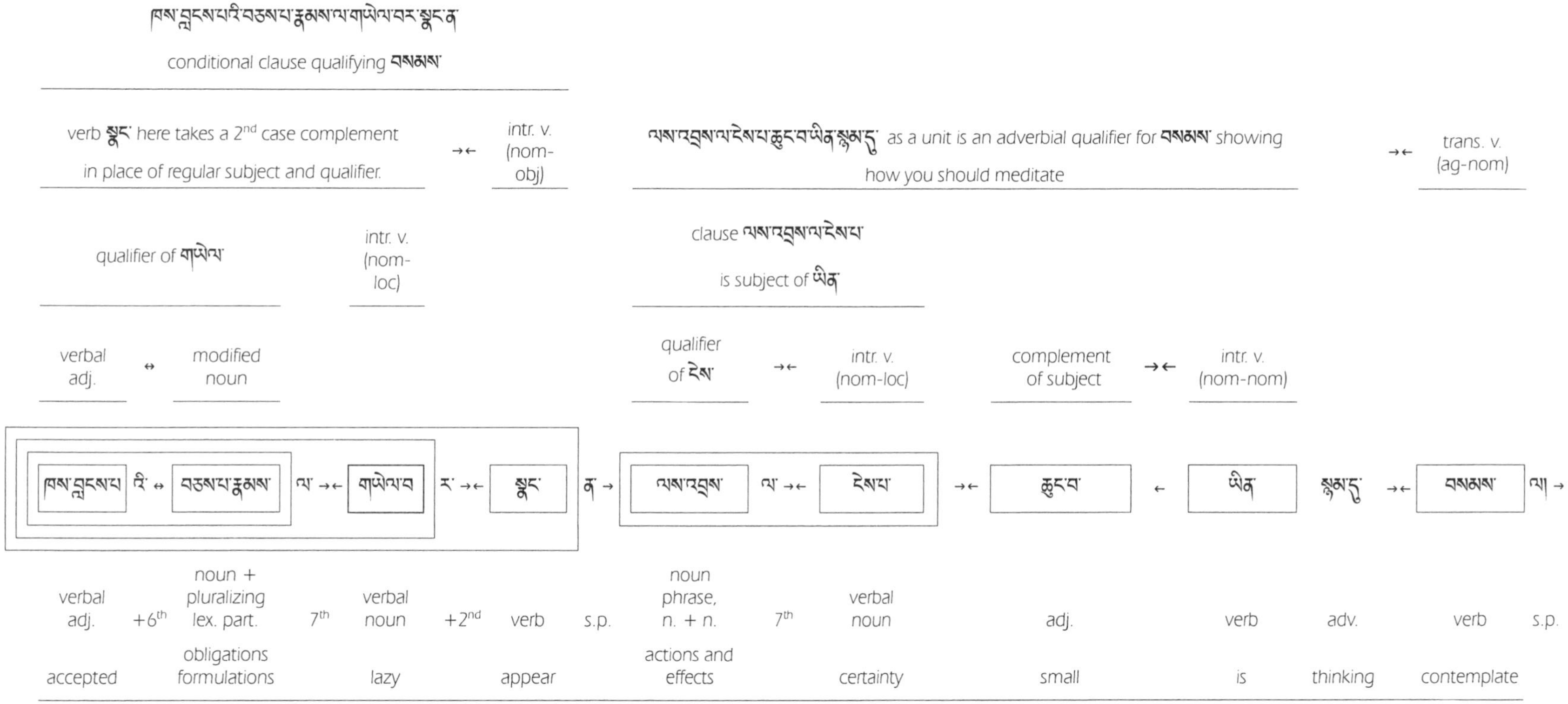

If it appears that you are lazy about [i.e., are deviating from] the [ethical] formulation that you have accepted, you should contemplate that your understanding of actions and [their] effects is shallow.

Glossary for Parts 10 and 11

ཁས་བླངས་ trans. v. (ag-nom), *promised, assert, accept;* literally, *hold by the mouth*
ཁས་ལེན། ཁས་བླངས། ཁས་བླང་། ཁས་ལོངས། ཐ་དད།

ཁས་བླངས་པའི་ verbal n. + 6th case particle fused to suffixless final syllable

འི་ particle fused to suffixless final syllable; either 1) a syntactic particle following a verb or verb phrase signifying conjunction or disjunction, or 2) a 6th case particle following nouns, pronouns, postpositions, and adjectives

ཁས་བླངས་པའི་བཅས་པ་ noun phrase (verbal adjective + 6th case particle + noun) *having promised*

བཅས་པ་ possessive lexical suffix particle having roots in the nom-s.p. verb of conjunction བཅས་

ཁས་བླངས་པའི་བཅས་པ་རྣམས་ *promises [you] have made*

རྣམས་ optional lexical pluralizing suffix particle

ཁས་བླངས་པའི་བཅས་པ་རྣམས་ལ་ noun phrase (verbal adjective + 6th case particle + noun) + 7th case particle indicating general referential context of action expressed by the verb གཡེལ་

ལ་ particle; either 1) a syntactic particle following a verb or verb phrase signifying conjunction or disjunction, or 2) a case particle following nouns, pronouns, postpositions, and adjectives marking the 2nd, 4th and 7th cases

གཡེལ་ intr. v. (nom-loc), *deviate from (be idle, be lazy)*
གཡེལ་གཡེལ་གཡེལ། ཐ་མི་དད།

གཡེལ་བ་ verbal noun, *deviation, laziness*

གཡེལ་བར་ verbal n. + 2nd case particle fused to suffixless syllable

ར་ particle fused to suffixless final syllable; either 1) a verb-modifying syntactic particle within a verb phrase, or 2) a case particle following nouns, pronouns, postpositions, and adjectives marking the 2nd, 4th and 7th cases

སྣང་ intr. v (nom-obj), *appear* སྣང་སྣང་སྣང་། ཐ་མི་དད།

སྣང་ན་ verb + conditional syntactic particle following a verb marking a conditional clause

ན་ particle; either 1) a rhetorical syntactic particle marking a conditional clause following a verb or verb phrase, or 2) a case particle following nouns, pronouns, postpositions, and adjectives marking the 2nd, 4th and 7th cases

ལས་ n., *actions*

ལས་ particle; either 1) syntactic particle marking adverbs, participles or disjunction, or 2) a case particle marking the 5th case

འབྲས་ n., *effect;* abbreviation for འབྲས་བུ

ལས་འབྲས་ལ་ noun phrase (n. + n.) + 7th case particle marking qualifier of verb ངེས་ *be certain, ascertain*

ལ་ particle; either 1) a syntactic particle following a verb or verb phrase signifying conjunction or disjunction, or 2) a case particle following nouns, pronouns, postpositions, and adjectives marking the 2nd, 4th and 7th cases

ངེས་ intr. v. (nom-loc), *be certain, ascertain* ངེས་ངེས་ངེས། ཐ་མི་དད།

ངེས་པ་ verbal n., *certainty, ascertainment*

ཆུང་བ་ adj., *small*

ཡིན་ intr. v. (nom-nom), *is, are* ཡིན་ཡིན་ཡིན་ཡིན། ཐ་མི་དད།

སྙམ་ trans. v. (ag-nom), *consider, think about, wonder about*
སྙམ་སྙམ་སྙམ། ཐ་མི་དད།

སྙམ་དུ་ adverb, *considering, thinking*

དུ་ particle; either 1) a verb-modifying syntactic particle within a verb phrase, or 2) a case particle following nouns, pronouns, postpositions, and adjectives marking the 2nd, 4th and 7th cases

བསམས་ trans. v. (ag-nom) (past tense), *think about, consider*
སེམས་བསམས་བསམ་སོམས། ཐ་དད།

བསམས་ལ། verb + conjunctive syntactic particle

Notes on Parts 10 and 11

ཁས་བླངས་པའི་བཅས་པ་རྣམས་ལ་ verbal adjective + noun + 7th case particle indicating general referential context of action expressed by the verb གཡེལ་

ལས་འབྲས་ལ་ངེས་པ་ཆུང་བ་ཡིན་སྙམ་དུ་ སྙམ་དུ་ functions to turn the clause it follows into an adverbial construction qualifying a later verb, here བསམས་, showing how you should contemplate, *[you should contemplate] how [your] understanding of causes and [their] effects is shallow.*

Part 12 is the conclusion of the sentence

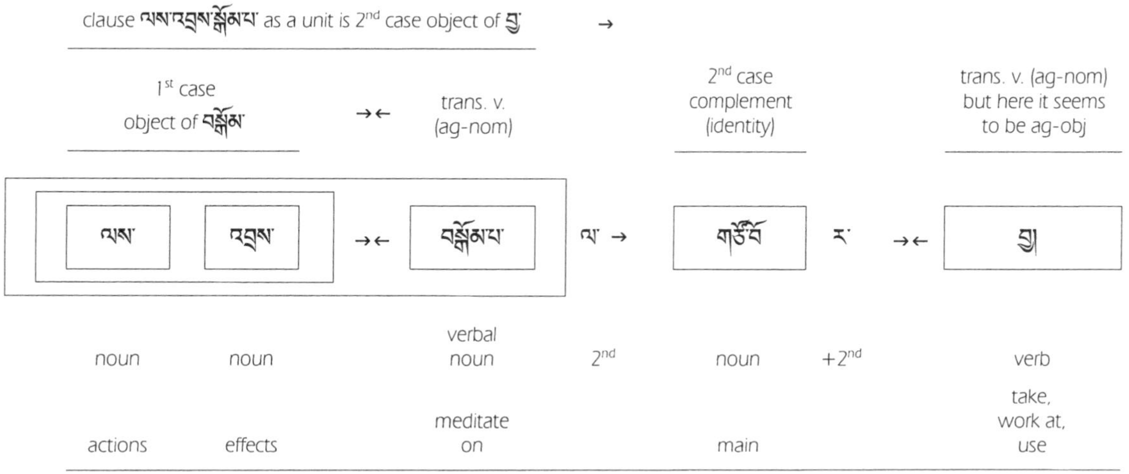

mainly work at meditating on actions and their effects.

Glossary for Part 12

ལས་ n., *actions*

འབྲས་ n., *effect;* abbreviation for འབྲས་བུ་

སྒོམ་པ་ n., *cultivation*

ལས་འབྲས་སྒོམ་པ་ verbal noun clause (object + trans. v.), *meditation on actions and [their] effects*

ལས་འབྲས་སྒོམ་པ་ལ་ verbal noun clause (object + trans. v.) + 2nd case particle marking the 2nd, 4th and 7th cases; here: I'm seeing this as an irregular 2nd case object of the normally ag-nom verb བྱ་

ལ་ particle; either 1) a syntactic particle following a verb or verb phrase signifying conjunction or disjunction, or 2) a case particle following nouns, pronouns, postpositions, and adjectives marking the 2nd, 4th and 7th cases

གཙོ་བོ་ n. or adj., *main, principal*

གཙོ་བོར་ n. + either fused syntactic particle or fused case particle; here: 2nd case adverbial identity as a complement to སྒོམ་པ་

བྱ་ trans. v. (ag-nom), *do, make, perform, take* བྱེད་བྱས་བྱ་བྱོས། ཐ་དད།

Further clarification of the conclusion of Part 12

ལས་འབྲས་ abbreviation for noun phrase composed of nouns in a list: ལས་དང་འབྲས་བུ་ *actions and effects*

གཙོ་བོར་གྱུ the ར་ fused on the end of གཙོ་བོ་ is a case particle fused to a suffixless syllable. This is an identity construction, called in Tibetan དེ་ཉིད་
There are three types of identity constructions: adverbial identity, existential identity, and transformed identity.

Parts 13, 14, and 15

13 འཁོར་བ་མཐའ་དག་ལ་སྐྱོ་ཤས་ཆུངས་ན་

14 ཐར་པ་དོན་གཉེར་གྱི་བློ་ཚིག་ཙམ་དུ་འགྲོ་བས་

15 འཁོར་བའི་ཉེས་དམིགས་རྣམས་བསམ།

Part 13 is a conditional clause qualifying Part 14; Parts 13 and 14 together state a reason qualifying Part 15; and Part 15 is the conclusion.

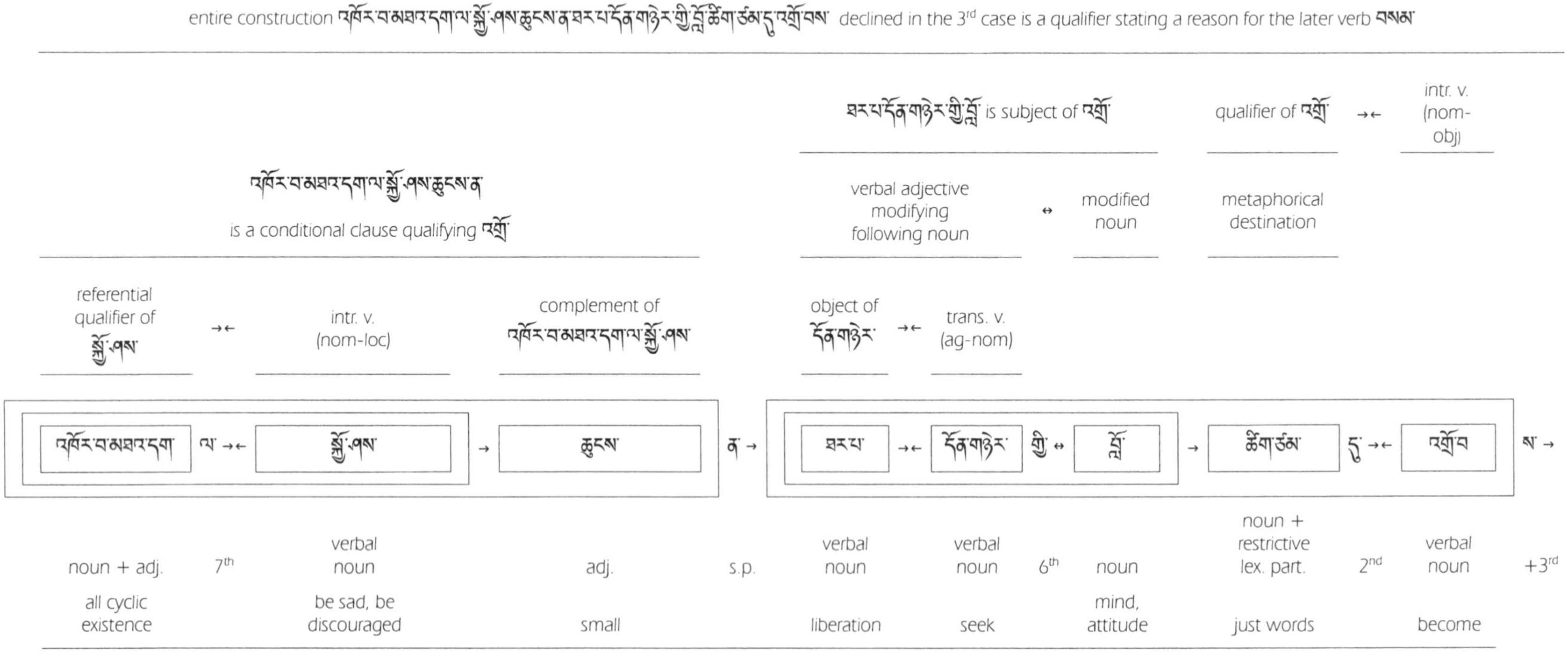

If you have little discouragement with respect to all of cyclic existence, then your attitude of seeking liberation has become just words. Therefore...

Glossary for Parts 13 and 14

འཁོར་བ་ n., *cyclic existence*

མཐའ་དག་ adj., *all*

འཁོར་བ་མཐའ་དག་ noun phrase (noun + adj.), *all of cyclic existence*

འཁོར་བ་མཐའ་དག་ལ་ noun phrase + 7th case particle marking qualifier of the nom-loc attitude verb སྐྱོ་ *be discouraged [about* something marked with the 7th case]

ལ་ particle; either 1) a syntactic particle following a verb or verb phrase signifying conjunction or disjunction, or 2) a case particle following nouns, pronouns, postpositions, and adjectives marking the 2nd, 4th and 7th cases

སྐྱོ་ intr. v. (nom-loc), *be discouraged, be sad about something*

སྐྱོ་སྐྱོ་སྐྱོ། ཐ་མི་དད།

སྐྱོ་ཤས་ verbal noun, *perspective of discouragement, attitude of discouragement*

ཆུངས་ adj., *very small*

སྐྱོ་ཤས་ཆུངས་ན་ verbal clause with implicit linking verb ཡིན་ and conditional syntactic particle, *if your discouragement is small*

ན་ particle; either 1) a rhetorical syntactic particle marking a conditional clause following a verb or verb phrase, or 2) a case particle following nouns, pronouns, postpositions, and adjectives marking the 2nd, 4th and 7th cases

ཐར་ intr. v. (nom-s.p. verb of separation), *be liberated* [from some state]. Verbs of separation are classified as a nom-s.p. verbs together with verbs of absence, conjunction and disjunction, but its qualifier, that from which the subject is liberated, is marked with a true 5th case particle.

ཐར་ཐར་ཐར། ཐ་མི་དད།

ཐར་པ་ verbal n., *liberation*

དོན་གཉེར་ trans. v. (ag-nom), abbreviation for དོན་དུ་གཉེར་ *seek*

དོན་དུ་གཉེར་ trans. phrasal v. (ag-nom), *seek*

གཉེར་གཉེར་གཉེར་གཉེར། ཐ་དད།

ཐར་པ་དོན་གཉེར་ verbal clause (object + transitive verbal noun), *seeking liberation*

ཐར་པ་དོན་གཉེར་གྱི་ verbal adjective (verbal clause + 6th case particle), *which seeks liberation,* modifying the following noun བློ་ *mind, awareness*

ཐར་པ་དོན་གཉེར་གྱི་བློ་ noun phrase (verbal adjective + 6th case particle + modified noun), *the attitude of seeking liberation*

བློ་ n., *mind, awareness*

ཚིག་ n., *word*

ཙམ་ n. and adj., *mere, only*

ཚིག་ཙམ་ noun phrase (n. + adj.), *mere words*

ཚིག་ཙམ་དུ་ noun phrase + 2nd case particle signifying the metaphorical destination of verb འགྲོ་, *(becomes) just words*

དུ་ particle; either 1) a verb-modifying syntactic particle within a verb phrase, or 2) a case particle following nouns, pronouns, postpositions, and adjectives marking the 2nd, 4th and 7th cases

འགྲོ་ intr. v., *go,* often used by extension in the sense of *turns into* or *becomes*

འགྲོ་ཕྱིན་འགྲོ་སོང་། ཐ་མི་དད། སོང་ is also an alternate past form

འགྲོ་བ་ verbal noun, *goer, migrator*

འགྲོ་བས་ n. + 3rd case particle fused to suffixless final syllable

ས་ abbreviation of the particle འིས་ (when འིས་ is fused to a suffixless final syllable, the འི goes away and all that's left is a fused ས་); either 1) syntactic particle creating an adverbial construction, 2) syntactic particle marking the qualifier of an intransitive nom-s.p. verb of absence, or 3) case particle marking the 3rd case

གིས་ཀྱིས་གྱིས་འིས་ཡིས་ are equivalent particles, marking the 3rd case and also marking syntactic adverbial relationships.

Part 13 is a conditional clause which acts like it has an implicit linking verb

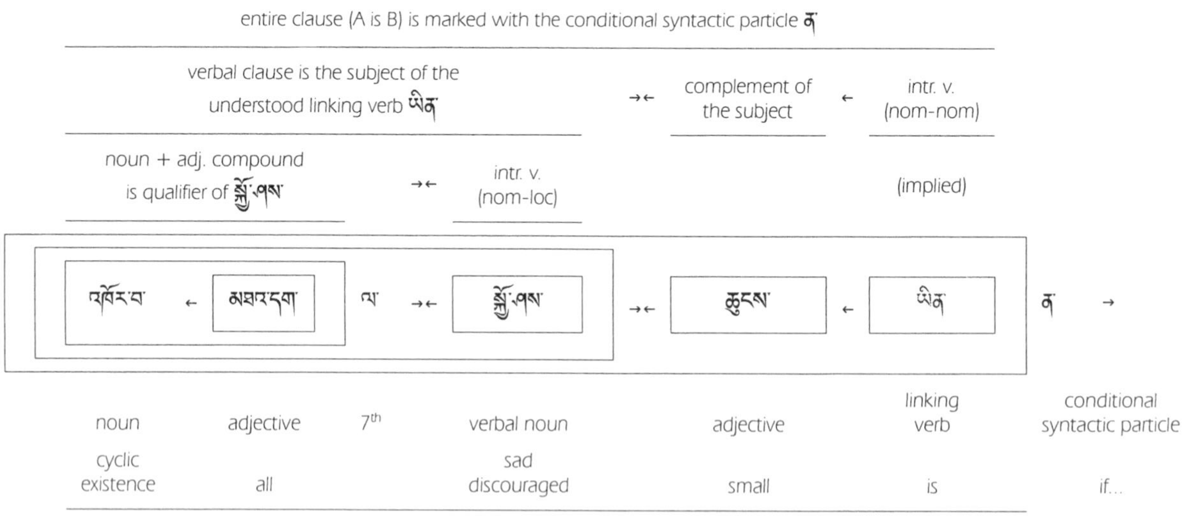

If [your] attitude of discouragement towards cyclic existence is small, ...

Grammar review • Complements with the subjects of intransitive linking verbs

སྐྱོ་	intr. v. (nom-loc), *be discouraged, be sad about something* སྐྱོ་སྐྱོ་སྐྱོ། ཐ་མི་དད།
སྐྱོ་ཤས་	verbal noun, *perspective of discouragement, attitude of discouragement*
འཁོར་བ་མཐའ་དག་ལ་སྐྱོ་ཤས་	nom-loc attitude verbs often occur, as here, without a subject. The verb is qualified by that with respect to which the attitude is directed.
ཐར་པ་དོན་གཉེར་གྱི་བློ་	the verbal adjective ཐར་པ་དོན་གཉེར་ + the 6th case clause connective གྱི་ modifies the following noun བློ་ adjectivally
ཐར་པ་དོན་གཉེར་གྱི་བློ་ཚིག་ཙམ་དུ་འགྲོ་	here the meaning of the nom-obj verb of motion འགྲོ་ *go* has been extended from "go to some place" to "become something else," *the mind seeking liberation has become just words*
ཐར་པ་དོན་གཉེར་གྱི་བློ་	noun phrase (verbal adjective + noun) is the subject (in the 1st case) of the nom-obj verb of motion འགྲོ་ *go*
ཚིག་ཙམ་དུ་	noun phrase (noun + adjective) in the 2nd case is the metaphorical destination of the nom-obj verb of motion འགྲོ་ *becomes*
ཐར་པ་དོན་གཉེར་གྱི་བློ་ཚིག་ཙམ་དུ་འགྲོ་བས་	verbal clause (subject + 2nd case qualifier + intr. nom-obj verb of motion) declined in 3rd case becomes a qualifier stating a reason

Part 15

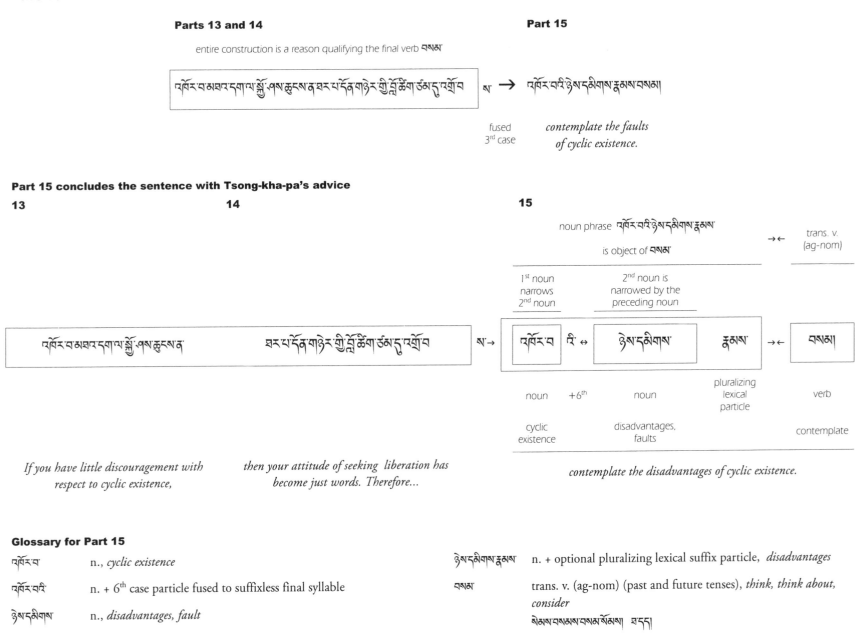

Parts 13 and 14

entire construction is a reason qualifying the final verb བསམ་

འཁོར་བ་མཐར་དག་ལ་སྐྱོ་ཤས་ཆུངས་ན་ཐར་པ་དོན་གཉེར་གྱི་བློ་ཚིག་ཙམ་དུ་འགྲོ་བ ས་ →

fused 3rd case

Part 15

འཁོར་བའི་ཉེས་དམིགས་རྣམས་བསམས།

contemplate the faults of cyclic existence.

Part 15 concludes the sentence with Tsong-kha-pa's advice

13

འཁོར་བ་མཐར་དག་ལ་སྐྱོ་ཤས་ཆུངས་ན

If you have little discouragement with respect to cyclic existence,

14

ཐར་པ་དོན་གཉེར་གྱི་བློ་ཚིག་ཙམ་དུ་འགྲོ་བ ས་→

then your attitude of seeking liberation has become just words. Therefore...

15

noun phrase འཁོར་བའི་ཉེས་དམིགས་རྣམས་ is object of བསམ་ →← trans. v. (ag-nom)

1st noun narrows 2nd noun | 2nd noun is narrowed by the preceding noun

འཁོར་བ འི་ ↔ ཉེས་དམིགས་ རྣམས་ →← བསམས།

འཁོར་བ	འི་	ཉེས་དམིགས་	རྣམས་	བསམས།
noun	+6th	noun	pluralizing lexical particle	verb
cyclic existence		disadvantages, faults		contemplate

contemplate the disadvantages of cyclic existence.

Glossary for Part 15

འཁོར་བ — n., *cyclic existence*

འཁོར་བའི་ — n. + 6th case particle fused to suffixless final syllable

ཉེས་དམིགས་ — n., *disadvantages, fault*

ཉེས་དམིགས་རྣམས་ — n. + optional pluralizing lexical suffix particle, *disadvantages*

བསམ་ — trans. v. (ag-nom) (past and future tenses), *think, think about, consider*
སེམས་བསམས་བསམ་སོམས། ཐ་དད།

16
ཅི་བྱེད་སེམས་ཅན་གྱི་དོན་དུ་བྱེད་པའི་བློ་ཤུགས་དྲག་མི་སྣང་ན

17
ཐེག་ཆེན་གྱི་རྩ་བ་འཆད་པས

18
སྨོན་སེམས་རྒྱུ་དང་བཅས་པ་ལ་མང་དུ་སྦྱང་།

The sentence composed of Parts 16, 17, and 18 begins with a conditional clause stated by Part 16

The subject of the conditional clause beginning this sentence is a noun + adjective compound modified by a verbal adjective clause

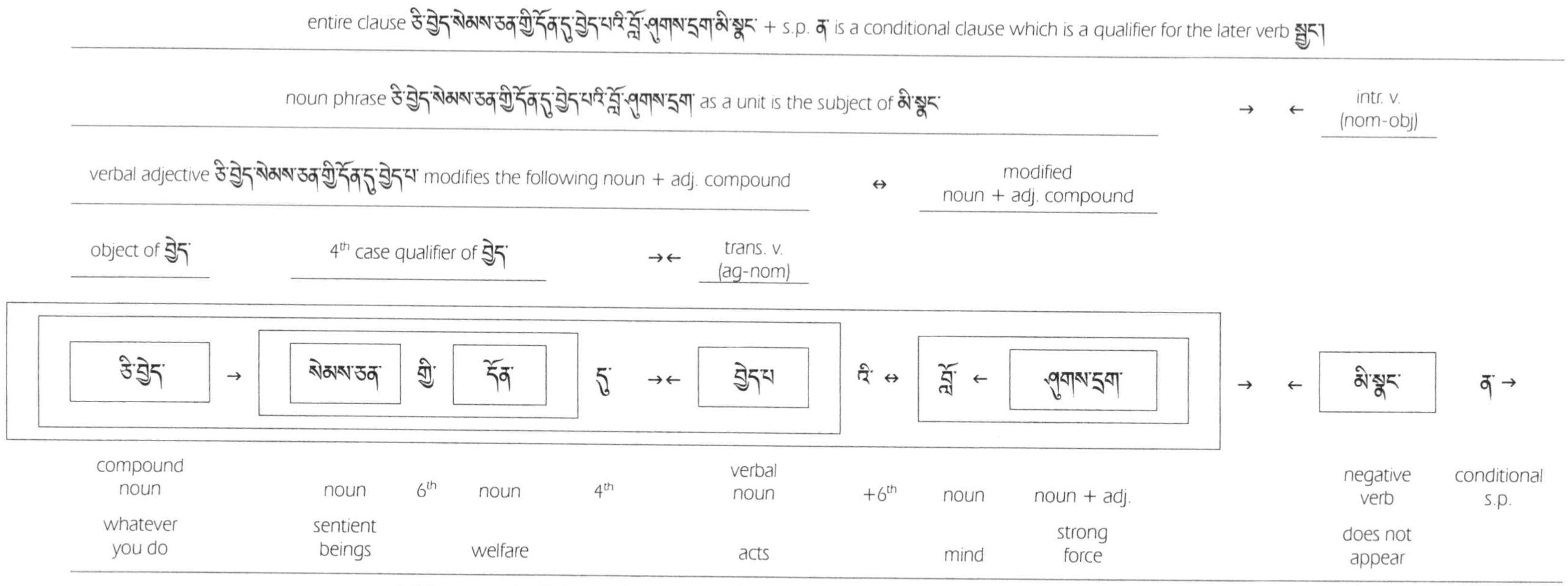

If the attitude of doing whatever you do for the welfare of sentient beings doesn't seem strong...

Glossary for Part 16

ཅི་	general relative and interrogative pronoun, *what, which*
བྱེད་	trans. v. (ag-nom), *do, make, perform, take;* also the strong present auxiliary བྱེད་བྱས་བྱ་བྱོས། ཐ་དད།
སེམས་ཅན་	n., *sentient being* (literally, *mind-possessing*)
ཅན་	lexical suffix particle indicating possession
སེམས་ཅན་གྱི་	n. + 6th case particle connecting noun to the following noun
དོན་	n., *object, purpose, welfare*
སེམས་ཅན་གྱི་དོན་	compound n., *welfare of sentient beings*
སེམས་ཅན་གྱི་དོན་དུ་	noun phrase + case particle marking the 2nd, 4th and 7th cases; here: 4th case signifying purpose
དུ་	particle; either 1) a verb-modifying syntactic particle within a verb phrase, or 2) a case particle following nouns, pronouns, postpositions, and adjectives marking the 2nd, 4th and 7th cases
བྱེད་	trans. v. (ag-nom), *do, make, perform, take* བྱེད་བྱས་བྱ་བྱོས། ཐ་དད།
བྱེད་པའི་	verbal n. + 6th case particle fused to suffixless final syllable
འི་	particle fused to suffixless final syllable; either 1) a syntactic particle following a verb or verb phrase signifying conjunction or disjunction, or 2) a 6th case particle following nouns, pronouns, postpositions, and adjectives
བློ་	n., *mind, awareness*
ཤུགས་	n., *force, strength, power*
དྲག་	adj., *hard, heavy, strong*
མི་སྣང་	negative lexical prefix particle + intr. v. (nom-obj), *not appear*
སྣང་	intr. v. (nom-obj), *appear* སྣང་སྣང་སྣང་། ཐ་མི་དད།
སྣང་ན་	verb + conditional syntactic particle following a verb marking a conditional clause
ན་	particle; either 1) a rhetorical syntactic particle marking a conditional clause following a verb or verb phrase, or 2) a case particle following nouns, pronouns, postpositions, and adjectives marking the 2nd, 4th and 7th cases

Notes on Part 16

ཅི་བྱེད་	interrogative pronoun + verbal noun (a verbal clause actually) *whatever [you] do*
སེམས་ཅན་གྱི་དོན་	*welfare of sentient beings*
སེམས་ཅན་གྱི་དོན་དུ་བྱེད་པའི་	*done for the welfare of sentient beings,* a verbal adjective clause modifying the noun + adj. compound བློ་ཤུགས་དྲག་ *strong force of mind*

Are Buddhas སེམས་ཅན་ ?

Although this word literally means *mind-possessor,* it is used with reference only to those whose minds have obstructions yet to be removed. Buddhas do not have any obstructions, thus Buddhas are not སེམས་ཅན་

Parts 17 and 18

16 ཅི་བྱེད་སེམས་ཅན་གྱི་དོན་དུ་བྱེད་པའི་བློ་ཤུགས་དྲག་མི་སྣང་ན་ **17** ཐེག་ཆེན་གྱི་རྩ་བ་ཆད་པས་ **18** སྨོན་སེམས་རྒྱུ་དང་བཅས་པ་ལ་མང་དུ་སྦྱང་།

This sentence concludes with a qualifying verbal in the 3rd case stating a reason, followed by a transitive verb and its object

Part 16

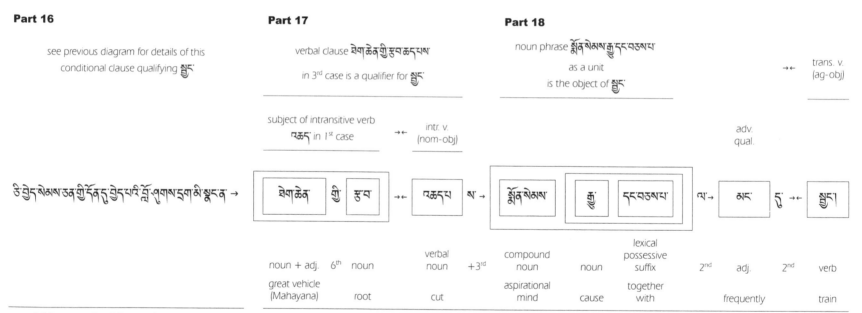

see previous diagram for details of this conditional clause qualifying སྦྱང་

Part 17

verbal clause ཐེག་ཆེན་གྱི་རྩ་བ་ཆད་པས་ in 3rd case is a qualifier for སྦྱང་

subject of intransitive verb འཆད་ in 1st case →← intr. v. (nom-obj)

Part 18

noun phrase སྨོན་སེམས་རྒྱུ་དང་བཅས་པ་ as a unit is the object of སྦྱང་

adv. qual.

→← trans. v. (ag-obj)

ཅི་བྱེད་སེམས་ཅན་གྱི་དོན་དུ་བྱེད་པའི་བློ་ཤུགས་དྲག་མི་སྣང་ན་ → [ཐེག་ཆེན་] གྱི་ [རྩ་བ་] →← [ཆད་པ] ས་ → [སྨོན་སེམས་] [རྒྱུ་] [དང་བཅས་པ་] ལ་→ [མང་] དུ་ →← [སྦྱང་།]

ཐེག་ཆེན་	གྱི་	རྩ་བ་	ཆད་པ	ས་	སྨོན་སེམས་	རྒྱུ་	དང་བཅས་པ་	ལ་	མང་	དུ་	སྦྱང་།
noun + adj.	6th	noun	verbal noun	+3rd	compound noun	noun	lexical possessive suffix	2nd	adj.	2nd	verb
great vehicle (Mahayana)		root	cut		aspirational mind	cause	together with		frequently		train

If the attitude of doing whatever you do for the welfare of sentient beings doesn't seem strong...

then since the root of the Great Vehicle has been severed, train frequently in the aspirational altruistic intention to become a Buddha as well as its causes.

Glossary for Parts 17 and 18

ཐེག་ཆེན་	n. + adj., *Great Vehicle = Mahayana*
ཐེག་ཆེན་གྱི་	n. + 6th case particle connecting noun to the following noun
གྱི་	particle; either 1) a syntactic particle following a verb or verb phrase signifying conjunction or disjunction, or 2) a 6th case particle following nouns, pronouns, postpositions, and adjectives
རྩ་བ་	n., adj., *root, main, principal*
འཆད་	intr. v. (nom-obj), *be severed, be cut* འཆད་ཆད་འཆད། ཐ་མི་དད།
འཆད་	trans. v. (ag-nom), *explain* འཆད་བཤད་བཤད་ཤོད། ཐ་དད།
འཆད་པ་	verbal noun, *cut, severed*
འཆད་པས་	verbal n. + 3rd case particle fused to suffixless final syllable
ས་	abbreviation of the particle འིས་ (when འིས་ is fused to a suffixless final syllable, the འི goes away and all that's left is a fused ས་); either 1) syntactic particle creating an adverbial construction, 2) syntactic particle marking the qualifier of an intransitive nom-s.p. verb of absence, or 3) case particle marking the 3rd case
གིས་ཀྱིས་གྱིས་འིས་ཡིས་	are equivalent particles, marking the 3rd case and also marking syntactic adverbial relationships.
ཐེག་ཆེན་གྱི་རྩ་བ་ཆད་པས་	verbal clause in 3rd case qualifies the action expressed by the verb སྦྱང་ by showing the reason for the action. 3rd case qualifiers stating reasons can in general be translated in two ways. First, by ending the sentence: *...you have cut the root of the Great Vehicle. Therefore, ...* Alternately, state the reason first: *because you have cut the root of the Great Vehicle, ...*
སྨོན་	trans. v. (ag-obj), *aspire, aspire to* སྨོན་སྨོན་སྨོན་སྨོན། ཐ་དད།
སེམས་	trans. v. (ag-nom), *think about, consider* སེམས་བསམས་བསམ་སོམས། ཐ་དད།
སེམས་	n., *mind*
སྨོན་སེམས་	comp. n., *aspirational mind [of enlightenment]*
རྒྱུ་	n., *cause*
རྒྱུ་དང་བཅས་པ་	noun phrase (noun + possessive lexical suffix particle), *together with [its] causes*
དང་བཅས་པ་	possessive lexical suffix particle, *together with;* actually, it's a verbal phrase
བཅས་	intr. v. (nom-s.p. verb of conjunction)
སྨོན་སེམས་རྒྱུ་དང་བཅས་པ་ལ་	noun phrase (noun + verbal noun) + 2nd, 4th or 7th case particle; here: 2nd case particle marking object of verb སྦྱང་
ལ་	particle; either 1) a syntactic particle following a verb or verb phrase signifying conjunction or disjunction, or 2) a case particle following nouns, pronouns, postpositions, and adjectives marking the 2nd, 4th and 7th cases
མང་	adj., *many*
མང་དུ་	adj. + 2nd case particle followed by a verb creates an adverbial qualifier for following verb, the adjective *many* becomes *frequently*
དུ་	particle; either 1) a verb-modifying syntactic particle within a verb phrase, or 2) a case particle following nouns, pronouns, postpositions, and adjectives marking the 2nd, 4th and 7th cases
སྦྱང་	trans. v. (ag-obj), *train in* སྦྱོང་སྦྱངས་སྦྱང་སྦྱོངས། ཐ་དད།

Chapter Nine Self Test

Write out the passage, boxing and identifying every syntactic element.

དེ་རྣམས་བསྒོམ་པའི་ཚེ་ཡང་རྟོག་པ་སྦྱང་བར་བྱས་ནས་བློ་རྣམས་ཆ་མཉམ་དགོས་ཏེ། འདི་ལྟར་ལམ་ལ་འཁྲིད་པའི་བཤེས་གཉེན་ལ་གུས་པ་ཆུང་བར་སྣང་ན་ལེགས་ཚོགས་ཐམས་ཅད་ཀྱི་རྩ་བ་འཆད་པས་བསྟེན་ཚུལ་ལ་འབད། དེ་བཞིན་དུ་སྒྲུབ་པ་ལ་སྤྲོ་ཤུགས་ཆུང་ན་དལ་འབྱོར་གྱི་སྙོར་དང་ཚེ་འདི་ལ་མངོན་ཞེན་ཆེ་བར་སོང་ན་མི་རྟག་པ་དང་ངན་འགྲོའི་ཉེས་དམིགས་སྒོམ་པ་ལ་གཙོ་བོར་བྱ་དགོས། ཁས་བླངས་པའི་བཅས་པ་རྣམས་ལ་གཡེལ་བར་སྣང་ན་ལས་འབྲས་ལ་ངེས་པ་ཆུང་བ་ཡིན་སྙམ་དུ་བསམས་ལ། ལས་འབྲས་སྒོམ་པ་ལ་གཙོ་བོར་བྱ། འཁོར་བ་མཐའ་དག་ལ་སྐྱོ་ཤས་ཆུང་ན་ཐར་པ་དོན་གཉེར་གྱི་བློ་ཚིག་ཙམ་དུ་འགྲོ་བས་འཁོར་བའི་ཉེས་དམིགས་རྣམས་བསམ། ཅི་བྱེད་སེམས་ཅན་གྱི་དོན་དུ་བྱེད་པའི་བློ་ཤུགས་དྲག་མི་སྣང་ན་ཐེག་ཆེན་གྱི་རྩ་བ་འཆད་པས་སྨོན་སེམས་རྒྱུ་དང་བཅས་པ་ལ་མང་དུ་སྦྱང་།

Vocabulary

For each word, can you identify what part of speech it is (noun, pronoun, adjective, verb, adverb, postposition) and what it means?
For each syntactic particle, can you identify what class of syntactic particle it belongs to and how it is used?

སྙོར་	སྙེ་	གྲུབ་	ཤུགས་
རྩ་བ་	སྙམ་དུ་	བྱེད་	ལེགས་ཚོགས་
སྤྲོ་	སྙམ་	བྱས་	ལེགས་
སྒྲུབ་པ་	སྒོམ་པ་	བྱ་	ལས་
སྦྱང་བར་བྱས་	སྒོམ་	གྱི་	ལམ་
སྦྱང་	རྒྱུ་	ཀྱི་	ལ་
སྐྱོ་ཤས་	རྣམས་	ཀྱང་ཡང་འང་	ཡིན་
སྐྱོ་	རྟོག་པ་	ཀྱང་	ཡང་
དང་བཅས་པ་ལ་	རྟོག་	སོང་	འི་
སྨོན་སེམས་	རྟེན་	སེམས་ཅན་གྱི་དོན་	འབྲས་
སྨོན་	བློ་	སེམས་ཅན་	འགྲོ་བ་
སྣང་	དྲག་	སེམས་	འགྲོ་

འཁྲིད་པ་
འཁྲིད་
འབབ་
འདི་ལྟར་
འདི་
འཆད་པ་
འཆད་
འང་
འཁོར་བ་
འཁོར་
ཞེན་
ཚོགས་
ཚེ་འདི་
ཚེ་
ཚུལ་
ཚིག་
ཙམ་
མི་སྣང་

མི་རྟག་པ་
མཐའ་དག་
མངོན་ཞེན་
མངོན་པར་ཞེན་
མངོན་པར་
མང་དུ་
མང་
བསྒྲུབ་
བསྟེན་ཚུལ་
བསྟེན་
བསྒོམ་པ་
བསྒོམ་
བསམས་
བསམ་
བཤེས་གཉེན་
བཅས་པ་
ནས་
ན་

དུ་
དོན་དུ་གཉེར་
དོན་གཉེར་
དོན་
དེ་བཞིན་དུ་
དེ་
དལ་འབྱོར་
དང་བཅས་པ་
དང་
དགོས་
ཐེག་ཆེན་
ཐར་པ་
ཐར་
ཐམས་ཅད་
ཏེ་ སྟེ་ and དེ་
ཉེས་དམིགས་
ཆེ་བ་
ཆུངས་

ཆུང་བ་
ཆ་མཉམ་
ཆ་
ཅི་
ཅན་
ངེས་པ་
ངེས་
ངན་འགྲོ་
གུས་པ་
གུས་
གོམས་
གིས་ཀྱིས་གྱིས་འིས་ཡིས་
གཡེལ་བ་
གཡེལ་
གཙོ་བོར་བྱ་
གཙོ་བོ་
ཁས་བླངས་

དེ་རྣམས་བསྒོམ་པའི་ཚེ་ཡང་རྟོག་པ་སྦྱང་བར་བྱས་ནས་བློ་རྣམས་ཆ་མཉམ་དགོས་ཏེ། འདི་ལྟར་ལམ་ལ་འཁྲིད་པའི་བཤེས་གཉེན་ལ་གུས་པ་ཆུང་བར་སྣང་ན་ལེགས་ཚོགས་ཐམས་ཅད་ཀྱི་རྩ་བ་འཆད་པས་བསྟེན་ཚུལ་ལ་འབད། དེ་བཞིན་དུ་སྒྲུབ་པ་ལ་སྤྲོ་ཤུགས་ཆུང་ན་དལ་འབྱོར་གྱི་སྐོར་དང་ཚེ་འདི་ལ་མངོན་ཞེན་ཆེ་བར་སོང་ན་མི་རྟག་པ་དང་ངན་འགྲོའི་ཉེས་དམིགས་སྒོམ་པ་ལ་གཙོ་བོར་བྱ་དགོས། ཁས་བླངས་པའི་བཅས་པ་རྣམས་ལ་གཡེལ་བར་སྣང་ན་ལས་འབྲས་ལ་ངེས་པ་ཆུང་བ་ཡིན་སྙམ་དུ་བསམས་ལ། ལས་འབྲས་སྒོམ་པ་ལ་གཙོ་བོར་བྱ། འཁོར་བ་མཐའ་དག་ལ་སྐྱོ་ཤས་ཆུང་ན་ཐར་པ་དོན་གཉེར་གྱི་བློ་ཚིག་ཙམ་དུ་འགྲོ་བས་འཁོར་བའི་ཉེས་དམིགས་རྣམས་བསམ། ཅི་བྱེད་སེམས་ཅན་གྱི་དོན་དུ་བྱེད་པའི་བློ་ཤུགས་དྲག་མི་སྣང་ན་ཐེག་ཆེན་གྱི་རྩ་བ་འཆད་པས་སྨོན་སེམས་རྒྱུ་དང་བཅས་པ་ལ་མང་དུ་སྦྱང་།

Also, when those are cultivated in meditation, you need a balanced attitude, having become skilled in analysis. If it appears that you have little respect for the spiritual guide leading you on the path, since the root of the collections of goodness is severed, you should strive at the mode of reliance [on a spiritual guide]. Similarly, if you have little force of enthusiasm for practice, work at the topics of leisure and fortune. If you come to have great attachment to this life, mainly work at meditating on impermanence and the faults of bad migrations. If it appears that you are deviating from the [ethical] formulation that you have accepted, mainly work at meditating on actions and their effects. If you have little discouragement with respect to cyclic existence, then since your seeking of liberation has become merely verbal, contemplate the faults of cyclic existence. If the attitude of doing whatever you do for the welfare of sentient beings doesn't seem strong, then since the root of the Great Vehicle has been severed, train frequently in the aspirational altruistic intention to become a Buddha as well as its causes.

Annotations for Tsong-kha-pa's text in Chapter Nine

Here is Tsong-kha-pa's text as supplemented by *The Four Interwoven Annotations,* 833.6-835.1

གསུམ་པ་རྟོག་ཞིབ་མོས་གནད་དུ་བསྣུན་ཚུལ་ནི།

། དེ་ལྟ་བུའི་ལུས་ཡོངས་སུ་རྫོགས་པའི་ལམ་ དེ་རྣམས་བསྒོམ་ པར་བྱེད་ པའི་ཚེ་ ན་ ཡང་ བློས་བསྒོམ་པ་དེ་ཙམ་ལམ་བཞག་པར་གང་ལ་གང་དགོས་པའི་ཕྱོགས་ཐམས་ཅད་ ནས་རིགས་ངེས་པའི་ རྟོག་པ་སྦྱང་ ཞིང་གྲུབ་ བར་བྱས་ནས་ ལམ་བསྒོམ་པའི་ བློ་ གོང་འོག་བར་མ་ རྣམས་ ཐམས་ཅད་ ཆ་མཉམ་ དུ་བསྒྲུབ་ དགོས་ཏེ། དེ་ལྟར་ཆ་མཉམ་དུ་བསྒྲུབ་པའི་ཚུལ་ནི་ འདི་ལྟར་ ཡིན་ཏེ་ཐོག་མར་རང་ཉིད་ ལམ་ལ་འཁྲིད་པར་བྱེད་ པའི་བཤེས་གཉེན་ དམ་པ་དེ་བསྟེན་ཚུལ་ ལ་གུས་པ་ སྐྱེ་ལུགས་དེ་ཉིད་ལམ་གཞན་ལས་བསྐྱེད་ ཆུང་བར་སྣང་ན་ ནི་གུས་པ་དེ་མེད་པ་དེ་ཉིད་འདི་ཕྱིའི་ ལེགས་ པའི་འབྲས་བུ་འབྱུང་བའི་ ཚོགས་ཐམས་ཅད་ཀྱི་རྩ་བ་ གཞི་ནས་ འཆད་ ཅིང་གཏོར་བ་ཡིན་ པས་ ན་བཤེས་གཉེན་ བསྟེན་ཚུལ་ གྱི་ཆོས་སྐོར་ ལ་ ཅི་ནས་གལ་པོ་ཆེར་ འབད་ དགོས་པ་ཡིན། ཚུལ་ དེ་བཞིན་དུ་ སྙིང་པོའི་དོན་ལག་ཏུ་ལེན་པའི་བསྒྲུབ་པ་ལ་སྤྲོ་ཤུགས་ཆུངས་ བ་ཡིན་པ་འདུག་ ན་ ནི་དེའི་རྒྱུ་ དལ་འབྱོར་གྱི་ ཆོས་ སྐོར་ ལ་འབད་འབུངས་འདོན་པ་ དང་ གང་ཏེ་ ཚེ་འདི་ལ་མངོན་ཞེན་ རིས་གྱིས་ ཆེ་བར་སོང་ འདུག་ ན་ དེའི་གཉེན་པོ་འཆི་བ་ མི་རྟག་པ འི་སྐོར་ དང་ངན་འགྲོའི་ཉེས་དམིགས་བསྒོམ་པ འི་སྐོར་གཉིས་ ལ་ འབད་པ་ གཙོ་བོར་བྱ་དགོས། གལ་ཏེ་རང་གིས་ ཁས་བླངས་པའི་བཅས་པ འི་མཚམས་ རྣམས་ལ་གཡེལ་ ཏེ་བསྲུབ་པ་ལ་མི་སྤྲོ་ བར་སྣང་ན་ དེའི་གཉེན་པོར་ ལས་འབྲས་ལ་ངེས་པ་ཆུང་ ནས་ཡིད་མ་ཆེས་པས་ལན་ བ་ཡིན་སྙམ་དུ་བསམས་ པར་བྱས་ ལ། ལས་འབྲས་བསྒོམ་པ་ལ་གཙོ་བོར་ འབད་པར་ བྱ་ དགོས། གལ་ཏེ་ འཁོར་བ་མཐའ་དག་ལ་སྐྱོ་ཤས་ཆུངས་ འདུག་ ན་ དེའི་དབང་གིས་ ཐར་པ་དོན་གཉེར་གྱི་བློ་ དེ་ཉིད་ ཚིག་ཙམ་དུ་འགྲོ་བ་ ཡིན་པ ས་ ན། དེ་འདྲའི་སྐྱོ་ཤས་སྐྱེལ་བའི་ཕྱིར་དུ་ འཁོར་བའི་ཉེས་དམིགས་རྣམས་ བློ་ཐམས་ཅད་ནས་ བསམ་ དགོས་པ་ཡིན། གལ་ཏེ་རང་གི་བྱ་བ་ ཅི་བྱེད་ ཐམས་ཅད་ སེམས་ཅན་གྱི་དོན་དུ་བྱེད་པའི་བློ་ཤུགས་དྲག་ པོ་ མི་སྣང་ན་ དེ་འདྲའི་བློ་ཤུགས་དྲག་པོ་མེད་པ་ནི་ ཐེག་ཆེན་གྱི་རྩ་བ་འཆད་ ཅིང་ཉམས་པ་ཡིན་ པས་ ན་དེ་བསྐྱེད་པའི་ཕྱིར་དུ་ སྨོན་ པའི་ སེམས་བསྐྱེད་ཀྱི་ རྒྱུ་ སྙིང་རྗེ་གཞི་ དང་བཅས་པ་ལ་ སྙིང་ནས་ལན་ མང་དུ་སྦྱངས་ པ་ཞིག་དགོས།

Three: how to develop special emphasis through fine analysis

Also, while you are cultivating the thoroughly complete body of the paths, all the attitudes of cultivating the paths—the earlier, middle and end—must be achieved equally through analyzing with certain reasoning all the factors pertaining to what is needed for a particular meditative cultivation to be posited as a path. The proper way to accomplish this equality is as follows.

If it appears that your respect is small for your excellent spiritual guide leading you on the path—how respect is generated is produced from other paths—then it is extremely important that you work at the topics of proper reliance on your spiritual guide as best as you can, because just your lacking this respect severs and scatters the basic root for all the collections whereby later good effects are accomplished.

Similarly, if you have little force of enthusiastic practice—making the most of the essence [of leisure and opportunity]—you should work at its causes, meditating on the topics of leisure and opportunity, striving through the three doors. If you come to have great attachment to this life, mainly work at meditating on the two topics of its antidotes: the impermanence of death and the faults of bad migrations.

If it appears that you are forgetting about the boundaries of the [ethical] formulations that you have accepted, i.e., they have not permeated your practice, mainly work at meditating on actions and their effects.

If you have little discouragement with respect to cyclic existence, then due to that your seeking of liberation has become merely verbal. Therefore, in order to extend such, contemplate the faults of cyclic existence from all points of view.

If it appears that you do not have a strong force of mind turning everything you do for the welfare of sentient beings, then since that absence of strong determination severs the root of the Mahayana, in order to generate it train frequently in the causes of generating the aspirational altruistic intention to become a Buddha as well as its basis, compassion, through taking them to heart.

Chapter Ten

རྒྱལ་སྲས་ཀྱི་སྡོམ་པ་བླངས་ནས་སྤྱོད་པ་ལ་སློབ་པ་ནའང་མཚན་མར་འཛིན་པའི་འཆིང་བ་ཤུགས་དྲག་པར་སྣང་ན་རིགས་ཤེས་ཀྱིས་མཚན་མར་འཛིན་པའི་བློས་བཟུང་བའི་དམིགས་གཏད་ཐམས་ཅད་བཤིག་ལ། ནམ་མཁའ་ལྟ་བུ་དང་སྒྱུ་མ་ལྟ་བུའི་སྟོང་ཉིད་ལ་བློ་སྦྱོང་། སེམས་དགེ་བའི་དམིགས་པ་ལ་མི་སྡོད་པའི་རྣམ་གཡེང་གི་དབང་དུ་གྱུར་པར་སྣང་ན་རྩེ་གཅིག་པའི་གནས་ཆ་ལ་གཙོ་བོར་སྐྱོང་བར་གོང་མ་རྣམས་གསུང་སྟེ། དེས་མཚོན་ནས་མ་བཤད་པ་རྣམས་ཀྱང་ཤེས་པར་བྱ་ལ། མདོར་ན་ཕྱོགས་རེ་བར་མ་སོང་བར་རྒྱུད་དགེ་བའི་ཕྱོགས་ཐམས་ཅད་ལ་བཀོལ་དུ་རུང་བ་ཞིག་དགོས་སོ། །

Division of the passage into units to facilitate the analysis of the syntax

I have divided this final text section into seven meaning units.

1

རྒྱལ་སྲས་ཀྱི་སྡོམ་པ་བླངས་ནས་སྤྱོད་པ་ལ་སློབ་པ་ནའང་མཚན་མར་འཛིན་པའི་འཆིང་བ་ཤུགས་དྲག་པར་སྣང་ན

2

རིགས་ཤེས་ཀྱིས་མཚན་མར་འཛིན་པའི་བློས་བཟུང་བའི་དམིགས་གཏད་ཐམས་ཅད་བཤིག་ལ།

3

ནམ་མཁའ་ལྟ་བུ་དང་སྒྱུ་མ་ལྟ་བུའི་སྟོང་ཉིད་ལ་བློ་སྦྱོང་།

4

སེམས་དགེ་བའི་དམིགས་པ་ལ་མི་སྡོད་པའི་རྣམ་གཡེང་གི་དབང་དུ་གྱུར་པར་སྣང་ན

5

རྩེ་གཅིག་པའི་གནས་ཆ་ལ་གཙོ་བོར་སྐྱོང་བར་གོང་མ་རྣམས་གསུང་སྟེ།

6

དེས་མཚོན་ནས་མ་བཤད་པ་རྣམས་ཀྱང་ཤེས་པར་བྱ་ལ།

7

མདོར་ན་ཕྱོགས་རེ་བར་མ་སོང་བར་རྒྱུད་དགེ་བའི་ཕྱོགས་ཐམས་ཅད་ལ་བཀོལ་དུ་རུང་བ་ཞིག་དགོས་སོ། །

Part 1 • རྒྱལ་སྲས་ཀྱི་སྡོམ་པ་བླངས་ནས་སྤྱོད་པ་ལ་སློབ་པ་ན་འང་མཚན་མར་འཛིན་པའི་འཆིང་བ་ཤུགས་དྲག་པར་སྣང་ན

Part 1 is a conditional clause that qualifies the later verb བཞིག

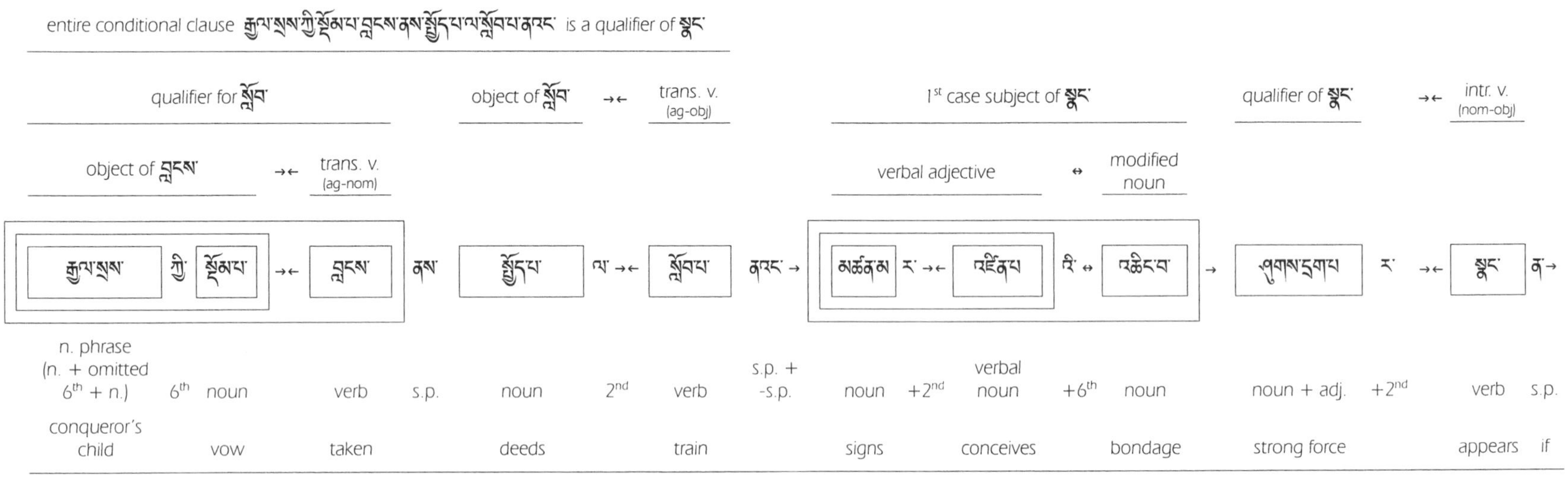

Also, if it appears that you have the fetters of the conceptions of signs [inherent existence] in strong force when training in the [Bodhisattva] deeds having taken the Bodhisattva vow, ...

Glossary for Part 1

རྒྱལ་ intr. v. (nom-s.p.), *be victorious, win, conqueror, subdue;* this verb of separation is classified as a nom-s.p. verb together with verbs of absence, conjunction and disjunction, but its qualifier, that over which the subject is victorious, is marked with a true 5th case.

རྒྱལ་ n., *conqueror;* abbreviation for རྒྱལ་བ་ (i.e., Buddha)

སྲས་ n., *child, son*

རྒྱལ་སྲས་ noun phrase, *conqueror's children, children of the conqueror (i.e., Bodhisattvas);* abbreviation for རྒྱལ་བའི་སྲས་

རྒྱལ་སྲས་ཀྱི་ noun phrase + 6th case particle; here: possessive use of 6th case

ཀྱི་ particle; either 1) a syntactic particle following a verb or verb phrase signifying conjunction or disjunction, or 2) a 6th case particle following nouns, pronouns, postpositions, and adjectives

སྡོམ་ trans. v. (ag-nom), *vow*

སྡོམ་བསྡམས་བསྡམ་སྡོམས། ཐ་དད། སྡོམ་བསྡོམས་བསྡོམ་སྡོམས། ཐ་དད།

སྡོམ་པ་ n., *vow*

བླངས་ trans. v. (ag-nom) (past tense), *take* ལེན་བླངས་བླང་ལོངས། ཐ་དད།

བླངས་ནས་ verb in past tense + continuative s.p. = past participle, *having taken*

ནས་ particle; either 1) a syntactic particle following verbs and verb phrases marking adverbs, participles or disjunction, or 2) a case particle marking the 5th case

སྤྱོད་ trans. v. (ag-nom), *use* སྤྱོད་སྤྱད་སྤྱད་སྤྱོད། ཐ་དད།

སྤྱོད་པ་ n., *deeds*

སྦྱོང་པ་ལ་ n. + 2nd case particle marking the object of the transitive verb སློབ་ *train in*

ལ་ particle; either 1) a syntactic particle following a verb or verb phrase signifying conjunction or disjunction, or 2) a case particle following nouns, pronouns, postpositions, and adjectives marking the 2nd, 4th and 7th cases

སློབ་ trans. v. (ag-obj), *train in* སློབ་བསླབས་བསླབ་སློབས། ཐ་དད།

སློབ་ན་ verb + conditional syntactic particle makes the clause ending in the verb སློབ་ a conditional clause, *if [you] train...*

སློབ་ན་འང་ verb + conditional syntactic particle + conjunctive or disjunctive syntactic particlke fused to a suffixless final syllable, *even if [you] train...*

ན་འང་ 2 fused syntactic particles: ན་ and འང་, *even if...*

འང་ conjunctive and disjunctive syntactic particle used after nouns, pronouns, adjectives, verbs, and verb phrases, *but, even, also.* འང་ follows words with suffixless final syllables.

མཚན་མ་ n., *sign, mark* (generally indicating a level of wrongly reified perception)

མཚན་མར་ noun + 2nd case particle fused to a suffixless syllable

མཚན་མར་འཛིན་པ་ verbal clause, *conception of signs [i.e., true existence]*

འཛིན་ trans. v. (ag-nom), *grasp, hold;* by extension: *apprehend, conceive*

འཛིན་བཟུང་གཟུང་ཟུང་། ཐ་དད།

འཛིན་པ་ verbal noun, *held, apprehended, conception*

འཛིན་པའི་ verbal noun + 6th case particle fused to suffixless syllable

འི་ particle fused to suffixless final syllable; either 1) a syntactic particle following a verb or verb phrase signifying conjunction or disjunction, or 2) a 6th case particle following nouns, pronouns, postpositions, and adjectives

འཆིང་ trans. v. (ag-nom), *bind, tie up* འཆིང་བཅིངས་བཅིང་འཆིངས། ཐ་དད།

འཆིང་བ་ n., *bondage, fetters*

ཤུགས་ n., *force, strength, power*

དྲག་ adj., *hard, heavy, strong*

དྲག་པར་ adj. + 2nd case particle fused to suffixless final syllable

ར་ particle fused to suffixless final syllable; either 1) a verb-modifying syntactic particle within a verb phrase, or 2) a case particle following nouns, pronouns, postpositions, and adjectives marking the 2nd, 4th and 7th cases

སྣང་ intr. v. (nom-obj), *appear* སྣང་སྣང་སྣང་། ཐ་མི་དད།

སྣང་ན་ verb + conditional syntactic particle makes the clause ending in the verb སྣང་ a conditional clause, *if [it] appears...*

ན་ particle; either 1) a rhetorical syntactic particle marking a conditional clause following a verb or verb phrase, or 2) a case particle following nouns, pronouns, postpositions, and adjectives marking the 2nd, 4th and 7th cases

Notes on Part 1

རྒྱལ་སྲས་ཀྱི་སྡོམ་པ་བླངས་ནས་ verbal clause + syntactic particle ནས་ creating a participle, *having taken the Bodhisatva vows...*

ནས་ particle; either 1) a syntactic particle following verbs and verb phrases marking adverbs, participles or disjunction, or 2) a case particle marking the 5th case

མཚན་མར་འཛིན་པ་ *conception of signs, i.e., the conception of inherent existence.* Rather than translating མཚན་མར་འཛིན་པ་ as *grasping signs,* a **physical relationship**, མཚན་མར་འཛིན་པ་ is better understood as signifying a **cognitive relationship** translated as *conceiving signs [of true existence],* i.e., the superimposition of a mode of existence which, although strongly believed in, does not exist.

Part 2 • རིགས་ཤེས་ཀྱིས་མཚན་མར་འཛིན་པའི་བློས་བཟུང་བའི་དམིགས་གཏད་ཐམས་ཅད་བཞིག་ལ།

Parts 2 and 3 complete the sentence by stating the conclusion; here is Part 2

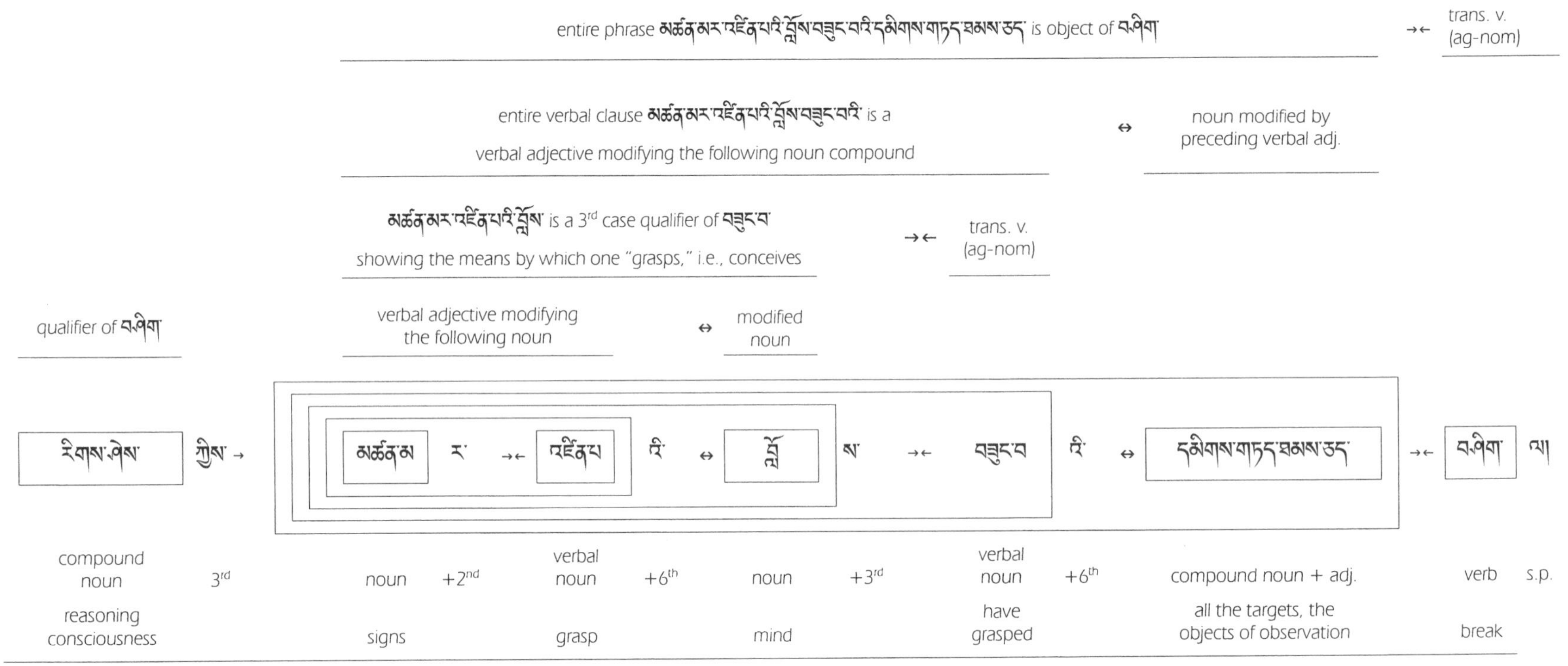

[...if it appears you have the conception of inherent existence], break down all the targets of the conception of signs through a reasoning consciousness;

Glossary for Part 2

རིགས་ཤེས་ compound noun, *reasoning consciousness*

ཀྱིས་ either syntactic or case particle; here: 3rd case particle

མཚན་མ་ n., *sign*

མཚན་མར་ noun + 2nd, 4th or 7th case particle fused to a suffixless syllable

ར་ particle fused to suffixless final syllable; either 1) a verb-modifying syntactic particle within a verb phrase, or 2) a case particle following nouns, pron., post., and adjectives marking the 2nd, 4th and 7th cases

མཚན་མར་འཛིན་པ་ *conception of signs, i.e., the conception of inherent existence.* Rather than translating མཚན་མར་འཛིན་པ་ as *grasping signs,* a **physical relationship,** མཚན་མར་འཛིན་པ་ is better understood as signifying a **cognitive relationship** translated as *conceiving signs [of true existence],* i.e., the superimposition of a mode of existence which, although strongly believed in, does not exist.

འཛིན་ trans. v. (ag-nom), *grasp, hold;* by extension: *apprehend, conceive*

འཛིན་པའི་ verbal noun + 6th case particle fused to suffixless syllable

འི་ particle fused to suffixless final syllable; either 1) a syntactic particle following a verb or verb phrase signifying conjunction or disjunction, or 2) a 6th case particle following nouns, pronouns, postpositions, and adjectives

བློ་ n., *mind, awareness*

བློས་ noun + 3rd case particle fused to suffixless syllable

ས་ abbreviation of the particle ཡིས་ (when ཡིས་ is fused to a suffixless final syllable, the ཡི goes away and all that's left is a fused ས་); either 1) syntactic particle creating an adverbial construction, 2) syntactic particle marking the qualifier of an intransitive nom-s.p. verb of absence, or 3) case particle marking the 3rd case

བཟུང་ trans. v. (ag-nom) (past-tense), *grasp, hold;* by extension: *apprehend, conceive*

འཛིན་བཟུང་གཟུང་ཟུང་། ཐ་དད།

བཟུང་བའི་ verbal noun + 6th case particle fused to suffixless syllable

འི་ particle fused to suffixless final syllable; either 1) a syntactic particle following a verb or verb phrase signifying conjunction or disjunction, or 2) a 6th case particle following nouns, pronouns, postpositions, and adjectives

དམིགས་ trans. v. (ag-nom), *observe.* དམིགས་དམིགས་དམིགས་དམིགས། ཐ་དད།

དམིགས་ n., *object of observation*

གཏད་ trans. v. (ag-nom), *aim, focus, concentrate; delegate, entrust*

གཏོད་གཏད་གཏད་གཏོད། ཐ་དད།

དམིགས་གཏད་ compound noun, *target.* This word is used to talk about the mistaken way we think things exist. The idea here is that what you're conceiving—in this case inherently existent mind and body—doesn't exist at all. However, the conception does exist, thereby creating all the problems of cyclic existence. You attack the target—the object as you conceive it—with a reasoning consciousness, eventually coming to understand that mind and body don't exist in the way you had been conceiving them to exist.

ཐམས་ཅད་ adj., *all*

བཤིག་ trans. v. (ag-nom) (past and future), *destroy, break down*

འཇིག་བཤིག་བཤིག་ཤིགས། ཐ་དད།

བཤིག་ལ། verb + syntactic particle signifying conjunction or disjunction; here; conjunction *and*

ལ་ particle; either 1) a syntactic particle following a verb or verb phrase signifying conjunction or disjunction, or 2) a case particle following nouns, pronouns, postpositions, and adjectives marking the 2nd, 4th and 7th cases

Notes on Part 2

རིགས་ཤེས་ཀྱིས་ qualifier of བཤིག showing the means by which one is to destroy the conceived-to-exist-inherently objects of observation

མཚན་མར་འཛིན་པའི་བློ་ a verbal clause + a fused 6th case particle acting as a verbal adjective modifying the following noun བློ་ *the mind which conceives signs*

མཚན་མར་འཛིན་པའི་བློས་བཟུང་བའི་དམིགས་གཏད་ཐམས་ཅད་ a verbal clause + a fused 6th case particle acting as a verbal adjective modifying the following noun + adj. compound དམིགས་གཏད་ཐམས་ཅད་ *all the targets of a mind conceiving signs*

དམིགས་གཏད་ compound n., *target.* The idea here is that what you're conceiving—inherently existent mind and body—doesn't exist at all. The conception does exist, creating all the problems of cyclic existence, so you attack the conception with a reasoning consciousness, eventually coming to understand that **mind and body don't exist in the way you had been conceiving them to exist.**

Part 3 is the conclusion of the sentence begun with Part 2

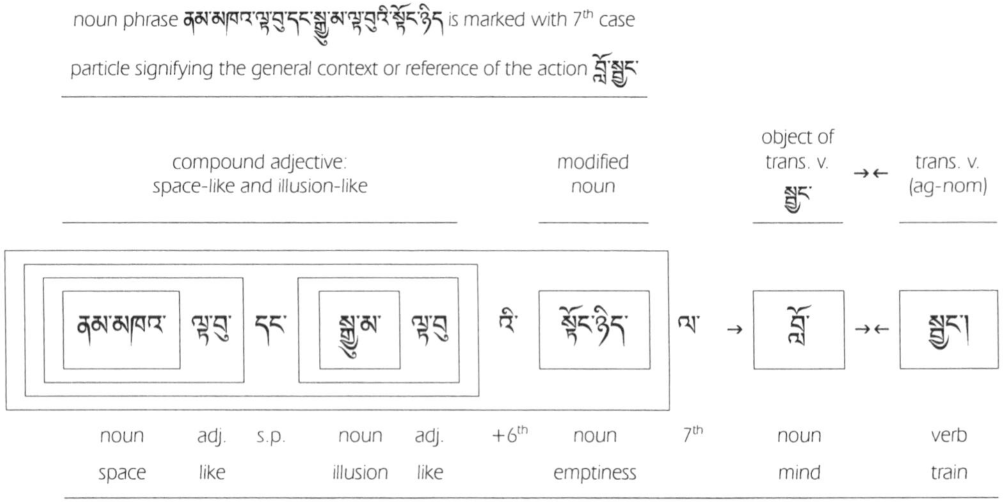

and train in space-line and illusion-like emptiness.

Glossary for Part 3

ནམ་མཁའ་ n., *space*

ལྟ་བུ་ adj., *like*

དང་ particle; used three ways: 1) continuative syntactic particle used following nouns and noun phrases (*and*, or with negative verb, *or*); 2) syntactic particle marking the qualifier of an intr. nom-s.p. v. of conjunction, as in ང་རང་མི་སྡུག་པ་དང་ཕྲད་ན་ *if we meet with unpleasantness;* and 3) syntactic particle marking the qualifier of an intr. nom-s.p. v. of disjunction, as in རྟོག་པ་དང་བྲལ་ *free from conceptuality*

སྒྱུ་མ་ n., *illusion*

ལྟ་བུ་ adj., *like*

སྒྱུ་མ་ལྟ་བུ་ noun phrase (n. + adj.), *illusion-like*

སྒྱུ་མ་ལྟ་བུའི་ n. + 6th case particle fused to suffixless final syllable

འི་ particle fused to suffixless final syllable; either 1) a syntactic particle following a verb or verb phrase signifying conjunction or disjunction, or 2) a 6th case particle following nouns, pronouns, postpositions, and adjectives

སྟོང་ intr. v. (nom-s.p.), *be empty;* this intransitive verb of absence takes a subject in the 1st case and a qualifier—that of which the subject is empty—marked with one of the particles that also marks the 3rd case: གིས་ཀྱིས་གྱིས་འིས་ཡིས་
སྟོང་སྟོངས་སྟོང་། ཐ་མི་དད།

སྟོང་ཉིད་ n., *emptiness*

ཉིད་ restrictive lexical suffix syllable, *-ness*

སྟོང་ཉིད་ལ་ noun + 7th case particle signifying the general context or reference of the action བློ་སྦྱང་།

ལ་ particle; either 1) a syntactic particle following a verb or verb phrase signifying conjunction or disjunction, or 2) a case particle following nouns, pronouns, postpositions, and adjectives marking the 2nd, 4th and 7th cases

བློ་ n., *awareness, mind*

སྦྱང་ trans. v. (ag-nom), *train*

སྦྱོང་སྦྱངས་སྦྱང་སྦྱོངས། ཐ་དད།

Notes on Part 3

ནམ་མཁའ་ལྟ་བུའི་སྟོང་ཉིད་ noun phrase, *space-like emptiness*

སྒྱུ་མ་ལྟ་བུའི་སྟོང་ཉིད་ noun phrase, *illusion-like emptiness*

སྟོང་ intr. v. (nom-s.p.), *be empty;* this intransitive verb of absence takes a subject in the 1st case and a qualifier—that of which the subject is empty—marked with one of the particles that also mark the 3rd case: གིས་ཀྱིས་གྱིས་འིས་ཡིས་

གིས་ཀྱིས་གྱིས་འིས་ཡིས་ equivalent particles; either 1) syntactic particle creating an adverbial construction, 2) syntactic particle marking the qualifier of an intransitive nom-s.p. verb of absence, or 3) case particle marking the 3rd case

སྟོང་ཉིད་ལ་བློ་སྦྱང་། noun phrase ནམ་མཁའ་ལྟ་བུ་དང་སྒྱུ་མ་ལྟ་བུའི་སྟོང་ཉིད is marked with 7th case particle signifying the general context or reference of the action བློ་སྦྱང་།

It is not the place of activity where the training occurs (that would be in the 2nd case); rather it is that with respect to which one trains the mind, indicated by a general referential use of the 7th case.

Parts 4 and 5 • སེམས་དགེ་བའི་དམིགས་པ་ལ་མི་སྡོད་པའི་རྣམ་གཡེང་གི་བྲན་དུ་གྱུར་པར་སྣང་ན་རྩེ་གཅིག་པའི་གནས་ཆ་ལ་གཙོ་བོར་སྐྱོང་བར་གོང་མ་རྣམས་གསུང་ངོ་།

In basic form Parts 4 and 5 are: A said that if B, then you should sustain C. We'll look at B first.

B	C				A	said
སེམས་དགེ་བའི་དམིགས་པ་ལ་མི་སྡོད་པའི་རྣམ་གཡེང་གི་བྲན་དུ་གྱུར་པར་སྣང་ན་	རྩེ་གཅིག་པའི་གནས་ཆ་	ལ་	གཙོ་བོར་སྐྱོང་བ	ར་	གོང་མ་རྣམས་	གསུང་ངོ་།

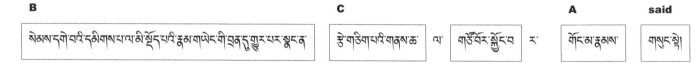

Part 4 begins with a conditional clause

the whole verbal clause སེམས་དགེ་བའི་དམིགས་པ་ལ་མི་སྡོད་པའི་རྣམ་གཡེང་གི་བྲན་དུ་གྱུར་པར་སྣང་ plus the s.p. ན་ is a conditional clause qualifying སྐྱོང་ (seen on the next page)

verbal clause སེམས་དགེ་བའི་དམིགས་པ་ལ་མི་སྡོད་པའི་རྣམ་གཡེང་གི་བྲན་དུ་གྱུར་པར་ is the qualifier of སྣང་
If you see *that your mind has become a distracted servant—not staying on virtuous objects of observation*
→← intr. v. (nom-obj)

subject of གྱུར་ → noun phrase དགེ་བའི་དམིགས་པ་ལ་མི་སྡོད་པའི་རྣམ་གཡེང་གི་བྲན་ is qualifier for གྱུར། →← intr. v. (nom-obj)

དགེ་བའི་དམིགས་པ་ལ་མི་སྡོད་པའི་ is a verbal adjective modifying following compound རྣམ་གཡེང་གི་བྲན་ ↔ modified adj. + noun compound

qualifier of མི་སྡོད་ (place of living) →← intr. v. (nom-loc)

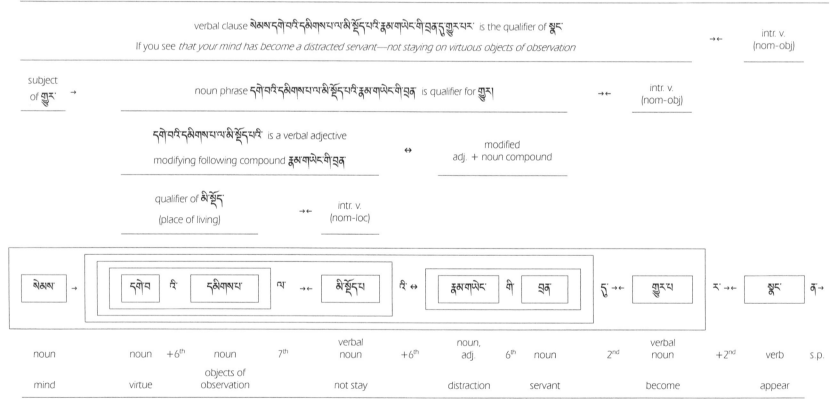

སེམས་ →	དགེ་བ	འི་	དམིགས་པ་	ལ་ →←	མི་སྡོད་པ	འི་ ↔	རྣམ་གཡེང་	གི་	བྲན་	དུ་ →←	གྱུར་པ	ར་ →←	སྣང་	ན་ →
noun	noun	+6th	noun	7th	verbal noun	+6th	noun, adj.	6th	noun	2nd	verbal noun	+2nd	verb	s.p.
mind	virtue		objects of observation		not stay		distraction		servant		become		appear	

If [your] mind appears to have become a distracted servant—not staying on virtuous objects of observation, ...

Glossary for Part 4

སེམས་	n., *mind*
དགེ་བ་	n., *virtue*
དགེ་བའི་	noun + 6th case particle
འི་	particle fused to suffixless final syllable; either 1) a syntactic particle following a verb or verb phrase signifying conjunction or disjunction, or 2) a 6th case particle following nouns, pronouns, postpositions, and adjectives
དམིགས་	trans. v. (ag-nom), *observe, look at* དམིགས་དམིགས་དམིགས་དམིགས། ཐ་དད།
དམིགས་པ་	n., *object of observation*
དམིགས་པ་ལ་	n. + case particle marking the 2nd, 4th and 7th cases; here: 7th case, place of living
ལ་	particle; either 1) a syntactic particle following a verb or verb phrase signifying conjunction or disjunction, or 2) a case particle following nouns, pronouns, postpositions, and adjectives marking the 2nd, 4th and 7th cases
མི་སྡོད་	negative intr. v. (nom-loc), *not stay, not remain*
མི་	negative lexical prefix particle
མ་མི་	negative lexical prefix particles that precede the word they negate
མིན་མེད་	negative lexical suffix particles that follow the word they negate
མི་	n., *man, human, person*
སྡོད་	intr. v. (nom-loc), *stay, remain* སྡོད་བསྡད་བསྡད་སྡོད། ཐ་མི་དད།
མི་སྡོད་པ་	verbal n., *not remaining, not staying*
མི་སྡོད་པའི་	verbal noun + 6th case particle fused to suffixless syllable
འི་	particle fused to suffixless final syllable; either 1) a syntactic particle following a verb or verb phrase signifying conjunction or disjunction, or 2) a 6th case particle following nouns, pronouns, postpositions, and adjectives
རྣམ་གཡེང་	n., *distraction*
རྣམ་གཡེང་གི་	n. + 6th case particle
གི་	particle; either 1) a syntactic particle following a verb or verb phrase signifying conjunction or disjunction, or 2) a 6th case particle following nouns, pronouns, postpositions, and adjectives
བྲན་	n., *servant*
བྲན་དུ་	n. + 2nd case particle marking metaphorical destination of the intransitive nom-obj verb གྱུར་ *become*
དུ་	particle; either 1) a verb-modifying syntactic particle within a verb phrase, or 2) a case particle following nouns, pronouns, postpositions, and adjectives marking the 2nd, 4th and 7th cases
གྱུར་	intr. v. (nom-obj) (past tense), *became;* also the weak auxiliary འགྱུར་གྱུར་འགྱུར། ཐ་མི་དད།
གྱུར་པ་	verbal noun
གྱུར་པར་	verbal noun + 2nd case particle fused to suffixless syllable
ར་	particle fused to suffixless final syllable; either verb-modifying syntactic particle within a verb phrase, or a case particle marking the 2nd, 4th and 7th cases following nouns, pronouns, postpositions, and adjectives
སྣང་	intr. v. (nom-obj), *appear* སྣང་སྣང་སྣང་། ཐ་མི་དད།
སྣང་ན་	verb + syntactic particle marking a conditional clause
ན་	particle; either 1) a rhetorical syntactic particle marking a conditional clause following a verb or verb phrase, or 2) a case particle following nouns, pronouns, postpositions, and adjectives marking the 2nd, 4th and 7th cases

Part 5 • རྩེ་གཅིག་པའི་གནས་ཆ་ལ་གཙོ་བོར་སྐྱོང་བར་གོང་མ་རྣམས་གསུང་ངོ་།

A said that if B, then mainly sustain C.

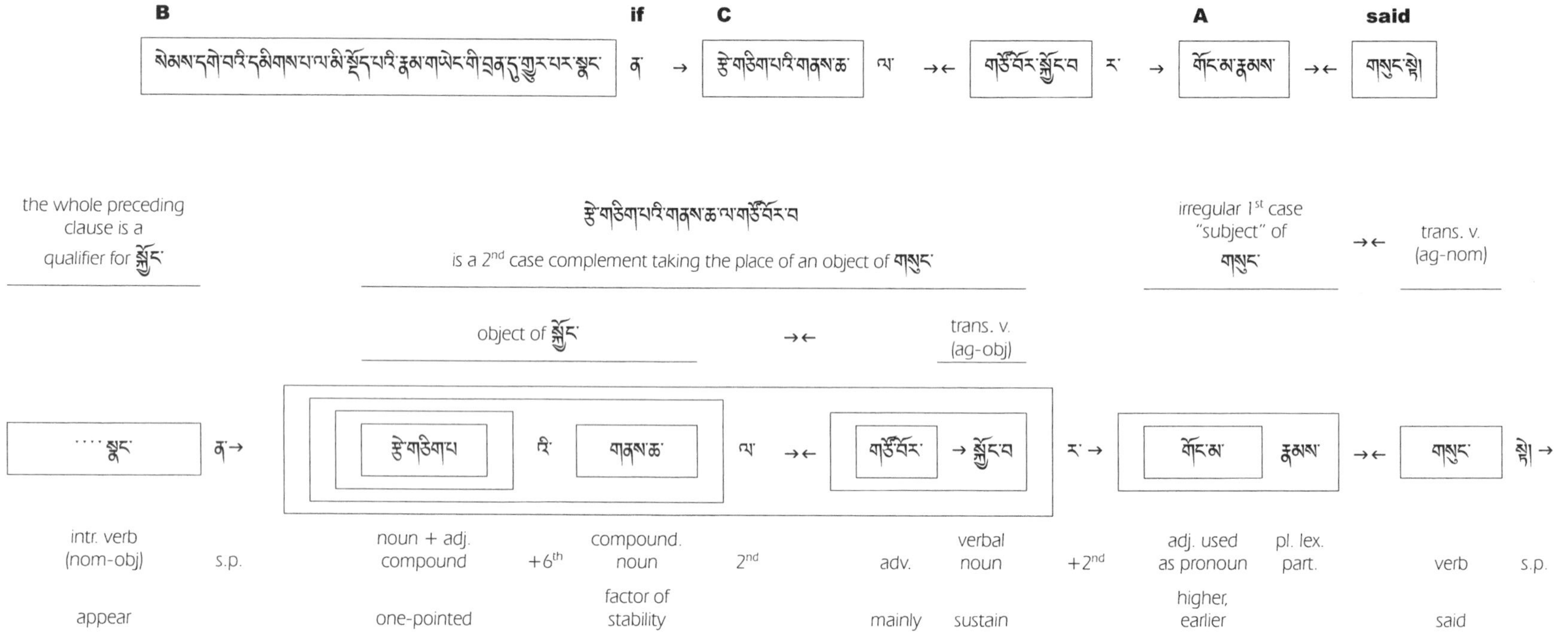

[If it appears that your mind...], the earlier [teachers of the stages of the path lineage] said that you should mainly sustain the factor of one-pointed stability.

Glossary for Part 5

རྩེ n., *point*

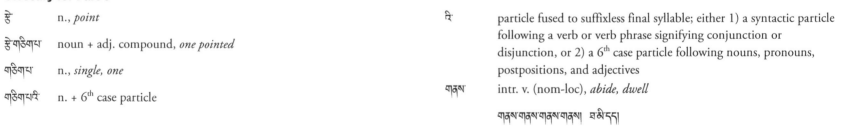

རྩེ་གཅིག་པ noun + adj. compound, *one pointed*

གཅིག་པ n., *single, one*

གཅིག་པའི n. + 6th case particle

འི particle fused to suffixless final syllable; either 1) a syntactic particle following a verb or verb phrase signifying conjunction or disjunction, or 2) a 6th case particle following nouns, pronouns, postpositions, and adjectives

གནས intr. v. (nom-loc), *abide, dwell*

གནས་གནས་གནས་གནས། ཐ་མི་དད།

གནས་ n., *place, abode, location,* and also *status, state, situation, source, object, topic* and *basis*

ཆ་ n., *part, factor*

གནས་ཆ་ compound n., *factor of stability*

གནས་ཆ་ལ་ noun + 2nd case particle marking object of སྐྱོང་

ལ་ particle; either a syntactic particle (following a verb) signifying conjunction or disjunction, or a case particle marking the 2nd, 4th and 7th cases following nouns, pronouns, postpositions, and adjectives

གཙོ་བོ་ n., *main, principal*

གཙོ་བོར་ n. + 2nd case particle, here signifying adverbial identity

ར་ particle fused to suffixless final syllable; either 1) a verb-modifying syntactic particle within a verb phrase, or 2) a case particle following nouns, pronouns, postpositions, and adjectives marking the 2nd, 4th and 7th cases

སྐྱོང་ trans. v. (ag-obj), *sustain, look after* or *nurse*

སྐྱོང་བསྐྱངས་བསྐྱང་སྐྱོངས། ཐདད།

སྐྱོང་བ་ verbal noun, *sustaining, training*

སྐྱོང་བར་ verbal noun + 2nd case particle marking complement

ར་ particle fused to suffixless final syllable; either 1) a verb-modifying syntactic particle within a verb phrase, or 2) a case particle following nouns, pronouns, postpositions, and adjectives marking the 2nd, 4th and 7th cases

གོང་མ་ adj., *upper, superior, higher;* by extention: *earlier*

རྣམས་ optional pluralizing lexical suffix particle

གསུང་ honorific trans. v. (ag-nom), *say*

གསུང་གསུངས་གསུང་གསུངས། ཐདད།

གསུང་སྟེ། verb phrase + continuative syntactic particle showing sequence by indicating that more relevant information will follow.

ཏེ་ སྟེ་ དེ་ are equivalent syntactic particles; either 1) continuative syntactic particles following verbs and verb phrases showing sequence, or 2) punctuational syntactic particles following words or phrases marking appositives

ཏེ་ follows words ending with suffix letters ནར་ལ་ས་

སྟེ་ follows suffixless words and words ending with suffix letters གང་བ་མ་འ་

དེ་ follows words ending with suffix letter ད་

Grammar review • Direct quote compared to attributive syntax

གསུང་ this is an honorific transitive (ag-nom) verb.

We see it here with a syntactically irregular but frequently seen subject in the 1st case. This is not a direct quote, *The earlier [teachers] said, "you should work at sustaining the factor of stability."* Rather it is a step away from a direct quote. Tsong-kha-pa is reporting the general thrust of their advice, much as we would say—without meaning it as a direct quote— *My teachers said to work hard.*

Parts 6 and 7 are a compound sentence; we will look at Part 6 first

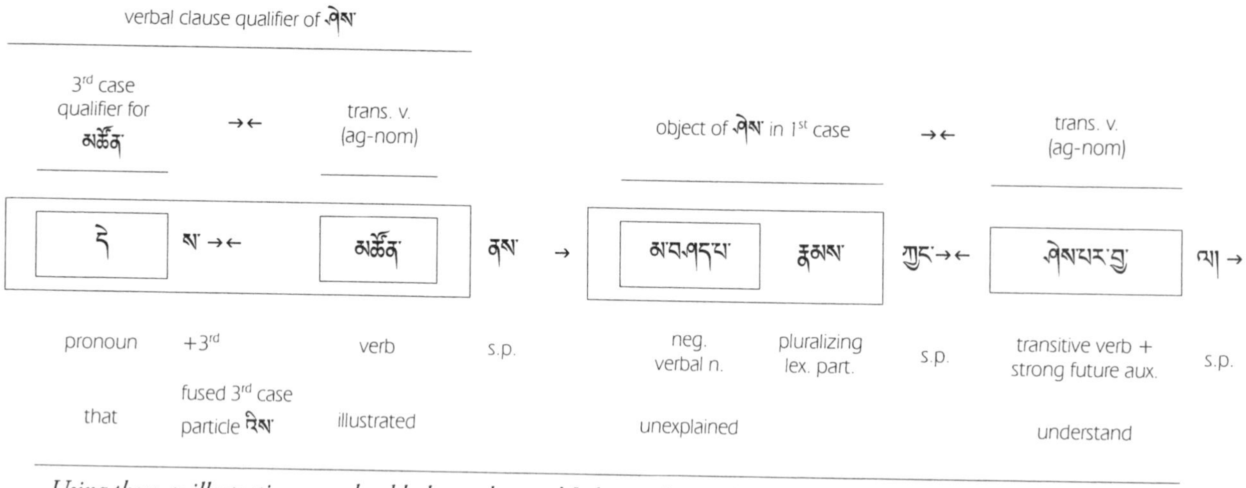

Using those as illustrations you should also understand [what to do in other situations] which have not been explained.

Glossary for Part 6

དེ་	limiting adj. used as pronoun, *that, those*
དེས་	pronoun + 3rd case particle fused to suffixless final syllable
ས་	abbreviation of the particle ཡིས་ (when ཡིས་ is fused to a suffixless final syllable, the ཡི goes away and all that's left is a fused ས་); either 1) syntactic particle creating an adverbial construction, 2) syntactic particle marking the qualifier of an intransitive nom-s.p. verb of absence, or 3) case particle marking the 3rd case
མཚོན་	trans. v. (ag-nom), *define, make known, illustrate*
	མཚོན་མཚོན་མཚོན་མཚོན། ཐ་དད།
མཚོན་ནས་	verb + continuative s.p. following core verb indicating a sequence of actions, *through illustrating, having illustrated*
མ་བཤད་	negative trans. v. (ag-nom) (past tense), *not explained*
	འཆད་བཤད་བཤད་ཤོད། ཐ་དད།
མ་མི་	negative lexical prefix particles that precede the word they negate
མིན་མེད་	negative lexical suffix particles that follow the word they negate
བཤད་པ་	verbal noun, *explanation*
རྣམས་	optional lexical pluralizing suffix particle
ཀྱང་	conjunctive syntactic particle occurring after nouns, pronouns, adverbs, and verbs; *but, even, also*
ཀྱང་ཡང་འང་	are equivalent conjunctive and disjunctive syntactic particles used after nouns, pronouns, adjectives, verbs, and verb phrases, *but, even, also*
ཀྱང་	follows words ending with the letters གདབས
ཡང་	follows words ending with the letters ངནམའརལ and after suffixless words
འང་	follows suffixless words

ཤེས་ trans. v. (ag-nom), *know, understand.* This verb is listed in the *Great Word Treasury* as ཐ་མི་དད།, but I think it is a transitive ag-nom verb. ཤེས་ཤེས་ཤེས། ཐ་མི་དད།

ཤེས་པར་བྱ་ verb phrase (verbal infinitive + strong future auxiliary), *[I] will understand* or *[you] should understand*

ཤེས་པར་ verbal infinitive; here, the fused ར་ is a syntactic particle modifying a verb to create a verbal infinitive within the verb phrase ཤེས་པར་བྱ་ *[I] will understand [something], [you] should understand [something];* it is **not** a case particle marking the 2nd, 4th or 7th cases because it does not follow a noun—it is within a verb phrase

བྱ་ trans. v. (ag-nom) (future tense), *do, make, perform, take;* also strong future auxiliary བྱེད་བྱས་བྱ་བྱོས། ཐ་དད།

ཤེས་པར་བྱ་ལ། verb phrase + conjunctive or disjunctive syntactic particle

ལ་ particle; either 1) a syntactic particle following a verb or verb phrase signifying conjunction or disjunction, or 2) a case particle following nouns, pronouns, postpositions, and adjectives marking the 2nd, 4th and 7th cases

Part 7 • མདོར་ན་ཕྱོགས་རེ་བར་མ་སོང་བར་རྒྱུད་དགེ་བའི་ཕྱོགས་ཐམས་ཅད་ལ་བཀོལ་དུ་རུང་བ་ཞིག་དགོས་སོ།

Part 7 is the conclusion of the sentence begun in Part 6

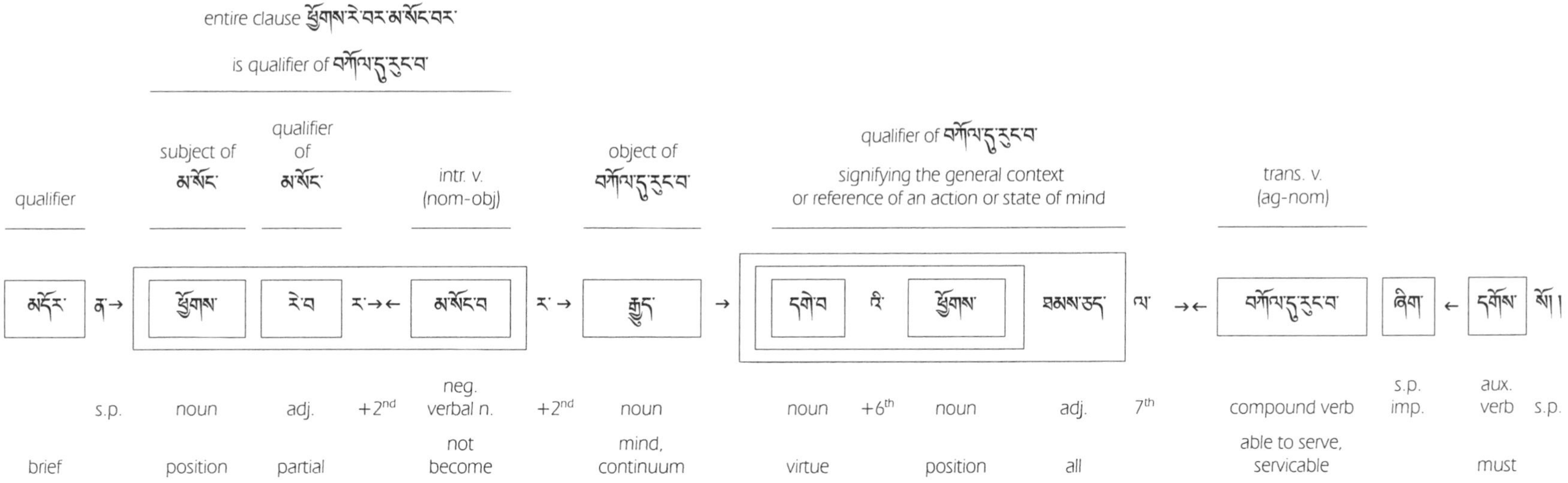

In brief, without becoming partial, your continuum should be serviceable for all virtuous directions.

Glossary for Part 7

མདོ་ n., *discourse, rule, axiom;* translation of Sanskrit *sútra*

མདོར་ n. + 2nd case particle, *in brief*

མདོར་ན་ n. + 2nd case particle + omitted verb + conditional syntactic particle, *in brief, in general;* abbreviation for མདོར་བསྡུ་ན་

ན་ particle; either 1) a rhetorical syntactic particle marking a conditional clause following a verb or verb phrase, or 2) a case particle following nouns, pronouns, postpositions, and adjectives marking the 2nd, 4th and 7th cases

ཕྱོགས་ intr. v. (nom-obj.), *be diverted, be turned, go aside*

ཕྱོགས་ ཕྱོགས་ ཕྱོགས། ཐ་མི་དད།

ཕྱོགས་ n., *position, portion, direction, faction, side*

རེ་བ་ n., *partial*

རེ་ adj., pron., *each*

མ་སོང་བར་ negative lexical prefix particle + intr. verb + fused 2nd case particle, *without having gone*

ར་ particle fused to suffixless final syllable; either 1) a verb-modifying syntactic particle within a verb phrase, or 2) a case particle following nouns, pronouns, postpositions, and adjectives marking the 2nd, 4th and 7th cases

རྒྱུད་ n., *stream, continuum*

དགེ་བ་ n., *virtue*

དགེ་བའི་ noun + 6th case particle, *virtuous*

འི་ particle fused to suffixless final syllable; either 1) a syntactic particle following a verb or verb phrase signifying conjunction or disjunction, or 2) a 6th case particle following nouns, pronouns, postpositions, and adjectives

ཕྱོགས་ n., *position, portion, direction, faction, side*

ཐམས་ཅད་ adj., *all*

ཕྱོགས་ཐམས་ཅད་ noun phrase (n. + adj.), *all directions*

ཕྱོགས་ཐམས་ཅད་ལ་ noun phrase (n. + adj.) + 7th case particle

ལ་ particle; either 1) a syntactic particle following a verb or verb phrase signifying conjunction or disjunction, or 2) a case particle following nouns, pronouns, postpositions, and adjectives marking the 2nd, 4th and 7th cases

དགེ་བའི་ཕྱོགས་ཐམས་ཅད་ལ་ qualifier in 7th case signifying the general context or reference of an action or state of mind: one's own mental continuum must become serviceable *in terms of all virtuous endeavors, for all virtuous endeavors*

བཀོལ་ trans. v. (ag-nom), *serve* བཀོལ་བཀོལ་བཀོལ་ཁོལ། ཐ་དད།

བཀོལ་དུ་རུང་བ་ compound verb phrase (infinitive + verb), *serviceable;* notice the compound verb uses the infinitive composed of the core verb + verb-modifying syntactic particle དུ་

བཀོལ་དུ་ here, the particle དུ་ is a verb-modifying syntactic particle modifying a verb to create an infinitive within the compound verb phrase བཀོལ་དུ་རུང་བ་ *[it] is serviceable;* it is **not** a case particle marking the 2nd, 4th or 7th cases because it does not follow a noun—it is within a verb phrase

རུང་ intr. v. (nom-obj), *be suitable* རུང་རུང་རུང་། ཐ་མི་དད།

ཞིག་ s.p., makes preceding word, phrase or clause into an adverbial construction

དགོས་ intr. v. (b/p-nom), *need, must, require*

དགོས་དགོས་དགོས། ཐ་མི་དད།

དགོས་སོ།། verb + sentence-terminating syntactic particle following word with suffix letter ས.

སོ་ sentence-terminating syntactic particle following word with suffix letter ས.

Chapter Ten Self Test

Write out the passage, boxing and identifying every syntactic element.

རྒྱལ་སྲས་ཀྱི་སྡོམ་པ་བླངས་ནས་སྤྱོད་པ་ལ་སློབ་པ་ནའང་མཚན་མར་འཛིན་པའི་འཆིང་བ་ཤུགས་དྲག་པར་སྣང་ན་རིགས་ཤེས་ཀྱིས་མཚན་མར་འཛིན་པའི་བློས་བཟུང་བའི་དམིགས་གཏད་ཐམས་ཅད་བཤིག་ལ། ནམ་མཁའ་ལྟ་བུ་དང་སྒྱུ་མ་ལྟ་བུའི་སྟོང་ཉིད་ལ་བློ་སྦྱང་། སེམས་དགེ་བའི་དམིགས་པ་ལ་མི་སྡོད་པའི་རྣམ་གཡེང་གི་བྲན་དུ་གྱུར་པར་སྣང་ན་རྩེ་གཅིག་པའི་གནས་ཆ་ལ་གཙོ་བོར་སྐྱོང་བར་གོང་མ་རྣམས་གསུང་སྟེ། དེས་མཚོན་ནས་མ་བཤད་པ་རྣམས་ཀྱང་ཤེས་པར་བྱ་ལ། མདོར་ན་ཕྱོགས་རེ་བར་མ་སོང་བར་རྒྱུད་དགེ་བའི་ཕྱོགས་ཐམས་ཅད་ལ་བཀོལ་དུ་རུང་བ་ཞིག་དགོས་སོ། །

Vocabulary

For each word, can you identify what part of speech it is (noun, pronoun, adjective, verb, adverb, postposition) and what it means?
For each syntactic particle, can you identify what class of syntactic particle it belongs to and how it is used?

རྩེ་གཅིག་པ་	ལྟ་	དྲག	ལ་
རྩེ་	ལྟ་བུ་	བྱ་	རེ་བ་
སྦྱང་	རྒྱུད་	ཕྱོགས་ཐམས་ཅད་	རེ་
སྤྱོད་པ་	རྒྱལ་སྲས་	ཕྱོགས་	རུང་བ་
སྤྱོད	རྒྱལ་	གྱུར་པ་	རུང་
སྒྱུ་མ་	རྣམས་	གྱུར་	རིགས་ཤེས་
སྐྱོང་བ་	རྣམ་གཡེང་	ཀྱིས་	ཡང་
སྐྱོང་	སློབ་	ཀྱི་	འི་
སྣང་	བློས་	ཀྱང་ཡང་འང་	འཛིན་པ་
སྡོམ་པ་	བློ་	སོ་	འཛིན་
སྡོམ་	བླངས་	སེམས་	འཆིང་བ་
སྡོད་	སྲས་	ཤུགས་	འཆིང་
སྟོང་ཉིད་	བྲན་དུ་	ཤེས་པར་བྱ་	འང་
སྟོང་	བྲན་	ཤེས་	ཞིག་

མིན་	མ་བཤད་	དེས་	ཆ་
མེད་	བཤིག་	དེ་	གོང་མ་
མི་སྡོད་པ་	བཤད་པ་	དམིགས་པ་	གིས་ཀྱིས་གྱིས་འིས་ཡིས་
མི་སྡོད་	བཟུང་	དམིགས་གཏད་	གི་
མི་	བཀོལ་དུ་རུང་བ་	དམིགས་	གསུང་
མཚོན་	བཀོལ་	དང་	གཙོ་བོ་
མཚན་མར་འཛིན་པ་	ནས་	དགོས་	གནས་ཆ་
མཚན་མ་	ནའང་	དགེ་བ་	གནས་
མདོར་	ནམ་མཁའ་	ཐམས་ཅད་	གཅིག་པ་
མ་སོང་	ན་	ཏེ་ སྟེ་ དེ་	
མ་	དུ་	ཉིད་	

Translation of Tsong-kha-pa's text

རྒྱལ་སྲས་ཀྱི་སྡོམ་པ་བླངས་ནས་སྤྱོད་པ་ལ་སློབ་པ་ནའང་མཚན་མར་འཛིན་པའི་འཆིང་བ་ཤུགས་དྲག་པར་སྣང་ན་རིགས་ཤེས་ཀྱིས་མཚན་མར་འཛིན་པའི་བློས་བཟུང་བའི་དམིགས་གཏད་ཐམས་ཅད་བཤིག་ལ། ནམ་མཁའ་ལྟ་བུ་དང་སྒྱུ་མ་ལྟ་བུའི་སྟོང་ཉིད་ལ་བློ་སྦྱང་། སེམས་དགེ་བའི་དམིགས་པ་ལ་མི་སྡོད་པའི་རྣམ་གཡེང་གི་བྲན་དུ་གྱུར་པར་སྣང་ན་རྩེ་གཅིག་པའི་གནས་ཆ་ལ་གཙོ་བོར་སྐྱོང་བར་གོང་མ་རྣམས་གསུང་སྟེ། དེས་མཚོན་ནས་མ་བཤད་པ་རྣམས་ཀྱང་ཤེས་པར་བྱ་ལ། མདོར་ན་ཕྱོགས་རེ་བར་མ་སོང་བར་རྒྱུད་དགེ་བའི་ཕྱོགས་ཐམས་ཅད་ལ་བཀོལ་དུ་རུང་བ་ཞིག་དགོས་སོ། །

Also, if it appears that you have the fetters of the conceptions of signs [inherent existence] in strong force when training in the [Bodhisattva] deeds having taken the Bodhisattva vow, break down all the targets of the conception of signs through a reasoning consciousness and train in space-like and illusion-like emptiness.

If [your] mind appears to have become a distracted servant—not staying on virtuous objects of observation, mainly train in the factor of one-pointed stability. This is what the earlier [great masters] said.

Using those as illustrations, you should also understand [what to do in other situations] which have not been explained. In brief, without becoming partial, your continuum should be serviceable for all virtuous directions.

Annotations for Tsong-kha-pa's text in Chapter Ten

Here is Tsong-kha-pa's text as supplemented by *The Four Interwoven Annotations,* 835.1-836.1

གལ་ཏེ་ རྒྱལ་སྲས་ཀྱི་སྨོན་པ་བླངས་ནས་ དེའི་བསླབ་བྱ་རྒྱལ་སྲས་ཀྱི་ སྤྱོད་པ་ལ་སློབ་པ་ འི་ཚེ་ ནའང་ ལྷག་མཐོང་གི་མི་མཐུན་ཕྱོགས་བདེན་འཛིན་གྱི་ མཚན་མར་འཛིན་པའི་ བདེན་ཞེན་གྱི་ འཆིང་བ་ཞུགས་དྲག་པར་སྣང་ན་ ནི་དོན་དམ་ལ་དཔྱོད་པའི་ རིགས་ཤེས་ཀྱིས་མཚན་མར་འཛིན་པའི་བློ་ བདེན་འཛིན་དེ་ ས་ ཇི་ལྟར་ བཟུང་བའི་ འཛིན་སྟངས་ཀྱི་ དམིགས་གཏད་ཐམས་ཅད་བཤིག་ལ། བདེན་ཞེན་གྱི་གཏད་སོ་མེད་པར་བྱས་ཏེ་དགག་བྱ་བཀག་ཙམ་གྱི་སྟོང་སང་ ནམ་མཁའ་ལྟ་བུ་ འི་སྟོང་པ་འཆར་ཚུལ་ དང་ དེའི་རྗེས་ཐོབ་ཏུ་སྣང་སྟོང་གཉིས་ཚོགས་ཀྱི་ སྒྱུ་མ་ལྟ་བུའི་སྟོང་ཉིད་ གཉིས་ ལ་བློ་སྦྱང་ པ་གཙོ་བོར་བྱ་དགོས། གལ་ཏེ་རང་གི་ སེམས་དགེ་བའི་དམིགས་པ་ལ་མི་སྡོད་པའི་རྣམ་གཡེང་གི་དབང་དུ་གྱུར་ཏེ་རྣམ་གཡེང་དེས་ བྲན་ གཡོག་བཀོལ་བ་བཞིན་ དུ་གྱུར་པར་སྣང་ན་ ནི་རྣམ་གཡེང་དེའི་གཉེན་པོར་དྲན་ཤེས་དང་རྩོལ་བ་བསྐྱེད་དེ་སེམས་རྩེ་གཅིག་པའི་གནས་ཆ་ སྒྲུབ་པ་ ལ་གཙོ་བོར་སྐྱོང་ དགོས་ པར་ ལམ་རིམ་འདིའི་བླ་མ་ གོང་མ་རྣམས་གསུང་ངོ་།

བཞི་པ་ཉམས་ལེན་ཕྱོགས་རེ་བར་མ་སོང་བར་གདམས་པ་ན།

ཆ་མཉམ་ལུགས་གོང་གི་ ངེས་མཚོན་ནས་ འདིར་དངོས་སུ་ མ་བཤད་པ་རྣམས་ཀྱང་ བློ་སྦྱིམ་པོས་གང་དང་གང་ཤས་ཆུང་བར་སོང་བ་དེ་དང་དེའི་ཆ་མཉམ་ལུགས་ ཤེས་པར་བྱ་ དགོས་པ་ཡིན་ ལ། དེ་ཐམས་ཅད་ཀྱི་དོན་ མདོར་ བསྡུ་ ན་ ལམ་གྱི་ཆ་ ཕྱོགས་རེ་བར་མ་སོང་བར་ བྱས་ནས་རང་གི་སེམས་ རྒྱུད་དགེ་བའི་ཕྱོགས་ཐམས་ཅད་ལ་ བསྐུལ་ཐུབ་པའི་སྒོ་ནས་ བཀོལ་དུ་རུང་བ་ འི་ལས་རུང་ ཞིག་ ཅི་ནས་ཀྱང་ དགོས་སོ། །

If upon taking the vow of conqueror's children, you train in the deeds of precepts of conqueror's children and it appears that you have the fetters of a consciousness adhering to true existence—the conception of signs [conceiving persons and other phenomena] to truly exist, the class discordant to special insight—in strong force, then your reasoning consciousness analyzing the ultimate must break down the target of the mode of apprehension wherein the mind conceiving signs—conceiving true existence—conceives in that way. You will find that the target aimed at by the consciousness adhering to true existence does not exist. Then you must train in the mode of appearance of space-like emptiness, wherein the vacuity that is the mere elimination of the object to be negated [true existence] dawns like space, and [in meditative states] subsequent to meditative equipoise [on emptiness] you must train in illusion-like emptiness, a composite of [a conventional awareness of] appearance [—it not being that there is no appearance at all—and a reasoning consciousness to which the object appears to be] empty [of existing in the way it appears].[2]

If it appears that your mind has come under the power of distraction, not staying on virtuous objects of observation, and has become a servant of distraction, as an antidote generate mindfulness and exertion: mainly train in the factor of achieving one-pointed stability. This is what the earlier gurus of the stages of the path lineage said.

Four: advice to keep your practice from being partial

Using those as illustrations of how to practice equally, you should also understand whatever has become weak by force of mind and the way to equalize it.

To condense the meaning of all these, without letting any part of the path become marginalized, your continuum should be serviceable in the sense of its ability to urge you on in all virtuous directions.

[2] Bracketed material is from Tri-jang Rinpoche's annotation heading from *The Middle Length Stages of the Path,* 212b (Mundgod: Ganden Shardzay, n.d., edition including outline of topics by Trijang Riunpoche).

འདི་ལ་སྣང་བ་གཏན་མེད་མིན་པར་སྣང་བའི་ཐ་སྙད་པའི་བློ་དང་། སྣང་བ་ལྟར་གྱི་དོན་ཡོད་པས་སྟོངས་པར་འཆར་བའི་རིགས་ཤེས་གཉིས་ཚོགས་དགོས་པ།

The need for a composite of two [factors], a conventional awareness of appearance—it not being that there is no appearance at all—and a reasoning consciousness to which [the object] appears to be empty of existing in the way it appears.

Appendix

Alphabetical Glossary of All Particles and Words

ཀ་ ཁ་ ག་ ང་
ཅ་ ཆ་ ཇ་ ཉ་
ཏ་ ཐ་ ད་ ན་
པ་ ཕ་ བ་ མ་
ཙ་ ཚ་ ཛ་ ཝ་
ཞ་ ཟ་ འ་ ཡ་
ར་ ལ་ ཤ་ ས་
ཧ་ ཨ་

Order of verb forms:

ད་ལྟ་བ་ **present** • འདས་པ་ **past** • མ་འོངས་པ་ **future** • སྐུལ་ཚིག **imperative**.
Verbs can have one, two, three or four forms.
Often intransitive verbs do not have an imperative form.

Verbs are either ཐ་དད། **transitive** (trans.) or ཐ་མི་དད། **intransitive** (intr.)

༄༅	ཡིག་མགོ a head ornament at beginning of a text
་	ཚེག *tsek;* separates syllables; metaphorically we speak of 8 "uses" of the *tsek*, meaning the eight possible relationships between any two syllables.
།	ཤད་ *shay;* vertical line ending a sentence, clause, line of poetry, and even a single word; put negatively, the presence of a ཤད་ doesn't necessarily mean the end of a sentence.

ཀ་	1st letter of Tibetan alphabet
ཀྱང་	conjunctive and disjunctive syntactic particle used after nouns, pronouns, adjectives, verbs, and verb phrases, *but, even, also.* ཀྱང་ follows words ending with the letters ག་ད་བ་ས
ཀྱི་	particle; either 1) a syntactic particle following a verb or verb phrase signifying conjunction or disjunction, or 2) a 6th case particle following nouns, pronouns, postpositions, and adjectives
ཀྱིན་	syntactic particle following verb signifying (recent) continuative. ཀྱིན་གྱིན་གིན་ are three equivalent syntactic particles used following verbs to signify continuous action
ཀྱིས་	particle; either 1) a syntactic particle creating an adverbial construction, 2) a syntactic particle marking the qualifier of an intransitive nom-s.p. verb of absence, or 3) case particle marking the 3rd case. གིས་ཀྱིས་གྱིས་འིས་ཡིས་ are five equivalent particles
དཀའ་བ་	n., adj., *difficult*
དཀར་	adj. *white, wholesome;* abbreviation for དཀར་པོ་
དཀར་པོ་	adj. *white, wholesome*
བཀོལ་	trans. v. (ag-nom), *serve* བཀོལ་བཀོལ་བཀོལ་ཁོལ། ཐ་དད།
སྐབས་	n., *occasion, context,* by extension *chapter*
སྐོར་	trans. v. (ag-nom), *turn* སྐོར་བསྐོར་བསྐོར་སྐོར། ཐ་དད།
སྐོར་	n., *topic*
སྐྱབས་	n., *refuge*
སྐྱབས་འགྲོ་	n., *go for refuge*

སྐྱེ་ intr. v. (nom-obj), *be born, arise, be created*

སྐྱེ་སྐྱེས་སྐྱེ། ཐ་མི་དད།

སྐྱེད་ trans. v. (ag-nom), *produce, generate, create, give birth to*

སྐྱེད་བསྐྱེད་བསྐྱེད་སྐྱེད། ཐ་དད།

སྐྱེས་ intr. v. (nom-obj) (past tense), *was born, arose, was created*

སྐྱེ་སྐྱེས་སྐྱེ། ཐ་མི་དད།

སྐྱེས་བུ་ n., *being*

སྐྱེས་བུ་གསུམ་ n. + adj. compound. *beings of the three [capacities]*

སྐྱོ་ intr. v. (nom-loc), *be discouraged, be sad about something*

སྐྱོ་སྐྱོ་སྐྱོ། ཐ་མི་དད།

སྐྱོང་ trans. v. (ag-obj), *sustain, look after* or *nurse*

སྐྱོང་བསྐྱངས་བསྐྱང་སྐྱོངས། ཐ་དད།

སྐྱོང་བ་ verbal noun, *sustaining, nursing*

སྐྱོང་བར་ verbal noun + 2nd, 4th or 7th case particle fused to suffixless syllable བ་

བསྐྱང་ trans. v. (ag-obj) (future tense), *sustain, look after* or *nurse*

སྐྱོང་བསྐྱངས་བསྐྱང་སྐྱོངས། ཐ་དད།

བསྐུལ་ trans. v. (ag-obj) (future and past tenses), *urge on*

སྐུལ་བསྐུལ་བསྐུལ་སྐུལ། ཐ་དད།

བསྐུལ་བས་ verbal + 3rd case particle fused to suffixless final syllable

བསྐྱེད་ trans. v. (ag-nom) (past and future tenses), *produce, generate, create, give birth to*

སྐྱེད་བསྐྱེད་བསྐྱེད་སྐྱེད། ཐ་དད།

བསྐྱེད་རིམ་ comp. n., *stages of generation*

ཁ་

2nd letter of Tibetan alphabet

ཁ་ n., *mouth*

ཁས་ n. + fused 3rd case particle, *by the mouth*

ཁས་བླངས་ trans. v. (ag-nom), *assert, accept;* literally, *hold by the mouth*

ཁས་ལེན། ཁས་བླངས། ཁས་བླང་། ཁས་ལོངས། ཐ་དད།

ཁྱད་པར་ n. and adv.; as noun, *attribute, feature, qualification, difference;* as adverb, *in particular, especially*

ཁྱད་པར་དུ་ n. + 2nd case particle, *in particular*

མཁས་ intr. v. (nom-loc), *be skilled*

མཁས་མཁས་མཁས། ཐ་མི་དད།

མཁས་པར་བྱས་ verb phrase (verbal infinitive + strong past auxiliary), *[I, you] have become skilled.* མཁས་པར་ is a verbal infinitive; here, the fused ར་ is a syntactic particle modifying a verb to create a verbal infinitive within the verb phrase མཁས་པར་བྱ་ *[I, you] have become skilled;* it is **not** a case particle marking the 2nd, 4th or 7th cases because it does not follow a noun—it is within a verb phrase. བྱས་ is a trans. v. (ag-nom) (past tense), *do, make, perform, take;* here it is the strong past auxiliary

འཁོར་ intr. v. (nom-obj), *be turned*

འཁོར་འཁོར་འཁོར། ཐ་མི་དད།

འཁོར་བ་ n., *cyclic existence*

འཁྱམ་ intr. v. (nom-obj), *wander*

འཁྱམ་འཁྱམས་འཁྱམ་འཁྱོམས། ཐ་མི་དད།

འཁྱམ་ཚུལ་ compound n., *mode of wandering*

འཁྲིད་ trans. v. (ag-nom), *guide*

འཁྲིད་ཁྲིད་འཁྲིད་ཁྲིད། ཐ་དད།

འཁྲིད་པ་ n., *guide*

ག་ 3rd letter of Tibetan alphabet

གང་ relative and interrogative pronoun, *what, which*

གི་ particle; either 1) a syntactic particle following a verb or verb phrase signifying conjunction or disjunction, or 2) a 6th case particle following nouns, pronouns, postpositions, and adjectives. གི་ཀྱི་གྱི་འི་ཡི་ are the five equivalent particles marking the 6th case (connective).

གིས་ particle; either 1) a syntactic particle creating an adverbial construction, 2) a syntactic particle marking the qualifier of an intransitive nom-s.p. verb of absence, or 3) case particle marking the 3rd case. གིས་ཀྱིས་གྱིས་འིས་ཡིས་ are the five equivalent particles marking the 3rd case.

གུས་ intr. v. (nom-loc), *be respectful of*

གུས་གུས་གུས། ཐ་མི་དད།

གུས་པ་ n., *respect*

གོ་ trans. v., (ag-nom), *know, understand.* This verb is listed in the *Great Word Treasury* as ཐ་མི་དད།, but I think it is a transitive verb (ag-nom).

གོ་གོ་གོ ཐ་མི་དད།

གོ་བ་ n., *understanding*

གོང་མ་ adj., *upper, superior, higher;* by extention: *earlier*

གོང་མ་གོང་མ་ adj., *higher, higher and higher*

གོམས་ intr. v. (nom-loc), *be accustomed to*

གོམས་གོམས་གོམས། ཐ་མི་དད།

གོས་ intr. v. (nom-loc), *be polluted*

གོས་གོས་གོས། ཐ་མི་དད་

གོས་པ་ n., *pollution*

གྱི་ particle; either 1) a syntactic particle following a verb or verb phrase signifying conjunction or disjunction, or 2) a 6th case particle following nouns, pronouns, postpositions, and adjectives. གི་ཀྱི་གྱི་འི་ཡི་ are the five equivalent particles marking the 6th case (connective)

གྱིས་ particle; either 1) a syntactic particle creating an adverbial construction, 2) a syntactic particle marking the qualifier of an intransitive nom-s.p. verb of absence, or 3) case particle marking the 3rd case. གིས་ཀྱིས་གྱིས་འིས་ཡིས་ are five equivalent particles

གྱུར་ intr. v. (nom-obj), *become;* also the weak auxiliary

འགྱུར་གྱུར་འགྱུར། ཐ་མི་དད།

གྱུར་པ་ verbal noun, *becoming*

གྱུར་པར་ verbal noun + 2nd, 4th or 7th case particle fused to suffixless syllable

གྲུབ་ intr. v. (nom-obj) (past tense), *be established, be proven, exist*

འགྲུབ་གྲུབ་འགྲུབ། ཐ་མི་དད།

གྲོལ་ intr. v. (nom-s.p.), *be released*
This verb of separation is classified as a nom-s.p. verb together with verbs of absence, conjunction and disjunction, but its qualifier, that from which the subject is separated, is marked with a true 5th case.

གྲོལ་གྲོལ་གྲོལ། ཐ་མི་དད་

དགེ་བ་ n., *virtuous (actions)*

དགེ་བའི་ noun + 6th case particle fused to suffixless final syllable

དགེ་བའི་བཤེས་གཉེན་ n., Tibetan translation of the Sanskrit *kalyānamitra, spiritual friend*

དགེ་མི་དགེ་ comp. n., *virtuous and non-virtuous (actions)*

དགོས་ intr. v. (b/p-nom), *be necessary, need, require*

དགོས་དགོས་དགོས། ཐ་མི་དད།

དགོས་པ་ n., *need, purpose*

འགྱུར་	intr. v. (nom-obj), *become;* also the weak auxiliary
	འགྱུར་གྱུར་འགྱུར། ཐ་མི་དད།
འགྲོ་	intr. v. (nom-obj), *go;* often used by extension in the metaphorical sense of *turns into* or *becomes*
	འགྲོ་ཕྱིན་འགྲོ་སོང་། ཐ་མི་དད། སོང་ is also used as the past form
འགྲོ་བ་	verbal noun, *goer*, *migrator*
རྒྱ་མཚོ་	n., *ocean*
རྒྱ་མཚོར་	n. + 2nd, 4th or 7th case particle fused to suffixless syllable
རྒྱལ་	intr. v. (nom-s.p.), *be victorious, win, conqueror, subdue;* this verb of separation is classified as a nom-s.p. verb together with verbs of absence, conjunction and disjunction, but its qualifier, that over which the subject is victorious, is marked with a true 5th case.
	རྒྱལ་རྒྱལ་རྒྱལ་རྒྱལ། ཐ་མི་དད།
རྒྱལ་	n., *conqueror*
རྒྱུ་	n., *cause*
རྒྱུད་	n., *stream, continuum*
རྒྱུན་	n., *stream, continuum*
རྒྱུན་དུ་	n. + 2nd case particle; here: adverbial sense, *continuously*
རྒྱུན་དུ་བསྒྲུབ་པ	phrasal verbal noun, *practice*
སྒོ་	n., *door, approach*
སྒོམ་	trans. v. (ag-nom), *meditate on, cultivate*
	སྒོམ་བསྒོམས་བསྒོམ་སྒོམས། ཐ་དད།
སྒོམ་པ་	n., *cultivation, meditation*
སྒྱུ་མ་	n., *illusion*
སྒྲུབ་	trans. v. (ag-nom), *achieve, attain, accomplish, complete; prove*
	སྒྲུབ་བསྒྲུབས་བསྒྲུབ་སྒྲུབས། ཐ་དད།
སྒྲུབ་པ་	n., *accomplishment, achievement, proof*
བསྒོམ་	trans. v. (ag-nom), *meditate on, cultivate*
	སྒོམ་བསྒོམས་བསྒོམ་སྒོམས། ཐ་དད།
བསྒོམ་	trans. v. (ag-nom) (future tense), *meditate on, cultivate*
བསྒོམས་	trans. v. (ag-nom) (past tense), *meditate on, cultivate*
བསྒྲུབ་	trans. v. (ag-nom) (future tense), *achieve, establish, accomplish*
	སྒྲུབ་བསྒྲུབས་བསྒྲུབ་སྒྲུབས། ཐ་དད།
ང་	4th letter of Tibetan alphabet
ངན་འགྲོ་	n., *bad migrations*
ངན་འགྲོར་	n. + 2nd, 4th or 7th case particle fused to suffixless syllable
ངེས་	intr. v. (nom-loc), *be certain, ascertain*
	ངེས་ངེས་ངེས། ཐ་མི་དད།
ངེས་པ་	verbal n., *certainty, ascertainment*
ངོ་	terminating syntactic particle ending the sentence following the suffix ང་.
ངོ་བོ་	n., *entity, nature, character*
ངོས་བཟུང་	trans. v. (ag-nom) (past tense), *identify*
	ངོས་འཛིན། ངོས་བཟུང་། ངོས་གཟུང་། ངོས་ཟུང་། ཐ་དད།
ངོས་བཟུང་ནས་	v. + continuative s.p., *having identified*
མངོན་པར་	lexical prefix syllable, trans. Sanskrit *abhi-*, *exceptionally, extensively*
མངོན་པར་ཞེན་	intr. v. (nom-loc), *cling, adhere, strongly adhere*
མངོན་ཞེན་	abbreviation of མངོན་པར་ཞེན་ *adhere, strongly adhere*
སྔ་མ་	adj., *former*

ཅ་	5th letter of Tibetan alphabet
ཅན་	lexical suffix particle indicating possession, *having X, possessing X*
ཅི་	indefinite and general relative pronoun, and interrogative pronoun, *what, which, however, whatever*
ཅི་ཡང་	indefinite and general relative pronoun, *whatever, any, at all*
ཅི་ཡང་མེད་	verb phrase, *without any, not at all*
ཅི་ཡང་མེད་པར་	indefinite and general neg. relative pronoun, *without any, not at all*
ཅིག་	following nouns, adj., modified form of གཅིག་, *one; a, some, a little*
ཅིག་	following verbs, an imperative marking syntactic particle
ཅིང་	continuative syntactic particle used following verbs and verb phrases
ཅུང་ཟད་	adv., *slightly, a little, briefly*
གཅིག་པ་	n., *single, one*
བཅད་	trans. v. (ag-nom) (past tense), *cut, eliminate, decide, judge*
	གཅོད་བཅད་གཅད་ཆོད། ཐ་དད།
བཅས་	possessive lexical suffix particle, *having X, possessing X*
བཅུ་	n. or adj., *ten*
བཅུའི་	n. + 6th case particle fused to suffixless, single-syllable word
བཅོ་བརྒྱད་	n. or adj., *eighteen*
བཅོས་	trans. v. (ag-nom) (past tense), *fabricate, make up*
	འཆོས་བཅོས་བཅོས་ཆོས། ཐ་དད།
བཅོས་མ་	n., *simulated* (in the sense of made up or fabricated)
བཅོས་མ་མིན་པ་	n., *non-simulated, non-fabricated*
བཅོས་མིན་	adj., *non-simulated*

ཆ་	6th letter of Tibetan alphabet
ཆ་	n., *part, factor*
ཆ་མཉམ་	adj., *equal, balanced*
ཆད་	intr. v. (nom-obj) (past tense), *be severed, be cut*
	འཆད་ཆད་འཆད། ཐ་མི་དད།
ཆད་མཐའ་	compound n., *extreme of annihilation*
ཆུང་ངུ་	adj., *small*
ཆུང་བ་	adj., *small*
ཆུངས་	adj., *small*
ཆེ་	adj., *great, big*
ཆེར་	adj. + 2nd, 4th or 7th case particle fused to suffixless syllable
ཆེ་བ་	adj., *great*
ཆེན་པོ་	adj., *big, large, great*
ཆོ་ག་	n., *rite*
ཆོ་གས་	n. + 3rd case particle fused to suffixless final syllable
ཆོས་	n., *phenomenon; religion, Doctrine* (what Buddha taught), and many other meanings. This is the Tibetan translation of the Sanskrit *dharma*
ཆོས་སྐོར་	comp. n., *topics of practice*
འཆད་	trans. v. (ag-nom), *explain*
	འཆད་བཤད་བཤད་ཤོད། ཐ་དད།
འཆད་	intr. v. (nom-obj), *be severed, be cut*
	འཆད་ཆད་འཆད། ཐ་མི་དད།
འཆིང་	trans. v. (ag-nom) *bind, tie up* འཆིང་འཅིངས་འཅིང་འཆིངས། ཐ་དད།

འཆིང་ n., *bondage*

འཆོས་ trans. v. (ag-nom), *fabricate, make up*

འཆོས་བཅོས་བཅོས་ཆོས། ཐ་དད།

ཇ་

7th letter of Tibetan alphabet

ཇི་འདྲ་བ་ adverbial pronoun, *just like*

ཇེ་ adv., indicates increase

ཇེ་ + adj. + 2nd case particle an adverbial comparative construction where ཇེ་ is an adverb modifying the adjective following it

ཇེ་ཆེ་ adv. + adj., *bigger*

ཇེ་ཆེར་ adv. + adj. + 2nd case particle, *bigger*

འཇིག་ trans. v. (ag-nom), *destroy, break*

འཇིག་བཤིག་གཞིག་ཤིགས། ཐ་དད།

འཇིག་ intr. v. (nom-obj), *disintegrate*

འཇིག་ཞིག་འཇིག ཐ་མི་དད།

འཇིག་རྟེན་ compound n., *the world;* literally, *disintegrating basis*

འཇིགས་ intr. v. (nom-loc), *fear, be afraid*

འཇིགས་འཇིགས་འཇིགས། ཐ་མི་དད།

འཇིགས་པ་ verbal n., *fright*

འཇུག་ this is the present tense of both the transitive verb and the intransitive verb.

འཇུག་ trans. v. (ag-obj), causative in sense of *make something happen*

འཇུག་འཙུག་གཞུག་ཆུག ཐ་དད།

འཇུག་ intr. v. (nom-obj), *enter, engage, apply;* by extension: *supplement*

འཇུག་ཞུགས་འཇུག་ཞུགས། ཐ་མི་དད།

འཇུག་སྡོམ་ compound n., *vow of practice*

འཇོག་ trans. v. (ag-nom), *posit, put, set, designate;* this verb has two sets of tense spellings:

འཇོག་བཞག་གཞག་ཞོག ཐ་དད།

འཇོག་བཞོགས་གཞོག་ཞོགས། ཐ་དད།

རྗེས་ postposition, *after*

བརྗོད་ trans. v. (ag-nom), *set forth, express, say*

རྗོད་བརྗོད་བརྗོད་རྗོད། ཐ་དད།

བརྗོད་པར་བྱ་ verb phrase (verbal infinitive + strong future auxiliary), *[I] will express, [you] should express.* བརྗོད་པར་ is a verbal infinitive; here, the fused ར་ is a syntactic particle modifying a verb to create a verbal infinitive within the verb phrase བརྗོད་པར་བྱ་ *[I] will express* or *[you] should express;* it is **not** a case particle marking the 2nd, 4th or 7th cases because it does not follow a noun—it is within a verb phrase. བྱ་ is a trans. v. (ag-nom) (future tense), *do, make, perform, take;* here it is the strong future auxiliary.

ཉ་

8th letter of Tibetan alphabet

ཉན་ trans. v. (ag-obj), *listen to*

ཉན་མཉན་མཉན་ཉོན། ཐ་དད།

ཉམས་སུ་བླང་ trans. v. (ag-nom), *practice, train*

ཉམས་སུ་ལེན། ཉམས་སུ་བླངས། ཉམས་སུ་བླང་། ཉམས་སུ་ལོངས། ཐ་དད།

ཉེས་དམིགས་ n., *fault*

ཉེས་བྱས་ comp. n., *secondary faults*

ཉེས་བྱས་བཞི་བཅུ་ཞེ་དྲུག	comp. n. + adj., *forty-six secondary faults*
ཉོན་མོངས་	n., *affliction*
གཉིས་	n. or adj., *two*
མཉན་	trans. v. (ag-nom) (past and future tenses), *listen to* ཉན་མཉན་མཉན་ཉོན། ཐ་དད།
རྙེད་	intr. v. (nom-obj), *be found* རྙེད་རྙེད་རྙེད། ཐ་མི་དད།
རྙེད་པ་	n., *found*
སྙམ་	trans. v. (ag-nom), *consider, think about, wonder about.* This verb is listed in the *Great Word Treasury* as ཐ་མི་དད། but I think it is a transitive ag-nom verb. སྙམ་སྙམ་སྙམ། ཐ་མི་དད།
སྙམ་དུ་	adv., *considering, thinking*
སྙིང་	n., *heart, essence*
སྙིང་པོ་	n., *heart*
སྙིང་རྗེ་	n., *compassion*

ཏ་

9th letter of Tibetan alphabet

ཏིང་ངེ་འཛིན་	n., *meditative stabilization*
ཏེ་	either conditional s.p. (follows a verb or aux.) or punctuational s.p. (follows words or phrases)
གཏད་	trans. v. (ag-nom), *aim, focus, concentrate; delegate, entrust* གཏོད་གཏད་གཏད་གཏོད། ཐ་དད།
གཏན་པ་	verbal n. and adj., *stable*
བཏགས་	trans. v. (ag-nom) (past tense), *designated, imputed* འདོགས་བཏགས་གདགས་ཐོགས། ཐ་དད།

རྟག་	n. or adj., abbreviation for རྟག་པ་ *permanent phenomena, permanent*
རྟག་པ་	n. or adj., *permanent phenomena, permanence*
རྟག་མཐར་	compound n., *extreme of permanence*
རྟེན་	intr. v. (nom-loc), *depend on, rely on* རྟེན་བརྟེན་བརྟེན་རྟེན། ཐ་མི་དད།
རྟེན་	n., *basis, support*
རྟོག་	trans. v. (ag-nom), *think about, consider* རྟོག་བརྟགས་བརྟག་རྟོགས། ཐ་དད།
རྟོག་པ་	n., (conceptual) *thought*
རྟོག་པ་སྦྱོང་	verbal compound: *thought purification*
ལྟ་	trans. v. (ag-obj), *look at, regard,* and by extension: *consider* ལྟ་བལྟས་བལྟ་ལྟོས། ཐ་དད།
ལྟ་བ་	n., *view*
ལྟ་བུ་	adj., *like*
ལྟ་བུའི་	n. + 6th case particle fused to suffixless final syllable
ལྟུང་	intr. v. (nom-obj), *fall* ལྟུང་ལྟུངས་ལྟུང་། ཐ་མི་དད།
ལྟོས་	intr. v. (nom-loc), *depend; be contingent on, be within the context of* ལྟོས་བལྟོས་ལྟོས། ཐ་མི་དད།
སྟེ་	either conditional s.p. (follows a verb or aux.) or punctuational s.p. (follows words or phrases)
སྟེན་	trans. v. (ag-obj), *adhere to, rely on, stay close to* སྟེན་བསྟེན་བསྟེན་བསྟེན། ཐ་དད།

སྟོང་ intr. v. (nom-s.p.), *be empty [of something]*

སྟོང་སྟོངས་སྟོང་། ཐ་མི་དད།

སྟོང་ཉིད་ n., *emptiness*

སྟོན་ trans. v. (ag-nom), *teach*

སྟོན་བསྟན་བསྟན་སྟོན། ཐ་དད།

སྟོན་པ་ verbal n., *teacher*

སྟོབས་བཞི་ n. phrase, *the four powers;* abbreviation for གཉེན་པོ་སྟོབས་བཞི་:

རྟེན་གྱི་སྟོབས་ *the power of reliance*

གཉེན་པོའི་སྟོབས་ *the power of [overcoming non-virtues by] antidotes*

རྣམ་པར་སུན་འབྱིན་པའི་སྟོབས་ *the power of repentance*

ཉེས་པ་ལས་སླར་ལྡོག་པའི་སྟོབས་ *the power of not engaging in non-virtues again*

སྟོན་པའི་ verbal n. + fused 6th case particle

བརྟན་ trans. v. (ag-nom), *make stable, make firm*

རྟོན་བརྟན་བརྟན་རྟོན། ཐ་དད།

བརྟན་པར་བྱ་ verb phrase (verbal infinitive + strong future auxiliary), *[you] should make (it) stable.* བརྟན་པར་ is a verbal infinitive; here, the fused ར་ is a syntactic particle modifying a verb to create a verbal infinitive within the verb phrase བརྟན་པར་བྱ་ *[you] should make (it) stable;* it is **not** a case particle marking the 2nd, 4th or 7th cases because it does not follow a noun—it is within a verb phrase. བྱ་ is a trans. v. (ag-nom) (future tense), *do, make, perform, take;* here: the strong future auxiliary

བརྟན་པར་བྱས་ verb phrase (verbal infinitive + strong past auxiliary), *[I, you] have made [something] stable.* བརྟན་པར་ is a verbal infinitive; here, the fused ར་ is a syntactic particle modifying a verb to create a verbal infinitive within the verb phrase བརྟན་པར་བྱས་ *[you] should have made [it] stable;* it is **not** a case particle marking the 2nd, 4th or 7th cases because it does not follow a noun—it is within a verb phrase. བྱས་ is a trans. v. (ag-nom) (past tense), *do, make, perform, take;* here: the strong past auxiliary

བརྟན་བྱ་ abbreviation for བརྟན་པར་བྱ་

བརྟེན་ intr. v. (nom-loc) (past tense), *depend on, rely on*

རྟེན་བརྟེན་བརྟེན་རྟེན། ཐ་མི་དད།

བསྟེན་ trans. v. (ag-obj) (past and future tenses), *adhere to, rely on, stay close to*

སྟེན་བསྟེན་བསྟེན་བསྟེན། ཐ་དད།

བསྟེན་ཚུལ་ comp. n., *mode of reliance*

ཐ་

10th letter of Tibetan alphabet

ཐ་མ་ adj., *last*

ཐག་པ་ n., *distance, depth*

ཐན་ཐུན་ adj., *a little*

ཐམས་ཅད་ adj., *all*

ཐར་ intr. v. (nom-s.p. verb of separation), *be liberated [from something or from somewhere].* X Y ལས་ཐར། *X is liberated from Y.* This verb of separation is classified as a nom-s.p. verb together with verbs of absence, conjunction and disjunction, but its qualifier, that from which the subject is liberated, is marked with a true 5th case particle.

ཐར་ཐར་ཐར། ཐ་མི་དད།

ཐར་པ་ verbal n., *liberation*

ཐུག་ intr. v. (nom-obj), *meet, meet back, derive from*

ཐུག་ཐུག་ཐུག། ཐ་མི་དད་ intransitive

ཐུག་པ་ verbal n., *meeting, deriving*

ཐུག་པས་ verbal n. + fused 3rd case particle

ཐུན་མོང་བ་ adj., *common, shared*

ཐེག་ཆེན་	n. + adj., abbreviation for ཐེག་པ་ཆེན་པོ་ *Great Vehicle.* Sanskrit, *Måhåyana*
ཐོག་	n., *top,* and by extension: *context*
ཐོག་བྲེད་པ་	n., *roof*
ཐོག་མ་	n., *the beginning*
ཐོག་མར་	n. + fused 7th case particle signifying time: *at the beginning*
ཐོབ་	intr. v. (nom-obj) (past tense), *attain, obtain, get* འཐོབ་ཐོབ་འཐོབ། ཐ་མི་དད།
ཐོབ་པ་	n., *acquisition, attainment*
མཐའ་	n., *end, limit*
མཐོང་	trans. v. (ag-nom), *see, preceive.* This verb is listed in the *Great Word Treasury* as ཐ་མི་དད། but I think it is a transitive verb (ag-nom). མཐོང་མཐོང་མཐོང་། ཐ་མི་དད།
འཐོབ་	intr. v. (nom-obj), *attain, obtain, get* འཐོབ་ཐོབ་འཐོབ། ཐ་མི་དད།

ད་

11th letter of Tibetan alphabet

ད་	adv., *now*
དང་	particle; used three ways: 1) continuative syntactic particle used following nouns and noun phrases (*and,* or with negative verb, *or*); 2) syntactic particle marking the qualifier of an intr. nom-s.p. v. of conjunction, as in ང་རང་མི་སྡུག་པ་དང་ཕྲད་ན *if we meet with unpleasantness;* and 3) syntactic particle marking the qualifier of an intr. nom-s.p. v. of disjunction, as in རྟོག་པ་དང་བྲལ་ *free from conceptuality*
དང་བཅས་པ་	possessive lexical suffix particle, *together with;* actually, it's a verbal phrase
དད་	intr. v. (nom-loc), *have faith in, be interested in* དད་དད་དད། ཐ་མི་དད།
དད་པ་	n., *faith*
དལ་བ་	n., *leisure*
དལ་འབྱོར་	comp. n., *the (eight) leisures and (ten) endowments.* Abbreviation for དལ་བ་དང་འབྱོར་བ་
དུ་	particle; either verb-modifying syntactic particle within verb phrases, or case particle marking the 2nd, 4th and 7th cases
དུ་མ་	adj., *many*
དེ་	syntactic particle; either cont. s.p. (follows verb or aux.) or punct. s.p.(follows words or phrases)
དེ་	limiting adj. and pronoun, *that, those*
དེ་ལྟར་	adv. pronoun, *such, thus (in that way)*
དེ་དག་	limiting adj. (often used as pronoun) + lexical pluralizing particle, *those*
དེ་འདྲ་	limiting adj. used as pronoun, *such, like that*
དེ་འདྲ་བ་	limiting adjective used as an adverbial pronoun, *such, like that*
དེ་འདྲ་བའི་	pronoun + 6th case particle fused to suffixless final syllable
དེ་ནས་	a syntactic particle translated *then;* literally, *after that.* དེ་ནས་ is often glossed as དེའི་རྗེས་སུ་ *after that*
དེ་མེད་ན་	conditional clause (pronoun + v. + conditional s.p.); with verb of possession: *If [you] don't have that;* or, with verb of existence: *If that doesn't exist*
དེ་བཞིན་དུ་	adverbial pronoun, *thus, so, in that way*
དེ་ལ་	adj. or pronoun + 2nd, 4th or 7th case particle
དེའི་	adj. or pronoun + 6th case particle fused to a suffixless syllable
དེའི་རྗེས་སུ་	pronoun + 6th case particle + postposition + fused 7th case particle, *after that*
དེར་	adj. or pronoun + 2nd, 4th or 7th case particle fused to a suffixless syllable
དེས་	adj. or pronoun + fused 3rd case particle

དོ་	terminating s.p. following word ending with the suffix letter ད་
དོན་	n., *object, meaning, purpose*
དོན་གཉེར་	trans. v. (ag-nom), abbreviation for དོན་དུ་གཉེར་ *seek*
དོན་དུ་གཉེར་	trans. phrasal v. (ag-nom), *seek* གཉེར་གཉེར་གཉེར་གཉེར། ཐ་དད།
དོན་བསྡུ་བ་	comp. n., *summary, summation;* literally: *condensed meaning*
དྲག་	adj., *hard, heavy*
དྲག་པར་	adj. + 2nd 4th or 7th case particle fused to suffixless final syllable
དྲག་པོ་	adj., *strong*
དྲང་	trans. v. (ag-nom) (future tense), *induce, lead, draw; cite*
	འདྲེན་དྲངས་དྲང་དྲོངས། ཐ་དད།
དྲན་	trans. v. (ag-nom), *remember, be mindful of*
	དྲན་དྲན་དྲན་དྲན། ཐ་དད།
དྲུག་	n. or adj., *six*
དྲུག་པོ་	adj., *strong*
དྲུག་པོས་	adj. + fused 3rd case particle
བདག་	n., *self*
བདག་མེད་	n., *selfless, selflessness*
བདར་ཤ་བཅད་	phrasal verb (ag-nom), *take to heart, examine minutely*
མདོ་	n., *discourse, rule, axiom,* translation of Sanskrit *sátra*
མདོར་	n. + 2nd case particle, *in brief*
མདོར་ན་	n. + 2nd case particle + omitted verb + conditional syntactic particle, *in brief, in general;* abbreviation for མདོར་བསྡུ་ན
འདི་	limiting adj. used as a pronoun, *this*
འདི་ཡང་	s.p., introductory particle, *further*
འདི་ལྟར་	adverbial relative pronoun, *such, thus*
འདུས་	intr. v. (nom-obj) (past tense and imperative), *be gathered, be included*
	འདུད་འདུས་འདུ་འདུས། ཐ་མི་དད་
འདོགས་	trans. v. (ag-nom), *designate, impute*
	འདོགས་བཏགས་གདགས་ཐོགས། ཐ་དད།
འདོད་	trans. v. (ag-nom), *want, wish, assert.* This verb is listed in the *Great Word Treasury* as ཐ་མི་དད། but I think it is a transitive ag-nom verb. འདོད་འདོད་འདོད། ཐ་མི་དད།
འདོན་	trans. v. (ag-nom), *cause to come out, expel, recite*
	འདོན་འཏོན་གདོན་ཐོན། ཐ་དད།
འདྲ་	intr. v. (nom-s.p. verb of conjunction for which the qualifier is marked with a དང་), *be similar to*
	འདྲ་དྲས་དྲོས། ཐ་དད།
འདྲ་བར་འགྱུར་	verb phrase (verbal infinitive + weak present/future auxiliary), *[it] would/will be like [something].* འདྲ་བར་ is a verbal infinitive; here, the fused ར་ is a syntactic particle modifying a verb to create a verbal infinitive within the verb phrase འདྲ་བར་འགྱུར་ *would be similar, will be similar;* it is **not** a case particle marking the 2nd, 4th or 7th cases because it does not follow a noun—it is within a verb phrase. འགྱུར་ is an intr. v. (nom-obj), *become;* also the weak present/future auxiliary
འདྲོངས་	intr. v. (nom-loc) (past tense), *be induced*
	འདྲོང་འདྲོངས་འདྲོང་། ཐ་མི་དད།
ལྡོག་	intr. v. (nom-s.p.), *be isolated, be reversed.* This verb of separation is classified as a nom-s.p. verb together with verbs of absence, conjunction and disjunction, but its qualifier, that from which the subject is separated, is marked with a true 5th case particle, not a syntactic particle as the name of the class suggests.
	ལྡོག་ལྡོག་ལྡོག ཐ་མི་དད།

ལྡོག་པར་བྱ། verb phrase (verbal infinitive + strong future auxiliary), *[I] will turn, [you] should turn...* ལྡོག་པར་ is a verbal infinitive; here, the fused ར་ is a syntactic particle modifying a verb to create an infinitive within the verb phrase འབད་པར་བྱ་ *[you] should turn;* it is **not** a case particle marking the 2nd, 4th or 7th cases because it does not follow a noun—it is within a verb phrase བྱ་ trans. v. (ag-nom) (future tense), *do, make, perform, take;* here: the strong auxiliary

ལྡོག་བྱ། abbreviation for ལྡོག་པར་བྱ།

སྡོད་ intr. v. (nom-loc), *stay, remain, sit, dwell*

སྡོད་བསྡད་བསྡད་སྡོད། ཐ་མི་དད།

སྡོམ་ trans. v. (ag-nom), *bind, tie up; vow, promise*

སྡོམ་བསྡམས་བསྡམ་སྡོམས། ཐ་དད།

སྡོམ་པ་ n., *vow*

བསྡུ་ trans. v. (ag-nom) (future tense), *gather, collect*

སྡུད་བསྡུས་བསྡུ་སྡུས། ཐ་དད།

བསྡུ་བ་ n., *collection*

བསྡུ་བཞི་ noun phrase; *the four means of gathering [students]:*

མཁོ་པ་སྦྱིན་པ། *giving whatever is necessary;*

སྙན་པར་སྨྲ་བ། *speaking pleasantly (this means speaking about the paths leading to high status and definite goodness);*

དོན་མཐུན་པ། *purposeful behavior* (this means causing others to practice what is beneficial) and

དོན་སྤྱོད་པ། *concordant behavior* (this means to oneself practice what you recommend to others).

བསྔོས་ trans. v. (ag-nom), *risk*

སྔོ་བསྔོས་བསྔོ་སྔོས། ཐ་དད།

བསྔོས་པར་བྱ། verb phrase (verbal infinitive + strong future auxiliary), *[you] should risk.* བསྔོས་པར་ is a verbal infinitive; here, the fused ར་ is a syntactic particle modifying a verb to create a verbal infinitive within the verb phrase བསྔོས་པར་བྱ་ *[you] should risk;* it is **not** a case particle marking the 2nd, 4th or 7th cases because it does not follow a noun—it is within a verb phrase. བྱ་ is a trans. v. (ag-nom) (future tense), *do, make, perform, take;* also strong future auxiliary

བསྔོས་བྱ། abbreviation for བསྔོས་པར་བྱ་ *[you] should risk.*

ན་

12th letter of Tibetan alphabet

ན་ particle; either syntactic particle (following a verb) marking a conditional clause, or case particle (following a noun) marking the 2nd, 4th and 7th cases

ནང་ postposition, *in, inside*

ནང་ནས་ postposition + 5th case particle (source), *from within*

ནམ་མཁའ་ n., *space*

ནའང་ 2 fused s.p. = ན་ + འང་ *even if...*

ནས་ particle; either 1) a syntactic particle following verbs and verb phrases marking adverbs, participles or disjunction, or 2) a case particle marking the 5th case

ནས་ n., *barley*

ནི་ punctuation s.p., sets off a word or n. phrase for rhetorical emphasis without changing the declension.

ནུས་ intr. v. (nom-loc), *be able* ནུ་ནུས་ནུ་ནུས། ཐ་དད།

ནུས་པ་ n., *capacity, ability*

ནོ་ a terminating syntactic particle which follows words ending with a ན་ suffix.

གནད་ n., *essential, important point*

གནད་དུ་ n. + 2nd, 4th or 7th case particle

གནད་དུ་འགྲོ་ verbal phrase, *be successful*

འགྲོ་ཕྱིན་འགྲོ་སོང་། ཐ་མི་དད།

གནས་ intr. v. (nom-loc), *abide, dwell*

གནས་གནས་གནས་གནས། ཐ་མི་དད།

གནས་ n., *place, abode, location,* and also *status, state, situation, source, object, topic* and *basis*

གནས་ཆ་ compound n., *factor of stability*

གནས་པ་ verbal n., *dwelling, remaining, one who dwells* or *remains*

རྣམ་པ་ n., *aspect*

རྣམས་ optional lexical pluralizing particle

རྣམ་དག adj., *pure, very pure, complete;* abbreviation for རྣམ་པར་དག་པ་

རྣམ་གཡེང་ intr. v. (nom-loc), *be distracted*

གཡེང་གཡེང་གཡེང་། ཐ་མི་དད།

རྣལ་མ་ adj., *natural*

སྣང་ intr. v. (nom-obj), *appear;* by extension: *imagine*

སྣང་སྣང་སྣང་། ཐ་མི་དད།

པ་

13th letter of Tibetan alphabet

པའི་ either syntactic particle or 6th case particle fused to suffixless final syllable པ་

པས་ either syntactic particle or 3rd case particle fused to suffixless final syllable པ་

སྤོང་ trans. v. (ag-nom), *abandon* སྤོང་སྤངས་སྤང་སྤོངས། ཐ་དད།

སྤྱི་ n., *generality, universal*

སྦྱིན་པ་ n., *generosity* (1st of the six perfections)

སྤྱིའི་ n. + fused 6th case particle

སྤྱོད trans. v. (ag-nom), *practice, use, enjoy*

སྤྱོད་སྤྱད་སྤྱད་སྤྱོད། ཐ་དད།

སྤྱོད་པ་ n., *deeds*

སྤྲུག་ trans. v. (ag-nom), *shake off, shake*

སྤྲུག་སྤྲུགས་སྤྲུག་སྤྲུགས། ཐ་དད།

སྤྲོ་ trans. v. (ag-nom), *spread out*

སྤྲོ་སྤྲོས་སྤྲོ་སྤྲོས། ཐ་དད།

སྤྲོ་ intr. v. (nom-obj), *be spread out*

སྤྲོ་སྤྲོ་སྤྲོ། ཐ་མི་དད།

ཕ་

14th letter of Tibetan alphabet

ཕར་ཕྱིན་ n., *perfection;* contraction for ཕ་རོལ་ཏུ་ཕྱིན་པ་ literally, a verbal clause employing the past tense of the verb *go, gone to the [other] side.* The intransitive verb of motion འགྲོ་ is often used by extension in the metaphorical sense of *turns into* or *becomes.* འགྲོ་ཕྱིན་འགྲོ་སོང་། ཐ་མི་དད། སོང་ is also an alternate past form

ཕ་རོལ་ཏུ་ཕྱིན་པ་ n., *perfection*, literally a verbal clause *gone to the other side*

ཕྱི་མ་ adj., *later*

ཕྱིན་ intr. v. (nom-obj) (past tense), *went;* often used by extension in the metaphorical sense of *turned into* or *became.* འགྲོ་ཕྱིན་འགྲོ་སོང་། ཐ་མི་དད། སོང་ is also an alternate past form

ཕྱིན་དྲུག n. + adj. compound, *the six perfections:*

སྦྱིན་པ་ n., *generosity*

ཚུལ་ཁྲིམས་ n., *ethics*

བཟོད་པ་ n., *patience*

བརྩོན་འགྲུས་ n., *effort*

	བསམ་གཏན་ n., *concentration*
	ཤེས་རབ་ n., *wisdom*
ཕྱིར་	adverb, *again, back*
ཕྱིར་	postposition indicating intention, *for the sake of, for the purpose of, because*
ཕྱིར་དུ་	post. + 4th case particle signifying purpose
ཕྱིར་འཆོས་པ་	verbal n., *restoration of vows (through confession of transgressed vows ceremony)*
ཕྱོགས་	intr. v. (nom-obj), *be diverted, be turn, go aside, be inclined (towards)* ཕྱོགས་ ཕྱོགས་ ཕྱོགས། ཐ་མི་དད།
ཕྱོགས་	n., *position, portion, direction, faction, side*
ཕྱོགས་རི་བ་	comp. n., *partisan*

བ་

15th letter of Tibetan alphabet

བའི་	either syntactic particle or 6th case particle fused to suffixless final syllable
བར་	2nd, 4th or 7th case particle fused to suffixless final syllable
བོར་	2nd, 4th or 7th case particle fused to suffixless final syllable
བས་	either syntactic particle or 3rd case particle fused to suffixless final syllable
བྱ་	trans. v. (future tense) (ag-nom), *do, make, perform, take;* as an auxiliary, this is the strong future auxiliary frequently seen meaning *will* or *must* བྱེད་བྱས་བྱ་བྱོས། ཐ་དད།
བྱང་ཆུབ་	n., *enlightenment*
བྱང་ཆུབ་ཀྱི་སེམས་	compound n., *the altruistic aspiration to enlightenment*
བྱང་སེམས་	n. *Bodhisattva;* abbreviation for བྱང་ཆུབ་སེམས་དཔའ་ *Bodhisattva*
བྱམས་	n., *love*
བྱས་	trans. v. (past tense) (ag-nom), *do, make, perform, take;* as an auxiliary, this is the strong past auxiliary བྱེད་བྱས་བྱ་བྱོས། ཐ་དད།
བྱུང་	intr. v. (nom-obj) (past tense), *arise, occur, come forth, occur* འབྱུང་བྱུང་འབྱུང་། ཐ་མི་དད།
བྱེ་བྲག་	n., *particular*
བྱེད་	trans. v. (ag-nom), *do, make, perform, take;* strong present auxiliary བྱེད་བྱས་བྱ་བྱོས། ཐ་དད།
བྲན་	n., *servant*
བྲན་དུ་	n. + 2nd, 4th or 7th case particle
བྲལ་	intr. v. (nom-s.p. verb of disjunction), *lack, be free of, be devoid of* འབྲལ་བྲལ་འབྲལ། ཐ་མི་དད།
བླངས་	trans. v. (ag-nom) (past tense), *take, obtain, grasp, seize, take up, appropriate* ལེན་བླངས་བླང་ལོངས། ཐ་དད།
བླངས་ནས་	trans. v. in past tense + v. modifying s.p. = past participle, *having taken*
བློ་	n., *mind, awareness*
བློས་	noun + 3rd case particle fused to suffixless syllable
བློ་ཁ་	n., *orientation*
འབད་	trans. v. (ag-obj), *strive to, strive at, make effort in* འབད་འབད་འབད་འབོད། ཐ་དད།

འབད་པར་བྱ་	verb phrase (verbal infinitive + strong future auxiliary), *[I] will strive, [you] should strive.* འབད་པར་ is a verbal infinitive; here, the fused ར་ is a syntactic particle modifying a verb to create a verbal infinitive within the verb phrase འབད་པར་བྱ་ *[I] will strive, [you] should strive;* it is **not** a case particle marking the 2nd, 4th or 7th cases because it does not follow a noun—it is within a verb phrase. བྱ་ is a trans. v. (ag-nom) (future tense), *do, make, perform, take;* also strong future auxiliary
འབྱུང་	intr. v. (nom-obj), *arise, come forth, emerge, occur, appear*
	འབྱུང་བྱུང་འབྱུང་། ཐ་མི་དད།
འབྱུང་བ་	n., *element, arising*
འབྱུང་བ་	verbal n., *arising, occurrence*
འབྱོར་བ་	n., *endowment*
འབྲས་	n., *effect;* abbreviation of འབྲས་བུ་
འབྲས་བུ་	n., *effect*
འབྲིང་	adj., *middle, the intermediate of a series of three*
སྦྱང་	trans. v. (ag-obj) (future tense), *wash, purify, train*
	སྦྱོང་སྦྱངས་སྦྱང་སྦྱོངས། ཐ་དད།
སྦྱང་བར་བྱས་	verb phrase (verbal infinitive + strong past auxiliary), *[I, you] have practiced purification.* སྦྱང་བར་ is a verbal infinitive; here, the fused ར་ is a syntactic particle modifying a verb to create a verbal infinitive within the verb phrase སྦྱང་བར་བྱས་ *having practiced purification;* it is **not** a case particle marking the 2nd, 4th or 7th cases because it does not follow a noun—it is within a verb phrase. བྱས་ is a trans. v. (ag-nom) (past tense), *do, make, perform, take;* here: the strong past auxiliary
སྦྱང་བར་བྱས་ནས་	verbal phrase + v. modifying s.p., *having practiced purification*
སྦྱངས་	trans. v. (ag-obj) (past tense), *washed, purified, trained in*
	སྦྱོང་སྦྱངས་སྦྱང་སྦྱོངས། ཐ་དད།
མ་	16th letter of Tibetan alphabet
མ་	n., *mother*
མ་	negative lexical prefix particle. མ་མི་ are negative lexical prefix particles that precede the word they negate. མིན་མེད་ are negative lexical suffix particles that follow the word they negate
མ་བཤད་	negative trans. v. (ag-nom) (past and future tenses), *not explained*
	འཆད་བཤད་བཤད་ཤོད། ཐ་དད།
མ་སོང་བ་	negative verbal noun derived from the past tense of the verb འགྲོ་ *go*
	འགྲོ་ཕྱིན་འགྲོ་སོང་། ཐ་མི་དད། སོང་ is also an alternate past form
མ་སོང་བར་	verbal noun + 2nd , 4th or 7th case particle
མང་	adj., *many, much.* Abbreviation of མང་པོ་
མང་པོ་	adj., *many, much*
མང་དུ་ + verb	adj. + 2nd case particle followed by a verb is most likely an adverbial construction, *frequently*
མི་	negative lexical prefix particle. མ་མི་ are negative lexical prefix particles that precede the word they negate. མིན་མེད་ are negative lexical suffix particles that follow the word they negate
མི་	n., *human, man*
མི་དགེ་	n., *non-virtuous (actions)*
མི་རྟག་པ་	n., *impermanent phenomena, impermanence*
མི་སྡོད་	negative lexical prefix particle + intr. v. (nom-loc), *not stay, not remain, not sit, not dwell*
	སྡོད་བསྡད་བསྡད་སྡོད། ཐ་མི་དད།
མི་སྡོད་པ་	n., *the non-remaining*
མི་སྡོད་པའི་	verbal noun + 6th case particle fused to suffixless syllable

མི་སྣང་	negative lexical prefix particle + intr. v. (nom-obj), *appear*
མིང་	n., *name*
མིན་	negative linking verb (nom-nom), *is not, are not*
མིན་	negative lexical suffix particle that follows the word it negates. མ་མི་ are negative lexical prefix particles that precede the word they negate. མིན་མེད་ are negative lexical suffix particles that follow the word they negate
མེད་	negative lexical verbal suffix particle. མ་མི་ are negative lexical prefix particles that precede the word they negate. མིན་མེད་ are negative lexical suffix particles that follow the word they negate
མེད་	intr. v. (nom-loc), *not exist.* Also a trans. v. (loc-nom), *not have*
	མེད་མེད་མེད་མེད། ཐ་མི་དད།
མྱོང་	intr. v. (nom-obj), *experience*
	མྱོང་མྱོང་མྱོང་། ཐ་མི་དད།
དམིགས་	trans. v. (ag-nom), *observe*
	དམིགས་དམིགས་དམིགས་དམིགས། ཐ་དད།
དམིགས་	n., *object of observation*
དམིགས་གཏད་	compound n., *target*
དམིགས་པ་	n., *object of observation*
རྨང་	n., *foundation*
རྨང་མེད་	n. + negative lexical suffix particle, *without a foundation*
སྨིན་	intr. v. (nom-obj), *be ripened*
	སྨིན་སྨིན་སྨིན། ཐ་མི་དད།
སྨིན་བྱེད་	verbal agent noun; *ripener*
སྨོན་	trans v. (ag-obj), *aspire to*
	སྨོན་སྨོན་སྨོན་སྨོན། ཐ་དད།
སྨོན་སེམས་	compound n., *aspirational mind (of enlightenment)*

ཙ

17th letter of Tibetan alphabet

ཙམ་	adj. and restrictive lexical suffix particle, *just, only, merely*
གཙོ་བོ་	n. or adj., *main, principal*
གཙོ་བོར་	n. + 2nd, 4th or 7th case particle fused to suffixless final syllable བོ་
རྩ་བ་	n., adj., *root, main, principal*
རྩ་བ་ཅན་	n., *having the root*
རྩ་ལྟུང་	compound n., *root downfalls*
རྩ་ལྟུང་བཅོ་བརྒྱད་	comp. n. + adj., *the eighteen root downfalls*
རྩེ་	n., *point*
རྩེ་གཅིག་པ་	noun + adj. compound, *one pointed*
བརྩོན་འགྲུས་	n., *effort, joyous effort, enthusiastic effort;* the 4th of the six perfections

ཚ

18th letter of Tibetan alphabet

ཚོགས་སུ་ཚུད་པ་	intr. phrasal verb (nom-obj), *be included, be involved, be internalized*
	ཚུད་ཚུད་ཚུད། ཐ་མི་དད།
ཚང་	intr. v. (nom-obj), *be complete* ཚང་ཚང་ཚང་། ཐ་མི་དད།
ཚང་བ་	adj., *complete*
ཚང་བར་	adj. + fused 2nd, 4th or 7th case particle
ཚིག་	n., *word*
ཚུལ་	n., *mode*

ཚུལ་ཁྲིམས་	n., *ethics;* 2nd of the six perfections
ཚེ་	n., *time, life, lifetime*
ཚོགས་	n., *collection, gathering, group*
མཚན་མ་	n., *sign, mark;* in the expression མཚན་མར་འཛིན་པ་ *conception of signs,* it indicates a reified status of phenomena which has been erroneously superimposed by a consciousness conceiving inherent existence
མཚམས་	n., *boundary*
མཚོ་	n., *ocean*
མཚོན་	trans. v. (ag-obj), *define, make known, illustrate*
	མཚོན་མཚོན་མཚོན་མཚོན། ཐ་དད།
མཚོན་ནས་	trans. v. + continuative s.p. following core verb indicating a particple, *illustrating, having illustrated*

ཛ་

19th letter of Tibetan alphabet

འཛིན་	trans. v. (ag-nom), *grasp, hold;* by extension: *apprehend, conceive* འཛིན་བཟུང་གཟུང་ཟུང་། ཐ་དད།
འཛིན་པ་	verbal noun, *holder, apprehender, conceiver, conception*
འཛིན་པའི་	verbal noun + 6th case particle fused to suffixless final syllable པ་
རྫོགས་	trans and intr. v., *complete; be included, be completed.* This verb is listed in the *Great Word Treasury* as ཐ་མི་དད།, but it is used in both transitive and intransitive senses. རྫོགས་རྫོགས་རྫོགས། ཐ་མི་དད།
རྫོགས་པ་	n., *completion*
རྫོགས་རིམ་	comp. n., *stages of completion*

ཝ་

20th letter of Tibetan alphabet

ཞ་

21st letter of Tibetan alphabet

ཞི་	intr. v. (nom-loc), *be peaceful, be calm* ཞི་ཞི་ཞི། ཐ་མི་དད།
ཞི་གནས་	comp. n., *calm abiding*
ཞི་གནས་དང་ལྷག་མཐོང་	comp. n. *calm abiding and special insight*
ཞི་ལྷག་	ཞི་གནས་དང་ལྷག་མཐོང་
ཞི་ལྷག་	abbreviated comp. n., *calm abiding and special insight*
ཞིག་	adv. s.p.; makes preceding word, phrase or clause into an adverbial construction
ཞིག་	following nouns, adj., a variant of གཅིག་, *one; a, some, a little*
ཞིང་	continuative syntactic particle used following verbs and verb phrases, *and*
ཞིང་	n., *field*
ཞུགས་	intr. v. (past tense) (nom-obj), *engage;* see འཇུག་ (present tense) འཇུག་ཞུགས་འཇུག་ཞུགས། ཐ་མི་དད།
ཞུགས་པ་ཞིག་བྱ་	trans. v. + imperative: *[You] should engage...*
ཞེན་	intr. v. (nom-loc), *cling, determine, conceive, adhere* ཞེན་ཞེན་ཞེན། ཐ་མི་དད།
གཞན་	n., adj., *other, the other one*
གཞི་	n., *basis*
བཞག་	trans. v. (ag-nom) (past, future), *posit, put, set, designate;* two sets of verb forms are seen: འཇོག་བཞག་གཞག་ཞོག ཐ་དད།

འཛོག་བཞོགས་གཞོག་ཞོགས། ཐ་དད།

བཞི་ — n., adj., *four*

བཞི་བཅུ་ཞེ་དྲུག — n., adj., *forty-six*

བཞུགས་ — intr. v. (nom-loc), *live* (honorific). This verb is the honorific used in place of གནས་ and སྡོད་
བཞུགས་བཞུགས་བཞུགས་བཞུགས། ཐ་མི་དད།

ཟ་

22nd letter of Tibetan alphabet

ཟག་པ་ — n., *contamination*

ཟུར་པ་ — n., *corner*

བཟུང་ — trans. v. (ag-nom) (past tense), *grasp, hold;* by extension: *apprehend, conceive*
འཛིན་བཟུང་གཟུང་ཟུང་། ཐ་དད།

བཟུང་བའི་ — verbal noun + 6th case particle fused to suffixless final syllable

བཟོད་ — intr. v. (nom-loc), *be patient*
བཟོད་བཟོད་བཟོད། ཐ་མི་དད།

བཟོད་པ་ — n., *patience;* 3rd of the six perfections

འ་

23rd letter of Tibetan alphabet

འང་ — conjunctive and disjunctive syntactic particle used after nouns, pronouns, adjectives, verbs, and verb phrases, *but, even, also.* འང་ follows words with suffixless final syllables.

འི་ — particle fused to suffixless final syllable; either 1) a syntactic particle following a verb or verb phrase signifying conjunction or disjunction, or 2) a 6th case particle following nouns, pronouns, postpositions, and adjectives

འིས་ — particle; either 1) a syntactic particle creating an adverbial construction, 2) a syntactic particle marking the qualifier of an intransitive nom-s.p. verb of absence, or 3) case particle marking the 3rd case

འོ་ — terminating syntactic particle fused to suffixless final syllable

འོག་མ་ — adj., *later, below, beneath, under, lower*

འོག་མ་འོག་མ་ — adj., *later, below, beneath, under, lower*

འོང་ — intr. v. (nom-obj), *come*
འོང་འོངས་འོང་། ཐ་མི་དད།

ཡ་

24th letter of Tibetan alphabet

ཡང་ — conjunctive and disjunctive syntactic particle used after declined nouns, pronouns, adjectives, and after verbs and verb phrases; conjunctively: *even, also;* disjunctively: *but, although.* ཡང་ follows words ending with the letters ང་ན་མ་འ་ར་ལ་

ཡིད་ཆེས་པའི་དད་པ་ — compound n., *faith of conviction*

ཡིག་མགོ་ — a beginning ornament ༄༅

ཡིད་ལ་བྱས་ — phrasal trans. v. (ag-nom) (past tense), *take to mind,* literally *put in mind*
བྱེད་བྱས་བྱ་བྱོས། ཐ་དད།

ཡིན་ — intr. v. (nom-nom), *is, are*
ཡིན་ཡིན་ཡིན་ཡིན། ཐ་མི་དད།

ཡོངས་སུ་ — lexical prefix particle, translates the Sanskrit prefix *pari-, completely, thoroughly*

ཡོངས་སུ་རྫོགས་པ་ — n., *completely*

ཡོན་ཏན་ — n., *good qualities*

གཡེལ་ — intr. v. (nom-loc), *deviate from (be idle, be lazy)*
གཡེལ་གཡེལ་གཡེལ། ཐ་མི་དད།

གཡེལ་བར་	verbal noun + 2nd, 4th or 7th case particle fused to suffixless final syllable བ་
ར་	25th letter of Tibetan alphabet
ར་	particle fused to suffixless final syllable; either 1) a verb-modifying syntactic particle within a verb phrase, or 2) a case particle following nouns, pronouns, postpositions, and adjectives marking the 2nd, 4th and 7th cases
རང་	reflexive pronoun, *itself, oneself*
རིགས་	intr. v. (nom-obj), *be correct, be reasonable*
	རིགས་རིགས་རིགས། ཐ་མི་དད།
རིགས་པ་	n., *reasoning*
རིགས་ཤེས་	compound n., *reasoning consciousness*
རིང་	adj., *long*
རིམ་	n., *stage*
རིམ་གཉིས་	n. + adj., *the two stages [of Highest Yoga Tantra]* (the stage of generation and the stage of completion)
རིམ་པ་	n., *stage*
རུང་	intr. v. (nom-obj), *be suitable*
	རུང་རུང་རུང་། ཐ་མི་དད།
རེ་	limiting adj. used as a pronoun, *each*
རེ་	intr. v. (nom-loc), *expect, hope*
	རེ་རེ་རེ། ཐ་མི་དད།
རླབས་	n., *wave*
ལ	26th letter of Tibetan alphabet
ལ་	particle; either a syntactic particle (following a verb) signifying conjunction or disjunction, or a case particle marking the 2nd, 4th and 7th cases following nouns, pronouns, postpositions, and adjectives
ལམ་	n., *path*
ལས་	either syntactic or 5th case particle
ལས་	n., *action;* Sanskrit *karma*
ལུགས་	n., *system*
ལེགས་	adj., *good*
ལེགས་ཚོགས་	adj. + noun compound, *good collections*
ལུས་	n., *body, corpus*
ལེན་	trans. v. (ag-nom), *take, obtain, grasp, seize, take up, obtain, appropriate* ལེན་བླངས་བླང་ལོངས། ཐ་དད།
ལོ་	n., *year*
ལོག་	intr. v. (nom-s.p.), *be reversed, be turned.* This intransitive verb is usually qualified by a noun in the 5th case from which the 1st case subject is separated ལོག་ལོག་ལོག ཐ་མི་དད།
ཤ	27th letter of Tibetan alphabet
ཤུགས་	n., *force, strength, power*
ཤས་ཆུངས་	adj., *very small*
ཤི་	intr. v. (nom-obj) (past tense), *die*
	འཆི་ཤི་འཆི་ཤི ཐ་མི་དད།
ཤི་ནས་	verb in past tense + verb modifying s.p. ནས་ indicating a past participle, *having died.* Here, ནས་ is **not** a 5th case particle because it follows a verb, not a noun

ཤིང་ continuative syntactic particle used following verbs and verb phrases

ཤིན་ཏུ་ adv., *very*

ཤེས་ trans. v. (ag-nom), *know, understand.* This verb is listed in the *Great Word Treasury* as ཐ་མི་དད།, but I think it is a transitive verb (ag-nom).
ཤེས་ཤེས་ཤེས། ཐ་མི་དད།

ཤེས་པར་བྱ་ verb phrase (verbal infinitive + strong future auxiliary), *[I] will understand* or *[you] should understand.* ཤེས་པར་ is a verbal infinitive; here, the fused ར་ is a syntactic particle modifying a verb to create a verbal infinitive within the verb phrase ཤེས་པར་བྱ་ *[I] will understand [something], [you] should understand [something];* it is **not** a case particle marking the 2nd, 4th or 7th cases because it does not follow a noun—it is within a verb phrase. བྱ་ is a trans. v. (ag-nom) (future tense), *do, make, perform, take;* also strong future auxiliary

ཤེས་པར་བྱས་ verb phrase (verbal infinitive + strong past auxiliary), *[I, you] have understood.* ཤེས་པར་ is a verbal infinitive; here, the fused ར་ is a syntactic particle modifying a verb to create a verbal infinitive within the verb phrase ཤེས་པར་བྱ་ *[I] will understand [something], [you] should understand [something];* it is **not** a case particle marking the 2nd, 4th or 7th cases because it does not follow a noun—it is within a verb phrase. བྱས་ is a trans. v. (ag-nom) (past tense), *do, make, perform, take;* here: strong past auxiliary

ཤེས་རབ་ n., *wisdom;* the 6th of the six perfections

བཤིག་ trans. v. (ag-nom) (past and future), *destroy, break down*
འཇིག་བཤིག་བཤིག་ཤིགས། ཐ་དད།

བཤེས་གཉེན་ n., *kalyānamitra, spiritual friend*

ས་

28th letter of Tibetan alphabet

ས་ n., *earth, ground*

ས་ abbreviation of the particle ཡིས་ (when ཡིས. is fused to a suffixless final syllable, the ཡི goes away and all that's left is a fused ས་); either a syntactic particle marking an adverbial construction, or a case particle marking the 3rd case.

སུ་ interrogative pronoun, *who*

སུ་ particle; either verb-modifying syntactic particle within a verb phrase, or case particle marking the 2nd, 4th and 7th cases following nouns, pronouns, postpositions, and adjectives

སེམས་ n., *mind*

སེམས་ trans. v. (ag-nom), *think about, consider*
སེམས་བསམས་བསམ་སོམས། ཐ་དད།

སེམས་ཅན་ n., *sentient being* (literally, *mind-possessing*)

སོ་ s.p., terminator following syllable ending with the suffix letter ས་

སོ་སོར་ lexical prefix particle, *separately, individually*

སོ་སོར་ཐར་པ་ verbal n., *individual liberation*

སོ་སོ་བ་ n., *individual*

སོགས་ s.p.; generalizing suffix particle indicating unstated members of list or class, *and so forth, etc.* སོགས་ indicates absent members of a known list, as in the phrase "the presidents of the United States, Washington, Jefferson, and so forth." Whereas in English "and so forth" often is used when we can't think of anything else but want to cover ourselves against a later criticism of under inclusion, སོགས་ references a specific list with specific members.

སོང་ intr. v. (nom-obj) (alternate past tense), *went;* often used by extension in the sense of *turned into* or *became.*
འགྲོ་ཕྱིན་འགྲོ་སོང་། ཐ་མི་དད། སོང་ is also an alternate past form

སོང་བ་ verbal noun (formed from past tense), *became*

སྲས་ n., *child, son*

སྲིད་ n., *existence, cyclic existence*

སྲོག་	n., *life*
སློབ་	trans. v. (ag-obj), *train in*
	སློབ་བསླབས་བསླབ་སློབས། ཐ་དད།
སློབ་པ་	n., *training*
གསུང་	honorific trans. v. (ag-nom), *say*
	གསུང་གསུངས་གསུང་གསུངས། ཐ་དད།
གསུམ་	n. or adj., *three*
གསེབ་	n., *the narrow interstices between things*
གསེབ་ནས་	n. + 5th case particle, *between, within*
བསམ་	trans. v. (ag-nom), *think, think about, consider*
	སེམས་བསམས་བསམ་སོམས། ཐ་དད།
བསམ་གཏན	n., *concentration;* 5th of the six perfections
བསམ་པ་	verbal n., *mind*
བསམས་	trans. v. (ag-nom) (past tense), *think about, consider*
	སེམས་བསམས་བསམ་སོམས། ཐ་དད།
བསྲུང་	trans. v. (ag-nom) (future tense), *protect, safeguard, maintain*
	སྲུང་བསྲུངས་བསྲུང་སྲུངས། ཐ་དད།
བསླབ་	trans. v. (ag-obj) (future tense), *train*
	སློབ་བསླབས་བསླབ་སློབས། ཐ་དད།
བསླབ་བྱ་	verbal object noun, *object of training*

ཧ་	29th letter of Tibetan alphabet
ལྷག	noun, adj., *special*
ལྷག་མཐོང་	n., *special insight*

ལྷུང་	intr. v. (nom-obj), *fall*
	ལྷུང་ལྷུང་ལྷུང་ལྷུངས། ཐ་མི་དད།
ཨ་	30th letter of Tibetan alphabet

Table of Related Pairs of Transitive and Intransitive Verbs

Often Tibetan has pairs of verbs related in meaning, one transitive (taking an agent separate from the object) and one intransitive (taking a subject and no object). When one member of a pair occurs in the reading, I have included the other member of the pair in the unit vocabulary to encourage you to memorize the pair. Here are all the pairs gathered together. Order of verb tenses: **present, past, future, imperative;** intransitive verbs often do not have an imperative form.

སྐྱེད་ trans. v. (ag-nom), *produce, generate, create, give birth to*

སྐྱེད་བསྐྱེད་བསྐྱེད་སྐྱེད། ཐ་དད།

སྐྱེ་ intr. v. (nom-obj), *be born, arise, be created*

སྐྱེ་སྐྱེས་སྐྱེ། ཐ་མི་དད།

སྡུད་ trans. v. (ag-nom), *gather, collect*

སྡུད་བསྡུས་བསྡུ་སྡུས། ཐ་དད།

འདུད་ intr. v. (nom-obj), *be gathered, be included*

འདུད་འདུས་འདུ་འདུས། ཐ་མིདད་

སྒྲུབ་ trans. v. (ag-nom), *achieve, attain, accomplish, complete; prove*

སྒྲུབ་བསྒྲུབས་བསྒྲུབ་སྒྲུབས། ཐ་དད།

འགྲུབ་ intr. v. (nom-obj), *be established, be proven, exists*

འགྲུབ་གྲུབ་འགྲུབ། ཐ་མི་དད།

སྒྲོལ་ trans. v. (ag-nom), *release*

སྒྲོལ་བསྒྲལ་བསྒྲལ་སྒྲོལ། ཐ་དད།

གྲོལ་ intr. v. (nom-s.p.), *be released*

གྲོལ་ གྲོལ་ གྲོལ། ཐ་མི་དད།

སྐོར་ trans. v. (ag-nom), *turn*

སྐོར་བསྐོར་བསྐོར་སྐོར། ཐ་དད།

འཁོར་ intr. v. (nom-obj), *be turned*

འཁོར་འཁོར་འཁོར། ཐ་མི་དད།

འཇུག་ trans. v. (ag-obj), causative in sense of *make something happen*

འཇུག་འཅུག་གཞུག་ཅུག ཐ་དད།

འཇུག་ intr. v. (nom-obj), *enter, engage, apply;* by extension: *be involved in*

འཇུག་ཞུགས་འཇུག་ཞུགས། ཐ་མི་དད།

སྒོམ་ trans. v. (ag-nom), *meditate on, cultivate*

སྒོམ་བསྒོམས་བསྒོམ་སྒོམས། ཐ་དད།

གོམས་ intr. v. (nom-loc), *be accustomed to*

གོམས་གོམས་གོམས། ཐ་མི་དད།

བྱེད་ trans. v. (ag-nom), *do, make, perform, take;* also strong auxiliary

བྱེད་བྱས་བྱ་བྱོས། ཐ་དད།

འགྱུར་ intr. v. (nom-obj), *become;* also the weak auxiliary

འགྱུར་གྱུར་འགྱུར། ཐ་མི་དད།

སྟེན་ trans. v. (ag-obj), *adhere to, rely on, stay close to*

སྟེན་བསྟེན་བསྟེན་བསྟེན། ཐ་དད།

རྟེན་ intr. v. (nom-loc), *depend on, rely on*

རྟེན་བརྟེན་བརྟེན་རྟེན། ཐ་མི་དད།

གཅོད་ trans. v. (ag-nom), *cut, eliminate, decide, judge*

གཅོད་བཅད་གཅད་ཆོད། ཐ་དད།

འཆད་ intr. v. (nom-obj), *be severed, be cut*

འཆད་ཆད་འཆད། ཐ་མི་དད།

འདྲེན་ trans. v. (ag-nom), *induce, lead, draw; cite*

འདྲེན་དྲངས་དྲང་དྲོངས། ཐ་དད།

འདྲོང་ intr. v. (nom-loc), *be induced*

འདྲོང་འདྲོངས་འདྲོང་། ཐ་མི་དད།

Abbreviations for Words and Particles

Tibetan consists of six types of words and three types of particles. The six types of words are nouns (n.), pronouns (p.n.), adjectives (adj.), verbs (v.), adverbs (adv.), and postpositions (post.) The three types of particles are case particles, syntactic particles, and lexical particles.

8 classes of verbs following Wilson's classification

Verb classification follows Wilson's excellent system of grouping verbs by the cases of their grammatical subjects and principal qualifier, complement, or—in the case of transitive verbs—object.

4 classes of intransitive verbs

(**nom-nom**) • subject in nom (1st case) and complement in nom (1st case)
(**nom-loc**) • subject in nom (1st case) and qualifier in locative (7th case)
(**nom-obj**) • subject in nom (1st case) and qualifier in objective (2nd case)
(**nom-s.p.**) • subject in nom (1st case) and qualifier marked with syntactic particle

2 classes of transitive verbs

(**ag-nom**) • agent in agentive (3rd case) and object in nom (1st case)
(**ag-obj**) • agent in agentive (3rd case) and object in objective (2nd case)

2 classes of specialized verb

(**b/p-nom**) • subject in bene./purposive (4th case) and object in nom (1st case)
(**loc-nom**) • subject in locative (7th case) and object in nom (1st case)

Order of verb forms: present • past • future • imperative

ད་ལྟ་བ་ **present** • འདས་པ་ **past** • མ་འོངས་པ་ **future** • སྐུལ་ཚིག་ **imperative**
Verbs can have one, two, three or four forms.
Often intransitive verbs do not have an imperative form.
Verbs are either ཐ་དད། **transitive** or ཐ་མི་དད། **intransitive.**

The three types of particles are case particles, syntactic particles, and lexical particles

8 classes of syntactic particles following Wilson's classification

introductory • begin phrases, clauses, and sentences.
terminating • end sentences.
rhetorical • end conditional and logical constructions.
punctuational • end quotes and set off words and phrases.
conjunctive and **disjunctive** • tie clauses and sentences together either conjunctively or disjunctively.
verb modifying • occur within verb phrases.
continuative • follow verbs to indicate sequence.
adverbial • follow noun or adj. making a word, phrase or clause into an adverbial construction.

19 case marking particles indicate relationships to nouns, pronouns, adjectives, and postpositions.

1st case • nominative • no particle
2nd case • objective • སུ་རུ་ཏུ་དུ་ན་ར་ལ་
3rd case • agentive • གིས་ཀྱིས་གྱིས་འིས་ཡིས་
4th case • beneficial/purposive • སུ་རུ་ཏུ་དུ་ན་ར་ལ་
5th case • originative • ནས་ལས་
6th case • connective • གི་ཀྱི་གྱི་འི་ཡི་
7th case • locative • སུ་རུ་ཏུ་དུ་ན་ར་ལ་
8th case • vocative • no particle

5 classes of lexical particles following Wilson's classification

prefix particles
negative prefix particles
final syllables
optional syllables
negative verbal particles

Abbreviations Used in the Glossaries and Diagrams

When diagramming sentences and in glossaries, space is often limited. I use the following abbreviations when space requires an abbreviated label.

1st	first case • nominative
2nd	second case • objective
$+2^{nd}$	fused second case particle
3rd	third case • agentive
$+3^{rd}$	fused third case particle
4th	fourth case • beneficial / purposive
5th	fifth case • originative
6th	sixth case • connective
$+6^{th}$	fused sixth case particle
7th	seventh case • locative
$+7^{th}$	fused seventh case particle
8th	eighth case • vocative
abbr.	abbreviation
adj.	adjective
adv.	adverb
adv. s.p.	adverbial syntactic particle • follow noun or adj. making word, phrase or clause into an adverbial construction.
ag.	agent(ive)
ag-nom	class of transitive verbs whose agent is in agentive (3rd) case and object is in the nominative (1st) case.
ag-obj	class of transitive verbs whose agent is in agentive (3rd) case and object is in the objective (2nd) case.
app.	apposition
attrib.	attributive syntax
attrib. loc-nom	syntactically irregular but frequently seen attributive syntax with normally agentive verbs: attributive subject in 7th (locative) case and object in 1st (nominative) case.
attrib. nom-loc	syntactically irregular but frequently seen attributive syntax with normally agentive verbs: attributive subject in 1st case (nominative) and object in the 7th case (locative).
aux.	auxiliary verb
b/p	beneficial/purposive
b/p-nom	beneficial/purposive-nom
b.v.	basic verb
c.c.	clause connective (6th case)
cl.	clause
comp.	compound
con.	connective case
condit.	conditional
conj.	conjunction
conj. s.p.	conjunctive syntactic particle • ties clauses and sentences together conjunctively.
cont. s.p.	continuative syntactic particle • follows verbs to indicate sequence.
contr.	contraction
def.	definite
disj. s.p.	disjunctive syntactic particle • ties clauses and sentences together disjunctively.
f.	future (tense)
fem.	feminine
freq.	frequent(ly)
fut.	future (tense)
gen.	general
imp.	implied
impers.	impersonal
indef.	indefinite
inf.	infinitive
instr.	instrumental
intr.	intransitive verb, i.e., a verb that has a subject but does not have an agent or object
intro. s.p.	introductory syntactic particle; begins phrases, clauses, and sentences.
irreg.	irregular

irreg. nom-s.p	syntactically irregular but frequently seen alternative syntax with normally agentive verbs: subject in 1st case and qualifier marked with a syntactic particle
irreg. s.p.-nom	syntactically irregular but frequently seen alternative syntax with normally agentive verbs: subject marked with a syntactic particle and qualifier in 1st case
lex. part.	lexical particle
lit.	literally
loc-nom	class of transitive verbs whose subject is in the locative (7th) case and object is in the nominative (1st) case.
masc.	masculine
mod.	modified
n.	noun
neg.	negative
nom.	nominative
nom-nom	class of intransitive verbs whose subject is in the nominative (1st) case and complement is in in the nominative (1st) case.
nom-loc	class of intransitive verbs whose subject is in nominative (1st) case and principal qualifier is in the locative (7th) case. These are verbs of existing, living, dependence, and verbs expressing attitudes and cognitive states.
nom-obj	class of intransitive verbs whose subject is in nominative (1st) case and principal qualifier is in the objective (2nd) case. These are nominative action verbs, verbs of motion, and rhetorical verbs.
nom-s.p.	class of intransitive verbs whose subject is in nominative (1st) case & principal qualifier is marked with a syntactic particle. These are verbs of separation, absence, conjunction and disjunction.
ns.	nouns
num.	numeral
obj.	object(ive)
opp.	(as) opposed (to); opposite
p.n.	pronoun
p.p.	past participle
part.	particle
parti.	(present) participle
pl.	plural
poss.	possessive
pref.	prefix
prep.	preposition
pres.	present (tense)
pron.	pronoun
punct. s.p.	punctuational syntactic particle • ends quotes and sets off words and phrases.
ref.	referential use of 7th (locative) case
refl.	reflexive
rel.	relative
rhet. s.p.	rhetorical syntactic particle • ends conditional and logical constructions.
s.p.	syntactic particle
+s.p.	fused syntactic particle
sent.	sentence
sim.	similar(ly)
Skr.	Sanskrit
st.	strong
subj.	subject
subst.	substantive
syl.	syllable(s)
t.	transitive
term. s.p.	terminating syntactic particle • ends sentences.
trans.	transitive: verb having different agent and object.
ult.	ultimately
uncert.	uncertain
unkn.	unknown
v.	verb
v. aux.	auxiliary verb
v. mod. s.p.	verb modifying syntactic particle • occurs within verb phrases.
vbl.	verbal
vbs.	verbs
w.	with
wd.	word

Colophon

I, Craig Preston, was inspired to complete this book for the sake of all people interested in translating the Dharma from the Tibetan language. I apologize for any errors and mistakes due to my ignorance and lack of ability. May all beings be free from suffering and the causes of suffering and enjoy well-being and happiness. I dedicate the merit of this book to the Great Enlightenment.

ཨོཾ་ཨ་ར་པ་ཙ་ན་དྷཱི། ཨོཾ་ཨ་ར་པ་ཙ་ན་དྷཱི། ཨོཾ་ཨ་ར་པ་ཙ་ན་དྷཱི། ཨོཾ་ཨ་ར་པ་ཙ་ན་དྷཱི། ཨོཾ་ཨ་ར་པ་ཙ་ན་དྷཱི།

ཨོཾ་ཨ་ར་པ་ཙ་ན་དྷཱི། ཨོཾ་ཨ་ར་པ་ཙ་ན་དྷཱི། ཨོཾ་ཨ་ར་པ་ཙ་ན་དྷཱི། ཨོཾ་ཨ་ར་པ་ཙ་ན་དྷཱི། ཨོཾ་ཨ་ར་པ་ཙ་ན་དྷཱི།

ཨོཾ་ཨ་ར་པ་ཙ་ན་དྷཱི། ཨོཾ་ཨ་ར་པ་ཙ་ན་དྷཱི།

ཨོཾ་ཨ་ར་པ་ཙ་ན་དྷཱི། ཨོཾ་ཨ་ར་པ་ཙ་ན་དྷཱི།

ཨོཾ་ཨ་ར་པ་ཙ་ན་དྷཱི། **ཨོཾ་ཨ་ར་པ་ཙ་ན་དྷཱི།** ཨོཾ་ཨ་ར་པ་ཙ་ན་དྷཱི།

ཨོཾ་ཨ་ར་པ་ཙ་ན་དྷཱི། ཨོཾ་ཨ་ར་པ་ཙ་ན་དྷཱི།

ཨོཾ་ཨ་ར་པ་ཙ་ན་དྷཱི། ཨོཾ་ཨ་ར་པ་ཙ་ན་དྷཱི།

ཨོཾ་ཨ་ར་པ་ཙ་ན་དྷཱི། ཨོཾ་ཨ་ར་པ་ཙ་ན་དྷཱི། ཨོཾ་ཨ་ར་པ་ཙ་ན་དྷཱི། ཨོཾ་ཨ་ར་པ་ཙ་ན་དྷཱི། ཨོཾ་ཨ་ར་པ་ཙ་ན་དྷཱི།

ཨོཾ་ཨ་ར་པ་ཙ་ན་དྷཱི། ཨོཾ་ཨ་ར་པ་ཙ་ན་དྷཱི། ཨོཾ་ཨ་ར་པ་ཙ་ན་དྷཱི། ཨོཾ་ཨ་ར་པ་ཙ་ན་དྷཱི། ཨོཾ་ཨ་ར་པ་ཙ་ན་དྷཱི།

༎ ཨོཾ་སྭ་སྟི་ ༎

༎ །དགེ་ལེགས་འཕེལ། ༎

Also available from Snow Lion
HOW TO READ CLASSICAL TIBETAN, Volume Two: Buddhist Tenets

by Craig Preston

How to Read Classical Tibetan, Volume Two: Buddhist Tenets continues Craig Preston's ground-breaking series of self-study materials designed for students learning to read Classical Tibetan on their own. This book serves a dual purpose: the student learns both grammar and philosophy at the same time.

With easy-to-understand diagrams, Preston shows how to find your way through Tibetan sentences. It is like having a personal tutor at your fingertips, allowing you to proceed at your own pace through a wealth of material. As you work your way through an actual Tibetan text, Preston offers guidance at every turn. He explains the meaning of new words as they arise. He also offers a complete glossary of all the words at the end of the book. As you encounter new grammatical constructions, he walks you through how to understand their meaning. He shows how to break down Tibetan sentences into small pieces, and then how to put those pieces back together to form clearly understandable English sentences.

The book also helps students of the Tibetan language gain entry into the genre of tenets, which is the comparative study of the original schools of Buddhist thought in India. He introduces the rich vocabulary of Buddhist philosophy without assuming any prior knowledge, offering simple, easy-to-understand explanations of complicated ideas.

Preston thus provides a complete language course. He teaches you how to read an actual Tibetan text and what it means. *How to Read Classical Tibetan* will take self-study students to the next level at their own speed.

"Teachers and students of Classical Tibetan were empowered when Craig Preston introduced Volume One of his 'How to Read' series. This year, Preston again favors intermediate Tibetan students, this time with How to Read Classical Tibetan, Volume Two: Buddhist Tenets. Volume Two is, surprisingly, even better than Volume One, with complete grammar, lists of vocabulary, elegant translation, and cogent discussions of difficult points of doctrine."
—Bill Magee, Assistant Professor of Tibetan Studies, Dharma Drum Buddhist College, Taiwan, and co-author of Fluent Tibetan

"Craig Preston has followed his extremely helpful How to Read Classical Tibetan, Volume One with a new book that takes the reader to the next level, analyzing a book on Buddhist philosophy. New students of written Tibetan, as well as many who are more experienced, will find his method of unpacking Tibetan sentences into their tiniest parts, using nested boxes, to be the key for which they have been searching."
—Daniel Cozort, Associate Professor of Religion at Dickinson College and co-editor, Journal of Buddhist Ethics

"Craig Preston should be congratulated for this outstanding contribution to Tibetan language learning materials. This book and its predecessor are invaluable resources for intermediate students who know the basics, but are not yet reading and translating on their own. This is the type of book I wished was available when I was learning Tibetan."
—James Blumenthal, Associate Professor of Buddhist Philosophy, Oregon State University